# Passive Solar Heating

by

J. Richard Williams

230 Collingwood, P.O. Box 1425, Ann Arbor, Michigan 48106

Library of Congress Catalog Card Number 82-72857
ISBN 0-250-40601-2

Manufactured in the United States of America


Butterworths, Ltd., Borough Green, Sevenoaks
Kent TN15 8PH, England

# PREFACE

Passive solar heating is one of the most economically attractive uses of solar energy today, particularly when well-designed passive heating systems are incorporated into new construction. Since passive solar techniques first became popular in the mid-1970s, a large number of books have been written on the topic, most of which are primarily descriptive—full of good ideas and pleasing photographs but bereft of information on proper design methodologies or techniques for accurate performance analysis. "Look-up tables" based on rules-of-thumb and crude correlations are often inadequate to provide the degree of accuracy required by builders and architects to obtain performance estimates of proposed systems. As far too many people have learned the hard way, an improperly designed passive solar building can be uncomfortably hot in the summer and cold in the winter, with utility bills exceeding those of conventional construction.

This is not a picture book of pretty passive solar homes, nor an exposition on the advantages and economics of passive heating. It is a practical handbook on the design of passive solar systems and the analysis of their performance. Various analytical tools are presented to permit the designer to select the most appropriate techniques for the job at hand. Examples are given to help the reader apply these tools.

The book begins with a brief description of the basic types of passive solar systems, then the following five chapters provide detailed descriptions of each of the five basic types. Examples of systems already installed are described, and analytical techniques are presented. Since the starting point for any solar system performance analysis is the characterization of the solar radiation environment, Chapter 7 discusses this topic in some detail. One of the most useful "look-up table" procedures for estimating performance of direct gain and storage wall systems is the Load Collector Ratio method described in Chapter 3; the data for U.S. and Canadian cities are given in Appendix A.

J. Richard Williams

**J. Richard Williams** is internationally recognized as one of the world's leading authorities on solar heating and cooling. His accomplishments include the development of the world's largest solar heated and air-conditioned building, several other commercial heating and cooling projects, numerous active and passive solar heated homes, and a variety of international solar heating and cooling projects that were the first of their kind. Dr. Williams currently is the Dean of Engineering at the University of Idaho. He is a registered Professional Engineer, holds an engineering PhD from the Georgia Institute of Technology, and is active in the National Society of Professional Engineers, the American Society of Mechanical Engineers (ASME), the International Solar Energy Society (ISES) and the American Society for Engineering Education. He has served as Director and Vice President of ISES (American Section), President of its Georgia chapter, and as a member of the Solar Energy Standards Committee of ASME. Dr. Williams is the author of *Solar Energy—Technology and Applications* and *Design and Installation of Solar Heating and Hot Water Systems,* both published by Ann Arbor Science.

# CONTENTS

# CHAPTER 1

# INTRODUCTION

Passive solar energy systems collect and utilize solar energy by natural means, and generally exclude the use of mechanical power or electronic controls to regulate the flow of heat. The thermal energy is transferred in and out of the structure, in and out of the storage medium and around and through the conditioned space by natural means. Control elements such as vents and dampers may be incorporated in passive designs to permit the occupant to restrict the flow of thermal energy. Passive solar energy systems are generally classified as:

1. direct-gain systems,
2. thermal storage walls,
3. thermal storage roofs,
4. attached greenhouses and
5. convective loops.

## DIRECT-GAIN SYSTEMS

In direct-gain systems, the solar radiation enters through a window and directly strikes the floor or wall or other objects within the heated space, which are heated by the solar radiation and in turn heat the air within the room. The thermal inertia of the conditioned space helps store this heat for periods of time when solar radiation is not available. Buildings with thick walls and massive contruction increase the thermal mass of the structure. Figure 1 is a simplified illustration of a direct-gain system with thermal heat storage in the rear wall and floor.

Virtually all of the solar radiation that enters through the window is converted into heat. The performance of direct-gain solar energy systems is improved if some means is used to cover the windows with thermal

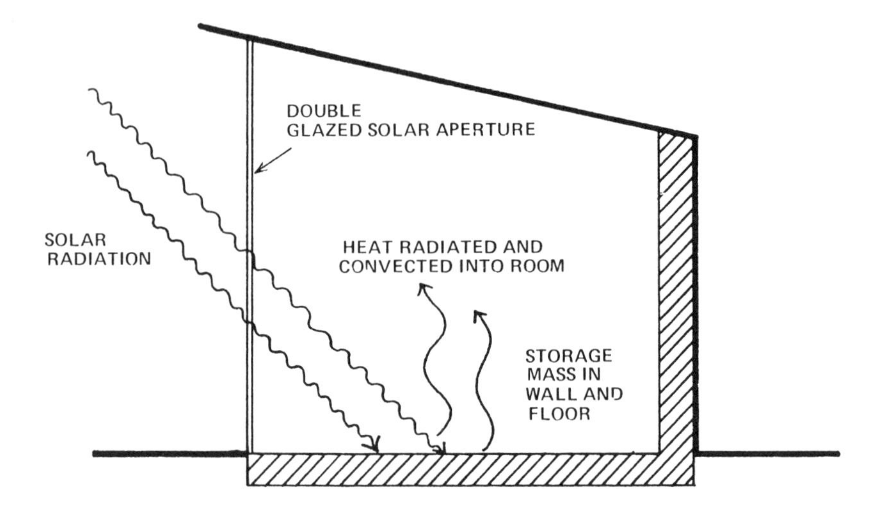


**Figure 1.** Direct-gain passive solar heating system with thermal storage in the rear wall and floor.

insulation during the periods in which the heat loss through the window would exceed the heat gain from solar radiation. During the heating season in the northern hemisphere, windows facing south take maximum advantage of the lower position of the sun in the sky during the winter. Overhangs above the windows provide shading in the summer when the sun is higher in the sky. The same effect can be accomplished somewhat by deciduous trees.

## THERMAL STORAGE WALL

The thermal storage wall utilizes a south-facing wall covered by one or two sheets of glass or plastic with air gaps between. The wall absorbs solar radiation and stores heat. There are several different types of thermal storage walls currently in use. One type, developed by Felix Trombe of France, consists of a thick wall of concrete or other massive structural material covered by two layers of glass (Figure 2). When the wall is heated by solar radiation, cool air from the room can circulate through the gap between the wall and the glazing, where it is heated, and the warm air then circulates into the room. A shutter on either the inlet or outlet vent prevents air from circulating when heat is not desired in the room. Also, an excess heat vent can be opened to vent hot air to the outside. Heat is transferred to the interior of the structure by convection and radiation from the warm south-facing wall.

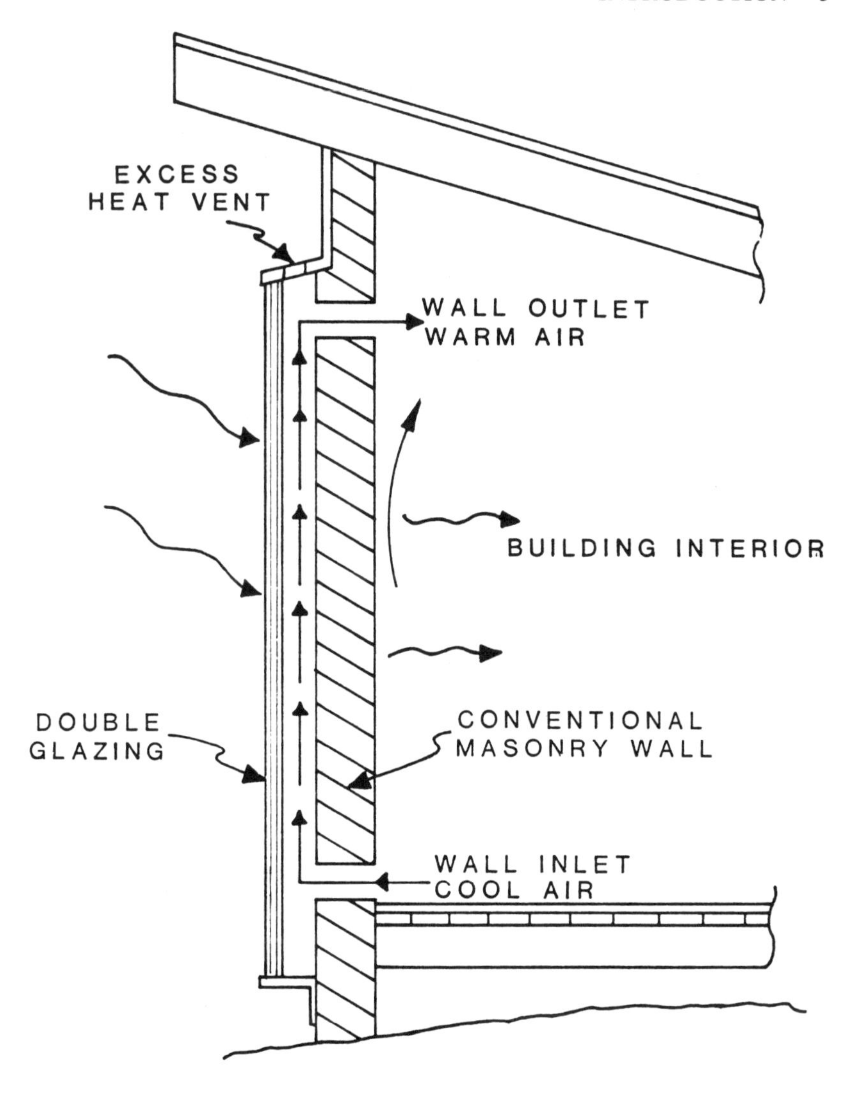


**Figure 2.** Trombe wall.

Another type of thermal storage wall, the drum wall, uses drums or barrels or other containers of water in place of the structural wall to store heat. In the case of the drum wall illustrated in Figure 3, solar radiation enters through the glass and strikes the drums. The drums are painted black to increase heat absorption; the water inside the drums is heated.

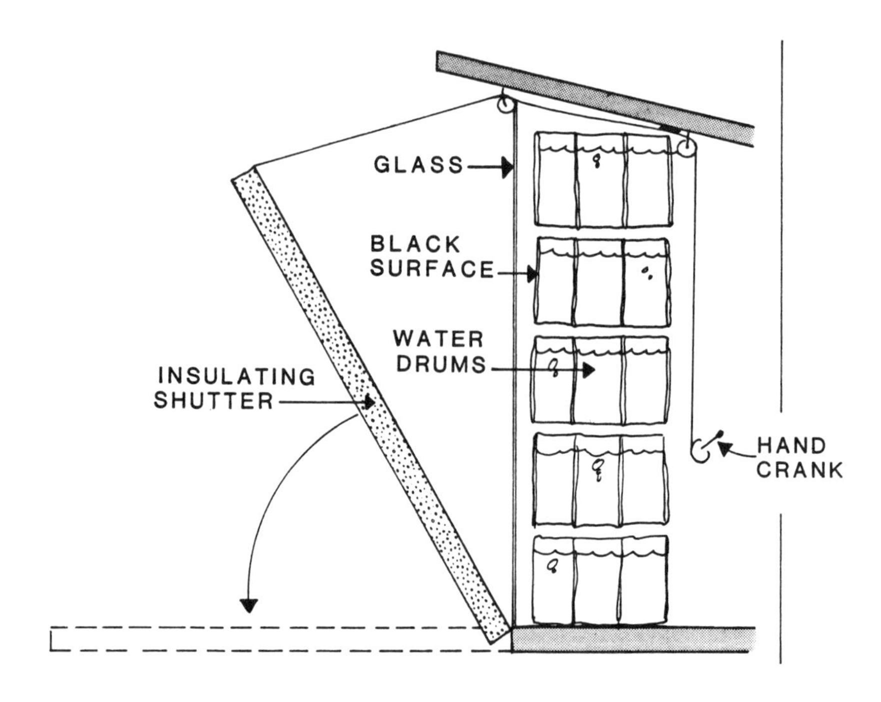


**Figure 3.** Drum wall.

An air gap within each drum accommodates changes in water volume due to temperature changes. An insulating shutter with a reflective upper surface reduces heat loss during periods of low or zero solar radiation and reflects additional solar radiation onto the drums when the sun is shining. In the latter case, the insulating shutter is lowered to its horizontal position, and its upper reflecting surface increases the total solar radiation reaching the drums. When the sun is not shining, the insulating shutter is raised with a hand crank (or photocell-activated motor) to cover the glass surface. The interior space then continues to be heated by the hot drums.

## THERMAL STORAGE ROOF

The thermal storage roof (Figure 4) is somewhat similar to the thermal storage wall, except that the storage mass is in the roof instead of a wall. Several different types of systems have been demonstrated that use bags

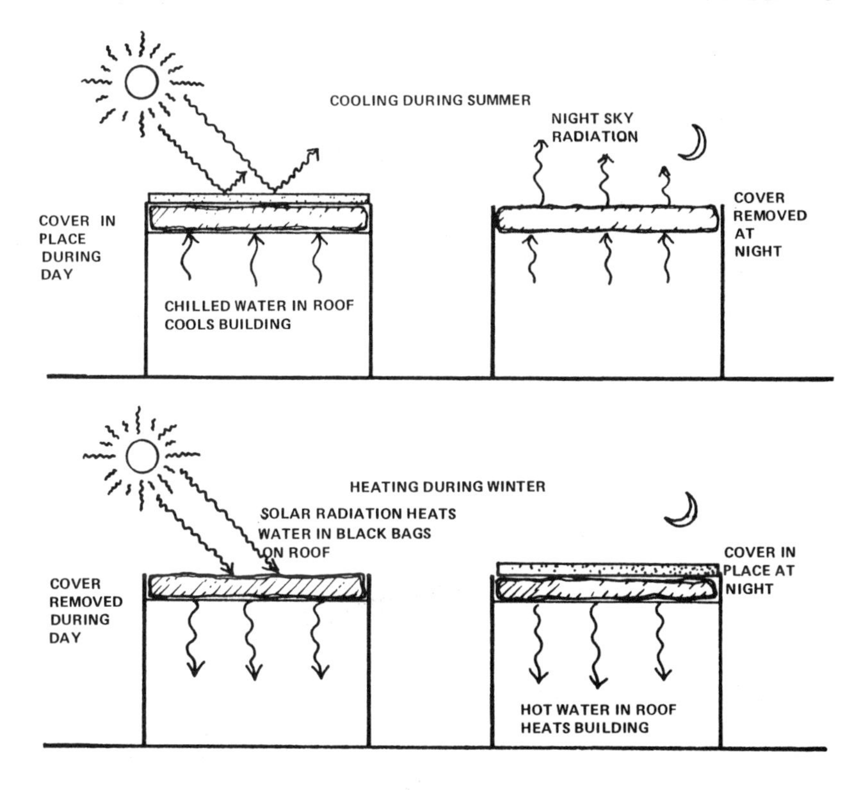


**Figure 4.** Thermal storage roof.

of water or other massive materials in the roof to store heat from solar radiation during the day for use at night or during other periods when the sun is not shining. Insulating shutters are pulled back during periods of high solar radiation to allow the blackened thermal storage mass to absorb this radiation and increase in temperature. The insulating shutters then slide over this thermal storage mass to prevent heat loss to the outside at night, just as the insulating shutter is used with the drum wall. Thus, the thermal storage mass in the roof keeps the heated space warm day and night. During the summer, this process can be reversed to provide cooling. The insulating shutters are withdrawn from the thermal storage mass at night to allow cooling of the roof by thermal radiation and/or evaporation. During the day the insulating shutters are put back in place over the thermal storage mass. The cool thermal storage mass in the roof then keeps the conditioned space cool both during the day and at night. This type of structure has been demonstrated to maintain comfortable indoor temperatures in dry climates even though the outside temperatures may range from $<0$ to $>40°C$.

## ATTACHED GREENHOUSE

The attached greenhouse or sunspace is a popular means of augmenting the heating of a structure (Figure 5). The greenhouse or sunspace serves a dual function in that it can also be used for growing plants. This structure acts not only as a collector of heat at certain times but also as a buffer that reduces heat loss from the building to the outside.

## CONVECTIVE LOOP

Several different types of convective loops have been used for passive solar heating. Figure 6 illustrates a simple convective-loop heater in which cooler air flows into the solar heater installed beneath the window, and warm air flows into the room. This particular type of heater as shown does not incorporate thermal storage mass and therefore provides heat only when a substantial amount of solar radiation is available; it has been used in office-type buildings, which require heat mainly during the day [Walton 1973]. Figure 7 illustrates a more sophisticated convective loop incorporating thermal storage mass in the form of a tank of stones. Solar radiation striking the collector causes warm air to rise and pass

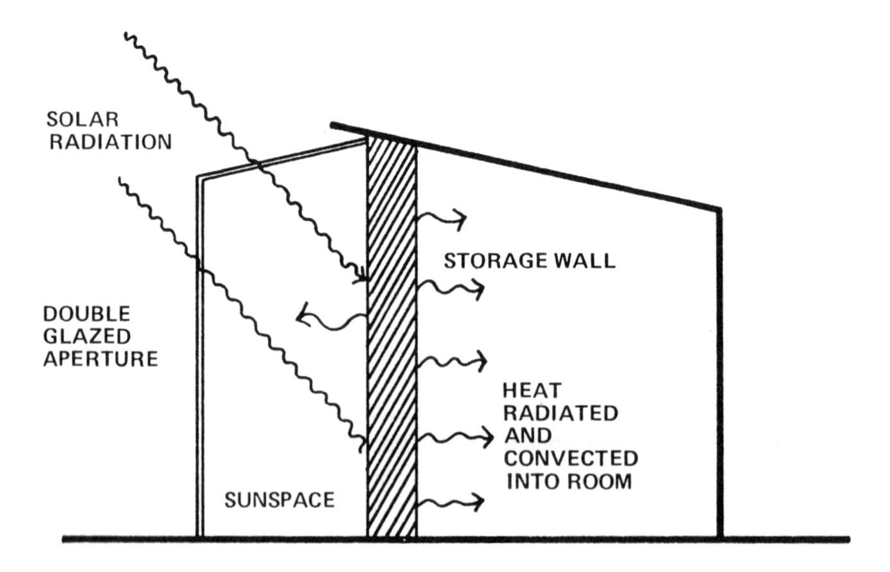


**Figure 5.** Attached greenhouse (sunspace).

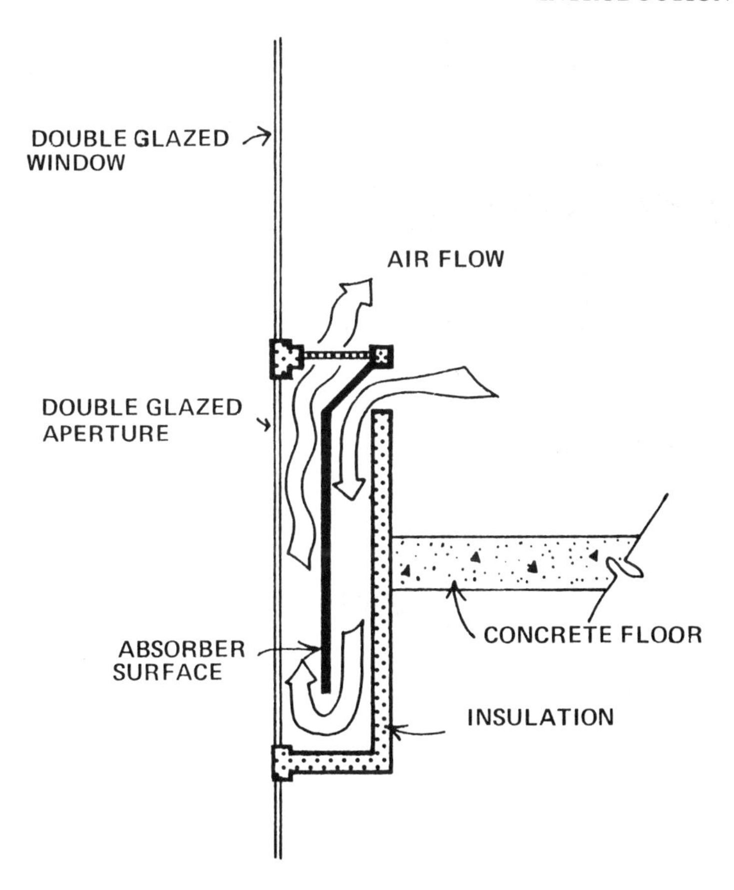


**Figure 6.** Simple convective-loop heater.

through the pebble bed or enter the heated space, and cool air from the pebble bed or heated space to return to the collectors. Figure 8 illustrates this system in more detail. Warm air is allowed to flow by natural convection into the heated space when a floor vent is open. If solar radiation is available, the warm air flows directly from the collector into the heated space, but if solar radiation is not available, warm air from the pebble bed flows into the heated space.

## ORIENTATION OF COLLECTORS/APERTURES

The collector aperture orientation for any of these systems may be classified as:

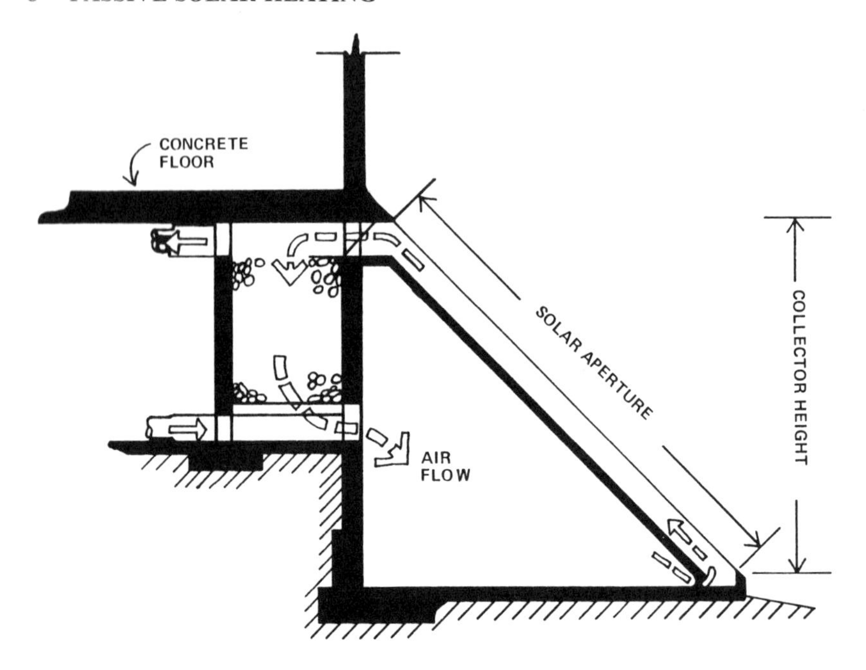


**Figure 7.** Convective-loop heating system with pebble bed storage.

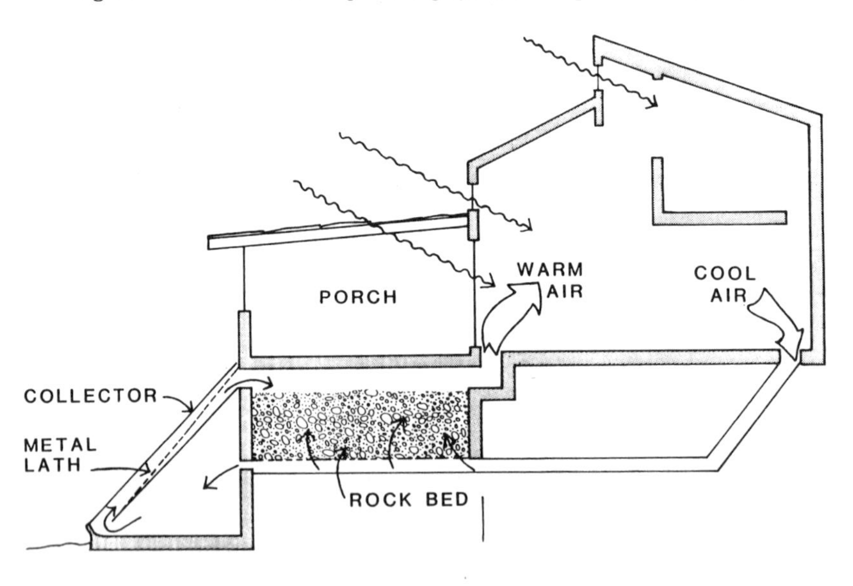


**Figure 8.** Thermosiphoning rock bed heating system.

1. south aperture,
2. shaded roof aperture,
3. roof aperture, or
4. remote aperture.

The south aperture consists of vertical glazing elements (direct gain, drum wall, convective loop) on the south wall of the structure. In the northern hemisphere this aperture preferentially receives winter solar radiation and, with an overhang, summer shade. For various reasons, if one wishes to receive direct radiation through the roof, a shaded roof aperture may be incorporated using either vertical or sloping glazing elements oriented to admit solar radiation into the heated space.

A roof aperture utilizes thermal storage mass and/or glazing elements on the roof, usually in combination with movable insulation. A remote aperture is not actually part of the building envelope. A remote aperture may be oriented at whatever angle is most advantageous to receive solar radiation.

## ENERGY DELIVERY OF PASSIVE SYSTEMS

In terms of energy delivery to the heated space, passive solar systems may be characterized as:

1. direct gain,
2. indirect heating and
3. isolated heating.

A direct-gain system admits solar radiation directly to the heated space where it is absorbed on interior surfaces. Absorption of solar radiation within the space results in heating of air within the space. An indirect heating system involves absorption of solar radiation on a surface external to the heated space. The heat is then transferred into the space by natural processes. An isolated heating system converts solar radiation to heat by absorption of solar radiation on an external surface in such a manner that the air temperature within the heated space can be regulated independently of the temperature of the absorber. Figure 9 illustrates examples of direct, indirect and isolated heating systems with south, shaded roof, roof and remote apertures. These combinations cover just about all of the passive heating concepts. Isolated heating systems provide maximum control over the thermal environment in the heated space; however, they tend to be less efficient. The most efficient is the

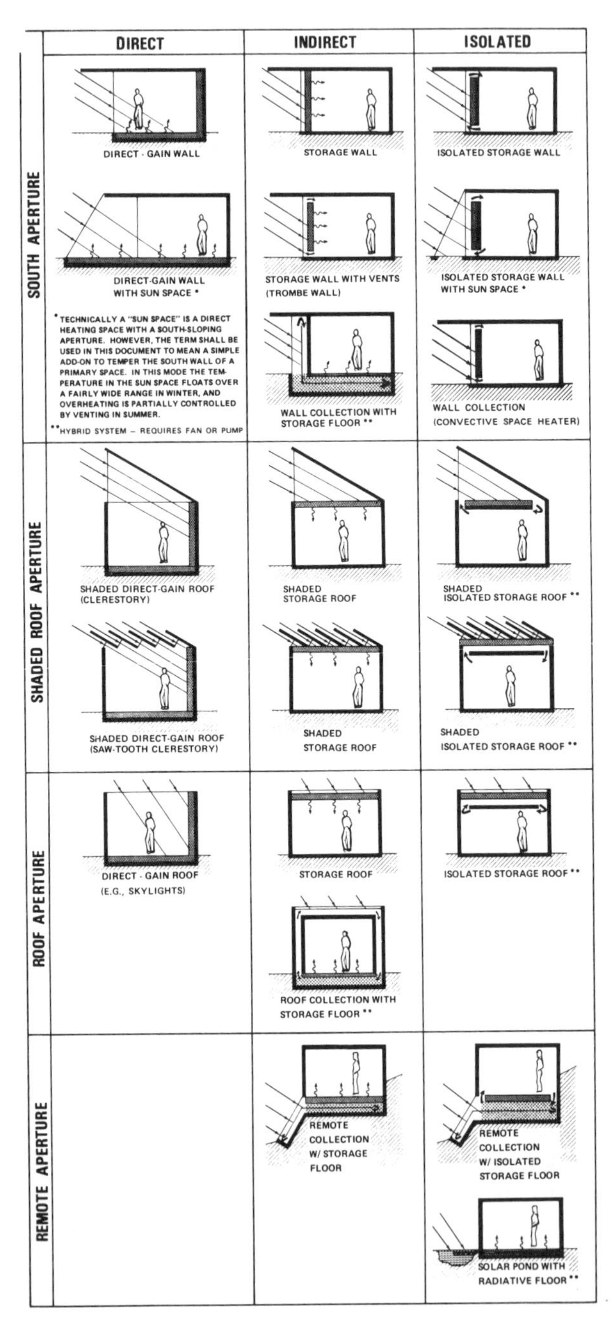


**Figure 9.** Direct, indirect and isolated passive heating systems with south, roof shaded, roof and remote apertures [DOE 1979].

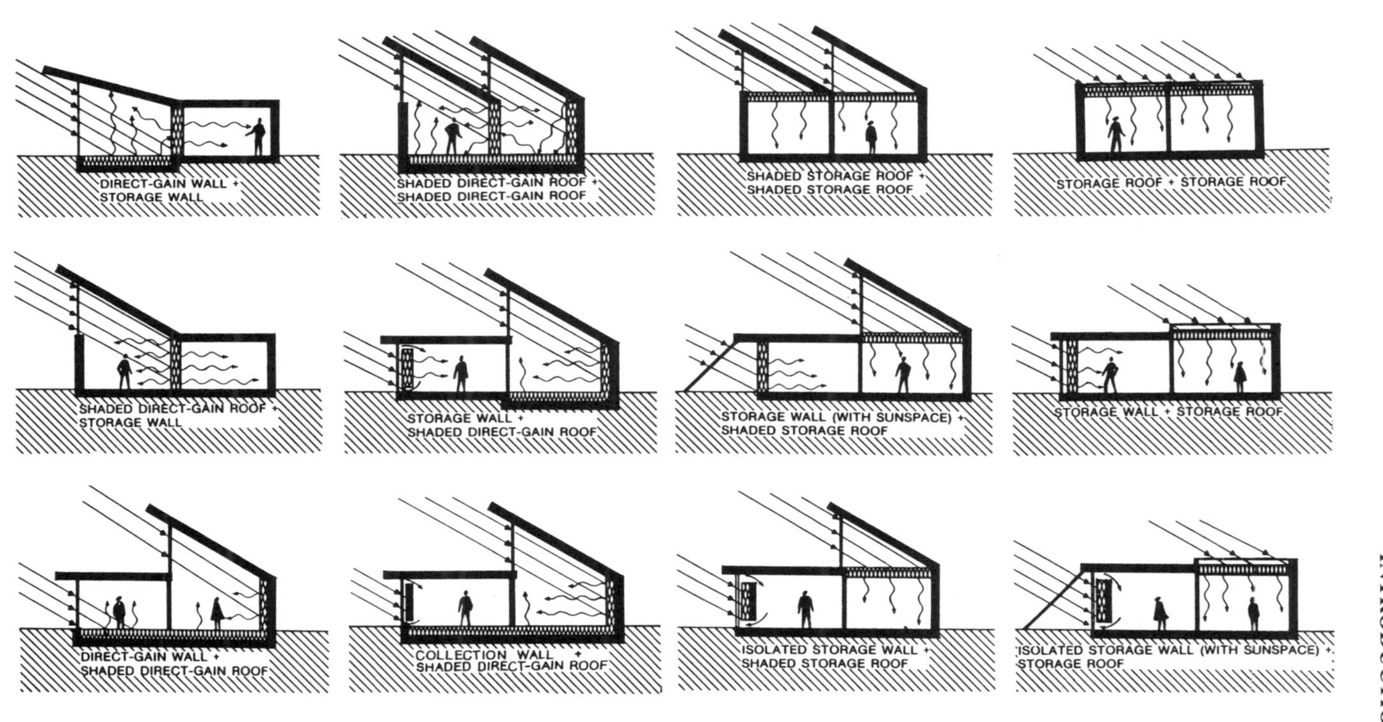


**Figure 10.** Examples of multizone passive solar systems [DOE 1979].

direct-gain system, but with this system, large temperature fluctuations within the heated space are frequently encountered.

Many passive systems incorporate several of the features illustrated in Figure 9. For example, direct-gain openings (windows) can be included in a south-facing thermal storage wall. Direct-gain elements are commonly combined with indirect heating or isolated heating units. There are a variety of multizone, single-story passive heating schemes such as those illustrated in Figure 10. These examples illustrate how several passive heating elements may be utilized to provide solar heating to a multiroom single-story structure.

## PASSIVE COOLING

Passive cooling involves selective rejection of heat to the cooler parts of the environment by natural means. Environmental heat sinks include the sky, the atmosphere, the ground and water.

Sky cooling involves reversing the solar collection processes for a sunspace, thermal storage wall or roof, or shaded roof aperture. Instead of receiving solar radiation through the aperture, heat at night is radiated from the aperture into the clear sky. Cooling to the atmosphere involves various means of providing ventilation. For example, if the excess heat vent (Figure 2) is open and the wall outlet closed, air from inside the room will be drawn upward and out through the outside heat vent, thereby helping to ventilate the room by pulling cooler air in from the north side of the structure. Atmospheric cooling works best in climates that experience large day/night temperature variations. Radiative cooling to the night sky works best in environments with clear skies and can sometimes produce cooling below the ambient air temperature. Since the thermal mass of the earth is quite large, ground and water temperatures during the summer are normally cooler than the average daytime ambient air temperature. Earth-sheltered buildings and structures with earth berms naturally benefit from ground cooling.

# CHAPTER 2

# DIRECT-GAIN SYSTEMS

The direct-gain passive heating system is by far the most common in the world, since the simplest direct-gain passive solar heating and cooling device is nothing more than a window. However, unless the normal window is carefully designed and installed, it may lose more heat than it gains. A double-glazed window facing south with an insulating shade to reduce heat loss at night can supply substantially more heat from solar radiation than is lost at night. An ordinary double-glazed south-facing window of this type can provide about as much heat per square foot of area as an active solar collector. In developing a numerical model of a direct-gain solar heating system, one may assume that all of the solar radiation transmitted through the collector aperture enters the heated space. The heat loss through the window is easily calculated.

## DESIGNING THE DIRECT-GAIN SYSTEM

The major design criteria for a direct-gain system [DOE 1980] are the time of the admission of solar radiation, the amount of solar heat gain, the type of glazing, heat losses from the glazing, and compatibility of the admission of sunlight with activities within the structure. Timing is important, since solar radiation must be allowed to enter only when heat is needed. More solar gain is normally required in the morning and in the winter than in the afternoon or in the summer. Thus, the timing of solar heat gain must correlate with the heat input needed to maintain the desired temperature within the heated space. The amount of solar heat gain must be selected to minimize excessive temperature fluctuations within the heated space.

## Type and Area of Glazing Requirements

Direct solar radiation should not be admitted if it interferes with activities within the heated space. Direct sunlight may interfere with office work, while diffuse light may be quite acceptable. Glazing may be clear to admit direct-beam solar radiation, or translucent material, such as diffusing glass, plastic films, fiberglass-based glazing and acrylics, may be used to admit solar radiation while diffusing direct sunlight. If the objective is to provide solar heating in the winter, heat losses through the glazing must be minimized by using multiple panes and/or insulating shutters.

Direct-gain systems are popular because they are relatively inexpensive and probably the most cost-effective type of solar system, provided they are designed to provide only a small portion of the total heating load. Direct-gain systems usually incorporate thermal storage mass within the heated space to moderate temperature fluctuations and permit a higher total solar heating fraction. The area of glazing is extremely important, since excessive glazing can result in undesirable temperature swings and large heat losses at night and in the winter, which can actually increase auxiliary energy requirements to exceed those required had a smaller glazing area been used.

Passive direct-gain apertures may face east, west, south, or any direction from east or west toward south. To reduce heat losses in cold climates, thermal shades, movable insulation or thick curtains should be used to cover the windows during periods of low or zero solar radiation. For example, to minimize heat loss, the insulating shade or curtains should be drawn on an east-facing window shortly before solar noon and opened on the west-facing window shortly after solar noon. This points out one of the disadvantages of passive solar systems: they commonly require some action of the building occupants to make the system effective. Control devices have been developed to open and close passive apertures automatically; even when these are used, the solar heating system is still considered passive since its thermal energy flows occur by passive means.

To provide direct-gain heating to rooms with no south-facing exterior walls, vertical windows in the roof are usually preferred to sloping skylights, since the former more easily accommodate summer shading. Whenever possible, massive objects should be located to ensure their exposure to direct sunlight. For example, a building with heavy floors and walls may include windows located to maximize the amount of direct solar radiation reaching the floor and wall surfaces. The incorporation of thermal storage mass into direct-gain heating systems is important in moderating extremes of temperature within the heated space.

## Thermal Storage Mass Requirements

Any structure that relies on a direct-gain passive heating system to supply a substantial portion of its heating needs will be subjected to significant temperature variations within the heated space, variations which the solar designer seeks to minimize. Generally, the greater the thermal mass and the greater the exposure of the thermal mass to direct solar radiation, the smaller will be the interior temperature fluctuations.

Two important characteristics of thermal storage mass are specific heat and thermal conductivity; both should be as high as possible. Obviously, the total amount of heat an object can release or absorb for a given temperature change is proportional to its specific heat. Likewise, the ability of an object to transfer this heat to its exterior surfaces depends on its thermal conductivity. Concrete will store about 28 Btu/ft$^3$-°F as compared with 62.4 for water. The building designer's challenge is to locate glazing apertures and thermal storage mass in an effective manner while creating an esthetically pleasing interior.

### *Choice of Material and Placement of Thermal Storage Mass*

Figure 11 illustrates three possible arrangements of thermal storage mass relative to the location of the vertical south-facing aperture. The upper-right figure has a surface area of thermal storage mass twice that of the upper-left figure, and in the lower figure the surface area has been increased six times. It has been shown that the lower arrangement with the greatest exposed surface area results in the smallest daily temperature fluctuations [DOE 1980], and that increased thermal conductivity of the thermal storage mass results in smaller temperature fluctuations. Table I lists the thermal conductivity, specific heat and density of concrete, brick, adobe and water. Adobe has the poorest conductivity and would result in the largest interior air-temperature fluctuations. Containers of water make an excellent thermal storage medium, since the water within the container is free to circulate and thereby maintain a relatively uniform temperature profile; the major mode of heat transfer is natural convection within the container. A general rule of thumb to follow in designing direct-gain systems is to supply enough thermal storage mass to store 30 Btu per degree Fahrenheit (57 kJ/°C) of temperature change for each square foot (0.091 m$^2$) of glazing aperture.

Thermal storage mass exposed to direct sunlight is about four times more effective than thermal storage mass in other locations in moderating temperature fluctuations. This is because the temperature change of room air is about half the change of the storage temperature if the storage mass is directly heated by solar radiation. If, on the other hand,

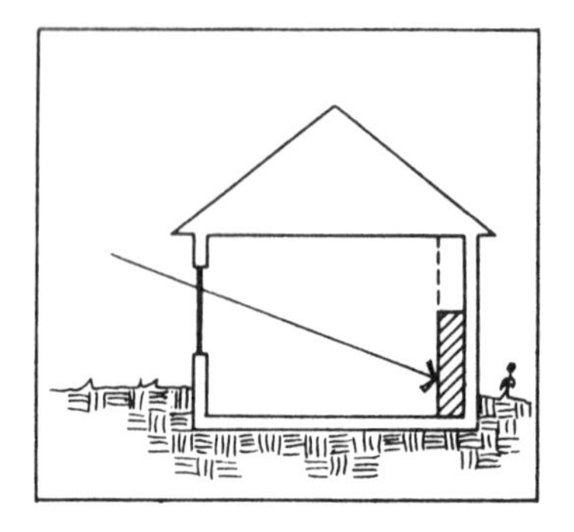

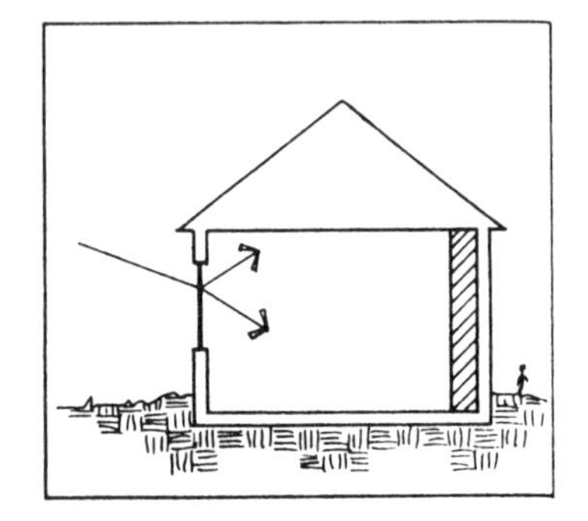

**Figure 11.** Three arrangements for locating thermal storage mass relative to direct-gain apertures.

**Table I. Thermal Storage Material Properties**

| Material | Conductivity, k [Btu/hr-ft$^2$-°F (W/m$^2$-°C)] | Specific Heat, $C_p$ [Btu/lb°F(kJ/kg-°C)] | Density, $\rho$ [lb/ft$^3$(kg/m$^3$)] |
|---|---|---|---|
| Concrete (Stone) | 12.0 (1.70) | 0.20 (0.84) | 140.0 (2240) |
| Brick (Common) | 5.0 (0.72) | 0.20 (0.84) | 120.0 (1920) |
| Brick (Magnesium Add.) | 26.4 (3.80) | 0.20 (0.84) | 120.0 (1920) |
| Adobe | 3.6 (0.52) | 0.24 (1.00) | 106.0 (1700) |
| Water (Isothermal) | | 1.00 (4.19) | 62.4 (1000) |

the storage mass is heated by the air, its temperature change is only about half that of the air. Storage mass is important for system efficiency, since excessive daytime temperatures usually result in increased ventilation, resulting in rejection of heat during the day which might otherwise have been absorbed by the storage mass and released at night when it is needed.

## Window Insulation Requirements

Since double-glazed windows have about 15 times the heat loss of an equal area of well insulated wall, some type of movable insulation is important in reducing the undesirable heat losses. Insulating materials include sheets of rigid insulation that can be inserted manually at night and removed in the morning; roller-shade devices using wood or plastic slates, Mylar®, cloth or other insulating materials; framed and hinged insulating panels; and shutters of various types. The heat loss factors for windows, with and without insulating covers, are given in Table II. One may estimate the energy savings factor by multiplying the difference in U-factors with and without covers by the number of degree-days (dd) of heating per year times 18. Insulating shutters and shades will not save as much energy as anticipated unless they seal reasonably well when closed.

**Table II. U-Values for Glazing with Movable Insulation**

| | Single Glass | Double Glass | Triple Glass |
|---|---|---|---|
| Solar Transmission Values | | | |
| Nominal Solar "Transmittance" | 0.87 | 0.76 | 0.66 |
| Approximate Seasonal Transmittance | 0.80–0.85 | 0.64–0.72 | 0.51–0.61 |
| U-Values (Winter) | | | |
| Nominal U-Value | 1.15 | 0.55 | 0.35 |
| With R-4 Insulating Cover | 0.21 | 0.17 | 0.14 |
| Average U-Values with R-4 Cover in Place, 16 hr/day (3/4 of the degree days) | 0.45 | 0.27 | 0.20 |
| Average U-Value with R-4 Cover in Place, 12 hr/day (2/3 of the degree days) | 0.52 | 0.29 | 0.21 |
| With R-10 Insulating Cover | 0.09 | 0.085 | 0.078 |
| Average U-Value with R-10 Cover in Place, 16 hr/day (3/4 of the degree days) | 0.36 | 0.20 | 0.15 |
| Average U-Value with R-10 Cover in Place, 12 hr/day (2/3 of the degree days) | 0.44 | 0.24 | 0.17 |

If air is allowed to circulate between the insulating cover and the glass, the heat loss is increased.

## MODELS OF DIRECT-GAIN SYSTEMS

An example of a direct-gain system is the Williamson house in Santa Fe, New Mexico, illustrated in Figures 12 and 13. The 1265-$ft^2$ house is basically rectangular with its long axis running east-west. The shaded roof aperture consists of five windows, each 46 in. high × 76 in. wide at 70° slope. Direct solar radiation entering this aperture falls on the north adobe wall of the house. Seven windows 76 in. high × 46 in. wide admit solar radiation through the south wall of the house, which falls on the brick floor and furnishings. All of the solar apertures are double glazed. The total aperture area is 310 $ft^2$.

All exterior walls are 10-in.-thick adobe with 2 in. of polystyrene foam insulation. The roof insulation is 4 in. of polystyrene foam covered with Celotex® and an asphalt coating. Thus, this house is well insulated with a fairly large direct-gain solar aperture and a large amount of direct-coupled thermal storage mass.

Figure 14 illustrates data recorded at this house between December 26 and January 8, 1979, a period including both sunny and cloudy days and cold nights. The inside temperature, as recorded using a thermocouple inside a black hollow copper sphere near the living room ceiling, ranged from 65 to 92°F while the ambient temperature ranged from 0 to 40°F. The solar heating fraction is about 72%; auxiliary heating is with electric

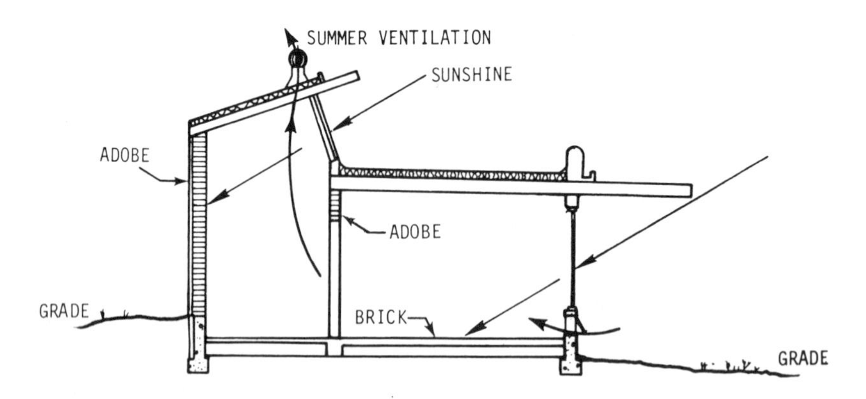


**Figure 12.** Cross section of Williamson house [Sandia 1979].

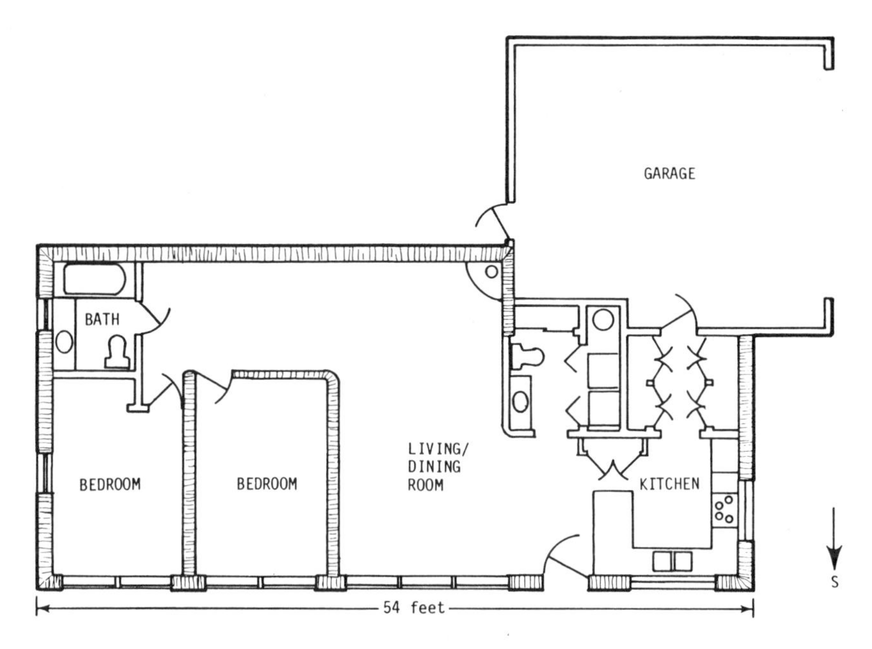


**Figure 13.** Floor plan of Williamson house [Sandia 1979].

baseboard heaters. The loss coefficient for the house is 14,000 Btu/dd, or about 11 Btu/ft$^2$-dd.

Another example of a direct-gain heating system is the Shankland house in White Rock, New Mexico [Zwarf 1978]. Figure 15 is a cross section of the house and Figure 16 is the floor plan of the ground floor. There are also three bedrooms, an office and bathroom on the second story, for a total of 2000 ft$^2$ of living area. The first floor is of 6-in.-thick concrete surfaced with red brick, and the walls up to the second story are of adobe. The second story has 6-in. stud walls with fiberglass insulation, plus an additional inch of insulating sheathing. The solar apertures are all double-glazed. There is 10 in. of fiberglass plus 1 in. of urethane foam insulation in the roof. The skylights have automatic louvers called Skylids®. The total solar aperture is 270 ft$^2$ on the south, 100 ft$^2$ on the east (to admit morning sun), and 30 ft$^2$ on the west. Fans circulate heated air from the loft through rock beds beneath the floor to provide additional thermal storage. The rock beds contain about 16 tons of rock. The fans can also circulate air from the house through the rock bed to provide additional heat when needed. Figure 17 shows performance data between February 21 and 25, 1978. The solar heating fraction has been

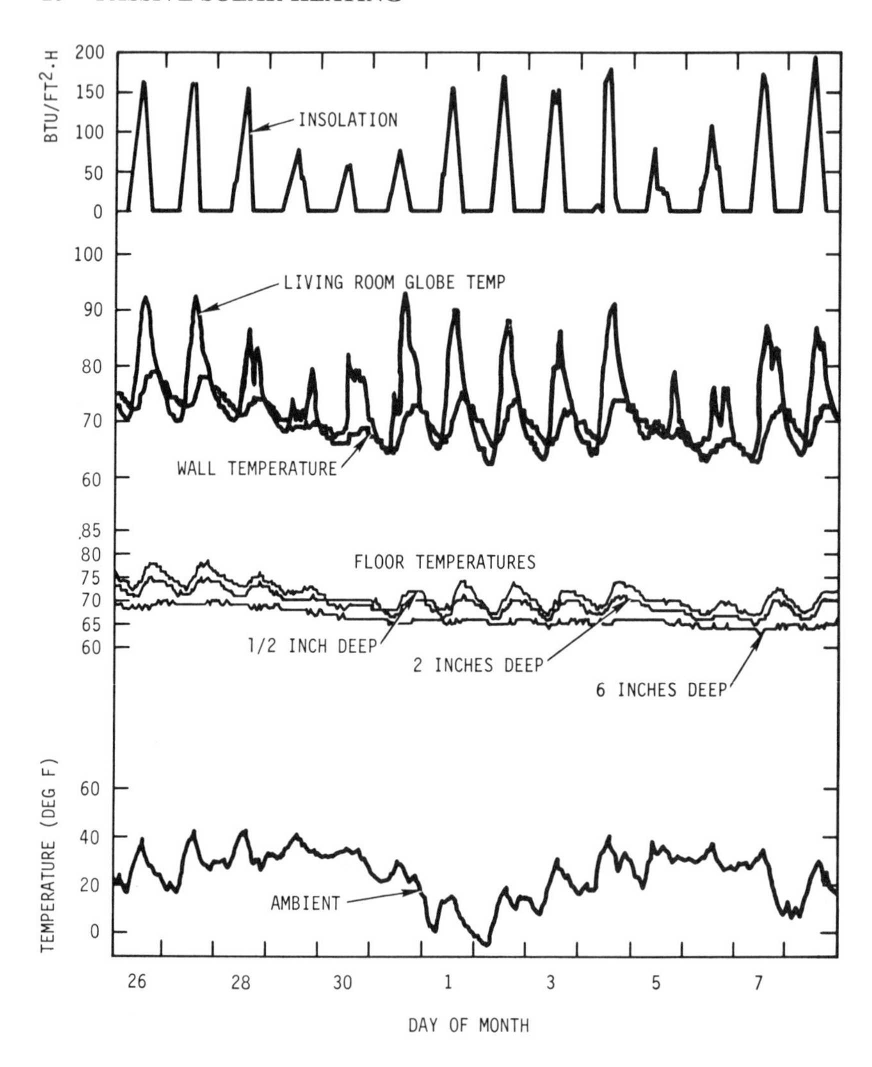


**Figure 14.** Data from Williamson house [Sandia 1979].

estimated to be 66%; the auxiliary heating source is wood stoves. The loss coefficient is 21,181 Btu/dd, or 10.6 Btu/ft$^2$-dd.

A direct-gain solar-heated warehouse was constructed by the Kalwall Corporation in Manchester, New Hampshire. Figures 18 and 19 illustrate the floor plan and cross section of the 40,000-ft$^2$ warehouse [Keller et al. 1978]. The south-facing solar aperture measures 125 × 15 ft, for a total area of 1650 ft$^2$ double-glazed with plastic sheets. The thermal storage

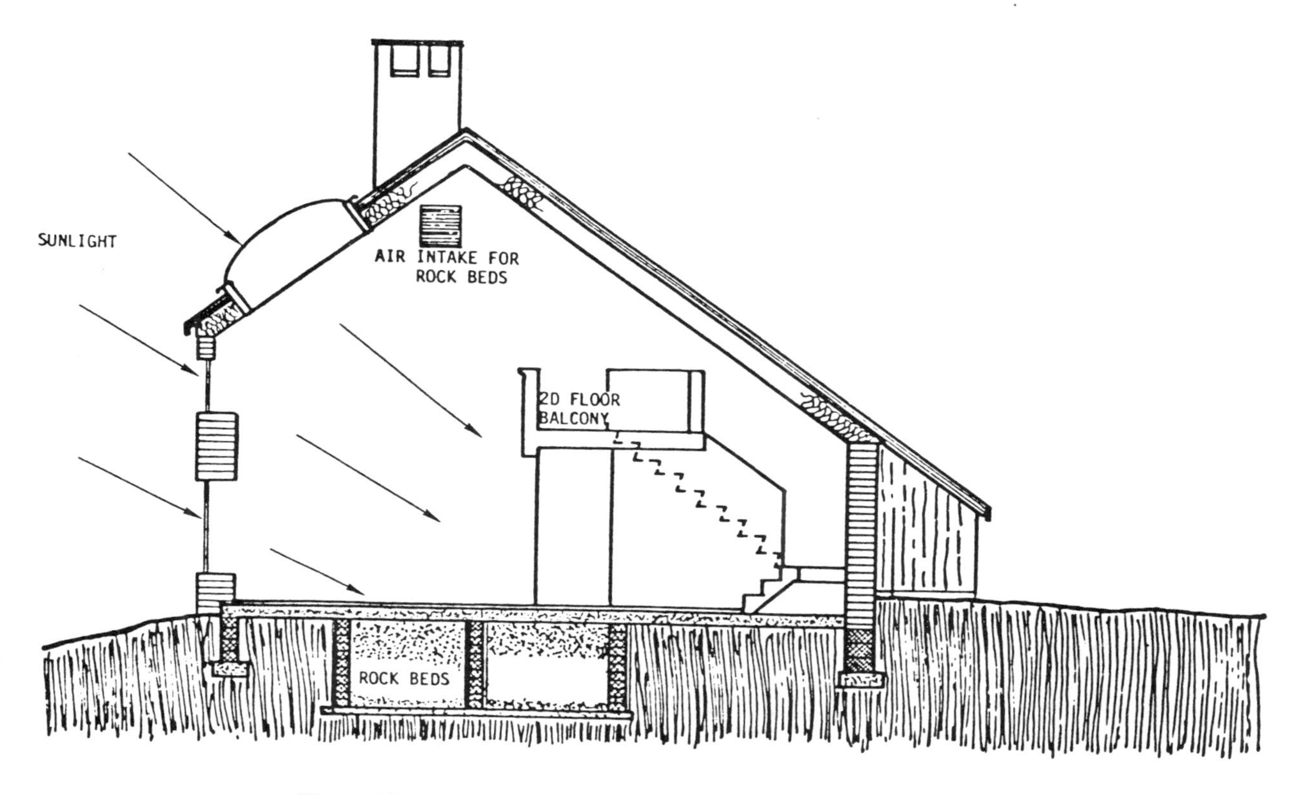


**Figure 15.** Cross section of Shankland house [Sandia 1979].

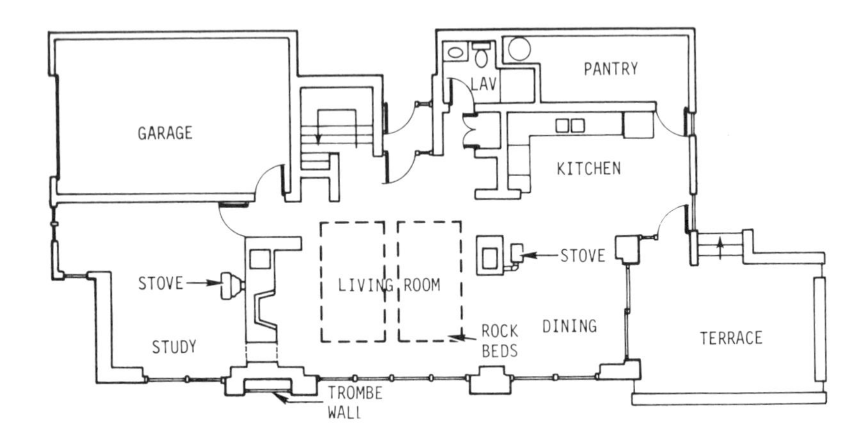


**Figure 16.** Floor plan of Shankland house [Sandia 1979].

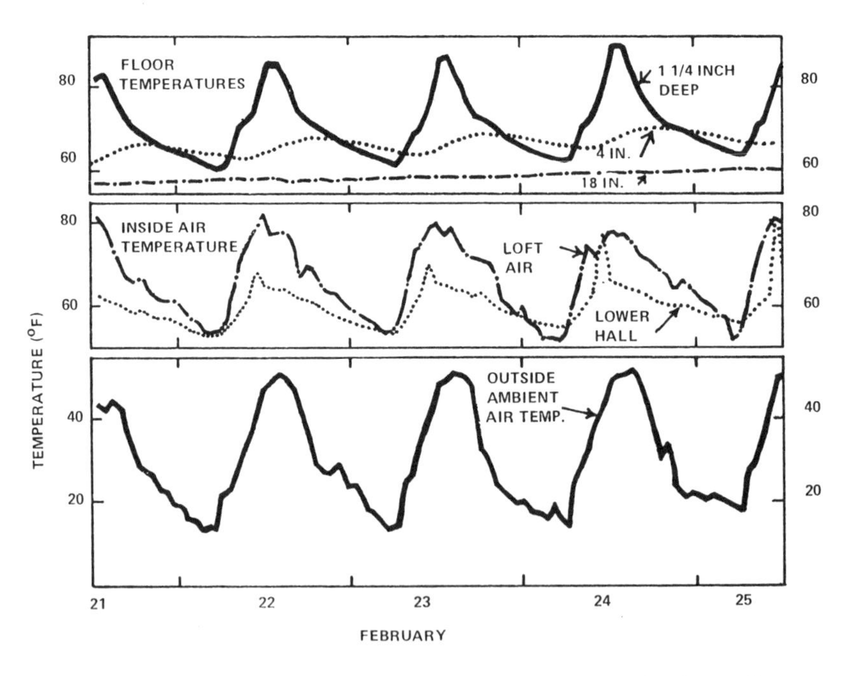


**Figure 17.** Performance data for Shankland house [Sandia 1979].

mass is the black concrete floor and the stored materials in the warehouse. Electric fans circulate air in the interior space. The warehouse is not heavily insulated. The solar heating fraction is about 55%.

The 960-ft$^2$ block and adobe Karen Terry House in Santa Fe, New Mexico, uses a 400-ft$^2$ shaded roof aperture [Terry 1976]. The tri-level

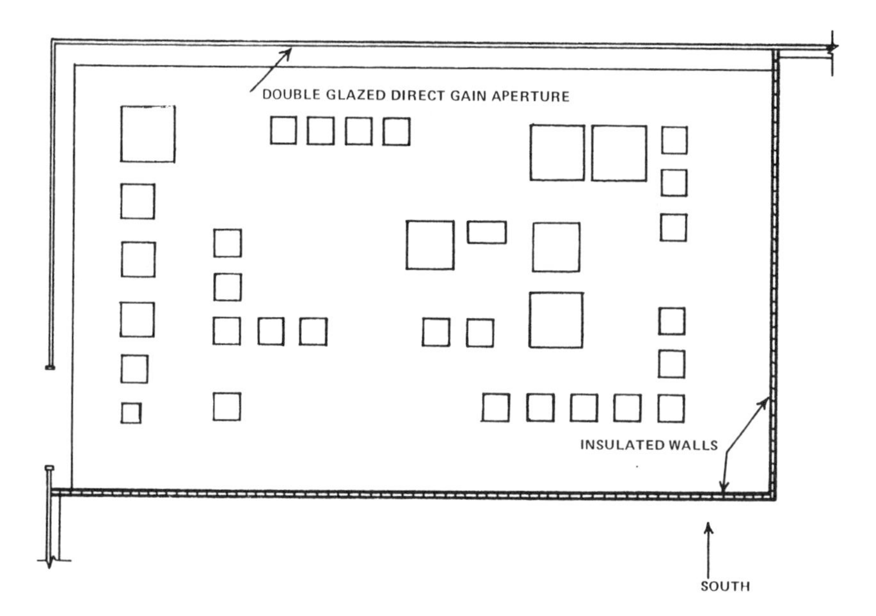


**Figure 18.** Floor plan for Kalwall warehouse.

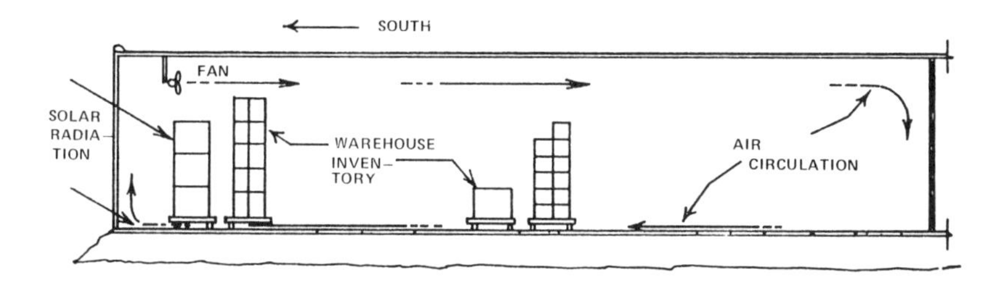


**Figure 19.** Cross section of Kalwall warehouse.

house has the bedroom and bath on the upper level, where the temperature is higher. The double glazing is of tempered glass and twenty-eight 55-gal drums of water provide direct-coupled thermal storage. The exterior walls are insulated on the outside with two inches of foam. Fixed louvers of 1- × 8-in. pine spaced 6 in. apart are manually installed outside over the aperture during the summer to block direct sunlight.

A four-story 267,000-ft$^2$ office building in Sacramento, California [Corsin 1978], uses direct-gain for heating and to enhance indoor lighting (Figure 20). Thermal storage is in two rock beds containing 1.35 million pounds of 1-in. (average) stones. The 4500-ft$^2$ solar aperture is tilted to the south at a 60° slope.

A large number of different types of direct-gain solar houses have been

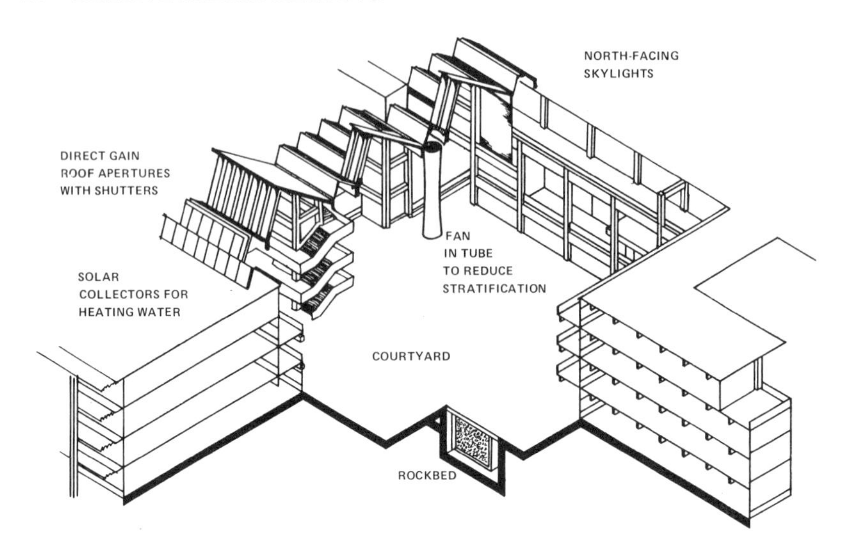


**Figure 20.** Direct-gain office building in Sacramento, California [Corsin 1978].

built during the past few years. A few of these are illustrated in Figure 21. The upper figure illustrates a house with a vertical roof aperture augmented by east and west apertures. The other illustrations show inclined and vertical south-facing wall and shaded roof apertures.

A house in Davis, California (Figure 22), uses a shaded roof aperture and south wall aperture with direct-coupled thermal storage mass (water) to provide 90% of its heating requirements. Direct-gain test buildings in Pullman, Washington, that used water barrels for heat storage maintained temperatures of 55–85°F while the outside temperatures ranged 27–58°F (Figure 23). An 866-ft$^2$ studio-classroom at the Massachusetts Institute of Technology (MIT) gets 59% of its heat from 180 ft$^2$ of double-glazed vertical south windows [Johnson 1978]. An earth-insulated 1100-ft$^2$ house in Ames, Iowa (Figures 24 and 25), gets about 85% of its heat by direct-gain through 500 ft$^2$ of south-facing wall and roof glazing [Block and Hodges 1979]. A direct-gain house in Santa Fe, New Mexico, is purported to get about 90% of its heating from solar [Rogers 1976], and direct-gain houses of nearly conventional design in Wisconsin are reported to get 44% of their heat from solar [Kieffer 1979]. An area of 860 ft$^2$ of south-facing windows provide about 70% of the heat for a 2000-ft$^2$ house (Figure 26) in Fayetteville, Arkansas [Lambeth 1978]. A direct-gain passive design for a 2650-ft$^2$ house in Oak Ridge, Tennessee (Figure 27), gets 42% of its heat from 248 ft$^2$ of south-facing double-glazed windows with insulating shutters [Reid et al. 1978].

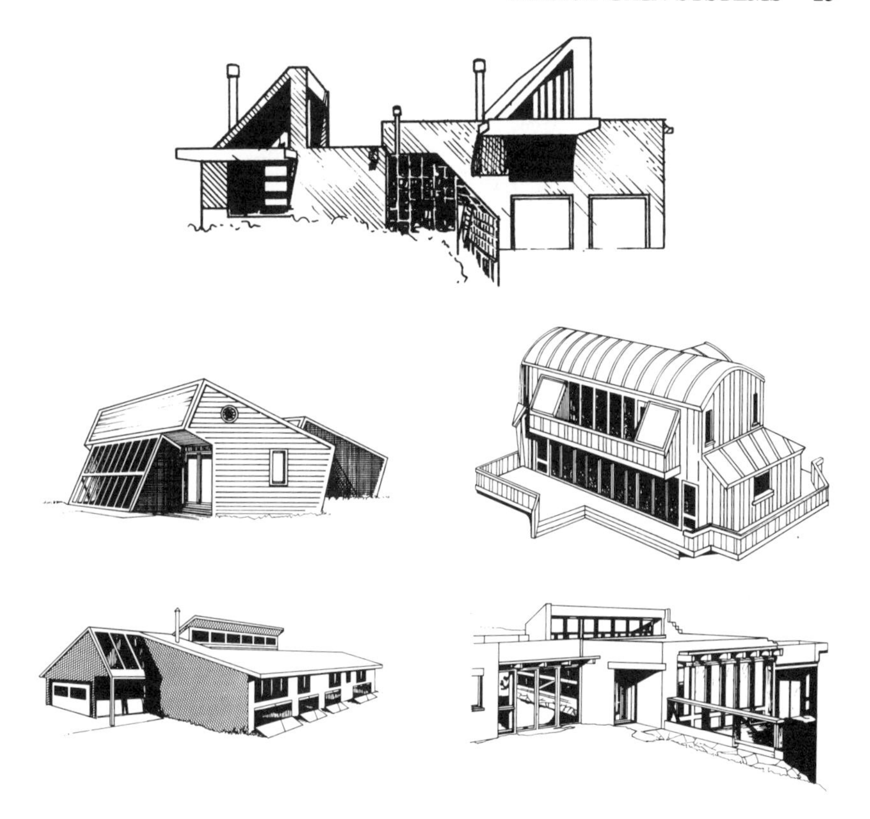

**Figure 21.** Some direct-gain solar houses [Loftness 1979].

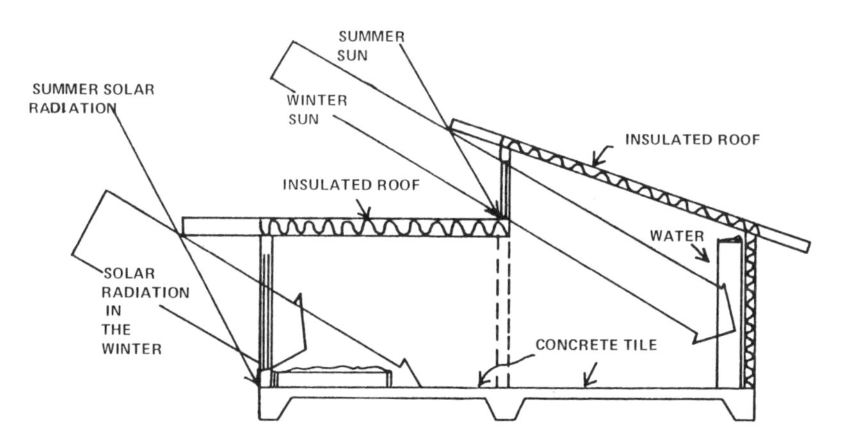


**Figure 22.** Davis, California, passive solar house.

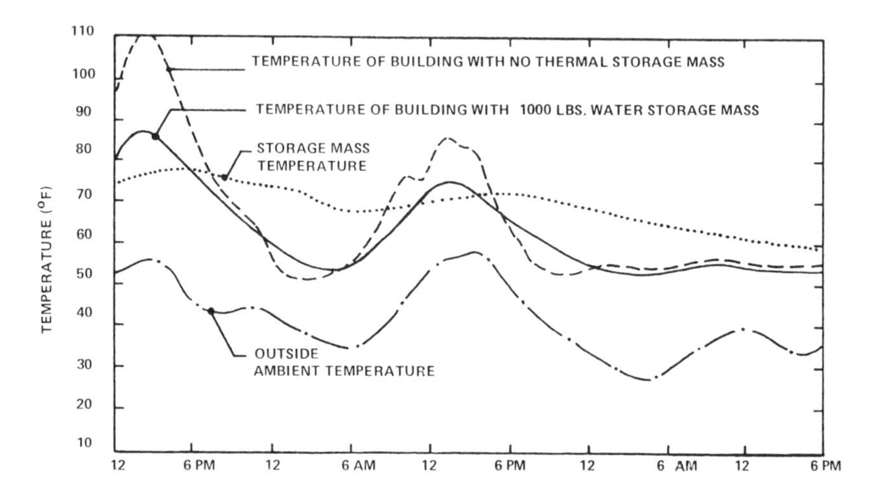


**Figure 23.** Temperature of direct-gain buildings in Pullman, Washington [Allen 1978].

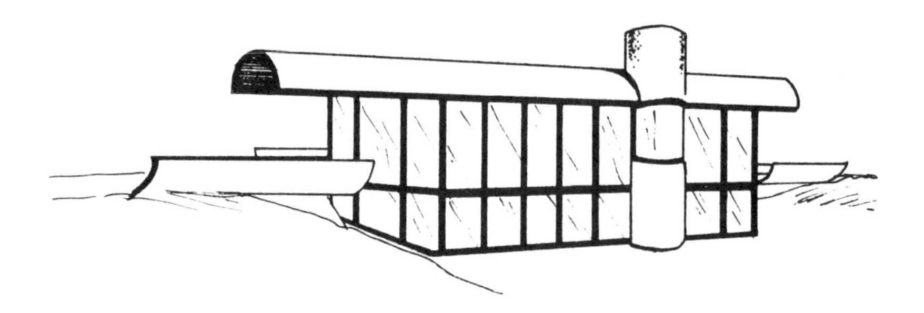

**Figure 24.** Ames, Iowa, direct-gain solar house [Block and Hodges 1979].

Some direct-gain residences circulate air through rock beds to moderate temperature fluctuations. An example is the 2100-ft$^2$ Lindeberg residence in Minneapolis, Minnesota [Pfister 1978], illustrated in Figures 28 to 30, which receives about half its heating from solar. The system uses 275 ft$^2$ of south-facing double-glazed windows with movable insulation and 75 ft$^2$ of south-facing skylights. Thermal storage is in the 32-ton concrete floor and 20-ton rock storage bin.

The Suncatcher house in Davis, California (Figure 31), gets about 70% of its heating from solar energy. Most of the solar gain is through a 96-ft$^2$ shaded vertical roof aperture (Figure 32) with a direct-coupled water wall for thermal storage. During the summer, direct sunlight is not admitted through the roof aperture (Figure 33). A manually operated insulating shutter inside the roof glazing reduces heat loss at night. The water wall consists of seven 2-ft-diameter galvanized steel tubes 10 ft high located 8 ft behind the windows. Three south-facing bedrooms are also heated by

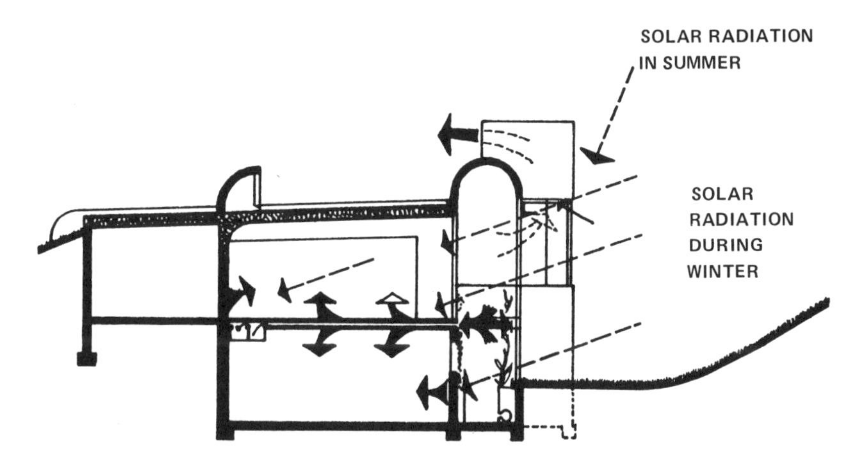


**Figure 25.** Cross section of Ames direct-gain house [Block and Hodges 1979].

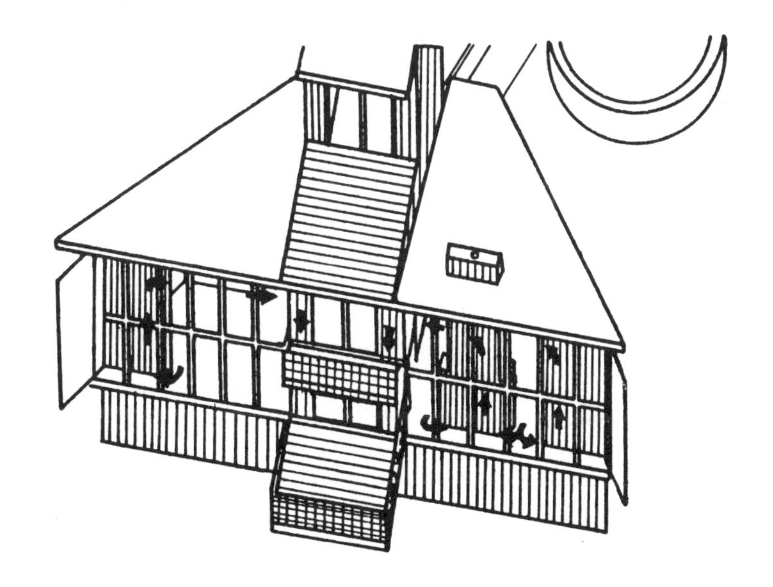

**Figure 26.** Direct-gain house in Fayetteville, Arkansas [Lambeth 1978].

**Figure 27.** Oak Ridge, Tennessee, direct-gain house [Reid et al. 1978].

**Figure 28.** Direct-gain house with rock bin storage.

direct gain through windows. This house was instrumented with more than 130 thermocouples [Maede et al. 1979a,b]. Temperature, solar radiation and various other parameters were recorded to determine system performance. The data were recorded using a microcomputer. Figure 34 illustrates a typical winter day, with the living room dry bulb temperature ranging 58–70°F and the outside temperature varying from 27 to 46°F.

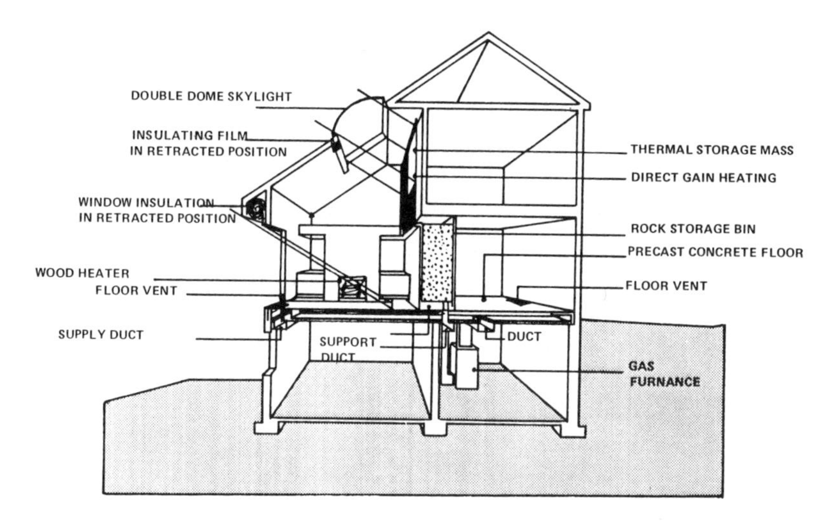


**Figure 29.** Cross section of direct-gain house with rock bin storage [Pfister 1978].

## HOW TO ANALYZE THE HEATING LOAD OF A BUILDING

A first step in analyzing the performance of a solar heating system is to determine the heating load of the building. The heating load is equal to the heat loss through the building envelope (or skin) plus the heat required to raise the temperature of outside air entering the building to the inside air temperature (infiltration load), less other sources of heat within the building envelope, such as lighting, appliances, equipment and people.

### Calculate Heat Loss Through Building Envelope

Heat losses through the building envelope for a month may be estimated using the degree-day method. The total UA factor for the building is multiplied by the average total number of heating degree-days for the month (Table III) times 24 hr/day. The UA factor is determined by the building geometry and the type of materials used for the structure and for insulation.

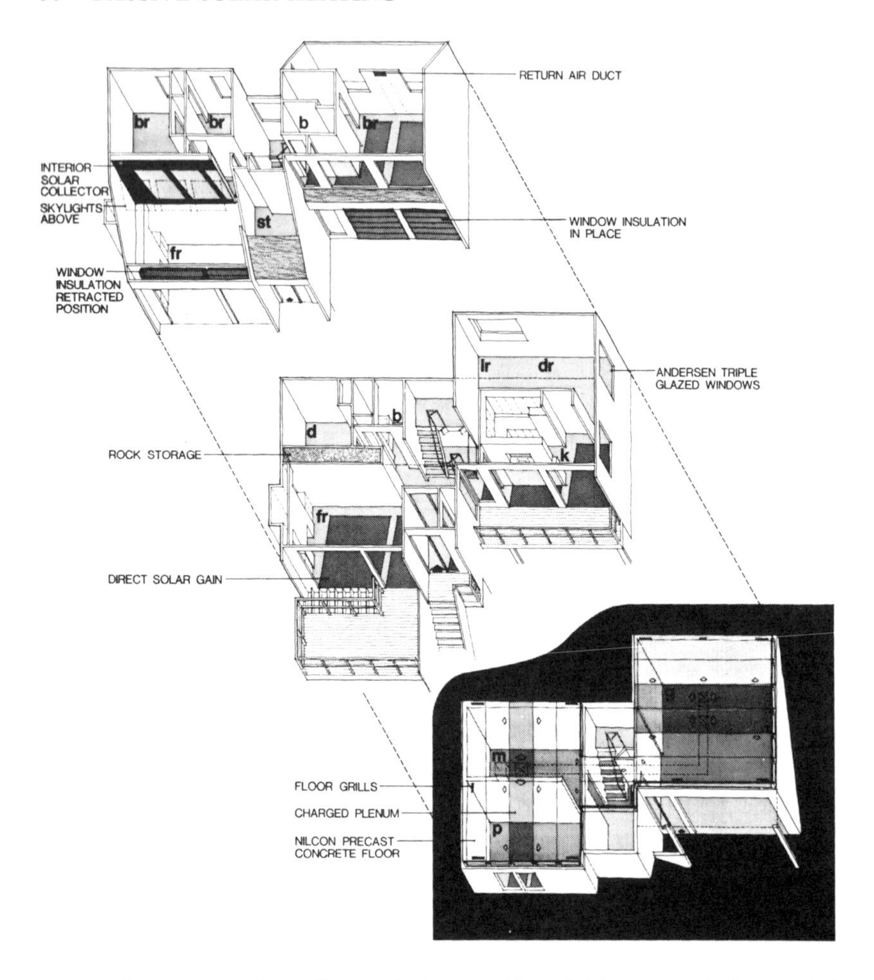


**Figure 30.** Isometric of direct-gain house with rock bin storage [Pfister 1978].

## *Reducing Heat Loss with Insulation*

Fiberglass and mineral wool insulation are commonly used insulators since they are nonflammable and relatively inexpensive. They must not be subjected to compression, since compression reduces the insulating value. Fireproof cellulose fill is even less expensive and is a useful insulation for a horizontal surface provided it never gets wet. Wet fiberglass recovers its insulating properties when it dries out; celulose fill does not. Also, cellulose and loose fiberglass cannot be piled higher than about 2 ft, since the insulation near the bottom will be compressed by the weight of insulation on top.

**Figure 31.** Suncatcher house with shaded roof aperture and water-wall heat storage [Meade 1979].

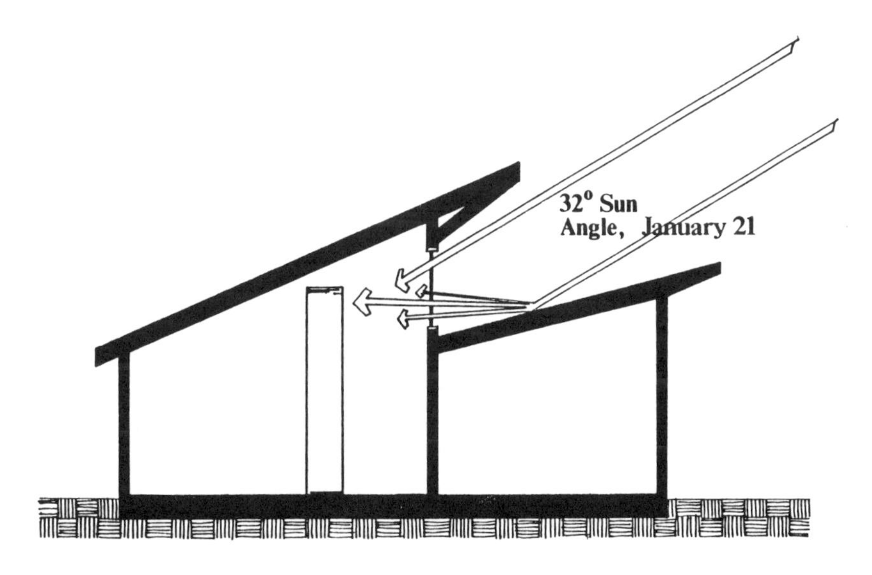


**Figure 32.** Suncatcher house receiving solar radiation in winter.

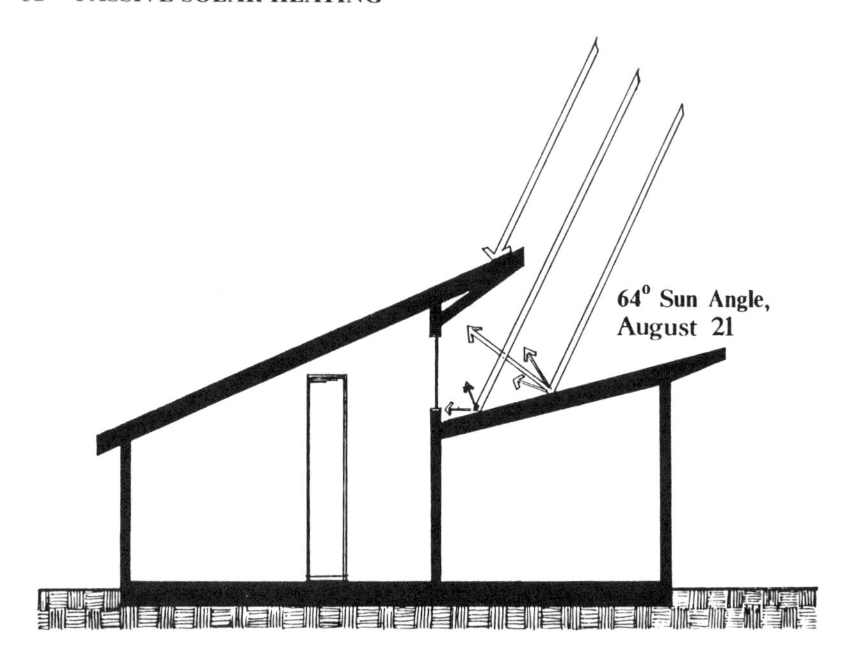


**Figure 33.** Suncatcher house blocking solar radiation in summer.

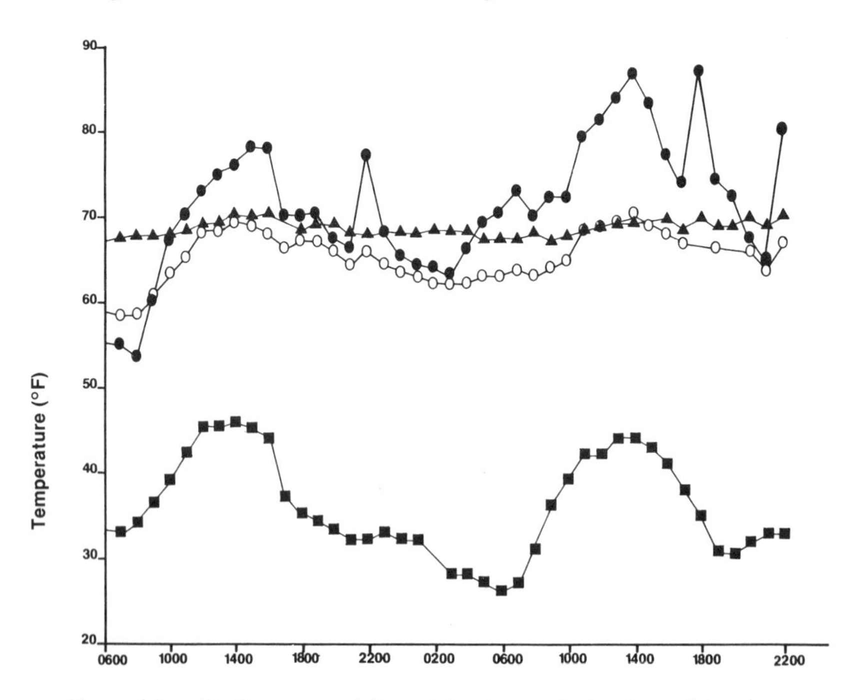


**Figure 34.** Performance of Suncatcher house during two winter days.

**Table III. Average Normal Total Heating Degree-Days (Base 65°)**

| State/City | Jan | Feb | Mar | Apr | May | Jun | Jul | Aug | Sep | Oct | Nov | Dec | Year |
|---|---|---|---|---|---|---|---|---|---|---|---|---|---|
| Alabama | | | | | | | | | | | | | |
| Birmingham | 592 | 462 | 363 | 108 | 9 | 0 | 0 | 0 | 6 | 93 | 363 | 555 | 2551 |
| Huntsville | 694 | 557 | 434 | 128 | 19 | 0 | 0 | 0 | 12 | 127 | 426 | 663 | 3070 |
| Mobile | 415 | 300 | 211 | 42 | 0 | 0 | 0 | 0 | 0 | 22 | 213 | 357 | 1560 |
| Montgomery | 543 | 417 | 216 | 90 | 0 | 0 | 0 | 0 | 0 | 68 | 330 | 527 | 2291 |
| Alaska | | | | | | | | | | | | | |
| Anchorage | 1631 | 1316 | 1293 | 879 | 592 | 315 | 245 | 291 | 516 | 930 | 1284 | 1572 | 10864 |
| Annette | 949 | 837 | 843 | 648 | 490 | 321 | 242 | 208 | 327 | 567 | 738 | 899 | 7069 |
| Barrow | 2517 | 2332 | 2468 | 1944 | 1445 | 957 | 803 | 840 | 1035 | 1500 | 1971 | 2362 | 20174 |
| Barter Is. | 2536 | 2369 | 2477 | 1923 | 1373 | 924 | 735 | 775 | 987 | 1482 | 1944 | 2337 | 19862 |
| Bethel | 1903 | 1590 | 1655 | 1173 | 806 | 402 | 319 | 394 | 612 | 1042 | 1434 | 1866 | 13196 |
| Cold Bay | 1153 | 1036 | 1122 | 951 | 791 | 591 | 474 | 425 | 525 | 772 | 918 | 1122 | 9880 |
| Cordova | 1299 | 1086 | 1113 | 864 | 660 | 444 | 366 | 391 | 522 | 781 | 1017 | 1221 | 9764 |
| Fairbanks | 2359 | 1901 | 1739 | 1058 | 555 | 222 | 171 | 332 | 642 | 1203 | 1813 | 2254 | 14279 |
| Juneau | 1237 | 1070 | 1073 | 810 | 601 | 381 | 301 | 338 | 483 | 725 | 921 | 1135 | 9075 |
| King Salmon | 1600 | 1333 | 1411 | 966 | 673 | 408 | 313 | 322 | 513 | 908 | 1290 | 1606 | 11343 |
| Kotzebue | 2192 | 1932 | 2080 | 1554 | 1057 | 636 | 381 | 446 | 723 | 1249 | 1728 | 2127 | 16105 |
| McGrath | 2294 | 1817 | 1758 | 1122 | 648 | 258 | 208 | 338 | 633 | 1184 | 1791 | 2232 | 14283 |
| Nome | 1879 | 1666 | 1770 | 1314 | 930 | 573 | 481 | 496 | 693 | 1094 | 1455 | 1820 | 14171 |
| Saint Paul | 1228 | 1168 | 1265 | 1098 | 936 | 726 | 605 | 539 | 612 | 862 | 963 | 1197 | 11199 |
| Shemya | 1045 | 958 | 1011 | 885 | 837 | 696 | 577 | 475 | 501 | 784 | 876 | 1042 | 9687 |
| Yakutat | 1169 | 1019 | 1042 | 840 | 632 | 435 | 338 | 347 | 474 | 716 | 936 | 1144 | 9092 |
| Arizona | | | | | | | | | | | | | |
| Flagstaff | 1169 | 991 | 911 | 651 | 437 | 180 | 46 | 68 | 201 | 558 | 867 | 1073 | 7152 |
| Phoenix | 474 | 328 | 217 | 75 | 0 | 0 | 0 | 0 | 0 | 22 | 234 | 415 | 1765 |
| Prescott | 865 | 711 | 605 | 360 | 158 | 15 | 0 | 0 | 27 | 245 | 579 | 797 | 4362 |
| Tucson | 471 | 344 | 242 | 75 | 6 | 0 | 0 | 0 | 0 | 25 | 231 | 406 | 1800 |

Table III, continued

| State/City | Jan | Feb | Mar | Apr | May | Jun | Jul | Aug | Sep | Oct | Nov | Dec | Year |
|---|---|---|---|---|---|---|---|---|---|---|---|---|---|
| Winslow | 1054 | 770 | 601 | 291 | 96 | 0 | 0 | 0 | 6 | 245 | 711 | 1008 | 4782 |
| Yuma | 363 | 228 | 130 | 29 | 0 | 0 | 0 | 0 | 0 | 0 | 148 | 319 | 1217 |
| Arkansas | | | | | | | | | | | | | |
| Fort Smith | 781 | 596 | 456 | 144 | 22 | 0 | 0 | 0 | 12 | 127 | 450 | 704 | 3292 |
| Little Rock | 756 | 577 | 434 | 126 | 9 | 0 | 0 | 0 | 9 | 127 | 465 | 716 | 3219 |
| Texarkana | 626 | 468 | 350 | 105 | 0 | 0 | 0 | 0 | 0 | 78 | 345 | 561 | 2533 |
| California | | | | | | | | | | | | | |
| Bakersfield | 546 | 364 | 267 | 105 | 19 | 0 | 0 | 0 | 0 | 37 | 282 | 502 | 2122 |
| Bishop | 874 | 666 | 539 | 306 | 143 | 36 | 0 | 0 | 42 | 248 | 576 | 797 | 4227 |
| Blue Canyon | 865 | 781 | 791 | 582 | 397 | 195 | 34 | 50 | 120 | 347 | 579 | 766 | 5507 |
| Burbank | 366 | 277 | 239 | 138 | 81 | 18 | 0 | 0 | 6 | 43 | 177 | 301 | 1646 |
| Eureka | 546 | 470 | 505 | 438 | 372 | 285 | 270 | 257 | 258 | 329 | 414 | 499 | 4643 |
| Fresno | 586 | 406 | 319 | 150 | 56 | 0 | 0 | 0 | 0 | 78 | 339 | 558 | 2492 |
| Long Beach | 375 | 297 | 267 | 168 | 90 | 18 | 0 | 0 | 12 | 40 | 156 | 288 | 1711 |
| Los Angeles | 372 | 302 | 288 | 219 | 158 | 81 | 28 | 22 | 42 | 78 | 180 | 291 | 2061 |
| Mt. Shasta | 983 | 784 | 738 | 525 | 347 | 159 | 25 | 34 | 123 | 406 | 696 | 902 | 5722 |
| Oakland | 527 | 400 | 255 | 355 | 180 | 90 | 53 | 50 | 45 | 127 | 309 | 481 | 2870 |
| Point Arguello | 474 | 392 | 403 | 339 | 298 | 243 | 202 | 186 | 162 | 205 | 291 | 400 | 3595 |
| Red Bluff | 605 | 428 | 341 | 168 | 47 | 0 | 0 | 0 | 0 | 53 | 318 | 555 | 2515 |
| Sacramento | 614 | 442 | 360 | 216 | 102 | 6 | 0 | 0 | 12 | 81 | 363 | 577 | 2773 |
| Sandberg | 778 | 661 | 620 | 426 | 264 | 57 | 0 | 0 | 30 | 202 | 480 | 691 | 4209 |
| San Diego | 313 | 249 | 202 | 123 | 84 | 36 | 6 | 0 | 15 | 37 | 123 | 251 | 1439 |
| San Francisco | 508 | 395 | 363 | 279 | 214 | 126 | 81 | 78 | 60 | 143 | 306 | 462 | 3015 |
| Santa Catalina | 353 | 308 | 326 | 249 | 192 | 105 | 16 | 0 | 9 | 50 | 165 | 279 | 2052 |
| Santa Maria | 459 | 370 | 363 | 282 | 233 | 165 | 99 | 93 | 96 | 146 | 270 | 391 | 2967 |

| | | | | | | | | | | | | | |
|---|---|---|---|---|---|---|---|---|---|---|---|---|---|
| Colorado | | | | | | | | | | | | | |
| Alamosa | 1476 | 1162 | 1020 | 696 | 440 | 168 | 65 | 99 | 279 | 639 | 1065 | 1420 | 8529 |
| Colorado Springs | 1128 | 938 | 893 | 582 | 319 | 84 | 9 | 25 | 132 | 456 | 825 | 1032 | 6423 |
| Denver | 1132 | 938 | 887 | 558 | 288 | 66 | 6 | 9 | 117 | 428 | 819 | 1035 | 6283 |
| Grand Junction | 1209 | 907 | 729 | 387 | 146 | 21 | 0 | 0 | 30 | 313 | 786 | 1113 | 5641 |
| Pueblo | 1085 | 871 | 772 | 429 | 174 | 15 | 0 | 0 | 54 | 326 | 750 | 986 | 5462 |
| Connecticut | | | | | | | | | | | | | |
| Bridgeport | 1079 | 966 | 853 | 510 | 208 | 27 | 0 | 0 | 66 | 307 | 615 | 986 | 5617 |
| Hartford | 1209 | 1061 | 899 | 495 | 177 | 24 | 0 | 6 | 99 | 372 | 711 | 1119 | 6172 |
| New Haven | 1097 | 991 | 871 | 543 | 245 | 45 | 0 | 12 | 87 | 347 | 648 | 1011 | 5897 |
| Delaware | | | | | | | | | | | | | |
| Wilmington | 980 | 874 | 735 | 387 | 112 | 6 | 0 | 0 | 51 | 270 | 588 | 927 | 4930 |
| Florida | | | | | | | | | | | | | |
| Apalachicola | 347 | 260 | 180 | 33 | 0 | 0 | 0 | 0 | 0 | 16 | 153 | 319 | 1308 |
| Daytona Beach | 248 | 190 | 140 | 15 | 0 | 0 | 0 | 0 | 0 | 0 | 75 | 211 | 879 |
| Fort Myers | 146 | 101 | 62 | 0 | 0 | 0 | 0 | 0 | 0 | 0 | 24 | 109 | 442 |
| Jacksonville | 332 | 246 | 174 | 21 | 0 | 0 | 0 | 0 | 0 | 12 | 144 | 310 | 1239 |
| Key West | 40 | 31 | 9 | 0 | 0 | 0 | 0 | 0 | 0 | 0 | 0 | 28 | 108 |
| Lakeland | 195 | 146 | 99 | 0 | 0 | 0 | 0 | 0 | 0 | 0 | 57 | 164 | 661 |
| Miami Beach | 56 | 36 | 9 | 0 | 0 | 0 | 0 | 0 | 0 | 0 | 0 | 40 | 141 |
| Orlando | 220 | 165 | 105 | 6 | 0 | 0 | 0 | 0 | 0 | 0 | 72 | 198 | 766 |
| Pensacola | 400 | 277 | 183 | 36 | 0 | 0 | 0 | 0 | 0 | 19 | 195 | 353 | 1463 |
| Tallahassee | 375 | 286 | 202 | 36 | 0 | 0 | 0 | 0 | 0 | 28 | 198 | 360 | 1485 |
| Tampa | 202 | 148 | 102 | 0 | 0 | 0 | 0 | 0 | 0 | 0 | 60 | 171 | 683 |
| West Palm Beach | 87 | 64 | 31 | 0 | 0 | 0 | 0 | 0 | 0 | 0 | 6 | 65 | 253 |
| Georgia | | | | | | | | | | | | | |
| Athens | 642 | 529 | 431 | 141 | 22 | 0 | 0 | 0 | 12 | 115 | 405 | 632 | 2929 |
| Atlanta | 639 | 529 | 437 | 168 | 25 | 0 | 0 | 0 | 18 | 127 | 414 | 626 | 2983 |
| Augusta | 549 | 445 | 350 | 90 | 0 | 0 | 0 | 0 | 0 | 78 | 333 | 552 | 2397 |
| Columbus | 552 | 434 | 338 | 96 | 0 | 0 | 0 | 0 | 0 | 87 | 333 | 543 | 2383 |

Table III, continued

| State/City | Jan | Feb | Mar | Apr | May | Jun | Jul | Aug | Sep | Oct | Nov | Dec | Year |
|---|---|---|---|---|---|---|---|---|---|---|---|---|---|
| Macon | 505 | 403 | 295 | 63 | 0 | 0 | 0 | 0 | 0 | 71 | 297 | 502 | 2136 |
| Rome | 710 | 577 | 468 | 177 | 34 | 0 | 0 | 0 | 24 | 161 | 474 | 701 | 3326 |
| Savannah | 437 | 353 | 254 | 45 | 0 | 0 | 0 | 0 | 0 | 47 | 246 | 437 | 1819 |
| Thomasville | 394 | 305 | 208 | 33 | 0 | 0 | 0 | 0 | 0 | 25 | 198 | 366 | 1529 |
| Idaho | | | | | | | | | | | | | |
| Boise | 1113 | 854 | 722 | 438 | 245 | 81 | 0 | 0 | 132 | 415 | 792 | 1017 | 5809 |
| Idaho Falls 46°W | 1538 | 1249 | 1085 | 651 | 391 | 192 | 16 | 34 | 270 | 623 | 1056 | 1370 | 8475 |
| Idaho Falls 42°NW | 1600 | 1291 | 1107 | 657 | 388 | 192 | 16 | 40 | 282 | 648 | 1107 | 1432 | 8760 |
| Lewiston | 1063 | 815 | 694 | 426 | 239 | 90 | 0 | 0 | 123 | 403 | 756 | 933 | 5542 |
| Pocatello | 1324 | 1058 | 905 | 555 | 319 | 141 | 0 | 0 | 172 | 493 | 900 | 1166 | 7033 |
| Illinois | | | | | | | | | | | | | |
| Cairo | 856 | 680 | 539 | 195 | 47 | 0 | 0 | 0 | 36 | 164 | 513 | 791 | 3821 |
| Chicago | 1209 | 1044 | 890 | 480 | 211 | 48 | 0 | 0 | 81 | 326 | 753 | 1113 | 6155 |
| Moline | 1314 | 1100 | 918 | 450 | 189 | 39 | 0 | 9 | 99 | 335 | 774 | 1181 | 6408 |
| Peoria | 1218 | 1025 | 849 | 426 | 183 | 33 | 0 | 6 | 87 | 326 | 759 | 1113 | 6025 |
| Rockford | 1333 | 1137 | 961 | 516 | 236 | 60 | 6 | 9 | 114 | 400 | 837 | 1221 | 6830 |
| Springfield | 1135 | 935 | 769 | 354 | 136 | 18 | 0 | 0 | 72 | 291 | 696 | 1023 | 5429 |
| Indiana | | | | | | | | | | | | | |
| Evansville | 955 | 767 | 620 | 237 | 68 | 0 | 0 | 0 | 66 | 220 | 606 | 896 | 4435 |
| Fort Wayne | 1178 | 1028 | 890 | 471 | 189 | 39 | 0 | 9 | 105 | 378 | 783 | 1135 | 6205 |
| Indianapolis | 1113 | 949 | 809 | 432 | 177 | 39 | 0 | 0 | 90 | 316 | 723 | 1051 | 5699 |
| South Bend | 1221 | 1070 | 933 | 525 | 239 | 60 | 0 | 6 | 111 | 372 | 777 | 1125 | 6439 |
| Iowa | | | | | | | | | | | | | |
| Burlington | 1259 | 1042 | 859 | 426 | 177 | 33 | 0 | 0 | 93 | 322 | 768 | 1135 | 6114 |
| Des Moines | 1398 | 1165 | 967 | 489 | 211 | 39 | 0 | 9 | 99 | 363 | 837 | 1231 | 6808 |
| Dubuque | 1420 | 1204 | 1026 | 546 | 260 | 78 | 12 | 31 | 156 | 450 | 906 | 1287 | 7376 |

| | | | | | | | | | | | | | |
|---|---|---|---|---|---|---|---|---|---|---|---|---|---|
| Sioux City | 1435 | 1198 | 989 | 483 | 214 | 39 | 0 | 9 | 108 | 369 | 867 | 1240 | 6951 |
| Waterloo | 1460 | 1221 | 1023 | 531 | 229 | 54 | 12 | 19 | 138 | 428 | 909 | 1296 | 7320 |
| Kansas | | | | | | | | | | | | | |
| Concordia | 1163 | 935 | 781 | 372 | 149 | 18 | 0 | 0 | 57 | 276 | 705 | 1023 | 5479 |
| Dodge City | 1051 | 840 | 719 | 354 | 124 | 9 | 0 | 0 | 33 | 251 | 666 | 939 | 4986 |
| Goodland | 1166 | 955 | 884 | 507 | 236 | 42 | 0 | 6 | 81 | 381 | 810 | 1073 | 6141 |
| Topeka | 1122 | 893 | 722 | 330 | 124 | 12 | 0 | 0 | 57 | 270 | 672 | 980 | 5182 |
| Wichita | 1023 | 804 | 645 | 270 | 87 | 6 | 0 | 0 | 33 | 229 | 618 | 905 | 4620 |
| Kentucky | | | | | | | | | | | | | |
| Covington | 1035 | 893 | 756 | 390 | 149 | 24 | 0 | 0 | 75 | 291 | 669 | 983 | 5265 |
| Lexington | 946 | 818 | 685 | 325 | 105 | 0 | 0 | 0 | 54 | 239 | 609 | 902 | 4683 |
| Louisville | 930 | 818 | 682 | 315 | 105 | 9 | 0 | 0 | 54 | 248 | 609 | 890 | 4660 |
| Louisiana | | | | | | | | | | | | | |
| Alexandria | 471 | 361 | 260 | 69 | 0 | 0 | 0 | 0 | 0 | 56 | 273 | 431 | 1921 |
| Baton Rouge | 409 | 294 | 208 | 33 | 0 | 0 | 0 | 0 | 0 | 31 | 216 | 369 | 1560 |
| Burrwood | 298 | 218 | 171 | 27 | 0 | 0 | 0 | 0 | 0 | 0 | 96 | 214 | 1024 |
| Lake Charles | 381 | 274 | 195 | 39 | 0 | 0 | 0 | 0 | 0 | 19 | 210 | 341 | 1459 |
| New Orleans | 363 | 258 | 192 | 39 | 0 | 0 | 0 | 0 | 0 | 19 | 192 | 322 | 1385 |
| Shreveport | 552 | 426 | 304 | 81 | 0 | 0 | 0 | 0 | 0 | 47 | 297 | 477 | 2184 |
| Maine | | | | | | | | | | | | | |
| Caribou | 1690 | 1470 | 1308 | 858 | 468 | 183 | 78 | 115 | 336 | 682 | 1044 | 1535 | 9767 |
| Portland | 1339 | 1182 | 1042 | 675 | 372 | 111 | 12 | 53 | 195 | 508 | 807 | 1215 | 7511 |
| Maryland | | | | | | | | | | | | | |
| Baltimore | 936 | 820 | 679 | 327 | 90 | 0 | 0 | 0 | 48 | 264 | 585 | 905 | 4654 |
| Frederick | 995 | 876 | 741 | 384 | 127 | 12 | 0 | 0 | 66 | 307 | 624 | 955 | 5087 |
| Massachusetts | | | | | | | | | | | | | |
| Blue Hill Observatory | 1178 | 1053 | 936 | 579 | 267 | 69 | 0 | 22 | 108 | 381 | 690 | 1085 | 6368 |
| Boston | 1088 | 972 | 846 | 513 | 208 | 36 | 0 | 9 | 60 | 316 | 603 | 983 | 5634 |
| Nantucket | 992 | 941 | 896 | 621 | 384 | 129 | 12 | 22 | 93 | 332 | 573 | 896 | 5891 |

Table III, continued

| State/City | Jan | Feb | Mar | Apr | May | Jun | Jul | Aug | Sep | Oct | Nov | Dec | Year |
|---|---|---|---|---|---|---|---|---|---|---|---|---|---|
| Pittsfield | 1339 | 1196 | 1063 | 660 | 326 | 105 | 25 | 59 | 219 | 524 | 831 | 1231 | 7578 |
| Worcester | 1271 | 1123 | 998 | 612 | 304 | 78 | 6 | 34 | 147 | 450 | 774 | 1172 | 6969 |
| Michigan | | | | | | | | | | | | | |
| Alpena | 1404 | 1299 | 1218 | 777 | 446 | 156 | 68 | 105 | 273 | 580 | 912 | 1268 | 8506 |
| Detroit | 1181 | 1058 | 936 | 522 | 220 | 42 | 0 | 0 | 87 | 360 | 738 | 1088 | 6232 |
| Escanaba | 1445 | 1296 | 1203 | 777 | 456 | 159 | 59 | 87 | 243 | 539 | 924 | 1293 | 8481 |
| Flint | 1330 | 1198 | 1066 | 639 | 319 | 90 | 16 | 40 | 159 | 465 | 843 | 1212 | 7377 |
| Grand Rapids | 1259 | 1134 | 1011 | 579 | 279 | 75 | 9 | 28 | 135 | 434 | 804 | 1147 | 6894 |
| Lansing | 1262 | 1142 | 1011 | 579 | 273 | 69 | 6 | 22 | 138 | 431 | 813 | 1163 | 6909 |
| Marquette | 1411 | 1268 | 1187 | 771 | 468 | 177 | 59 | 81 | 240 | 527 | 936 | 1268 | 8393 |
| Muskegon | 1209 | 1100 | 995 | 594 | 310 | 78 | 12 | 28 | 120 | 400 | 762 | 1088 | 6696 |
| Sault Ste. Marie | 1525 | 1380 | 1277 | 810 | 477 | 201 | 96 | 105 | 279 | 580 | 951 | 1367 | 9048 |
| Minnesota | | | | | | | | | | | | | |
| Duluth | 1745 | 1518 | 1355 | 840 | 490 | 198 | 71 | 109 | 330 | 632 | 1131 | 1581 | 10000 |
| International Falls | 1919 | 1621 | 1414 | 828 | 443 | 174 | 71 | 112 | 363 | 701 | 1236 | 1724 | 10606 |
| Minneapolis | 1631 | 1380 | 1166 | 621 | 288 | 81 | 22 | 31 | 189 | 505 | 1014 | 1454 | 8382 |
| Rochester | 1593 | 1366 | 1150 | 630 | 301 | 93 | 25 | 34 | 186 | 474 | 1005 | 1438 | 8295 |
| Saint Cloud | 1702 | 1445 | 1221 | 666 | 326 | 105 | 28 | 47 | 225 | 549 | 1065 | 1500 | 8879 |
| Mississippi | | | | | | | | | | | | | |
| Jackson | 546 | 414 | 310 | 87 | 0 | 0 | 0 | 0 | 0 | 65 | 315 | 502 | 2239 |
| Meridian | 543 | 417 | 310 | 81 | 0 | 0 | 0 | 0 | 0 | 81 | 339 | 518 | 2289 |
| Vicksburg | 512 | 384 | 282 | 69 | 0 | 0 | 0 | 0 | 0 | 53 | 279 | 462 | 2041 |
| Missouri | | | | | | | | | | | | | |
| Columbia | 1076 | 874 | 716 | 324 | 121 | 12 | 0 | 0 | 54 | 251 | 651 | 967 | 5046 |
| Kansas | 1032 | 818 | 682 | 294 | 109 | 0 | 0 | 0 | 39 | 220 | 612 | 905 | 4711 |
| St. Joseph | 1172 | 949 | 769 | 348 | 133 | 15 | 0 | 6 | 60 | 285 | 708 | 1039 | 5484 |

| | | | | | | | | | | | | | |
|---|---|---|---|---|---|---|---|---|---|---|---|---|---|
| St. Louis | 1026 | 848 | 704 | 312 | 121 | 15 | 0 | 0 | 60 | 251 | 627 | 936 | 4900 |
| Springfield | 973 | 781 | 660 | 291 | 105 | 6 | 0 | 0 | 45 | 223 | 600 | 877 | 4561 |
| Montana | | | | | | | | | | | | | |
| Billings | 1296 | 1100 | 970 | 570 | 285 | 102 | 6 | 15 | 186 | 487 | 897 | 1135 | 7049 |
| Glasgow | 1711 | 1439 | 1187 | 648 | 335 | 150 | 31 | 47 | 270 | 608 | 1104 | 1466 | 8996 |
| Great Falls | 1349 | 1154 | 1063 | 642 | 384 | 186 | 28 | 53 | 258 | 543 | 921 | 1169 | 7750 |
| Havre | 1584 | 1364 | 1181 | 657 | 338 | 162 | 28 | 53 | 306 | 595 | 1065 | 1367 | 8700 |
| Helena | 1438 | 1170 | 1042 | 651 | 381 | 195 | 31 | 59 | 294 | 601 | 1002 | 1265 | 8129 |
| Kalispell | 1401 | 1134 | 1029 | 639 | 397 | 207 | 50 | 99 | 321 | 654 | 1020 | 1240 | 8191 |
| Miles City | 1504 | 1252 | 1057 | 579 | 276 | 99 | 6 | 6 | 174 | 502 | 972 | 1296 | 7723 |
| Missoula | 1420 | 1120 | 970 | 621 | 391 | 219 | 34 | 74 | 303 | 651 | 1035 | 1287 | 8125 |
| Nebraska | | | | | | | | | | | | | |
| Grand Island | 1314 | 1089 | 908 | 462 | 211 | 45 | 0 | 6 | 108 | 381 | 834 | 1172 | 6530 |
| Lincoln | 1237 | 1016 | 834 | 402 | 171 | 30 | 0 | 6 | 75 | 301 | 726 | 1066 | 5864 |
| Norfolk | 1414 | 1179 | 983 | 498 | 233 | 48 | 9 | 0 | 111 | 397 | 873 | 1234 | 6979 |
| North Platte | 1271 | 1039 | 930 | 519 | 248 | 57 | 0 | 6 | 123 | 440 | 885 | 1166 | 6684 |
| Omaha | 1355 | 1126 | 939 | 465 | 208 | 42 | 0 | 12 | 105 | 357 | 828 | 1175 | 6612 |
| Scottsbluff | 1231 | 1008 | 921 | 552 | 285 | 75 | 0 | 0 | 138 | 459 | 876 | 1128 | 6673 |
| Valentine | 1395 | 1176 | 1045 | 579 | 288 | 84 | 9 | 12 | 165 | 493 | 942 | 1237 | 7425 |
| Nevada | | | | | | | | | | | | | |
| Elko | 1314 | 1036 | 911 | 621 | 409 | 192 | 9 | 34 | 225 | 561 | 924 | 1197 | 7433 |
| Ely | 1308 | 1075 | 977 | 672 | 456 | 225 | 28 | 43 | 234 | 592 | 939 | 1184 | 7733 |
| Las Vegas | 688 | 487 | 335 | 111 | 6 | 0 | 0 | 0 | 0 | 78 | 387 | 617 | 2709 |
| Reno | 1073 | 823 | 729 | 510 | 357 | 189 | 43 | 87 | 204 | 490 | 801 | 1026 | 6332 |
| Winnemucca | 1172 | 916 | 837 | 573 | 363 | 153 | 0 | 34 | 210 | 536 | 876 | 1091 | 6761 |
| New Hampshire | | | | | | | | | | | | | |
| Concord | 1358 | 1184 | 1032 | 636 | 298 | 75 | 6 | 50 | 177 | 505 | 822 | 1240 | 7383 |
| Mt. Washington Observatory | 1820 | 1663 | 1652 | 1260 | 930 | 603 | 493 | 536 | 720 | 1057 | 1341 | 1742 | 13817 |
| New Jersey | | | | | | | | | | | | | |
| Atlantic City | 936 | 848 | 741 | 420 | 133 | 15 | 0 | 0 | 39 | 251 | 549 | 880 | 4812 |

Table III, continued

| State/City | Jan | Feb | Mar | Apr | May | Jun | Jul | Aug | Sep | Oct | Nov | Dec | Year |
|---|---|---|---|---|---|---|---|---|---|---|---|---|---|
| Newark | 983 | 876 | 729 | 381 | 118 | 0 | 0 | 0 | 30 | 248 | 573 | 921 | 4859 |
| Trenton | 989 | 885 | 753 | 399 | 121 | 12 | 0 | 0 | 57 | 264 | 576 | 924 | 4980 |
| New Mexico | | | | | | | | | | | | | |
| Albuquerque | 930 | 703 | 595 | 288 | 81 | 0 | 0 | 0 | 12 | 229 | 642 | 868 | 4348 |
| Clayton | 986 | 812 | 747 | 429 | 183 | 21 | 0 | 6 | 66 | 310 | 699 | 899 | 5158 |
| Raton | 1116 | 904 | 834 | 543 | 301 | 63 | 9 | 28 | 126 | 431 | 825 | 1048 | 6228 |
| Roswell | 840 | 641 | 481 | 201 | 31 | 0 | 0 | 0 | 18 | 202 | 573 | 806 | 3793 |
| Silver City | 791 | 605 | 518 | 261 | 87 | 0 | 0 | 0 | 6 | 183 | 525 | 729 | 3705 |
| New York | | | | | | | | | | | | | |
| Albany | 1311 | 1156 | 992 | 564 | 239 | 45 | 0 | 19 | 138 | 440 | 777 | 1194 | 6875 |
| Binghamton (AP) | 1277 | 1154 | 1045 | 645 | 313 | 99 | 22 | 65 | 201 | 471 | 810 | 1184 | 7286 |
| Binghamton (PO) | 1190 | 1081 | 949 | 543 | 229 | 45 | 0 | 28 | 141 | 406 | 732 | 1107 | 6451 |
| Buffalo | 1256 | 1145 | 1039 | 645 | 329 | 78 | 19 | 37 | 141 | 440 | 777 | 1156 | 7062 |
| Central Park | 986 | 885 | 760 | 408 | 118 | 9 | 0 | 0 | 30 | 233 | 540 | 902 | 4871 |
| J. F. Kennedy Intl. Airport | 1029 | 935 | 815 | 480 | 167 | 12 | 0 | 0 | 36 | 248 | 564 | 933 | 5219 |
| LaGuardia | 973 | 879 | 750 | 414 | 124 | 6 | 0 | 0 | 27 | 223 | 528 | 887 | 4811 |
| Rochester | 1234 | 1123 | 1014 | 597 | 279 | 48 | 9 | 31 | 126 | 415 | 747 | 1125 | 6748 |
| Schenectady | 1283 | 1131 | 970 | 543 | 211 | 30 | 0 | 22 | 123 | 422 | 756 | 1159 | 6650 |
| Syracuse | 1271 | 1140 | 1004 | 570 | 248 | 45 | 6 | 28 | 132 | 415 | 744 | 1153 | 6756 |
| North Carolina | | | | | | | | | | | | | |
| Asheville | 784 | 683 | 592 | 273 | 87 | 0 | 0 | 0 | 48 | 245 | 555 | 775 | 4042 |
| Cape Hatteras | 580 | 518 | 440 | 177 | 25 | 0 | 0 | 0 | 0 | 78 | 273 | 521 | 2612 |
| Charlotte | 691 | 582 | 481 | 156 | 22 | 0 | 0 | 0 | 6 | 124 | 438 | 691 | 3191 |
| Greensboro | 784 | 672 | 552 | 234 | 47 | 0 | 0 | 0 | 33 | 192 | 513 | 778 | 3805 |
| Raleigh | 725 | 616 | 487 | 180 | 34 | 0 | 0 | 0 | 21 | 164 | 450 | 716 | 3393 |
| Wilmington | 546 | 462 | 357 | 96 | 0 | 0 | 0 | 0 | 0 | 74 | 291 | 521 | 2347 |
| Winston-Salem | 753 | 652 | 524 | 207 | 37 | 0 | 0 | 0 | 21 | 171 | 483 | 747 | 3595 |

| | | | | | | | | | | | | | |
|---|---|---|---|---|---|---|---|---|---|---|---|---|---|
| North Dakota | | | | | | | | | | | | | |
| Bismarck | 1708 | 1442 | 1203 | 645 | 329 | 117 | 34 | 28 | 222 | 577 | 1083 | 1463 | 8851 |
| Devils Lake | 1872 | 1579 | 1345 | 753 | 381 | 138 | 40 | 53 | 273 | 642 | 1191 | 1634 | 9901 |
| Fargo | 1789 | 1520 | 1262 | 690 | 332 | 99 | 28 | 37 | 219 | 574 | 1107 | 1569 | 9226 |
| Williston | 1758 | 1473 | 1262 | 681 | 357 | 141 | 31 | 43 | 261 | 601 | 1122 | 1513 | 9243 |
| Ohio | | | | | | | | | | | | | |
| Akron | 1138 | 1016 | 871 | 489 | 202 | 39 | 0 | 9 | 96 | 381 | 726 | 1070 | 6037 |
| Cincinnati | 970 | 837 | 701 | 336 | 118 | 9 | 0 | 0 | 54 | 248 | 612 | 921 | 4806 |
| Cleveland | 1159 | 1047 | 918 | 552 | 260 | 66 | 9 | 25 | 105 | 384 | 738 | 1088 | 6351 |
| Columbus | 1088 | 949 | 809 | 426 | 171 | 27 | 0 | 6 | 84 | 347 | 714 | 1039 | 5660 |
| Dayton | 1097 | 955 | 809 | 429 | 167 | 30 | 0 | 6 | 78 | 310 | 696 | 1045 | 5622 |
| Mansfield | 1169 | 1042 | 924 | 543 | 245 | 60 | 9 | 22 | 114 | 397 | 768 | 1110 | 6403 |
| Sandusky | 1107 | 991 | 868 | 495 | 198 | 36 | 0 | 6 | 66 | 313 | 684 | 1032 | 5796 |
| Toledo | 1200 | 1056 | 924 | 543 | 242 | 60 | 0 | 16 | 117 | 406 | 792 | 1138 | 6494 |
| Youngstown | 1169 | 1047 | 921 | 540 | 248 | 60 | 6 | 19 | 120 | 412 | 771 | 1104 | 6417 |
| Oklahoma | | | | | | | | | | | | | |
| Oklahoma City | 868 | 664 | 527 | 189 | 34 | 0 | 0 | 0 | 15 | 164 | 498 | 766 | 3725 |
| Tulsa | 893 | 683 | 539 | 213 | 47 | 0 | 0 | 0 | 18 | 158 | 522 | 787 | 3860 |
| Oregon | | | | | | | | | | | | | |
| Astoria | 753 | 622 | 636 | 480 | 363 | 231 | 146 | 130 | 210 | 375 | 561 | 679 | 5186 |
| Burns | 1246 | 988 | 856 | 570 | 366 | 177 | 12 | 37 | 210 | 515 | 867 | 1113 | 6957 |
| Eugene | 803 | 627 | 589 | 426 | 279 | 135 | 34 | 34 | 129 | 366 | 585 | 719 | 4726 |
| Meacham | 1209 | 1005 | 983 | 726 | 527 | 339 | 84 | 124 | 288 | 580 | 918 | 1091 | 7874 |
| Medford | 918 | 697 | 642 | 432 | 242 | 78 | 0 | 0 | 78 | 372 | 678 | 871 | 5008 |
| Pendleton | 1017 | 773 | 617 | 396 | 205 | 63 | 0 | 0 | 111 | 350 | 711 | 884 | 5127 |
| Portland | 825 | 644 | 586 | 396 | 245 | 105 | 25 | 28 | 114 | 335 | 597 | 735 | 4635 |
| Roseburg | 766 | 608 | 570 | 405 | 267 | 123 | 22 | 16 | 105 | 329 | 567 | 713 | 4491 |
| Salem | 822 | 647 | 611 | 417 | 273 | 144 | 37 | 31 | 111 | 338 | 594 | 729 | 4754 |
| Sexton Summit | 958 | 809 | 818 | 609 | 465 | 279 | 81 | 81 | 171 | 443 | 666 | 874 | 6254 |

**Table III, continued**

| State/City | Jan | Feb | Mar | Apr | May | Jun | Jul | Aug | Sep | Oct | Nov | Dec | Year |
|---|---|---|---|---|---|---|---|---|---|---|---|---|---|
| Pennsylvania | | | | | | | | | | | | | |
| Allentown | 1116 | 1002 | 849 | 471 | 167 | 24 | 0 | 0 | 90 | 353 | 693 | 1045 | 5810 |
| Erie | 1169 | 1081 | 973 | 585 | 288 | 60 | 0 | 25 | 102 | 391 | 714 | 1063 | 6451 |
| Harrisburg | 1045 | 907 | 766 | 396 | 124 | 12 | 0 | 0 | 63 | 298 | 648 | 992 | 5251 |
| Philadelphia | 1014 | 890 | 744 | 390 | 115 | 12 | 0 | 0 | 60 | 291 | 621 | 964 | 5101 |
| Pittsburgh | 1119 | 1002 | 874 | 480 | 195 | 39 | 0 | 9 | 105 | 375 | 726 | 1063 | 5987 |
| Reading | 1001 | 885 | 735 | 372 | 105 | 0 | 0 | 0 | 54 | 257 | 597 | 939 | 4945 |
| Scranton | 1156 | 1028 | 893 | 498 | 195 | 33 | 0 | 19 | 132 | 434 | 762 | 1104 | 6254 |
| Williamsport | 1122 | 1002 | 856 | 468 | 177 | 24 | 0 | 9 | 111 | 375 | 717 | 1073 | 5934 |
| Rhode Island | | | | | | | | | | | | | |
| Block Island | 1020 | 955 | 877 | 612 | 344 | 99 | 0 | 16 | 78 | 307 | 594 | 902 | 5804 |
| Providence | 1110 | 988 | 868 | 534 | 236 | 51 | 0 | 16 | 96 | 372 | 660 | 1023 | 5954 |
| South Carolina | | | | | | | | | | | | | |
| Charleston | 487 | 389 | 291 | 54 | 0 | 0 | 0 | 0 | 0 | 59 | 282 | 471 | 2033 |
| Columbia | 570 | 470 | 357 | 81 | 0 | 0 | 0 | 0 | 0 | 84 | 345 | 577 | 2484 |
| Florence | 552 | 459 | 347 | 84 | 0 | 0 | 0 | 0 | 0 | 78 | 315 | 552 | 2387 |
| Greenville | 648 | 535 | 434 | 120 | 12 | 0 | 0 | 0 | 0 | 112 | 387 | 636 | 2884 |
| Spartanburg | 663 | 560 | 453 | 144 | 25 | 0 | 0 | 0 | 15 | 130 | 417 | 667 | 3074 |
| South Dakota | | | | | | | | | | | | | |
| Huron | 1628 | 1355 | 1125 | 600 | 288 | 87 | 9 | 12 | 165 | 508 | 1014 | 1432 | 8223 |
| Rapid City | 1333 | 1145 | 1051 | 615 | 326 | 126 | 22 | 12 | 165 | 481 | 897 | 1172 | 7345 |
| Sioux Falls | 1544 | 1285 | 1082 | 573 | 270 | 78 | 19 | 25 | 168 | 462 | 972 | 1361 | 7839 |
| Tennessee | | | | | | | | | | | | | |
| Bristol | 828 | 700 | 598 | 261 | 68 | 0 | 0 | 0 | 51 | 236 | 573 | 828 | 4143 |
| Chattanooga | 722 | 577 | 453 | 150 | 25 | 0 | 0 | 0 | 18 | 143 | 468 | 698 | 3254 |
| Knoxville | 732 | 613 | 493 | 198 | 43 | 0 | 0 | 0 | 30 | 171 | 489 | 725 | 3494 |

| | | | | | | | | | | | | | |
|---|---|---|---|---|---|---|---|---|---|---|---|---|---|
| Memphis | 729 | 585 | 456 | 147 | 22 | 0 | 0 | 0 | 18 | 130 | 447 | 698 | 3232 |
| Nashville | 778 | 644 | 512 | 189 | 40 | 0 | 0 | 0 | 30 | 158 | 495 | 732 | 3578 |
| Oak Ridge (CO) | 778 | 669 | 552 | 228 | 56 | 0 | 0 | 0 | 39 | 192 | 531 | 772 | 3817 |
| Texas | | | | | | | | | | | | | |
| Abilene | 642 | 470 | 347 | 114 | 0 | 0 | 0 | 0 | 0 | 99 | 366 | 586 | 2624 |
| Amarillo | 877 | 664 | 546 | 252 | 56 | 0 | 0 | 0 | 18 | 205 | 570 | 797 | 3985 |
| Austin | 468 | 325 | 223 | 51 | 0 | 0 | 0 | 0 | 0 | 31 | 225 | 388 | 1711 |
| Brownsville | 205 | 106 | 74 | 0 | 0 | 0 | 0 | 0 | 0 | 0 | 66 | 149 | 600 |
| Corpus Christi | 291 | 174 | 109 | 0 | 0 | 0 | 0 | 0 | 0 | 0 | 120 | 220 | 914 |
| Dallas | 601 | 440 | 319 | 90 | 6 | 0 | 0 | 0 | 0 | 62 | 321 | 524 | 2363 |
| El Paso | 685 | 445 | 319 | 105 | 0 | 0 | 0 | 0 | 0 | 84 | 414 | 648 | 2700 |
| Fort Worth | 614 | 448 | 319 | 99 | 0 | 0 | 0 | 0 | 0 | 65 | 324 | 536 | 2405 |
| Galveston | 350 | 258 | 189 | 30 | 0 | 0 | 0 | 0 | 0 | 0 | 138 | 270 | 1235 |
| Houston | 384 | 288 | 192 | 36 | 0 | 0 | 0 | 0 | 0 | 6 | 183 | 307 | 1396 |
| Laredo | 267 | 134 | 74 | 0 | 0 | 0 | 0 | 0 | 0 | 0 | 105 | 217 | 797 |
| Lubbock | 800 | 613 | 484 | 201 | 31 | 0 | 0 | 0 | 18 | 174 | 513 | 744 | 3578 |
| Midland | 651 | 468 | 322 | 90 | 0 | 0 | 0 | 0 | 0 | 87 | 381 | 592 | 2591 |
| Port Arthur | 384 | 274 | 192 | 39 | 0 | 0 | 0 | 0 | 0 | 22 | 207 | 329 | 1447 |
| San Angelo | 567 | 412 | 288 | 66 | 0 | 0 | 0 | 0 | 0 | 68 | 318 | 536 | 2255 |
| San Antonio | 428 | 286 | 195 | 39 | 0 | 0 | 0 | 0 | 0 | 31 | 207 | 363 | 1549 |
| Victoria | 344 | 230 | 152 | 21 | 0 | 0 | 0 | 0 | 0 | 6 | 150 | 270 | 1173 |
| Waco | 536 | 389 | 270 | 66 | 0 | 0 | 0 | 0 | 0 | 43 | 270 | 456 | 2030 |
| Wichita Falls | 698 | 518 | 378 | 120 | 6 | 0 | 0 | 0 | 0 | 99 | 381 | 632 | 2832 |
| Utah | | | | | | | | | | | | | |
| Milford | 1252 | 988 | 822 | 519 | 279 | 87 | 0 | 0 | 99 | 443 | 867 | 1141 | 6497 |
| Salt Lake City | 1172 | 910 | 763 | 459 | 233 | 84 | 0 | 0 | 81 | 419 | 849 | 1082 | 6052 |
| Wendover | 1178 | 902 | 729 | 408 | 177 | 51 | 0 | 0 | 48 | 372 | 822 | 1091 | 5778 |
| Vermont | | | | | | | | | | | | | |
| Burlington | 1513 | 1333 | 1187 | 714 | 353 | 90 | 28 | 65 | 207 | 539 | 891 | 1349 | 8269 |

Table III, continued

| State/City | Jan | Feb | Mar | Apr | May | Jun | Jul | Aug | Sep | Oct | Nov | Dec | Year |
|---|---|---|---|---|---|---|---|---|---|---|---|---|---|
| Virginia | | | | | | | | | | | | | |
| Cape Henry | 694 | 633 | 536 | 246 | 53 | 0 | 0 | 0 | 0 | 112 | 360 | 645 | 3279 |
| Lynchburg | 849 | 731 | 605 | 267 | 78 | 0 | 0 | 0 | 51 | 223 | 540 | 822 | 4166 |
| Norfolk | 738 | 655 | 533 | 216 | 37 | 0 | 0 | 0 | 0 | 136 | 408 | 698 | 3421 |
| Richmond | 815 | 703 | 546 | 219 | 53 | 0 | 0 | 0 | 36 | 214 | 495 | 784 | 3865 |
| Roanoke | 834 | 722 | 614 | 261 | 65 | 0 | 0 | 0 | 51 | 229 | 549 | 825 | 4150 |
| Wash. Nat'l A. P. | 871 | 762 | 626 | 288 | 74 | 0 | 0 | 0 | 33 | 217 | 519 | 834 | 4224 |
| Washington | | | | | | | | | | | | | |
| Olympia | 834 | 675 | 645 | 450 | 307 | 177 | 68 | 71 | 198 | 422 | 636 | 753 | 5236 |
| Seattle | 738 | 599 | 577 | 396 | 242 | 117 | 50 | 47 | 129 | 329 | 543 | 657 | 4424 |
| Seattle Boeing | 831 | 655 | 608 | 411 | 242 | 99 | 34 | 40 | 147 | 384 | 624 | 763 | 4838 |
| Seattle Tacoma | 828 | 678 | 657 | 474 | 295 | 159 | 56 | 62 | 162 | 391 | 633 | 750 | 5145 |
| Spokane | 1231 | 980 | 834 | 531 | 288 | 135 | 9 | 25 | 168 | 493 | 879 | 1082 | 6655 |
| Stampede Pass | 1287 | 1075 | 1085 | 855 | 654 | 483 | 273 | 291 | 393 | 701 | 1008 | 1178 | 9283 |
| Tatoosh Island | 713 | 613 | 645 | 525 | 431 | 333 | 295 | 279 | 306 | 406 | 534 | 639 | 5719 |
| Walla Walla | 986 | 745 | 589 | 342 | 177 | 45 | 0 | 0 | 87 | 310 | 681 | 843 | 4805 |
| Yakima | 1163 | 868 | 713 | 435 | 220 | 69 | 0 | 12 | 144 | 450 | 828 | 1039 | 5941 |
| West Virginia | | | | | | | | | | | | | |
| Charleston | 880 | 770 | 648 | 300 | 96 | 9 | 0 | 0 | 63 | 254 | 591 | 865 | 4476 |
| Elkins | 1008 | 896 | 791 | 444 | 198 | 48 | 9 | 25 | 135 | 400 | 729 | 992 | 5675 |
| Huntington | 880 | 764 | 636 | 294 | 99 | 12 | 0 | 0 | 63 | 257 | 585 | 856 | 4446 |
| Parkersburg | 942 | 826 | 691 | 339 | 115 | 6 | 0 | 0 | 60 | 264 | 606 | 905 | 4754 |
| Wisconsin | | | | | | | | | | | | | |
| Green Bay | 1494 | 1313 | 1141 | 654 | 335 | 99 | 28 | 50 | 174 | 484 | 924 | 1333 | 8029 |
| La Crosse | 1504 | 1277 | 1070 | 540 | 245 | 69 | 12 | 19 | 153 | 437 | 924 | 1339 | 7589 |
| Madison | 1473 | 1274 | 1113 | 618 | 310 | 102 | 25 | 40 | 174 | 474 | 930 | 1330 | 7863 |
| Milwaukee | 1376 | 1193 | 1054 | 642 | 372 | 135 | 43 | 47 | 174 | 471 | 876 | 1252 | 7635 |

| | | | | | | | | | | | | | |
|---|---|---|---|---|---|---|---|---|---|---|---|---|---|
| Wyoming | | | | | | | | | | | | | |
| Casper | 1290 | 1084 | 1020 | 657 | 381 | 129 | 6 | 16 | 192 | 524 | 942 | 1169 | 7410 |
| Cheyene | 1228 | 1056 | 1011 | 672 | 381 | 102 | 19 | 31 | 210 | 543 | 924 | 1101 | 7278 |
| Lander | 1417 | 1145 | 1017 | 654 | 381 | 153 | 6 | 19 | 204 | 555 | 1020 | 1299 | 7870 |
| Sheridan | 1355 | 1154 | 1054 | 642 | 366 | 150 | 25 | 31 | 219 | 539 | 948 | 1200 | 7683 |

Glass foam is waterproof, fire-proof, withstands high temperatures (>400°C) and has a high compression strength, but is several times more expensive than fiberglass. Foamglass has been used to insulate beneath the bottom of a solar thermal storage tank. Foamglass is available in rigid slabs that can be cut with a saw but cannot be bent. Polystyrene foam is a very good insulator but is flammable, cannot withstand high temperatures and is easily compressed. It must be protected from weathering and sunlight. It is an excellent insulation for underground storage units. Urethane foam is similar to polystyrene foam, but has greater compressive strength.

Urea-formaldehyde foam (UFF) can be sprayed on in a two-part mixture. UFF has been under attack in recent years as a health hazard because it gradually releases toxic gases, and because it releases poisonous gases when burned. For this reason, UFF is not recommended for insulating interior spaces.

Foam insulation uses trapped air to restrict the flow of heat, so the R-value of a good insulating foam may approach that of still air, 0.386°C-m$^2$/W-cm (5.56°F-ft$^2$-hr/Btu-in.). Some foams are expanded with high-molecular-weight gases (refrigerants 11 or 12), which have a lower thermal conductivity than air. The R-value of these foams tends to decrease with age as the refrigerant gas diffuses out and is replaced by air. Moisture penetration of foam insulation can also reduce its R-value.

The effective R-value $R_e$ for multilayer materials is given by:

$$R_e = R_{si} + R_{so} + \sum R_i X_i \tag{1}$$

where $R_{si}$ = inside surface resistance (Table VI)
$R_{so}$ = outside surface resistance (Table VI)
$R_i$ = R-value of ith material (Tables IV and V)
$X_i$ = thickness of material i

Similarly, the effective heat loss coefficient for heat loss through j parallel paths is

$$U_e = \frac{\Sigma U_j A_j}{\Sigma A_j} \tag{2}$$

For example, consider a simple wall with 0.5-in. plaster board on the inside (R = 0.90) supported by 1.625-in.-wide by 3.5-in.-deep soft wood studs (R = 1.25) on 16-in. centers with 3.5-in. fiberglass insulation (R = 3.15) between and 0.05-in.-thick aluminum siding on the outside (R = 0.00065) with a 7.5-mph wind. What is the U-factor for this wall?

**Table IV. Density and R-Value of Insulation**

| Insulation | Density | | R-Value | |
|---|---|---|---|---|
| | kg/m$^3$ | lb/ft$^3$ | °C-m$^2$/W-cm | °F-ft$^2$-hr/Btu-in. |
| Acoustic Tile | 288 | 18.0 | 0.175 | 2.53 |
| Cellulose Fill | 40–48 | 2.5–3.0 | 0.257 | 3.70 |
| Fiberglass Batt | | | 0.218 | 3.15 |
| Glass Foam | 144 | 9.0 | 0.173 | 2.50 |
| Insulation Board | 288 | 18.0 | 0.182 | 2.63 |
| Mineral Board | | | 0.241 | 3.47 |
| Mineral Wool Batt | | | 0.231 | 3.33 |
| Low Density Particleboard | | | 0.128 | 1.85 |
| Perlite (R-11) | 80–128 | 5.0–8.0 | 0.187 | 2.70 |
| Polystyrene Beads | 16 | 1.0 | 0.248 | 3.57 |
| Polystyrene Board (air) | 29 | 1.8 | 0.277 | 4.00 |
| Polystyrene Board (R-12) | 35–56 | 2.2–3.5 | 0.347 | 5.00 |
| Polyurethane (R-11) | 25–40 | 1.5–2.5 | 0.433 | 6.25 |
| Urea Formaldehyde Foam | 11 | 0.7 | 0.289 | 4.17 |
| Vermiculite | 112–131 | 7.0–8.2 | 0.148 | 2.13 |

**Table V. Density and R-Values of Structural Materials**

| Material | Density | | R-Value | |
|---|---|---|---|---|
| | kg/m$^3$ | lb/ft$^3$ | °C-m$^2$/W-cm | °F-ft$^2$-hr/Btu-in. |
| Aluminum (1100 alloy) | 2740 | 171 | $45 \times 10^{-6}$ | $6.5 \times 10^{-4}$ |
| Brick (common) | 1920 | 120 | 0.014 | 0.20 |
| Brick (face) | 2080 | 130 | 0.0076 | 0.11 |
| Cement, Mortar, Plaster | 1860 | 116 | 0.014 | 0.20 |
| Concrete (heavy weight) | 2240 | 140 | 0.0076 | 0.11 |
| Concrete (medium weight) | 1280 | 80 | 0.028 | 0.40 |
| Concrete (light weight) | 481 | 30 | 0.077 | 1.11 |
| Gypsum, Plasterboard | 801 | 50 | 0.062 | 0.90 |
| Medium-Density Siding | 641 | 40 | 0.106 | 1.53 |
| Particleboard (high density) | | | 0.0055 | 0.08 |
| Particleboard (medium density) | | | 0.0076 | 0.11 |
| Particleboard (low density) | | | 0.128 | 1.85 |
| Steel (mild) | 7830 | 489 | $2.2 \times 10^{-4}$ | $3.2 \times 10^{-3}$ |
| Wood (hard) | 721 | 45 | 0.63 | 0.91 |
| Wood (soft) | 513 | 32 | 0.087 | 1.25 |

**Table VI. Surface Resistance of Nonreflective Surfaces**

| Wind Speed | | Surface Orientation | Direction of Heat Flow | Surface Resistance | |
|---|---|---|---|---|---|
| m/sec | mi/hr | | | °C-m²/W | °F-ft²-hr/Btu |
| 0 | 0 | Horizontal | Upward | 0.11 | 0.61 |
| 0 | 0 | 45° slope | Upward | 0.11 | 0.62 |
| 0 | 0 | Vertical | Horizontal | 0.12 | 0.68 |
| 0 | 0 | 45° slope | Downward | 0.13 | 0.76 |
| 0 | 0 | Horizontal | Downward | 0.16 | 0.92 |
| 3.4 | 7.5 | Any | Any | 0.030 | 0.17 |
| 6.7 | 15.0 | Any | Any | 0.044 | 0.25 |

Consider a 16-in.-wide segment of wall 1 ft high; the area of insulation is $14.375 \times 12$ in., or 1.198 ft², and the R-value is $0.68 + 0.17 + 0.90(0.5) + 3.15(3.5) + 0.00065(0.05)$, or 12.325. The face area of wall stud is $1.625 \times 12 = 19.5$ in.² $= 0.1354$ ft², and the R-value through this part of the wall is $0.68 + 0.17 + 0.90(0.5) + (1.25)(3.5) + 0.00065(0.05) = 5.675$. The loss coefficient for the wall is:

$$U_e = \frac{\dfrac{1.198}{12.325} + \dfrac{0.1354}{5.675}}{1.198 + 0.1354} = \frac{0.0972 + 0.0239}{1.3334} = 0.09082$$

and the R-value for the wall is $1/U_e - 11.01$ °F-ft²-hr/Btu.

The UA factor for the building is the sum of all the U values of exterior wall, windows, roof, doors, etc. times their respective areas, or

$$(UA) = \sum U_i A_i \qquad (3)$$

where $U_i$ = U value of ith exterior surface
$A_i$ = area of ith exterior surface

## Calculate Infiltration Load

The infiltration load is the product of the amount of air entering the building times the heat capacity of air (0.018 Btu/ft³-°F at sea level) times the inside/outside temperature differences. Table VII lists air properties as a function of altitude.

The internal load due to appliances, people, etc. is estimated for a specific situation. Such loads usually make a substantial contribution to the heat requirements of a building. The typical heat output of an adult human being is given by Table VIII. The heat output of electrical appliances, equipment, etc. is almost always equal to the electrical power consumed, so the heat generated from these sources may be estimated from the monthly electric bills.

The monthly heating load for a structure may therefore be estimated using the degree-day approach by:

$$L = (UA + mc_p)(DD)(24) - Q_{IH} \quad (4)$$

where $UA = \Sigma U_i A_i$ for building envelope
$mc_p$ = total thermal capacity of air flow/hour
$DD$ = number of degree days/month
$Q_{IH}$ = internal heat generation

**Table VII. Air Properties vs Altitude**

| Altitude (ft) | Density (lb/ft$^3$) | $C_p$ (Btu/ft$^3$-°F) | HC (Btu-hr/cfm-°F) |
|---|---|---|---|
| 0 | 0.0750 | 0.0180 | 1.08 |
| 1,000 | 0.0724 | 0.0174 | 1.04 |
| 2,000 | 0.0698 | 0.0167 | 1.01 |
| 3,000 | 0.0672 | 0.0161 | 0.97 |
| 4,000 | 0.0648 | 0.0155 | 0.93 |
| 5,000 | 0.0625 | 0.0150 | 0.90 |
| 6,000 | 0.0601 | 0.0144 | 0.86 |
| 8,000 | 0.0559 | 0.0134 | 0.81 |
| 10,000 | 0.0516 | 0.0124 | 0.74 |

**Table VIII. Typical Heat Output of an Adult Human Being**

| Activity | Heat Output (Btu/hr) |
|---|---|
| Sleeping | 260 |
| Awake, Lying | 300 |
| Sitting | 380 |
| Standing | 440 |
| Walking 2 mi/hr | 760 |
| Walking 4 mi/hr | 1400 |
| Heavy Work | 2000 |
| Very Heavy Work | 3000 |
| Max. Exertion | 4000 |

The internal heat generation from appliances, etc. occurs mostly during the day when there is less heat requirement, so if the heating load is primarily at night, the value of $Q_{IH}$ should be reduced to account for the fact that much of the internal heat generated is not available for heating at night.

## SIMPLIFIED METHOD FOR PREDICTING PERFORMANCE

Monson et al. [1981] reported a simplified method of predicting the performance of a direct-gain solar heating system. The monthly auxiliary energy required is

$$Q_{aux} = L - \overline{H}_T(\overline{\tau\alpha})_e A_c N \tag{5}$$

where
$L$ = monthly heating load
$\overline{H}_T$ = monthly average daily solar radiation on the aperture
$(\overline{\tau\alpha})_e$ = monthly average value of $(\tau\alpha)_e$
$A_c$ = aperture area
$N$ = number of days in the month

If $\overline{H}_T(\overline{\tau\alpha})_e A_c N > L$, then $Q_{aux}$ is zero, not a negative number. If the aperture is insulated at night, then UA for the building at night is different from UA during the day. The time-weighted average of UA may be defined as

$$(UA)_a = \frac{(UA)_u(DD)_d + (UA)_i(DD)_n}{DD} \tag{6}$$

where
$(UA)_u$ = thermal conductance of the building with the solar aperture uninsulated
$(UA)_i$ = thermal conductance of the building structure with the solar aperture insulated
$(DD)_d$ = monthly degree-days during the daytime
$(DD)_n$ = monthly degree-days at night
$DD$ = total monthly degree days (Table III)

The insulation installed during the night is assumed to be removed during the day so that it does not prevent solar radiation from entering the building.

Letting $Q_a$ represent the amount of auxiliary energy used for heating and L the total heating load of the building, then the fraction of the monthly heating load supplied by solar energy is

$$F_s = 1 - Q_a/L \tag{7}$$

$F_s$ is the solar heating fraction, as distinguished from the solar-load ratio $X_{sl}$, given by:

$$X_{sl} = \overline{H}_T(\overline{\tau\alpha})_e A_c N/L \tag{8}$$

which is the ratio of the total solar energy available to the building during the month to the monthly load L. $F_s$ is equal to $X_{sl}$ only if the instantaneous heating load is always greater than the energy content of the solar radiation entering the building through the direct-gain aperture, or the thermal storage mass is large enough to prevent excessive interior temperatures. If at any time during the month the solar energy transmitted through the aperture exceeds the instantaneous load, and the thermal storage mass is unable to absorb the excess, then the monthly solar heating fraction $F_s$ will be less than the monthly solar-load ratio $X_{sl}$. Ventilation is usually employed to reject excess heat from the building when interior temperatures become excessive.

Monson et al. [1981] carried out more than 500 monthly TRNSYS simulations of direct-gain solar systems to develop a correlation between the solar heating fraction $F_s$, the solar-load ratio $X_{sl}$ and the "storage-dump ratio" Y, defined as:

$$Y = C(\Delta T)/[\overline{\Phi}\overline{H}_T(\overline{\tau\alpha})_e A_c] \tag{9}$$

where $C$ = effective thermal capacitance
$\Delta T$ = difference between the set point of the auxiliary heating thermostat and the maximum temperature allowed in the space

This correlation is

$$F_s = PX_{sl} + (1 - P)(3{,}082 - 3.142\overline{\Phi})(1 - \exp(-0.329X_{sl})) \tag{10}$$

where

$$P = (1 - \exp(-0.294Y))^{0.652} \tag{11}$$

where $\overline{\Phi}$ = utilizability, calculated from Equation C.15 (see Appendix C)

The monthly load L is calculated using the degree-day approach with the skin loss and infiltration loads combined. The building interior is treated as a single zone with an effective thermal capacitance C. A typical value of C for conventional residential construction in the United States is 123 kJ/m$^2$-°C (6 Btu/ft$^2$-°F). The unit area is the building floor area of the heated space. Auxiliary energy is provided only if the temperature in the heated space drops to the minimum thermostat set point (turn-on temperature), and ventilation or air conditioning is employed to keep the interior from exceeding the maximum allowable temperature.

## Examples of Simplified Method

The following example calculation was adapted from Monson et al. [1981]. Consider a direct-gain solar heating system in Madison, Wisconsin (latitude 43.1°), in January. The building has a $(UA)_u$ of 265 W/°C, a south-facing aperture area of 25.6 $m^2$, an effective thermal capacitance of 23.5 MJ/°C, a $(\tau\alpha)_e$ of 0.7, and maximum/minimum interior temperatures of 23.9°C/18.3°C. The average daily horizontal solar radiation in January is 5.91 $MJ/m^2day$, $\overline{K_T} = 0.49$, and the average ambient temperature is −8.0°C. The ground reflectance (surface albedo) is 0.2, and the number of heating degree-days during the month is 828 day-°C. The typical day of the month is January 17. Calculate the solar heating fraction for the month and the amount of auxiliary energy required for the month.

### *Solution*

The solar heating fraction, $F_s$, is calculated from:

$$F_s = PX_{sl} + (1 - P)(3.082 - 3.142\Phi)[1 - \exp(-0.329X_{sl})] \qquad (10)$$

so the values of P, $X_{sl}$ and $\Phi$ must first be determined. Since $\Phi$ is required to calculate P, the solar-load ratio $X_{sl}$ is calculated first, then $\Phi$, then P.

$$X_{sl} = \overline{H_T}(\overline{\tau\alpha})_e A_c N/L \qquad (8)$$

$$\overline{H_T} = \bar{H}\bar{F} \qquad (12)$$

$$\bar{H} = 5.91 \text{ MJ/m}^2\text{day}$$

$$\bar{F} = (1 - \bar{D}/\bar{H})\overline{F_b} + (\bar{D}/\bar{H})(1 + \cos\beta)/2 + a(1 - \cos\beta)/2 \qquad (C.19)$$

$$\bar{D}/\bar{H} = 1.39 - 4.03\overline{K_T} + 5.53\overline{K_T}^2 - 3.11\overline{K_T}^3 \qquad (C.20)$$

$$\overline{K_T} = 0.49 \qquad \text{(given)}$$

$$\bar{D}/\bar{H} = 1.39 - 4.03(0.49) + 5.53(0.49)^2 - 3.11(0.49)^3 = 0.377 \quad (C.20)$$

$$\overline{F_b} = \frac{\cos(\phi - \beta)\cos\delta\sin\omega_s' + (\pi/180)\omega_s'\sin(\phi - \beta)\sin\delta}{\cos\phi\cos\delta\sin\omega_s + (\pi/180)\omega_s\sin\phi\sin\delta} \quad (C.21)$$

$$\omega_s' = \text{lesser of } \omega_s \text{ and } \arccos[-\tan(\phi - \beta)\tan\delta]$$

$$a = \text{albedo} = \text{reflectance of the earth}$$

$$\phi = 43.1°$$

$$\beta = 90°$$

$$\omega_s = \cos^{-1}(-\tan\phi\tan\delta) \quad (C.12)$$

$$\delta = 0.36 - 22.96\cos(0.9856n) - 0.37\cos(2 \times 0.9856n) - 0.15\cos(3 \times 0.9856n) + 4\sin 0.9856n \quad (141)$$

$$n = 17$$

$$\delta = 0.36 - 21.985 - 0.309 - 0.096 + 1.153 = -20.88°$$

$$\omega_s = \cos^{-1}[-\tan(43.1)\tan(-20.88)] = 69.1°$$

$$\omega_s' = \cos^{-1}[-\tan(\phi - \beta)\tan\delta] = \cos^{-1}[-\tan(43.1 - 90)\tan(-20.88)] = 114°$$

Set $\omega_s' = 69.1°$, and use Equation C.21 to calculate $\overline{F_b}$:

$$\overline{F_b} = \frac{\cos(-46.9)\cos(-20.88)\sin(69.1) + (\pi/180)(69.1)\sin(-46.9)\sin(-20.88)}{\cos(43.1)\cos(-20.88)\sin(69.1) + (\pi/180)(69.1)\sin(43.1)\sin(-20.88)}$$

$$= \frac{0.596 + 0.314}{0.637 - 0.294} = 2.65$$

Now

$$\bar{F} = (1 - 0.377)(2.65) + 0.377[1 + \cos(90)]/2 + 0.2[1 - \cos(90)]/2 \quad (C.19)$$

$$= 1.651 + 0.189 + 0.1 = 1.94$$

So $\overline{H_T}$ may now be calculated

$$\overline{H_T} = \bar{F}\bar{H} = 1.94(5.91\ \text{MJ/m}^2\text{-day}) = 11.5\ \text{MJ/m}^2\text{-day}$$

All that is now needed to get $X_{sl}$ is the load for the month L given by

$$L = (UA)_u (dd)_m$$

$$= (265\ \text{J/sec-°C})(828\ \text{day-°C})(86{,}400\ \text{sec/day}) = 18{,}870\ \text{MJ}$$

so using Equation 8 to calculate $X_{sl}$

$$X_{sl} = (11.5\ \text{MJ/m}^2\text{-day})(0.7)(25.6\ \text{m}^2)(31)/18{,}870\ \text{MJ} = 0.339$$

Now $\bar{\Phi}$ is calculated from

$$\bar{\Phi} = \exp\{[A + B(F_n/\bar{F})](X_c + CX_c^2)\} \qquad (C.15)$$

And since $\overline{K_T} = 0.49$

$$A = 2.943 - 9.271\overline{K_T} + 4.031\overline{K_T}^2 = -0.632 \qquad (C.16)$$

$$B = -4.34 + 8.853\overline{K_T} - 3.602\overline{K_T}^2 = -0.867 \qquad (C.17)$$

$$C = -0.170 - 0.306\overline{K_T} + 2.936\overline{K_T}^2 = 0.385 \qquad (C.18)$$

$F_n$ may be calculated from

$$F_n = \left[1 - \frac{R_{dn}}{R_{Tn}}\left(\frac{D}{H}\right)\right]F_{bn} + \frac{R_{dn}}{R_{Tn}}\left(\frac{D}{H}\right)\left(\frac{1 + \cos\beta}{2}\right) + a\left(\frac{1 - \cos\beta}{2}\right) \qquad (C.13)$$

where, for surfaces facing toward the equator, the ratio of beam radiation on a tilted surface to that on a horizontal surface at noon $F_{bn}$ is:

$$F_{bn} = \frac{\cos(\phi - \beta)\cos\delta + \sin(\phi - \beta)\sin\delta}{\cos\phi\cos\delta + \sin\phi\sin\delta} \qquad (C.14)$$

and D/H is given by

$$D/H = 1.0045 + 0.04349K_T - 3.5227K_T^2 + 2.6313K_T^3 = 0.490$$

using again a value of $\overline{K_T} = 0.49$

$$F_{bn} = \frac{\cos(-46.9)\cos(-20.88) + \sin(-46.9)\sin(-20.88)}{\cos(43.1)\cos(-20.88) + \sin(43.1)\sin(-20.88)}$$

$$= \frac{0.638 + 0.260}{0.682 - 0.244} = 2.05$$

$R_{Tn}$, the ratio of the solar radiation intensity at noon to the daily total radiation, is given by

$$R_{Tn} = R_{dn}[1.07 - 0.025\sin(\omega_s - 60)] \qquad (C.10)$$

where $R_{dn}$, the ratio of the diffuse radiation at noon to the daily diffuse radiation, is found from

$$R_{dn} = \left(\frac{\pi}{24}\right)\left[\frac{1 - \cos\omega_s}{\sin\omega_s - (\pi/180)\omega_s\cos\omega_s}\right] \qquad (C.11)$$

$$= \frac{\pi}{24}\left[\frac{1 - \cos(69.1)}{\sin(69.1) - (\nu/180)(69.1)\cos(69.1)}\right]$$

$$= 0.1309\left(\frac{0.643}{0.934 - 0.430}\right) = 0.167$$

$$R_{Tn} = 0.167[1.07 + 0.025\sin(9.1)] = 0.179 \qquad (C.10)$$

$F_n$ can now be calculated

$$F_n = \left[1 - \frac{0.167}{0.179}(0.490)\right]2.05 + \frac{0.167}{0.179}(0.490)(1 + \cos(90))/2$$
$$+ 0.2(1 - \cos(90))/2 = 1.113 + 0.229 + 0.1 = 1.442 \qquad (C.13)$$

$$X_c = \frac{H_{TC}}{R_{Tn}F_n\bar{H}} \qquad (C.9)$$

$$H_{TC} = \frac{U_L(T_i - T_a)}{(\tau\alpha)_e} = \frac{(265\ \text{W}/^\circ\text{C})(21.1 + 8.0^\circ\text{C})}{(0.7)(25.6\ \text{m}^2)} = 430\ \text{W/m}^2 \qquad (C.2)$$

$$X_c = \frac{430\ \text{J/m}^2\text{-sec}(3600\ \text{sec/hr})}{0.179(1.442)(5.91 \times 10^6\ \text{J/m}^2\text{-day})} = 1.0$$

keeping in mind that the 0.179 converts daily to hourly radiation.

$$\bar{\Phi} = \exp\left\{\left[-0.632 - 0.837\left(\frac{1.442}{1.94}\right)\right][1 + 0.385(1)^2]\right\}$$

$$= \exp[(-1.254)(1.385)] = 0.176$$

$$Y = \frac{C(\Delta T)}{\bar{\Phi}\bar{H}_T(\overline{\tau\alpha})_e A_c} \qquad (9)$$

$$= \frac{(23.5\ \text{MJ}/{}^\circ\text{C})(5.6^\circ\text{C})}{(0.176)(11.5\ \text{MJ/m}^2\text{-day})(0.7)(25.6\ \text{m}^2)} = 3.63$$

$$P = [1 - \exp(-0.294Y)]^{0.652} = 0.76 \qquad (11)$$

The solar heating fraction can now be determined from Equation 10

$$F_s = (0.76)(0.339) + (1 - 0.76)[3.082 - 3.142(0.176)]$$

$$\{1 - \exp[-0.329(0.339)]\}$$

$$= 0.258 + (0.607)(0.1055) = 0.32$$

and the auxiliary energy required for the month is

$$Q_a = L(1 - F_s) = 18{,}870\ \text{MJ}(1 - 0.32) = 12{,}830\ \text{MJ}$$

The value of $H_{TC}$ here was calculated using the average indoor temperature of 21.1°C (70°F). Monson et al. [1981] used the minimum indoor temperature of 18.3°C (65°F) to calculate $H_{TC}$, which resulted in a higher value of $\bar{\Phi}$ and a lower value of $F_s$. Table IX compares the results of their calculations with the results of more detailed TRNSYS simulation runs.

## Advantages of the Simplified Method

This analytical method for determining the performance of direct-gain systems is called the "unutilizability" method, since the solar radiant energy received above a certain threshold ($H_{TC}$) is lost or rejected, and the energy below this threshold is used. This is opposite to the situation for flat-plate collectors, which do not operate until the solar intensity threshold is reached, and then collect useful energy when the intensity is greater than this threshold. This concept of utilizability was developed by Klein [1978] to predict the performance of systems using conventional

**Table IX. Performance of Direct-Gain System in Madison, Wisconsin**

| Month | Degree-Days (°C-days) | $\overline{H}_T$ (MJ/day-m$^2$) | $\overline{\Phi}$ | $Q_{aux}$ (GJ) | $Q_{aux}$ (GJ) |
|---|---|---|---|---|---|
| January | 828 | 11.35 | 0.238 | 13.3 | 13.3 |
| February | 680 | 13.3 | 0.286 | 9.83 | 9.60 |
| March | 626 | 14.1 | 0.356 | 8.10 | 7.77 |
| April | 297 | 10.7 | 0.553 | 2.96 | 2.82 |
| May | 157 | 10.1 | 0.790 | 0.87 | 1.17 |
| June | 49 | 9.91 | 1.00 | 0.00 | 0.03 |
| July | 16 | 10.5 | 1.00 | 0.00 | 0.00 |
| August | 43 | 12.0 | 1.00 | 0.00 | 0.00 |
| September | 93 | 13.1 | 0.936 | 0.00 | 0.18 |
| October | 250 | 12.5 | 0.693 | 2.06 | 2.28 |
| November | 479 | 9.71 | 0.424 | 6.83 | 6.96 |
| December | 683 | 8.02 | 0.284 | 11.5 | 11.8 |
| Year | 4201 | 135.2 | | 55.4 | 55.9 |

flat-plate collectors; Monson, et al. [1981] later applied the utilizability concept in a different manner to predict the performance of direct-gain heating systems. They compared the results of detailed TRNSYS runs for eight cities around the United States with the results from the unutilizability method and found excellent agreement.

The unutilizability method for direct-gain systems, like the F-chart method for active solar heating and hot water systems, is not a numerical model in itself but a set of correlations developed from numerous calculations using a sophisticated numerical model for a generic type of system. These methods are quite useful and reasonably accurate when applied to the type of systems with the climatic conditions for which the correlations were developed.

## NUMERICAL METHOD FOR PREDICTING PERFORMANCE OF DIRECT–GAIN SYSTEMS

A variety of simple numerical models have been developed for direct-gain systems, such as the following by Niles [1978]. Niles assumed that the day/night temperature variations were sinusoidal in nature, so the temperature T could be given as

$$T = \overline{T} + T' \cos(2\pi t/24 + \phi) \tag{13}$$

and that there was sufficient thermal storage mass to absorb all of the excess heat during the day and release it at night. The solar radiation is also assumed to vary simusoidally. Niles' approach is aimed at estimating the amount of south-facing aperture needed for a direct-gain passive system and the resulting indoor temperature fluctuations. A single internal zone is considered with no auxiliary heating or cooling or internal heat generation.

In the case of indirect-coupled storage mass (Figure 35) or the direct-coupled case (Figure 36) the temperature is taken to be

$$T = \bar{T} + T' \angle \phi \tag{14}$$

and the solar transmitted radiation is

$$Q_s = \overline{Q_s} + Q_s' \angle \phi \tag{15}$$

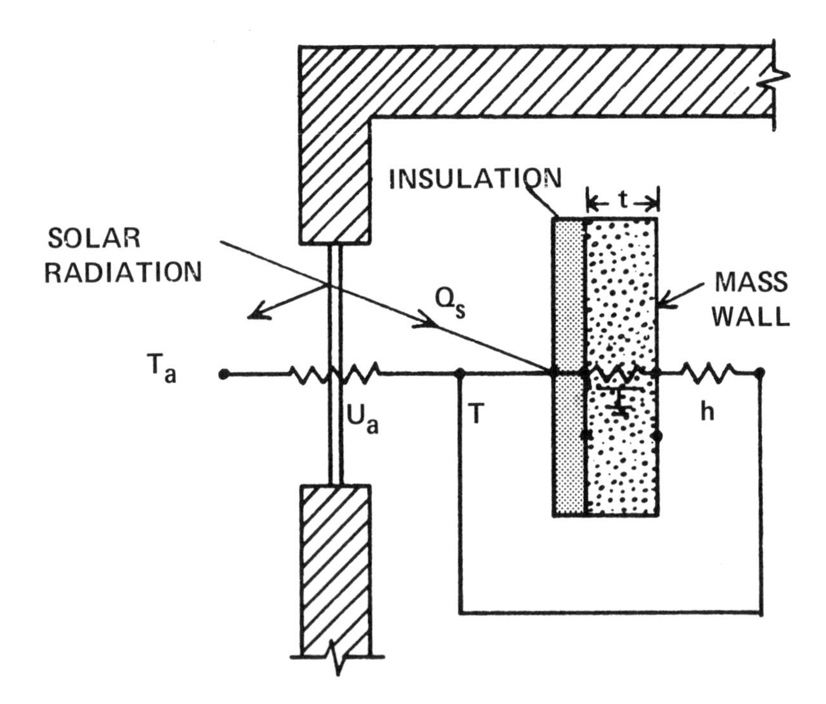


**Figure 35.** Indirect-coupled case. $A_{ST}$ = thermal storage well sunspace area; $U = UA + mC_p - U_2A_2$; T = inside temperature; $\tilde{A}$ = admittance of storage; t = thickness; h = surface conductance of thermal storage mass (Btu/ft$^2$-hr).

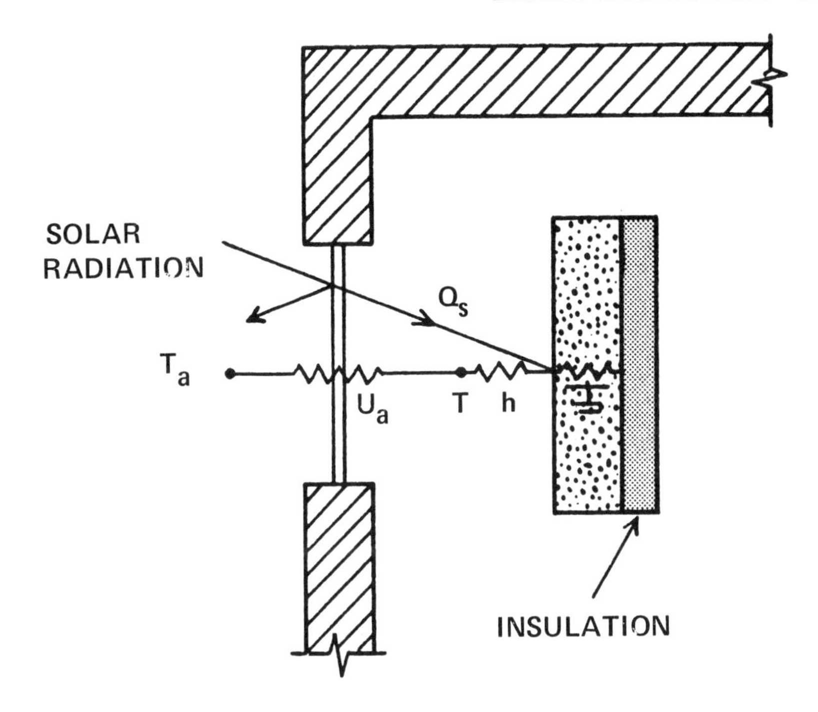


**Figure 36.** Direct-coupled case. $U = UA + mC_p - U_2A_2$; T = inside temperature; h = surface conductance of thermal storage mass (Btu/ft²-hr); $\tilde{A}$ = admittance of storage wall.

where $\angle\phi = \cos(2\pi t/24 + \phi)$
$t$ = time from solar noon
$\phi$ = phase angle with respect to solar noon
$\bar{T}$ = long-term average value of T
$T'$ = magnitude of sinusoidal component of T
$\overline{Q_s}$ = long-term average value of $Q_s(=H_tA_c)$
$Q_s'$ = magnitude of sinusoidal component of $Q_s$

Assuming that the room and storage mass temperatures respond immediately to the solar input and losses, the steady-state condition is reached when

$$\bar{T} = \overline{T_a} + \overline{Q_s}/[(UA) + mC_p] \tag{17}$$

where $T_a$ = average outside temperature
(UA) = UA factor for building envelope
$mC_p$ = thermal capacity of infiltration (see Equation 4)

The area of south-facing aperture $A_c$ is then

$$A_c = \frac{(\bar{T} - \bar{T}_a)U'}{\bar{H}_T\tau - (\bar{T} - \bar{T}_a)U_a} \tag{18}$$

where $U'$ = UA factor for the building, not including the direct gain aperture, plus $mC_p$

$t$ = transmittance of south direct-gain aperture

$U_a$ = loss coefficient for direct-gain aperture

$\bar{H}_T$ = average daily radiation on aperture

Equation 18 merely states the approximation that the average heat loss from the building is equal to the average heat gain through the direct-gain aperture. Table X lists values of transmittance $\tau$ for different types of glazing. Figure 37 is a plot of Equation 18 for a double-glazed aperture with a loss coefficient $U_a$ of 0.6 Btu/ft$^2$-hr-°F.

In the indirect-coupled case, the sinusoidal component of the room temperature is

$$\dot{T} = T'\angle\phi = \{\dot{Q}_s/[(UA) + mC_p] + \dot{T}_a\}/[1 + R_{sa}/(\overset{*}{U}/h + \overset{*}{U}/\dot{A})] \tag{19}$$

where $\dot{Q}_s = Q'_s\angle\phi$

$\dot{T}_a = T'_a\angle\phi$

$T'_a$ = magnitude of sinusoidal component of ambient temperature

$R_{sa}$ = ratio of thermal storage area to aperture area

$\overset{*}{U} = [(UA) + mC_p]/A_c$

$A_c$ = aperture area

$h$ = surface conductance of storage

$\dot{A}$ = storage wall admittance

If there is no storage mass, Equation 19 becomes

**Table X. Transmittance of Glazing**

| Glass | Normal Incidence $\tau$ | Multiplying Factor to Correct for Nonnormal |
|---|---|---|
| Single 0.05-in. Window Glass | 0.87 | 1.0 |
| Single 0.25-in. Plate | 0.77 | 0.87 |
| Single Heat-Absorbing Plate | 0.53 | 0.46 (0.56 in shade) |
| Double 0.125-in. Window Glass | 0.76 | 0.85 |
| Double 0.25-in. Plate | 0.60 | 0.66 (0.76 in shade) |
| Double Heat-Absorbing Plate | 0.35 | 0.37 (0.47 in shade) |

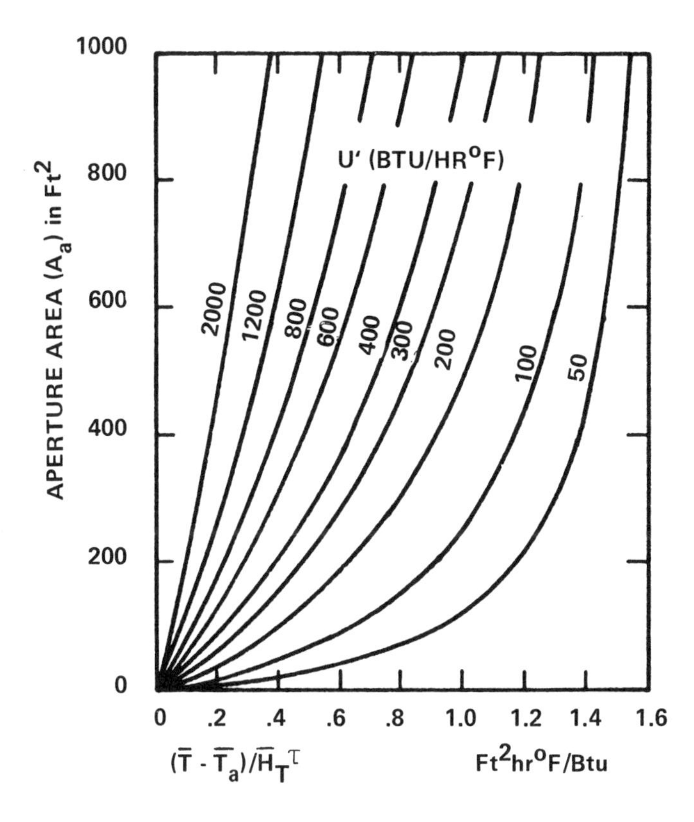


**Figure 37.** Aperture area vs U′ $(UA + mC_p - U_aA_c)$ and $(\bar{T} - \bar{T}_a)/\bar{H}_T\tau$, where $\bar{T}$ = average indoor temperature over a 24-hr time period (°F); $\bar{T}_a$ = average outside temperature over a 24-hr time period (°F); $\bar{H}_T$ = 24-hr average insulation; $\tau$ = transmittance of aperture.

$$\dot{T}_z = \dot{Q}_s/[(UA) + mC_p] + \dot{T}_a \tag{20}$$

Equation 20 can be written

$$\dot{T} = \dot{T}_z/[1 + R_{sa}/(\overset{*}{\dot{U}}/h + \overset{*}{\dot{U}}/\dot{A})] \tag{21}$$

Assuming that $\dot{T}_a$ always peaks at 3 p.m. ($\phi = -45°$) allows Equation 20 to be written

$$T_z = \frac{\overline{Q_s}}{(\overline{Q_s}/Q_s')[(UA) + mCp]}(\angle 0°) + T_a' \angle -45° \tag{22}$$

$\overline{Q_s}$ is given by Equation 17, so Equation 22 becomes

$$T_z = \frac{(\overline{T} - \overline{T_a})}{(\overline{Q_s}/Q_s')}(\angle 0°) + T_a' \angle -45° \quad (23)$$

so the amplitude of $\dot{T}_z$ is

$$|\dot{T}_z| = \{[(\overline{T} - \overline{T_a})/(\overline{Q_s}/Q_s')]^2 + T_a'^2 + \sqrt{2}T_a'(\overline{T} - \overline{T_a})/(\overline{Q_s}/Q_s')\}^{1/2} \quad (24)$$

It turns out that $\overline{Q_s}/Q_s' \simeq 0.6$. If it is assumed that the thermal storage mass has infinite thermal conductivity (or the walls are thin), then the admittance can be represented by

$$\dot{A} = \frac{2\pi C}{24} \angle 90° \quad (25)$$

Substituting this into Equation 21 and solving for the magnitude of $\dot{T}$ yields

$$|\dot{T}| = |\dot{T}_z|\{1 + [R_{sa}h(2 + R_{sa}h/\overset{*}{\dot{U}})/\overset{*}{\dot{U}}]/[1 + (24h/(2\pi C))^2]\}^{-1/2} \quad (26)$$

where $|\dot{T}_z|$ is given by Equation 24. This is the equation for the indirect-coupled case. For the direct-coupled case

$$\dot{T}_d = \frac{\dot{Q}_s/A_c}{\left[\dfrac{\overset{*}{\dot{U}}(1 + \dot{A})/h}{1 + R_{sa}\left(\dfrac{\overset{*}{\dot{U}}}{h} + \dfrac{\overset{*}{\dot{U}}}{\dot{A}}\right)}\right]} \quad (27)$$

so using the same approach

$$|\dot{T}_d| = \frac{|\dot{T}|}{|\dot{T}_z|}\left(\left\{\frac{\overline{T} - \overline{T_a}}{(\overline{Q_s}/Q_s')[1 + (2\pi C/(24h))^2]}\right\} \times \left[\frac{\overline{T} - \overline{T_a}}{\overline{Q_s}/Q_s'} + \sqrt{2}\,|\dot{T}_a|\left(1 + \frac{2\pi C}{24h}\right)\right] + |\dot{T}|^2\right)^{1/2} \quad (28)$$

when $|\dot{T}|$ and $|\dot{T}_z|$ are determined from Equations 24 and 26.

Figures 38 to 40 are plots of $|\dot{T}_z|$, $|\dot{T}|$ and $|\dot{T}_d|$ for the case of thermal storage in heavyweight concrete.

## Example of Numerical Method

The following example by Niles [1978] illustrates an application of this model. Consider a house with a loss coefficient, excluding the collector aperture, of 500 Btu-hr/°F, which is to be kept at an average daily indoor temperature of 65°F when the daily outdoor average temperature is 40°F with a sinusoidal amplitude of 10°F (30–50°F). The solar radiation falling on the south-facing aperture is 1500 Btu/ft²-day and the transmittance is 0.80. The thermal storage is three inches of heavyweight concrete with a surface area four times the aperture area. The thermal storage surface conductance h is 1 Btu-hr/ft²-°F. Referring to Figure 37, $\overline{H_T} = 1500/24$ and $(\bar{T} - \overline{T_a})/(\overline{H_T}\tau) = 25/50 = 0.5$; so, 340 ft² of aperture is required. According to Figure 38, $|\dot{T}_z|$ is 49°F. Since $R_{sa} = 4$, $(\bar{T} - \overline{T_a})R_{sa}h/(\overline{H_T}\tau) = 25(4)(1)/(50) = 2$; according to Figure 39, $|\dot{T}_z|/|\dot{T}| = 0.37$. Therefore, in the case of indirect-coupled thermal storage mass, the indoor air amplitude is $|\dot{T}| = 0.37(49) = 18$°F, and the indoor temperature fluctuates from 47°F at 3 a.m. to 83°F at 3 p.m. Referring to Figure 40, since $(\bar{T} - \overline{T_a})/|\dot{T}_a| = 25/10 = 2.5$ and the ratio of thickness to surface conductance is 3, then $|\dot{T}_d|/|\dot{T}| = 0.59$, so $|\dot{T}_d| = 0.59(18) = 11$°F; so, for the direct-coupled case, the inside temperature fluctuates from 54°F at 3 a.m. to 76°F at 3 p.m.

The Niles model has been compared with experimental results from a variety of direct-gain installations and found to be reasonably accurate. For example, an applicable direct-coupled system built in Butte, Montana, experienced an inside amplitude $|\dot{T}|$ of 5.2°F; this model predicted 5.9°F.

## OTHER MODELS FOR PREDICTING PERFORMANCE

More sophisticated models for calculating the performance of direct-gain passive systems are also available. The thermal balance method in-

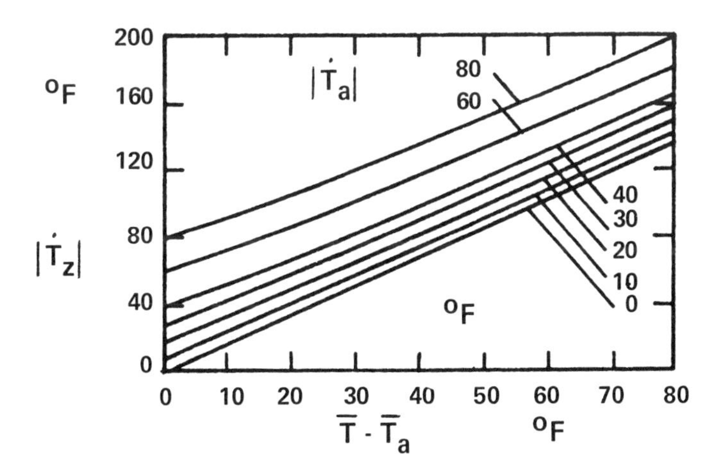


**Figure 38.** $|\dot{T}_z|$ vs $|\dot{T}_a|$ and $|\bar{T} - \overline{T_a}|$.

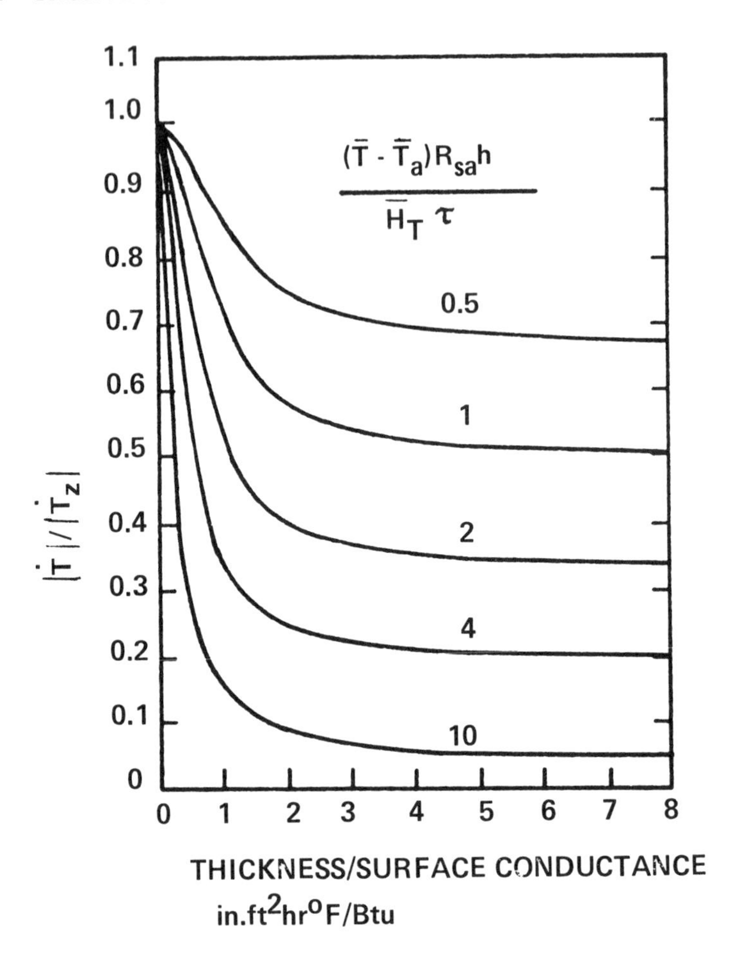


**Figure 39.** $|\dot{T}|/|\dot{T}_z|$ vs ratio of thickness (in.) to surface conductance (Btu/ft²-hr-°F) and $(T - T_a)R_{sa}h/H_T$. $\bar{T}$ = average indoor temperature over a 24-hr time period (°F); $\bar{T}_a$ = average outside temperature over a 24-hr time period (°F); $R_{sa}$ = ratio of storage mass surface area to direct-gain aperture area; h = surface conductance of thermal storage mass (Btu/ft²-hr).

volves performing thermal balance calculations on the inside and outside surfaces of the building envelope to determine inside surface temperatures and the inside air temperature. As an alternative to solving this involved set of heat balance equations, the weighting factor method uses weighting factors to estimate the contributions of component heat gains and losses to the total space heating or cooling load. The algebraic convolution method convolves the heating/cooling load with past values.

The Z-transform method uses the Laplace transform to determine the load. The thermal network method uses regions of uniform temperature within a building to define the processes that occur. The following summary of these methods was adapted from a DOE report prepared by CCB/Cumali Associates [1979].

## Thermal Balance Method

The thermal balance method employs a heat balance on each surface within the conditioned space to determine surface room temperatures

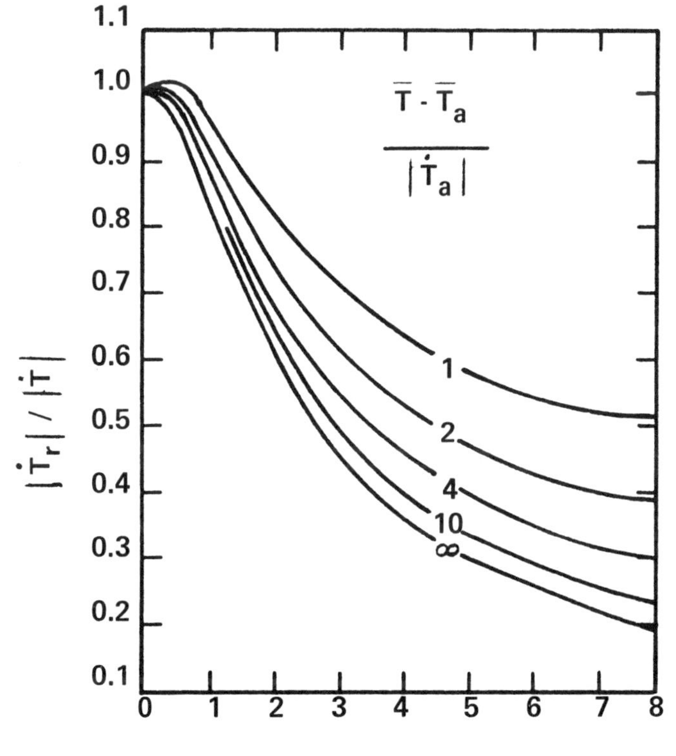


**Figure 40.** $|\dot{T}_r|/|\dot{T}|$ vs ratio of thickness (in.) to surface conductance (Btu/ft²-hr-°F) and $(\bar{T} - \bar{T}_a)/|\dot{T}_a|$.

and heating/cooling load. This approach was utilized earlier by Mitalas and Stephenson [1967a,b] to determine building loads.

A general equation for the heat balance at any internal surface i at time t is

$$q_{K_i}(t) = q_{C_i}(t) + q_{RS_i}(t) + q_{R_i}(t) \tag{29}$$

where
$q_{K_i}(t)$ = conduction heat gain at surface i
$q_{C_i}(t)$ = convection heat gain at surface i
$q_{RS_i}(t)$ = radiant heat gain at surface i from other surfaces
$q_{R_i}(t)$ = radiant heat gain from additional sources at surface i

The conductive heat gain $q_{K_i}(t)$ relates the outside and inside surface temperatures through the use of response factors applied to a time series of past temperature values:

$$q_{K_i}(t) = \left[ \sum_{j=0}^{n_i} X_i(j)T_i^I(t-j) - \sum_{j=0}^{n_i} Y_i(j)T_i^O(t-j) \right] A_i + C_i \cdot q_{K_i}(t-1) \tag{30}$$

where
$X_i(j)$ = internal surface time series response factors for surface i
$Y_i(j)$ = cross surface time series response factors for surface i
$A_i$ = area of surface i
$C_i$ = ratio for the above response factors
$n_i$ = number of response factor terms in the above time series
$T_i^I(t-j)$ = inside surface temperature history of surface i
$T_i^O(t-j)$ = outside surface temperature history of surface i

The convective heat gain $q_{C_i}(t)$ can be expressed as:

$$q_{C_i}(t) = h_i A_i [T_R - T_i^I(t)] \tag{31}$$

where
$h_i$ = convective heat transfer coefficient
$T_R$ = room air temperature

The radiant heat gain from other surfaces $q_{RS_i}(t)$ is

$$q_{RS_i}(t) = A_i \sum_{m=1}^{NS} G_{i,m}[T_m^I(t) - T_i^I(t)] \tag{32}$$

where
NS = number of surfaces within the space
$T_m^I(t)$ = inside surface temperature of surface m at time of t
$G_{i,m}$ = a term relating the heat exchange between surfaces i and m, expressed as

$$G_{i,m} = 4\epsilon_i F_{i,m} \sigma T_{REF}^3 \tag{33}$$

where $\epsilon_i$ = emissivity of surface i
$F_{i,m}$ = radiation view factor between surfaces i and m
$\sigma$ = Stefan-Boltzmann constant
$T_{REF}$ = reference temperature

The radiation view factor $F_{i,m}$ is

$$F_{i,m} = \frac{1}{A_i} \int_{A_i} \int_{A_m} \cos\phi_i \cdot \cos\phi_m \, dA_i \, dA_m \tag{34}$$

where $\phi_i$ and $\phi_m$ represent the appropriate geometrical relationships between the surfaces [Hutchinson 1962; Jakob 1957].

The radiant gain from other sources $q_{R_i}$ is a summation involving instantaneous solar radiation quantities, equipment, occupants and lights.

$$q_{R_i}(t) = q_{S_i}(t) + f_e q_e(t) + f_o q_o(t) + f_L q_L(t) \tag{35}$$

where $q_{S_i}(t)$ = radiation from the sun at surface i
$q_e(t)$ = radiation from equipment on surface i
$q_o(t)$ = radiation from occupants on surface i
$q_L(t)$ = radiation from lights on surface i
$f_e, f_o, f_L$ = radiative fractions of heat gain

Substitution of the above into Equation 29 yields

$$\left[ \sum_{j=0}^{n_i} X_i(j)T_i^I(t-j) - \sum_{j=0}^{n_i} Y_i(j)T_i^O(t-j) \right] A_i + C \cdot q_{K_i}(t-1)$$
$$= h_i A_i [T_R - T_i^I(t)] + A_i \sum_{m=1}^{NS} G_{i,m} [T_m^I(t) - T_i^I(t)] + q_{R_i}(t) \tag{36}$$

Isolating the inside surface temperatures results in

$$A_i \left[ X_i(O) + h_i + \sum_{m=1}^{NS} G_{i,m} \right] T_i^I(t) - A_i \left[ \sum_{m=1}^{NS} G_{i,m} \right] T_m^I(t)$$
$$= A_i \left[ - \sum_{j=1}^{n_i} X_i(j)T_i^I(t-j) + \sum_{j=0}^{n_i} Y_i(j)T_i^O(t-j) \right] - C \cdot q_{K_i}(t-1) + q_{R_i}(t) + h_i A_i T_R \tag{37}$$

for the constant room temperature case. With variable room temperature, an additional equation is needed. The room air heat balance at time t is obtained from surface temperatures, infiltration and supply mass flow rates, and convection heat gains from sources such as equipment, lights and occupants; so

$$q_{CS}(t) + q_{FL}(t) + q_{SP}(t) + q_{CO}(t) = 0 \tag{38}$$

where $q_{CS}(t)$ = convective gain due to all surface temperature changes
$q_{FL}(t)$ = heat gain from infiltration
$q_{SP}(t)$ = heat gain from supply air system
$q_{CO}(t)$ = convective heat gain from other sources

The convective heat gain due to all surface temperature changes is

$$q_{Cs}(t) = \sum_{i=1}^{NS} h_i A_i [T_i^I(t) - T_R(t)] \tag{39}$$

where $T_R(t)$ = room temperature at time t

The heat gain from the infiltration of outdoor air $q_{FL}(t)$ is

$$q_{FL}(t) = m_{FL}(t) C_P [T_o(t) - T_R(t)] \tag{40}$$

where $m_{FL}(t)$ = mass flowrate
$C_p$ = specific heat of air
$T_o(t)$ = outdoor dry bulb temperature at time t

$m_{FL}(t)$ may also be the volumetric flowrate if $C_P$ is then defined as the heat capacity per unit volume (Table VII). The heat gain due to supply air, $q_{SP}(t)$, is the same form as the infiltration gain above:

$$q_{SP}(t) = m_{SP}(t) C_P [T_S(t) - T_R(t)] \tag{41}$$

where $m_{SP}(t)$ = mass flowrate at time t (or volume flowrate if volumetric heat capacity is used)
$T_S(t)$ = supply air temperature at time t

The convective gain from other sources $q_{CO_L}(t)$ is

$$q_{CO_L}(t) = f_{ec} q_{ec}(t) + f_{oc} q_{oc}(t) + f_{LC} q_{LC}(t) + q_{bb}(t) + q_{sh}(t) \tag{42}$$

where $q_{ec}(t)$ = convective gain from equipment
$q_{oc}(t)$ = convective gain from occupants (Table VIII)
$q_{LC}(t)$ = convective gain from lights
$q_{bb}(t)$ = baseboard load
$q_{sh}(t)$ = solar energy absorbed by interior shades, plants or furniture and convected directly into the conditioned space
$f_{ec}, f_{oc}, f_{LC}$ = convective fractions of heat gain

The above f terms are obviously related to the radiation f terms by

$$f_{ec} = 1 - f_e, \text{etc.} \tag{43}$$

Substitution of the above into Equation 38 yields:

$$\sum_{i=1}^{NS} h_i A_i [T_i^I(t) - T_R(t)] + m_{FL}(t) C_P [T_o(t) - T_R(t)] + m_{SP}(t) C_P [T_S(t) - T_R(t)] + q_{CO}(t) = 0 \tag{44}$$

Rearranging terms to isolate the room air temperature

$$\sum_{i=1}^{NS} h_i A_i T_i^I(t) + \left[ -\sum_{i=1}^{NS} h_i A_i - m_{FL}(t) C_p - m_{SP}(t) C_P \right] T_R(t) = -m_{FL}(t) C_P T_o(t) - m_{SP}(t) C_P T_S(t) - q_{CO}(t) \tag{45}$$

Equations 37 and 45, when combined and put in matrix form, result in:

$$\begin{bmatrix} C_{1,1} & C_{1,2} & C_{1,3} \cdots\cdots & C_{1,NS+1} \\ C_{2,1} & \cdots\cdots\cdots\cdots & & C_{2,NS+1} \\ C_{3,1} & & & \\ \vdots & & & \\ C_{NS+1,1} & & & C_{NS+1,NS+1} \end{bmatrix} \begin{bmatrix} T_1^I(t) \\ T_2^I(t) \\ \\ \vdots \\ T_R(t) \end{bmatrix} = \begin{bmatrix} B_1 \\ B_2 \\ \\ \vdots \\ B_{NS+1} \end{bmatrix} \tag{46}$$

where

$$C_{i,i} = A_i \left[ X_i(O) + h_i + \sum_{m=1}^{NS} G_{i,m} \right]$$

$$C_{i,m} = -A_i G_{i,m} = C_{m,i} = -A_m G_{m,i}$$

$$C_{i,NS+1} = -h_i A_i = C_{NS+1,m} = -h_m A_m$$

$$C_{NS+1,NS+1} = -\sum_{i=1}^{NS} h_i A_i - m_{FL}(t) C_P - m_{SP}(t) C_P$$

$$B_i = A_i \left[ -\sum_{j=1}^{n_i} X_i(j) T_i^I(t-j) + \sum_{j=0}^{n_i} Y_i(j) T_i^O(t-j) \right] - C \cdot q_{K_i}(t-1) + q_{R_i}(t)$$

$$B_{NS+1} = -m_{FL}(t) C_P T_O(t) - m_{SP}(t) C_P T_S(t) - q_{CO}(t)$$

Once the surface temperature and room air temperatures are known, the zone load can be obtained from

$$Q(t) = \sum_{i=1}^{NS} h_i A_i [T_i^I(t) - T_R(t)] + m_{FL}(t) C_P [T_o(t) - T_R(t)] + q_{CO}(t) \tag{47}$$

which is the same expression as Equation 45, since the zone load is the heat picked up by the room air (or that lost by the room air) which has to be removed (or added) by the heating, ventilating and air-conditioning (HVAC) system.

## Weighting Factor Method

The weighting factor method used for determining zone loads was developed by Mitalas and Stephenson [1967a,b] of the National Research Council of Canada. Instead of solving a set of heat balance equations, as was done for the thermal balance method, in which the zone load is calculated by explicit solution of surface and room temperatures, each component of the heat gain contributing to the total load is determined by using weighting factors. Each component of heat gain is calculated independently of the others. The component heat gains are then weighted to estimate their contribution to the space load.

The weighting factor method assumes that the superposition principle applies to heat transfer processes occurring in a space, i.e., that the thermal processes can be described by linear differential equations. Therefore, one can use Green's function solutions to represent the time behavior of heat transfer within the space. This implies that one may calculate independently of the other heat gains the heat gain due to solar energy. A unit pulse is applied to the right hand side of the matrix Equation 45 from which is obtained the time history of the resulting loads $r_i(t)$. The solution for any arbitrary input $q_i(t)$ is then found by convolution with $r_i(t)$:

$$Q_i(t) = \sum_{j=0}^{\infty} q_i(t - j) r_i(j) \tag{48}$$

The weighting factors correspond to the values of the Green's function solution of the room thermal balance equations. The thermal balance and weighting factor methods are two distinct methods of solving the same set of heat balance equations. Given identical inputs, the resultant solutions should be nearly identical. The weighting factor method treats the relationship between the heat gain components due to conduction, convection and radiation and the total zone load. A load at constant room temperature is first computed using weighting factors for each of the above components. The variation in zone temperature is then derived from the computed zone load and an additional set of air temperature weighting factors. The conductive heat gain $q_{K_i}(t)$ is calculated from:

$$q_{K_i}(t) = -\left[\sum_{j=0}^{n_i} Y_i(j)T_i^O(t-j)\right]A_i + C_i \cdot q_{K_i}(t-1) \tag{49}$$

where
$Y_i(j)$ = cross surface time series response factor for surface i
$A_i$ = surface area of surface i
$C_i$ = common ratio for the above response factors
$n_i$ = number of response factor terms in the above time series
$T_i^O(t-j)$ = outside surface temperature history of surface i

The outside surface temperature history, $T_i^O(t-j)$, is generated by a heat balance at the outside surface relating the conduction equation to the heat gain by solar radiation incident on the surface. The effect of the response factor on the inside surface temperature [$T_i^I(t-j)$ in Equation 30] is dealt with by an additional layer of resistance in both Equation 49 and the outside surface temperature calculations. For a surface that is not delayed, the heat gain is

$$q_{K_i}(t) = U_i(T_{SOL} - T_R)A_i \tag{50}$$

where
$U_i$ = heat transfer coefficient of surface i
$T_{SOL}$ = air temperature of surface receiving solar radiation
$T_R$ = zone temperature

The convective heat gain is computed directly for each source. Usually, a specific magnitude is calculated or a percent convective gain is determined. Solar radiation data, both transmitted and absorbed, are necessary for definition of radiative heat gain, in addition to contributions arising from lights, equipment, occupants and infiltration.

Once the component heat gains are known, the zone load component at constant space temperature is calculated using weighting factors

$$Q(t) = V_0q(t) + V_1q(t-1) - W_1Q(t-1) \tag{51}$$

where
$Q(t)$ = component zone load at time t
$V_0, V_1, W_1$ = weighting factors
$q(t)$ = heat gain component at time t
$q(t-1)$ = heat gain component at time $t-1$
$Q(t-1)$ = component zone load at time t

The total load is the sum of component loads. The air temperature variation in the heated space with infiltration and ventilation is calculated by

$$\sum_{j=0}^{\infty} P_j[Q(t-j) - q(t-j)] = \sum_{j=0}^{\infty} G_j[T_R(t-j) - T_{RC}] \tag{52}$$

G and P are obtained by application of a pulse in room temperature $T_R$, which corresponds to a heat addition similar to the pulse for heat gain. Convolution of the resultant weighting factors with the time history of either heat extraction/addition or temperature yields the resulting space temperature distribution. Corrections must be applied to the formulation for infiltration and conductance. The magnitude of the infiltration is based on both outside air temperature and inside space temperature; as room temperature changes, the G terms must be corrected. Using Equation 52, the correction is

$$G_i(t) = G_i + P_i\left[1.1 \text{ cfm} + \sum_{i=1}^{NS} U_iA_i\right] \tag{53}$$

where $U_i$ = overall U-value for surface i
$A_i$ = surface area of surface i

The use of $\sum U_iA_i$ for conductance is correct in the asymptotic case, but for sudden fluctuations in temperature, it yields a low estimate. The weighting factor method is similar to the method employed in defining response factors, which is a well known procedure used in analyzing conduction heat transfer.

## Algebraic Convolution Method

The algebraic convolution method relates the cooling/heating load at any time t to the input heat gain/loss by an expression of the form:

$$Q(t) = \sum_{j=0}^{\infty} r(j)q(t-J) \tag{54}$$

where $Q(t)$ = cooling/heating load at time (t)
$q(t-j)$ = heat gain/heat loss at time $(t-j)$
$r(j)$ = response factors, which, for a unit input excitation, represent the actual cooling/heating load values.

This equation can be expanded using a finite number of terms as:

$$\begin{aligned} Q(t) = {} & r(0)q(t) + r(1)q(t-1) + r(2)q(t-2) + \ldots r(k)q(t-k) \\ & + r(k+1)q(t-k-1) + \ldots r(k+n)q(t-k-n) \end{aligned} \tag{55}$$

Since the responses are typically decaying exponentials, a relationship exists after k terms in which all succeeding r(j) terms are linear and related through the common ratio:

$$C = \frac{r(k+1)}{r(k)} \tag{56}$$

where C = common ratio

Thus, Equation 55 can be written as:

$$Q(t) = \sum_{j=0}^{k} r(j)q(t-j) + r(k)\sum_{j=k+1}^{\infty} C^j q(t-k-j) \tag{57}$$

A substantial reduction in solution time can be achieved by convolving the heating/cooling load Q(t) with past values. Substituting $t = t - 1$ into Equation 57 results in

$$Q(t) = \sum_{j=0}^{k} r'(j)q(t-j) + C \cdot Q(t-1) \tag{58}$$

which relates the cooling/heating load at time t, Q(t), to past values of cooling/heating load, $Q(t-1)$. The response factors, r′(j) are

$$r'(j) = r(j) - C \cdot r(j-1) \tag{59}$$

with

$$r'(0) = r(0) \tag{60}$$

The expression in Equation 58 is itself a time series which can be convolved in a similiar manner such that:

$$Q(t) = \sum_{j=0}^{k} r''(j)q(t-j) + C \cdot Q(t-1) + C' \cdot Q(t-2) \tag{61}$$

where

$$r''(j) = r'(j) - C' \cdot r'(j-1) \tag{62}$$

in which C′ is the common ratio of 58. Thus, the convolution can be carried as far as desired, and:

$$Q(t) = \sum_{j=0}^{k} V(j)q(t-j) + \sum_{j=1}^{k-1} W(j)Q(t-j) \tag{63}$$

where V = load response factors
W = common ratio after (k − 1) common ratios have been invoked

## Z-Transform Method

In the Z-transform method, the Laplace transform of a continuous function F(t), defined as

$$F(s) = \int_0^{\infty} e^{-st} F(t)\, dt \tag{64}$$

relates the time domain function F(t) to the complex plane domain function F(s). If the continuous function F(t) is sampled at regular intervals of time $m\Delta$, where $\Delta$ is a fixed time interval and m is an integer, one can relate the sampled output FO(t) to the input F(t) through a sampling function P(t) [Skinner 1964]. If the sampling function is a series of unit impulses expressed as:

$$P(t) = \sum_{m=0}^{\infty} \delta(t - m\Delta) \tag{65}$$

then the sampled output is

$$FO(t) = \sum_{m=0}^{\infty} F(m\Delta)\delta(t - m\Delta) \tag{66}$$

The Laplace transform of Equation 66 is

$$FO(s) = \sum_{m=0}^{\infty} F(m\Delta)e^{-(m\Delta)s} \tag{67}$$

Letting $Z = e^{s\Delta}$, where Z° is defined as the Z-transform of function F(t),

$$FO(Z) = \sum_{m=0}^{\infty} F(m\Delta)Z^{-m} \tag{68}$$

where the output depends only on the input values sampled at regular time intervals. Using this Z-transform, Equation 54 can be written as

$$Q(Z) = r(Z)q(Z) \tag{69}$$

The convolution in the time domain of function Q(t) is achieved in the Z-domain by multiplication and division of Equation 69 by the expression $(1 - C \cdot Z^{-1})$, where C is the common ratio of the r(Z) series; so

$$Q(Z)(1 - C \cdot Z^{-1}) = r(Z)(1 - C \cdot Z^{-1})q(Z) \tag{70}$$

which, when transformed, yields Equation 69. Successive applications of the same process lead to Equation 63.

## Thermal Network Method

The thermal network method uses regions of uniform temperature within a structure to define the heat transfer processes that occur. Each region is defined by a characteristic node and heat transfer between nodes is defined by a thermal conductance. By performing a heat balance at each node, a series of n-node equations are obtained that yield node solution temperatures. The following approach was taken by the Los Alamos Scientific Laboratory for its passive solar heating simulation program PASOLE [1978].

The heat balance equation at node i at time t is

$$\sum_{j=1}^{N} K_{i,j}(t)[T_i(t) - T_j(t)] + M_i(t)(dT/dt)_i = S_i(t) + B_i(t)T_i(t) \tag{71}$$

where
$K_{i,j}(t)$ = thermal conductance between nodes i and j
$T_i(t)$ = temperature at node i
$T_j(t)$ = temperature at node j
$M_i(t)$ = heat capacitance at node i
$S_i(t), B_i(t)$ = constants which define the heat source capacity of node i
N = number of nodes defining the system

The solution to this equation results in a matrix form similar to the thermal balance solution scheme, i.e.,

$$[C][T] = [B] \tag{72}$$

where

$$C_{i,i} = \frac{M_i(t)}{\Delta t} + -f\left[\sum_{j=1}^{N} K_{i,j}(t) - B_i(t)\right] \tag{73}$$

$$C_{i,j} = -fK_{i,j}(t) \tag{74}$$

$$B_i = M_i(t)T_i(t=0) + f\left[S_i(t) + \sum_{j=1}^{NF} K_{i,j}(t)T_j(t)\right]$$

$$+ (1-f)\left[\frac{M_i(t)}{M_i(t=0)}\right]\Big\{S_i(t=0) + B_i(t=0)T_i(t=0) \qquad (75)$$

$$+ \sum_{j=1}^{N} K_{i,j}(t=0)[T_j(t=0) - T_i(t=0)]\Big\}$$

where $f$ = constant, used to define the linear function solution to Equation 71
$NF$ = number of fixed temperature nodes

The above matrix is sized, of course, by the number of variable temperature nodes. The surface temperature heat balance Equation 37 can be rewritten

$$A_i\left[X_i(O) + h_i + \sum_{m=1}^{NS} G_{i,m}\right]T_i(t) - A_i\sum_{m=1}^{NS} G_{i,m}T_m(t)$$

$$= -A_i\sum_{j=1}^{t} X_i(j)T_i(t-j) + q_{R_i}(t) + h_iA_iT_R \qquad (76)$$

where the outside surface temperatures, $T_i^O(t)$, are assumed zero and the summation quantity on the right side deals with all past values of inside temperatures $T_i(t)$ to eliminate the use of past values of heat gain. In matrix form, Equation 76 is written

$$\begin{bmatrix} C_{1,1} & C_{1,2} \ldots & C_{1,NS} \\ C_{2,1} & & C_{2,NS} \\ \vdots & & \vdots \\ C_{NS,1} & & C_{NS,NS} \end{bmatrix} \begin{bmatrix} T_1(t) \\ T_2(t) \\ \vdots \\ T_{NS}(t) \end{bmatrix} = \begin{bmatrix} A_1h_1T_R + q_{R_1}(t) - \Phi_1(t) \\ \\ \vdots \\ A_{NS}h_{NS}T_R + q_{R_{NS}}(t) - \Phi_{NS}(t) \end{bmatrix}$$

or, using matrix notation,

$$[C] \cdot [T] = [B] \qquad (78)$$

where

$$C_{i,i} = A_i\left[X_i(O) + h_i + \sum_{m=1}^{NS} G_{i,m}\right] \qquad (79)$$

$$C_{i,m} = -A_iG_{i,m} = C_{m,i} = -A_mG_{m,i} \qquad (80)$$

$$B_i = A_i h_i T_R + q_{R_i}(t) - \Phi_i(t) \tag{81}$$

$$\Phi_i(t) = A_i \sum_{j=1}^{t} X_i(j) T_i(t - j) \tag{82}$$

Each of the terms in the [C] matrix are constant and independent of the solution temperatures $T_i$. The $B_i$ equation contains the excitation function, which for a unit radiation impulse is described as follows:

$$\sum_{i=1}^{NS} q_{R_i}(O) = 1 \quad \text{and} \quad q_{R_i}(t) = 0 \text{ at } t \geq 1 \tag{83}$$

In this case, the room air temperature $T_R$ is the lesser of zero and the outside air temperature. For a unit room air temperature pulse,

$$T_R = 1 \quad \text{and} \quad t = 0$$

$$T_R = 0 \quad \text{at} \quad t \geq 1$$

The solution of Equation 76 is obtained by inverting the [C] matrix; thus, using matrix notation,

$$[T] = [C]^{-1} \cdot [B] = [K] \cdot [B] \tag{84}$$

For $j = t$, the solution temperatures can be written as:

$$T_i(t - j) = T_i(O) = \sum_{n=1}^{NS} K_{i,n} B_n(O) \tag{85}$$

where

$$B_n(O) = A_n h_n T_R + q_{R_n}(O) \tag{86}$$

$$\Phi_n(O) = 0 \tag{87}$$

For $j < t$

$$T_i(t - j) = -\sum_{n=1}^{NS} K_{i,n} \Phi_n(t - j) \tag{88}$$

Substitution of Equations 85 and 88 into 82 yields:

$$\Phi_i(t) = -A_i \sum_{j=1}^{t-1} X_i(j) \sum_{n=1}^{NS} K_{i,n} \Phi_n(t - j) + A_i X_i(j) \sum_{n=1}^{NS} K_{i,n} B_n(O) \tag{89}$$

Weighting factors are determined by obtaining the heating/cooling load response to the impulse input heat gains. Specifically,

$$Q(t) = \sum_{m=1}^{NS} A_m h_m [T_R - T_m(t)] \tag{90}$$

A recursion relationship is developed by considering the load contribution from each surface; thus for $t \geq 1$,

$$Q_m(t) = A_m h_m \sum_{i=1}^{NS} K_{m,i} \Phi_i(t) \tag{91}$$

Substitution of Equation 89 into the expression yields

$$\begin{aligned} Q_m(t) = & -A_m h_m \sum_{i=1}^{NS} K_{m,i} \sum_{j=1}^{t-1} \frac{X_i(j)}{h_i} Q_i(t-j) \\ & + A_m h_m \sum_{i=1}^{NS} K_{m,i} A_i X_i(t) \sum_{n=1}^{NS} K_{i,n} B_n(O) \end{aligned} \tag{92}$$

so the total load is:

$$Q(t) = \sum_{m=1}^{NS} Q_m(t) \tag{93}$$

For all times after $t = 0$, the resultant load can be determined from past values of the load.

When analyzing the performance of direct-gain solar energy systems, the separate heat losses and gains from each source and the solar radiation input are summed over the period of the analysis. This allows one to calculate accurately the solar heating fraction and other performance parameters of interest.

# CHAPTER 3

# THERMAL STORAGE WALLS

## TROMBE WALLS

The Trombe wall, as illustrated in Figure 2, may be considered a modification of a direct-gain system with the thermal storage mass located adjacent to the solar aperture. This provides greater control over the amount of heat allowed to enter the conditioned space.

Trombe walls are characterized by one or more (usually two) layers of glass or transparent plastic located a few inches from the surface of a dark-colored wall. The dark wall is heated by solar radiation transmitted through the glazing. Vents are usually located in the bottom and top of the wall, as shown in Figure 2, to allow cool air from the conditioned space to rise in the gap between the wall and glazing and return to the conditioned space through the top vent. This type of thermal storage wall is known as the Trombe wall after Felix Trombe of Odeillo, France, who, working with architect Jacques Michel, built several homes in the French Pyrenees incorporating this design. The first Trombe walls were actually built by E. L. Morse in Salem, Massachusetts, in the 1880s, using slate covered by glass with both top and bottom vents and dampers. He received a patent for this concept.

A number of variations have been incorporated in Trombe walls to improve their efficiency or thermal control and to reduce heat losses. One variation combines movable insulation with the wall in the form of insulating shades or rigid insulating shutters that are hinged or slide across the aperture (Figure 41). Movable insulation to reduce heat losses at night and during cloudy weather are needed for colder climates. Another approach to reducing heat loss is triple glazing. Some Trombe walls are insulated on the inside so that when the damper is closed, heating of the interior space by the wall is almost completely eliminated. A

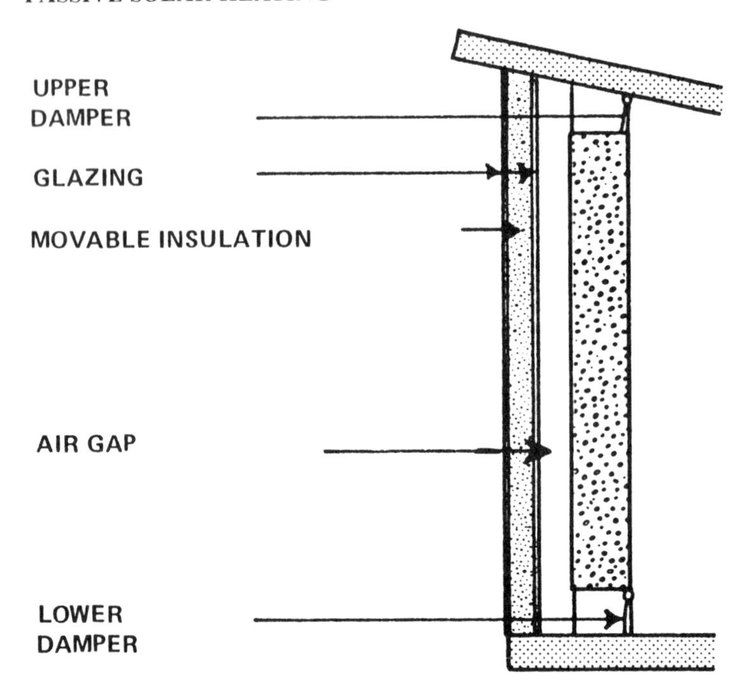


**Figure 41.** Movable insulation in a Trombe wall.

disadvantage of uninsulated Trombe walls is a tendency to radiate heat into the building during the summer, when the heat is not needed. On the other hand, the insulation on the wall greatly reduces radiant heating in the winter.

Another alternative to the solid concrete south-facing wall is the use of massive louvers, as illustrated in Figure 42. These louvers are oriented to admit solar radiation in the morning directly into the conditioned space and to store afternoon solar heat in the louvers. This is not a Trombe wall, but incorporates characteristics both of the Trombe wall and direct-gain system. It permits access to the inner surface of the glass for cleaning, and also facilitates the use of insulation between the glazing and the columns.

Thermal storage walls do not admit direct sunlight into the building as do direct-gain systems. This reduces sunlight damage to furnishings and eliminates the glare of sunlight, which may be distracting to building occupants. However, in some cases, direct sunlight may be desirable, and passive systems employing direct gain could be more appropriate. Trombe walls also provide greater security and structural stability and require very little maintenance. At higher latitudes, the vertical south wall provides good winter heating performance with little heating in the

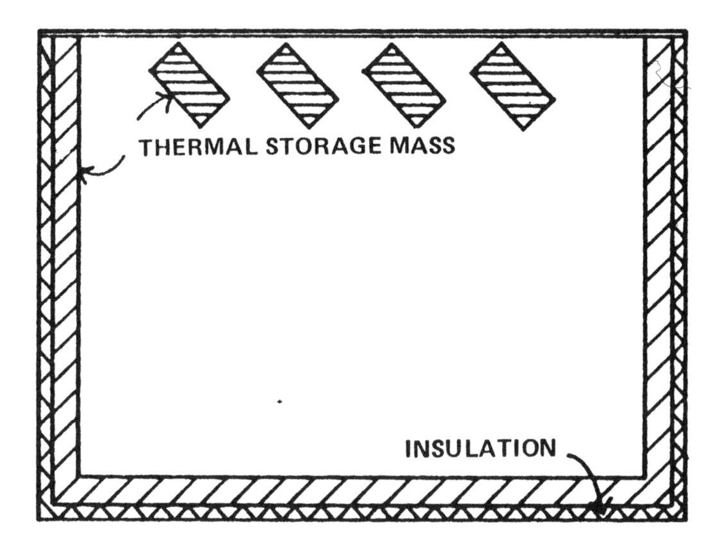


**Figure 42.** Vertical storage-mass louvers [Bier 1978].

summer. The optimum thickness is 6–12 in. Thicker walls are needed for heat delivery late at night; thinner walls are used for commercial buildings requiring primarily daytime heating. In fact, if the heat load occurs during the day, the direct-gain system or simple thermal siphoning loop (Figure 6) would be more suitable.

Figure 43 illustrates a conventional Trombe wall design of the type used in France and in many installations throughout the United States. This design consists of double glazing with an inner storage wall (usually of high-density concrete), backdraft dampers to control air flow through the vents and the structural components. The dampers are necessary not only to regulate heat flow into the building but to prevent reverse thermosiphoning, which can cause additional heat losses at night. Since the maximum stagnation temperature of the wall is about 180°F, heat-resistant plastics may also be used for glazing. Essentially, the wall is of conventional construction, except that air voids, which could reduce the thermal conductivity and heat capacity, are avoided, and the wall is thermally isolated from the metal frame of the glazing.

To allow a Trombe wall to heat by radiation as well as convection, the interior of the wall cannot be covered so as to reduce radiant heat loss. The interior color is not particularly important, since radiation into the room is in the far infrared region of the spectrum. Wood paneling or sheetrock should not be installed on the inside surface.

From a thermal performance standpoint, a good exterior coating for a Trombe wall is a flat black paint such as 3M's Nextel® black velvet. To

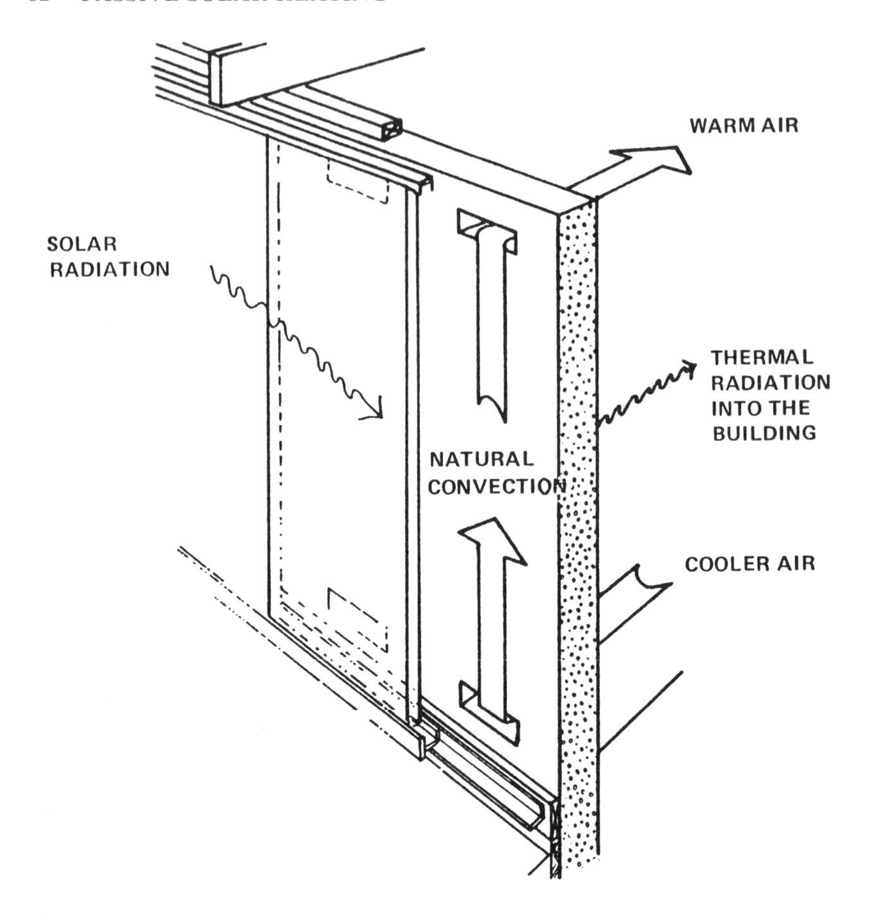


**Figure 43.** Conventional Trombe wall.

make the Trombe wall esthetically pleasing, however, architects often prefer to use a dark color other than black on the exterior surface. This results in an efficiency loss of a few percent. Vent holes are typically about 4 in. high × 15 in. wide and should be placed as close to the ceiling and floor as practicable. The glazing is typically mounted 3–4 in. from the exterior surface of the wall to provide adequate air flow.

## Kelbaugh House

One of the best known houses in the United States using a Trombe wall for heating is the Doug Kelbaugh house in Princeton, New Jersey [Kelbaugh 1976,1978; Kelbaugh and Tichy 1979]. This 1850-ft$^2$ two-story house incorporates 600-ft$^2$ of south-facing solar aperture, including the Trombe wall and attached greenhouse. Figure 44 is a cross section illustrating the convective and radiative heating of the two-story house by the south-facing Trombe wall. Windows in the Trombe wall provide a view to the south. Figure 45 illustrates the floor plan for the house with its 15-in.-thick concrete south wall. Additional thermal storage is provided by the concrete slab floor and the floor of the greenhouse, plus 55-gal drums of water in the greenhouse.

In this house, the ground floor is one continuous open space with the kitchen on the east end partially separated from the living and dining areas by the stairway. The three bedrooms on the second floor are located adjacent to the Trombe wall. A wide arch through the Trombe

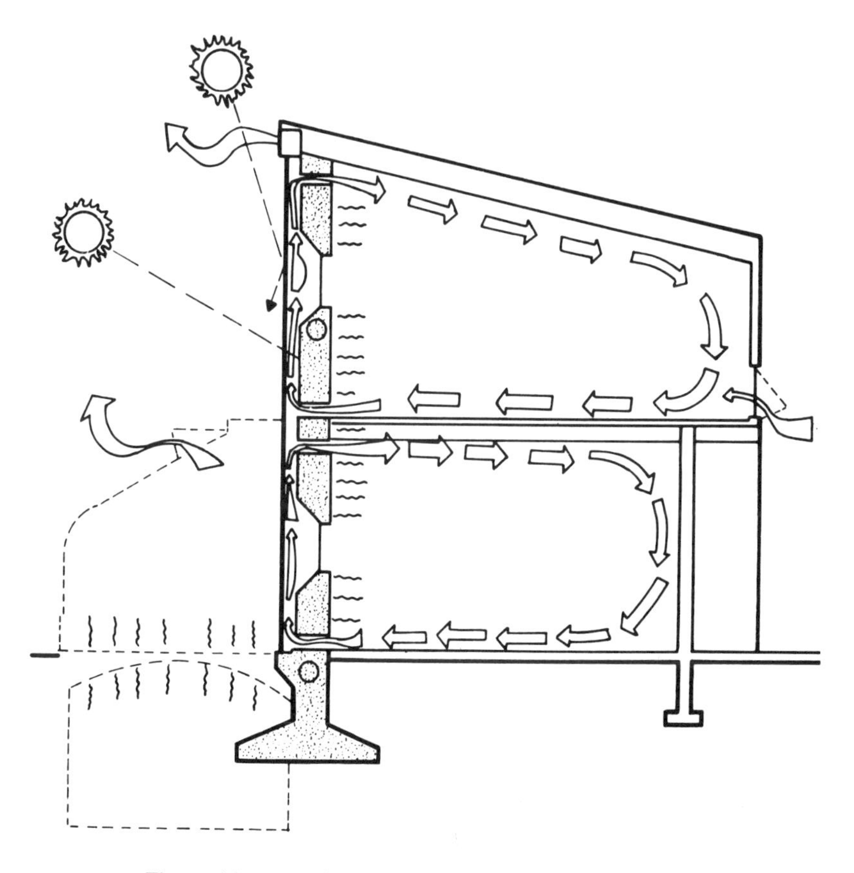

**Figure 44.** Passive circulation in the Kelbaugh house.

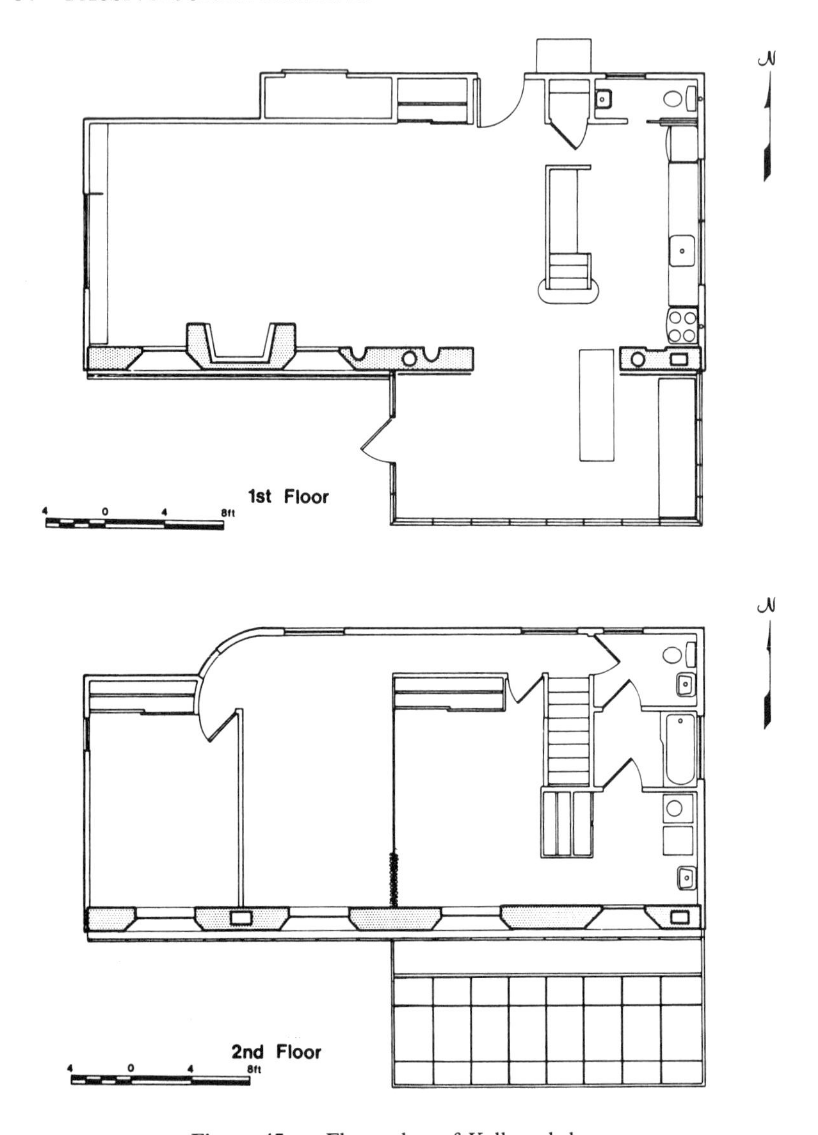


**Figure 45.** Floor plan of Kelbaugh house.

wall connects the greenhouse with the downstairs living area. The house is well insulated and equipped with 1-in.-thick styrofoam panels on the north windows to reduce heat loss at night. The backup heating system is a conventional gas furnace with ducts cast in the concrete wall. Two large deciduous trees reduce solar radiation on the Trombe wall in the summer.

Because of the large thermal storage mass, day/night temperatures fluctuate only 3–6°F. The solar-heating fraction was calculated to be 76%. Reverse thermal siphoning problems were initially encountered when the system was put into operation, but a simple backflow damper consisting of a wire mesh screen covered by a 0.5-mil plastic film solved the problem, since it permitted air circulation in one direction only. The building loss coefficient for this house was computed to be 13,093 Btu/degree day, or 6.89 Btu/ft$^2$-dd. The energy received by direct gain amounted to less than 9% of the total solar energy absorbed by the house. The calculated solar heating fraction of 76% is very close to what has been observed over the last few years. Figures 46 and 47 illustrate ambient and inside temperature data for a few days in July and a few days in December. It is seen that during the summer, the thermal mass inside the home results in interior temperatures about 10°F lower than the outside peak. During the winter, interior temperatures remain between 60 and 70°F, even though the outside ambient temperature falls as low as 10°F.

## Brookhaven House

Another house of more conventional design was built by the Brookhaven National Laboratory and uses the type of Trombe wall illustrated

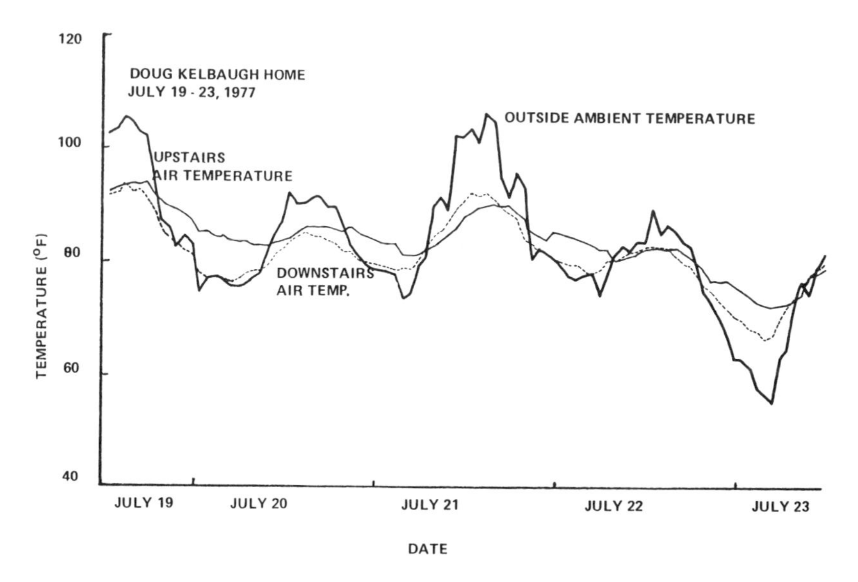


**Figure 46.** Temperature fluctuations in the Kelbaugh house in July.

in Figure 48. This wall has no vent to heat by convection, but provides radiant heating to the interior space. Double-glazed windows allow a view to the south, and a retractable canvas awning (Figure 49) shades the wall in the summer and is rolled up during the heating season.

The Trombe wall is triple-glazed to reduce heat loss, but in more southern climates, double-glazing would be more cost-effective. The commercial triple-glazed float glass panels are mounted in wood strips attached to the brick wall. Additional heat for the house is provided by a wood stove.

## Hunn House

The Bruce Hunn house in Los Alamos, New Mexico, is a 1955-ft$^2$ two-story house with a south-facing 250-ft$^2$ Trombe wall and 140 ft$^2$ of direct-gain aperture (Figure 50). Thermal storage is provided by the Trombe wall mass and a rock bed that is heated by air drawn from the Trombe wall. The Trombe wall has no windows, and heats the interior space by radiation and convection from its inner surface. From the interior of the house, the Trombe wall looks like a normal brick wall.

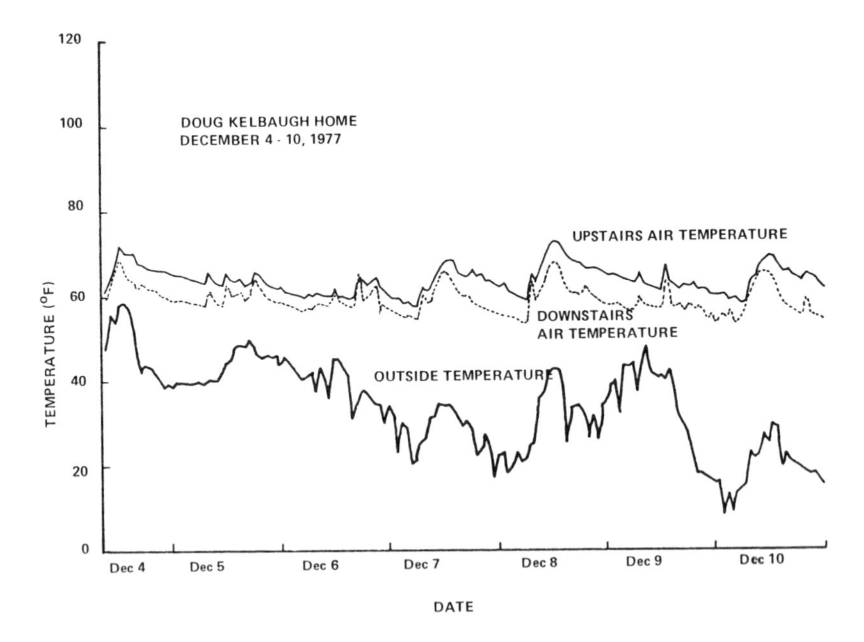


**Figure 47.** Temperature fluctuations in the Kelbaugh house in December.

**Figure 48.** Trombe wall of Brookhaven house.

The wall consists of 12 in. of open slump rock filled with cement and reinforced with rebar. The double glazing is of 3/16-in. plate glass with 1-in. spacing between the glass plates and a 2-in. space between the inner glazing and the rock wall. The outer surface of the wall is stained dark brown to an absorptance of 0.91.

**Figure 49.** Rendering of Brookhaven passive solar-heated house.

The first floor is a single open space which provides for free circulation of air. The exterior walls (other than the Trombe wall) are of $2 \times 6$ construction with R-19 fiberglass batts between the studs. The rafters are also $2 \times 6$ with R-19 batts in the roof. A 3-ft overhang on the south side shades the Trombe wall during the summer. The foundation of the house is insulated to a depth of 2 ft with a 2-in. layer of rigid expanded polystyrene. The rock bed is 3 ft deep, 6 ft long in the direction of air flow, and 12 ft wide. It rests on a concrete base and is framed with $2 \times 4$ studs sheathed with 0.75-in. plywood and insulated with 2-in. extruded polystyrene ($U = 0.11$). The 1040-ft$^2$ direct-gain aperture is double-glazed and there are two double-glazed 2- $\times$ 4-ft skylights on the roof. Data from about two weeks of operation during the winter are illustrated by Figure 51. It is seen that even though the wall temperature reaches 140°F and ambient temperatures below 0°F, the room temperature remains about 55–70°F. Figure 52 shows the floor plan of the house with the south-facing Trombe wall and direct-gain apertures to the south.

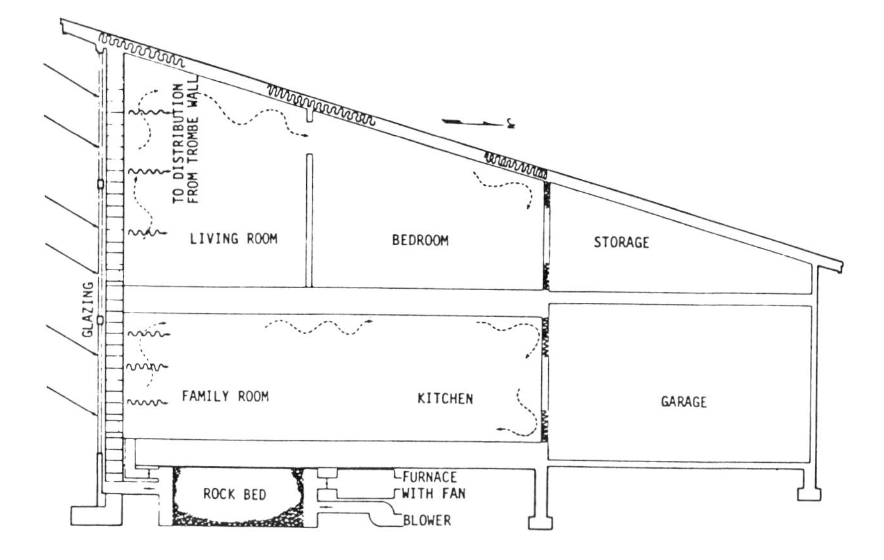


**Figure 50.** Cross section of Hunn house.

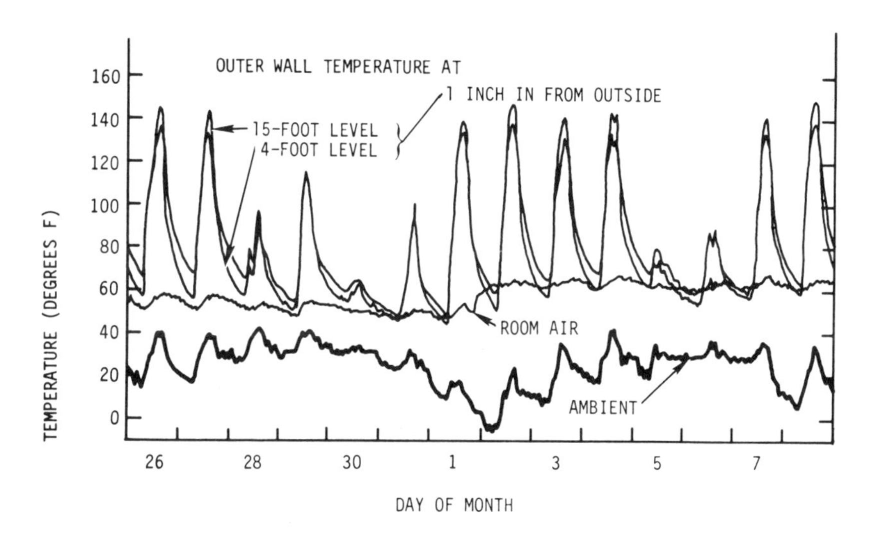


**Figure 51.** Winter temperature fluctuations in the Hunn house.

The recorded data illustrated in Figure 51 include both sunny and cloudy days; the days with low peak outer wall temperatures were cloudy. The outer wall temperature is a good indication of the total amount of solar energy falling on the wall at a given time. The building

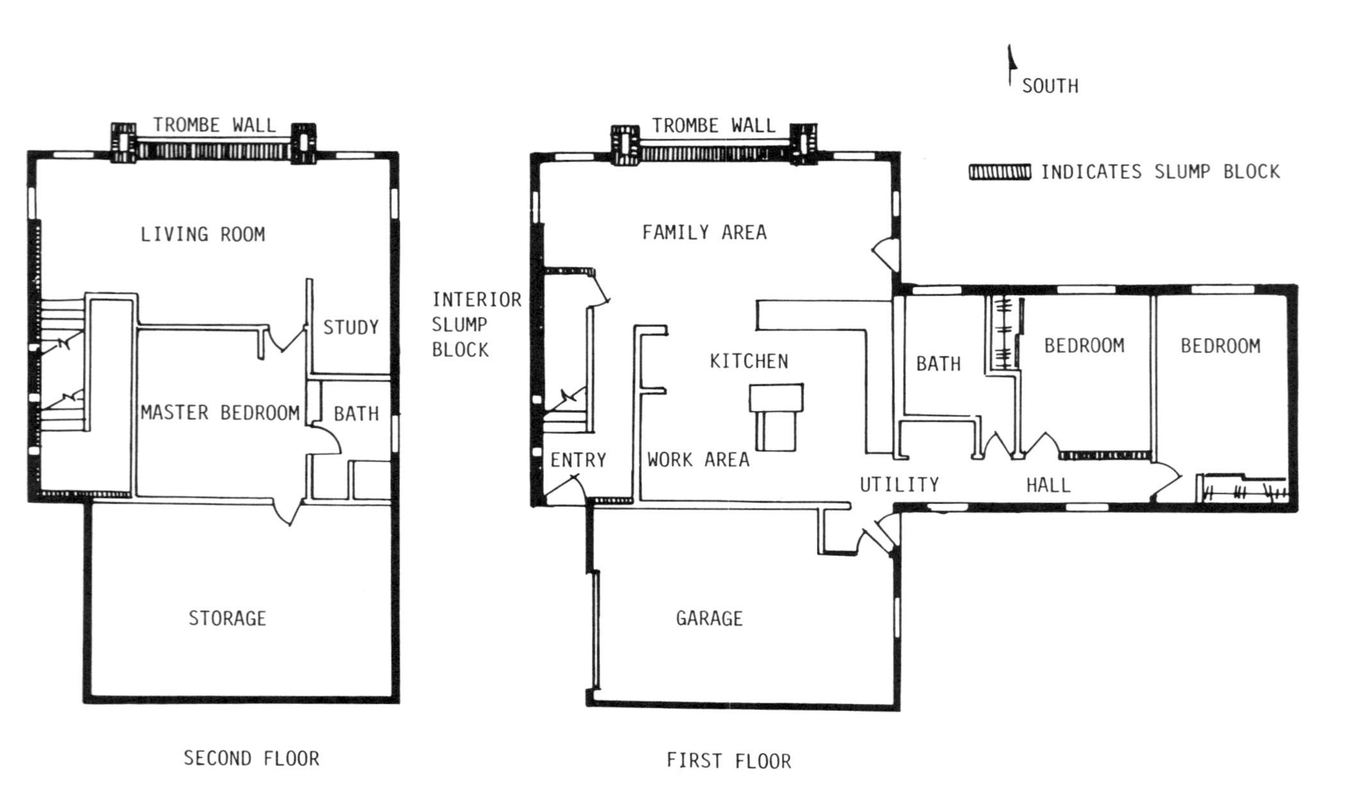


**Figure 52.** Floor plan of Hunn house with south-facing Trombe wall.

loss coefficient for this house was calculated to be 19,554 Btu/dd, which results in an annual load of about 93 million Btu. The solar-heating fraction was calculated to be 57%.

## Other Trombe Wall Examples

Two houses heated by Trombe walls in Odeillo, France, were built in 1967 by Felix Trombe and his colleagues. These houses use the type of Trombe wall illustrated in Figure 2. They are located a few blocks from the world's largest solar furnace. The 60-cm-thick heavy gravel concrete Trombe walls are double-glazed and painted on the outside with black acrylic paint. Thermal energy provided by one of these 80-$m^2$ Trombe walls was about 600 kWh/$m^2$-yr, which results in an energy cost (based on amortizing the cost of the wall) of 0.8¢/kWh. This type of system reduces the heating load by 60–70% [Trombe et al. 1975]. The volume of each house is about 300 $m^3$. The performance of the houses was calculated using finite difference techniques with 5-min time steps and 2.5 cm (1 in.) between nodes in the concrete slab [Ohanessian and Charters 1975].

A three-unit condominium was constructed near these houses in 1974 using Trombe walls of the type illustrated in Figures 53 and 54. The Trombe walls of each of the three attached dwelling units were painted a different dark color. Winter operation of the system (Figure 53) involves circulation of cool air down through the floor into the bottom of the wall and up through a vent at the top. During the summer, the exterior vent is opened, so that the Trombe wall ventilates the building by drawing in air from the north side. Exterior vents on Trombe walls must be tight fitting, or they can reduce substantially heating efficiency in the winter.

Parry [1979] reported the construction of a 1650-$ft^2$ tri-level home in Richland, Washington, with a 805-$ft^2$ Trombe wall. The 12-in.-thick wall was constructed of dense concrete block with filled cores. All other walls were of standard frame construction. The inner and outer surfaces of the Trombe wall were coated with a fibrous stucco to provide additional tensile strength and an esthetically pleasing surface texture. The outer surface was stained flat black while the inner layer of 3-mil Tedlar® film was separated by a 3/8-in. air gap from the outer glazing of translucent ultraviolet-stabilized corrugated fiberglass panel. The corrugated panel was chosen to provide resistance to high winds. The cross-sectional areas of the vents at the bottom of the first floor and near the ceiling of the second floor are about 14 in.$^2$ per lineal foot of wall. Thin plastic film backdraft preventers are mounted on the lower vents, and manually

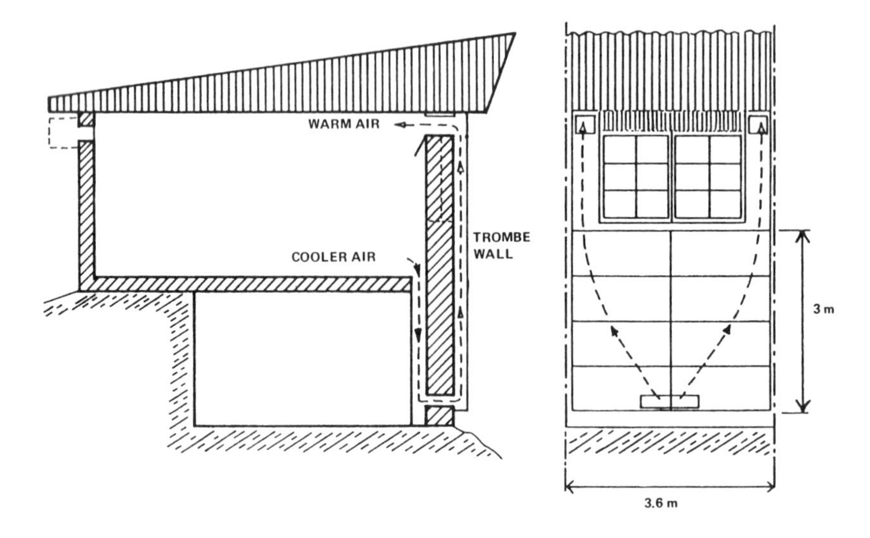


**Figure 53.** Trombe wall heating system for three-unit condominium in Odeillo, France.

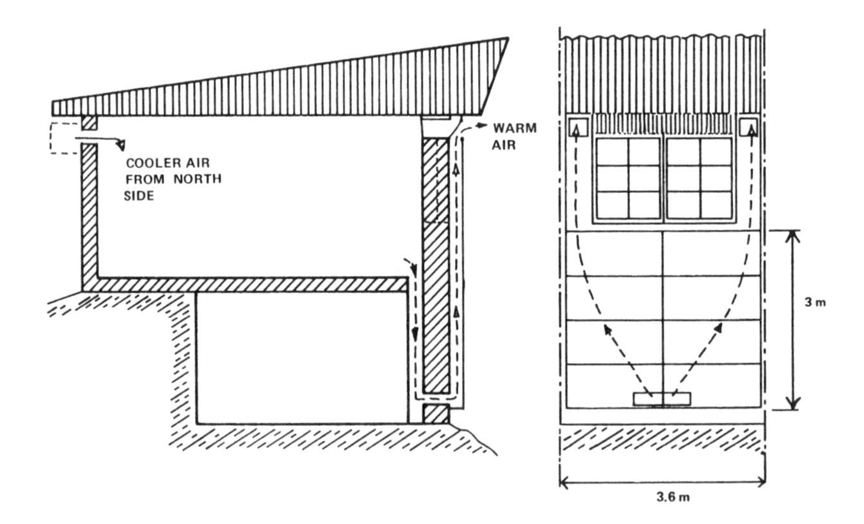


**Figure 54.** Trombe wall ventilating system for three-unit condominium in Odeillo, France.

operated dampers are fitted to the upper vents. The manually operated dampers are opened only when immediate daytime heating is needed; otherwise, they remain closed. Whenever overheating of the upper floors occurs due to thermal stratification, the central heating furnace fan is operated to circulate air throughout the house and maintain a uniform temperature. Heat from the wood stove in the living room is also distributed throughout the house in the same manner. The solar heating fraction is about 60%, and it has been found that the Trombe wall will supply all of the heating needs of the house on clear days with outside temperatures in the 20s. Overheating in the summer is minimized by using a small fan to circulate cool air at night over the outer surface of the wall, thereby reducing daytime wall temperatures.

The report by Parry et al. [1979] provides the following insight into some of the problems one might anticipate in constructing a house of unusual design, such as the first Trombe wall-heated house in a particular area. Because it was unusual, some of the subcontractors gave it a low priority and tended to assign the least skilled crew members to the job. On numerous occasions, subcontract work had to be redone; in one case, the owner and general contractor had to redo the wall and ceiling insulation. Clearly, when building a solar house in an area unaccustomed to solar houses, the general contractor should make every effort to identify subcontractors who are not only competent but also committed to the project.

Dobrovolny [1979] described an earth-insulated 1850-$ft^2$ residence in Eljebel, Colorado, which is heated by 294 $ft^2$ of south-facing 12-in.-thick Trombe wall, 155 ft of attached greenhouse and 165 $ft^2$ of south- and east-facing direct-gain aperture. The Trombe walls are painted a dark blue on the exterior to blend with sky and mountain reflections. The exterior glazing for the Trombe wall and the greenhouse glazing are standard tempered patio door glass. Inside temperatures typically are allowed to range 58–78°F in the winter. The solar-heating fraction is believed to be better than 90%.

## Techniques for Calculating Trombe Wall Performance

Balcomb and McFarland [1978] introduced a simple technique for calculating the yearly performance of Trombe or water wall heating systems to an accuracy of about 3% as compared with hour-by-hour simulations. This technique can be applied to storage walls of 45 Btu/°F of storage per $ft^2$ of aperture. The only data needed are the monthly values of solar radiation, the number of heating degree days and the thermal loss and gain characteristics of the building. The correlations were developed by performing a large number of detailed hour-by-hour simulations of storage wall systems for 29 different cities and for 6 building loads in each city. This method, which uses the load collector ratio (LCR), can be used for passive solar buildings with south-facing vertical double-glazed

($\tau = 0.747$) Trombe walls or water walls with or without night insulation. The night insulation was assumed to have $U = 0.11$ and to be in place from 5:00 p.m. to 9:00 a.m.

## *LCR Method*

The first step in the LCR method is to estimate the building loss coefficient in Btu/dd, which is the overall UA factor for the building plus the infiltration load (hourly air flow entering times $C_p$ for air), times 24 hr/day; however, the loss coefficient (UA factor) for the passive storage wall is not included. Having determined the loss coefficient, the load collector ratio is:

$$\text{LCR} = \frac{\text{building loss coefficient (Btu/dd)}}{\text{solar aperture area (ft}^2\text{)}} \tag{94}$$

Appendix A lists the LCR values that will result in a particular solar-heating fraction (SHF). Using the data for the city most representative of the local site, one can interpolate, if necessary, to determine the solar-heating fraction resulting from any LCR value. The auxiliary energy required is then:

$$\text{auxiliary energy required (Btu/yr)} = (1 - \text{SHF})(\text{dd})_a(\text{loss coefficient})$$

where $(\text{dd})_a$ is the annual number of heating days (Table III) and the loss coefficient is in Btu/dd.

The following example by Balcomb and McFarland [1978] illustrates the use of the model. A 72- × 24-ft building in Dodge City, Kansas, is heated by a south-facing 309-$\text{ft}^2$ double-glazed water wall. The transmittance is 0.74 and there are 45 lb water/$\text{ft}^2$ of collector aperture. The wall is double-glazed with sealed glass units with a transmittance of 0.74. There are 1107 $\text{ft}^2$ of walls ($U = 0.07$ Btu/$\text{ft}^2$-°F-hr), 120 $\text{ft}^2$ of windows ($U = 0.55$), 1728 $\text{ft}^2$ of roof ($U = 0.05$) and 1728 $\text{ft}^2$ of floor ($U = 0.05$). The building volume is 12,320 $\text{ft}^3$ and there is 0.5 air change each hour.

The UA factor for the building is calculated to be 316.3 Btu/hr-°F and the infiltration $mC_p$ is $(12{,}320 \text{ ft}^3)(0.5)(0.018) = 110.9$ Btu/hr-°F; so the total building loss coefficient is 427.2 Btu/hr-°F, or 10,250 Btu/dd. The load collector ratio (LCR) is, therefore, $10{,}250/309 = 33.2$. Table XI examines the relationship between SHF and LCR, and shows, by interpolation, that a LCR of 33.2 corresponds to a SHF of 0.48. Since the number of degree days is 4986, the useful energy supplied by solar is $(0.48)(10{,}250)(4986) = 24.5$ MBtu/yr. The auxiliary energy used is $(1 - 0.48)(10{,}250)(4986) = 26.6$ MBtu/yr.

**Table XI. $SHF_m/SLR_m$ Correlation Coefficients**

| Type of Storage Wall | A | B | C | D | W |
|---|---|---|---|---|---|
| Trombe Wall Without Night Insulation | 0.4520 | 1.0137 | 1.0392 | 0.7047 | 0.1 |
| Trombe Wall with Night Insulation | 0.7197 | 1.0074 | 1.1195 | 1.0948 | 0.5 |
| Water Wall Without Night Insulation | 0.5995 | 1.0149 | 1.2600 | 1.0701 | 0.8 |
| Water Wall with Night Insulation | 0.7642 | 1.0102 | 1.4027 | 1.5461 | 0.7 |

If monthly values of SHF are desired, the monthly LCR method may be used for estimating storage wall performance. The values in Table XI were actually derived using the monthly LCR method. The monthly solar load ratio is defined as:

$$SLR_m = \frac{\text{monthly solar radiation absorbed on the storage wall surface}}{\text{monthly load for the building including the storage wall}}$$

so

$$SLR_m = \frac{\overline{H}_T N \tau \alpha A_c}{\overset{*}{U}(dd)_m} = \frac{\overline{H}_T \tau/(dd)_m}{\overset{*}{U}/\alpha A_c} \qquad (95)$$

where
$\overline{H}_T$ = average daily solar radiation intensity on collectors
$N$ = number of days in the month
$\tau$ = transmittance of glazing
$\alpha$ = absorptance of storage wall surface
$A_c$ = aperture area of Trombe wall
$\overset{*}{U}$ = $\Sigma U_i A_i + mC_p$ = building loss coefficient including Trombe wall
$(dd)_m$ = number of heating degree days in the month

Although it is not rigorously correct to separate $\tau$ and $\alpha$, it is done here so one can define the solar capability index (SCI) as:

$$SCI = \overline{H}_T \tau (dd)_m \qquad (96)$$

the ratio of monthly solar radiation transmitted through to the wall surface to the monthly degree days. The modified load collector ratio (MLCR) is then defined as:

$$MLCR = \overset{*}{U}/(\alpha A_c) \qquad (97)$$

The SCI depends on the weather, and MLCR on the building structure. Typical average values of double-glazed storage walls (in Btu/ft$^2$-hr-°F) are 0.22 (uninsulated) and 0.12 (R-9 night insulation) for 18-in.-thick

Trombe wall, and 0.33 (uninsulated) and 0.18 (R-9 night insulation) for water walls. Balcomb and McFarland [1978] also showed that the ratio of $\overline{H_T\tau}$ for south-facing double glazing to $\bar{H}$ could be found from the following correlation:

$$(\overline{H_T\tau})_{sd}/\bar{H} = 0.2260 - 0.002512(L - D) + 0.0003075(L - D)^2 \qquad (98)$$

where $(\overline{H_T\tau})_{sd}$ = monthly (or average daily) solar radiation transmitted through south-facing double-glazed aperture
$\bar{H}$ = monthly (or average daily) solar radiation incident on a horizontal surface
L = latitude
D = solar declination at midmonth $\simeq 23.3\cos(30°M - 187°)$
M = number of month (January = 1, February = 2, etc.)

Equation 98 is plotted in Figure 55. If a horizontal specular reflector of 0.8 reflectance the same size as the storage wall is used, then $(\overline{H_T\tau})_{sd}$ is increased by up to 40%, as illustrated by Figure 56. The reflector is assumed to be positioned horizontally in front of the storage wall, so that the edge of the reflector is adjacent to the base of the wall. This would be the case if the reflector were also a rigid insulating wall cover hinged at

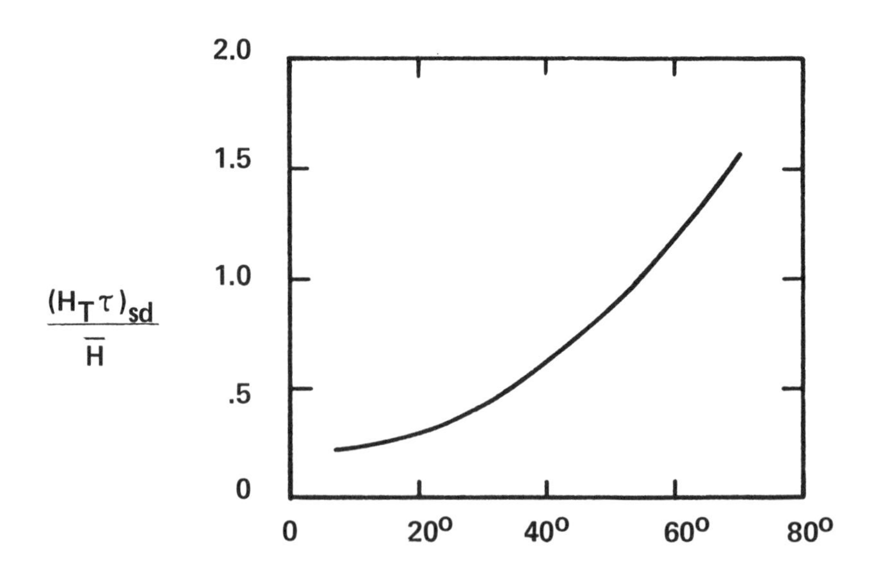


**Figure 55.** $(H_T\tau)_{sd}/\bar{H}$ vs L – D.

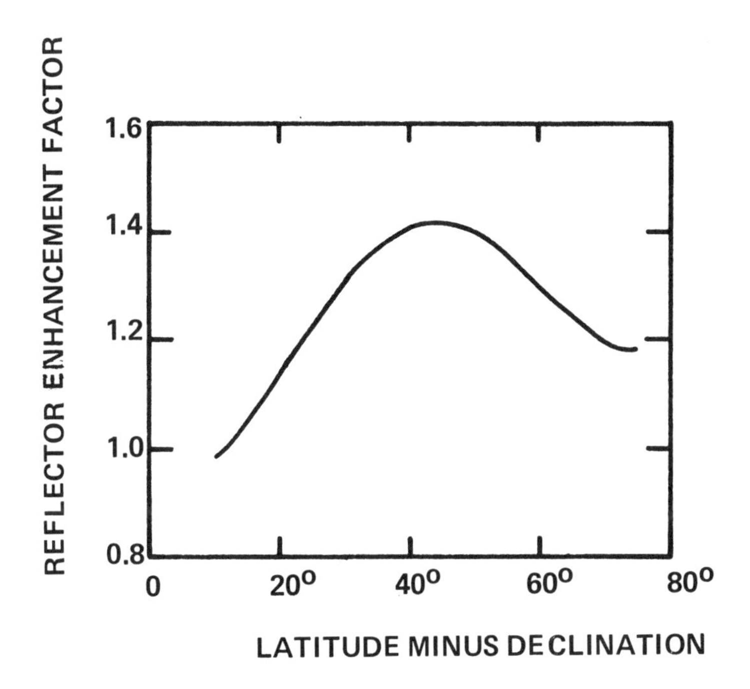


**Figure 56.** Reflector enhancement factor.

the base so it could be let down during the day and pulled up next to the wall at night, as illustrated in Figure 3. The curve of Figure 56 may be represented by:

$$\frac{(\bar{H}_T\tau)_{sd} \text{ with reflector}}{(\bar{H}_T\tau)_{sd} \text{ without reflector}} = 1.0083 - 0.01787(L - D) + 0.001916(L - D)^2 - 4.031 \times 10^{-5}(L - D)^3 + 2.466 \times 10^{-7}(L - D)^4 \quad (99)$$

For reflectances $\rho$ other than 0.8, this ratio is proportional to $\rho/0.8$.

In using the monthly LCR method, one first calculates the building loss coefficient $\overset{*}{U}$ and then determines the monthly $SLR_m$ from Equation 95. $\bar{H}$ is found from the tables, and then $(\bar{H}_T\tau)_{sd}/\bar{H}$ is determined from Equation 98. The monthly solar heating fraction $SHF_m$ is found from the monthly solar load ratio $SLR_m$, using Figure 57. The auxiliary energy used per month is then $(1 - SHF_m)(dd)_m\overset{*}{U}$. The annual auxiliary energy required is the sum of the monthly values, and the annual solar heating fraction is:

$$SHF = 1 - \frac{\text{annual auxiliary energy used}}{(\text{annual degree days}) \cdot \overset{*}{U}} \quad (100)$$

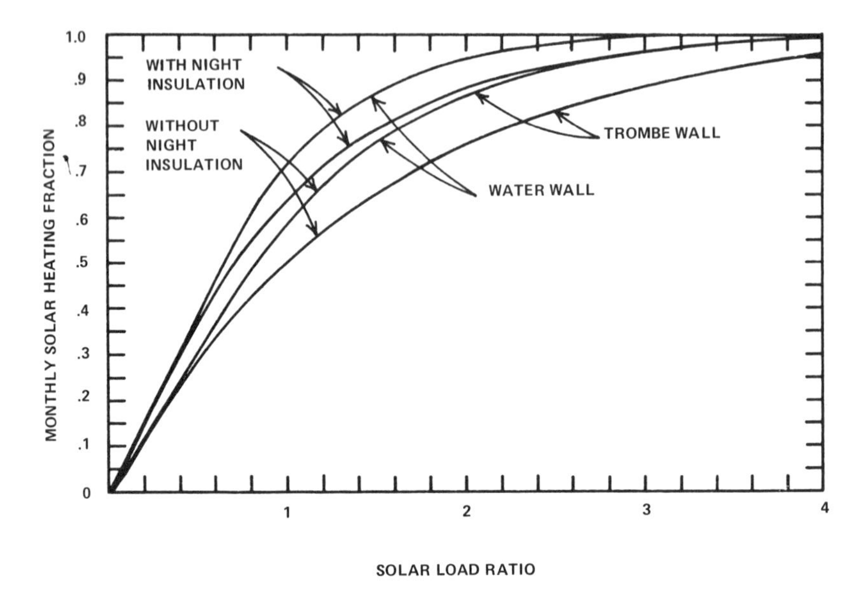


**Figure 57.** Monthly solar heating fraction vs monthly solar load ratios.

The curves of Figure 57 are plots of

$$(SHF)_m = A(SLR)_m \qquad \text{for SLR} \leq W \qquad (101)$$

$$(SHF)_m = B - C\exp[-D(SLR)_m] \qquad \text{for SLR} \geq W$$

when values of A, B, C, D and W are given in Table XI.

The SHF and monthly SHF evaluation procedures use correlations based on a large number of computer runs for several generic types of systems under a variety of climatic conditions. These techniques are believed to be accurate within a few percent when properly applied to the appropriate types of systems. Often, however, the designer will be faced with a system for which the above correlations are inappropriate, and for which parameters other than solar heating fractions are needed. In this case, a numerical model of the specific system may be necessary.

## *Numerical Method*

Trombe et al. [1976] developed a simple numerical model for their Trombe wall-heated houses at Odeillo, France (Figures 2, 53 and 54). Letting $\dot{m}$ be the mass flowrate of air through the Trombe wall, the heat transferred into the building is:

$$Q_t = \dot{m}C_p(T_{out} - T_{in}) \tag{102}$$

In addition, as illustrated in Figure 58, the heat transfer by convection from the inner surface of the wall is:

$$Q_c = h(T_t - T_b) \tag{103}$$

where $T_t$ = temperature of inner wall surface
$T_b$ = air temperature in the building $\simeq 20°C$
$h$ = convection coefficient $\simeq 5.108(T_t - T_b)^{1/3}$ kJ/m²-hr-°C

The radiant heating of one surface by another is:

$$Q_r = \frac{F_{mn}\sigma(T_m^4 - T_n^4)}{\dfrac{1}{\epsilon_m} + \dfrac{1}{\epsilon_n} - 1} \tag{104}$$

where $F_{mn}$ = the view factor between surfaces m and n
$\sigma$ = Stefan-Boltzmann constant = $20.4 \times 10^{-8}$ kj/m²-hr-°K⁴
$T_m$ = temperature of surface m
$T_n$ = temperature of surface n
$\epsilon_m$ = emittance of surface m
$\epsilon_n$ = emittance of surface n

Trombe showed that if $T_t$ is the temperature of the inner surface of the Trombe wall, and $T_w$ is the average temperature of the other surfaces of the room, then

$$Q = \frac{\epsilon}{2 - \epsilon}\sigma(T_t^4 - T_w^4) \tag{105}$$

Thus, knowing the room temperature, wall temperatures, and air flowrate, the total rate of heating of the building by the wall is calculated as the sum of $Q_t$, $Q_c$ and $Q_r$.

## *Akbari Method for Calculating Free Convective Flowrate*

A method of calculating the convective flowrate of air through a Trombe wall was developed by Akbari and Borgers [1978a,b], based on previous studies of laminar convection flow between parallel plates [Aihara 1963,1973; Aung and Aung 1972; Bodoia and Osterle 1962; Elenbass 1942; Engel and Mueller 1967; Kobayashi 1954; Miyatake and Fujii 1972; Siegel and Norris 1957]. Akbari and Borgers solved the equations of continuity, momentum and energy to obtain a relationship for the average volumetric flowrate ($m^3$/sec-m) up the wall to be:

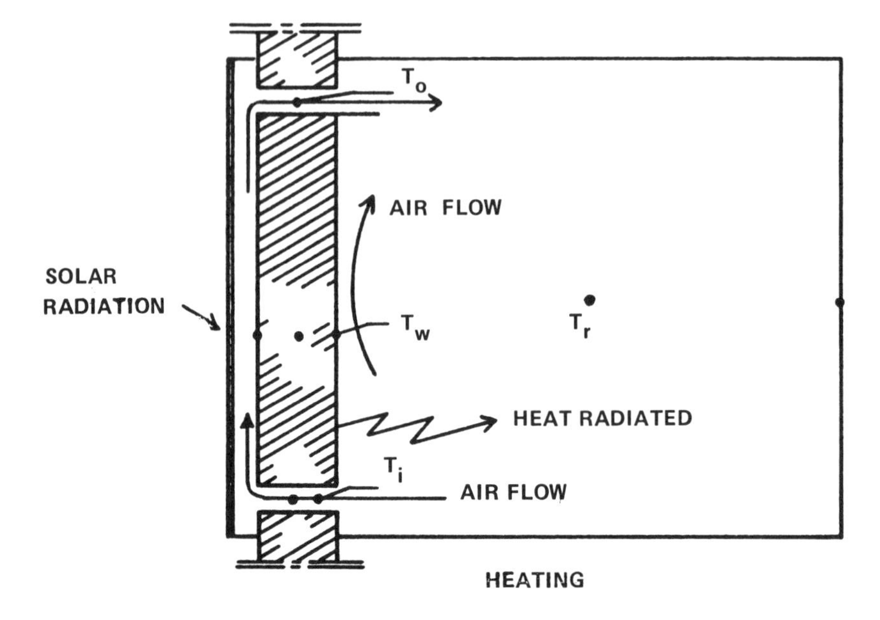


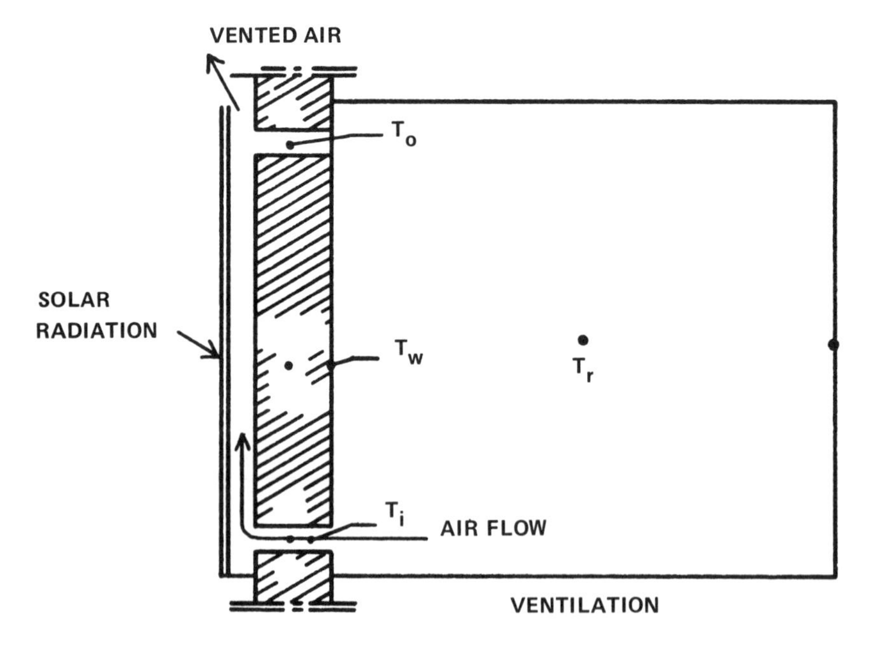


**Figure 58.** Trombe wall heat transfer [Trombe et al. 1976].

$$q = \nu \mathrm{Gr} 10^{[C_1 + C_2 \log L + C_3 (\log L)^2]} \tag{106}$$

where
$C_1 = 0.0851\{1 - \exp[-3.412(\theta_g - 0.4217)]\}^2 - 0.920$
$C_2 = 0.1331 + 0.6563 \exp(-8.521 \cdot \theta_g)$
$C_3 = -0.0619 + 0.07125 \exp(-6.762 \cdot \theta_g)$
$\nu$ = kinematic viscosity ($m^2/sec$)
$G\gamma = g\beta(T_m - T_o)b^3/\nu^2$ = Grashof number
b = distance between inner glazing and outer surface of Trombe wall (m)
$g$ = acceleration of gravity = 9.801 $m/sec^2$
$\beta$ = coefficient of volumetric thermal expansion ($m^3/°K$)
$T_m$ = temperature of the warmer surface (wall or glass)
$T_o$ = inlet temperature
$\theta_g = (T_g - T_o)/(T_m - T_o)$
$T_g$ = glass temperature
$L = \ell/(\mathrm{Gr} \cdot b)$ = dimensionless channel height
$\ell$ = height of channel (m)

The volume flowrate is $\bar{u}$ times the cross-sectional area of the channel between the wall and inner glazing, and the mass flowrate is the volume flowrate times the density of air.

The heat absorbed by the air passing through the channel $\dot{H}_L$ is [Akbari and Borgers 1978a,b]:

$$\dot{H}_L = L \cdot \overline{Nu_t}/\mathrm{Pr} \tag{107}$$

where
$\overline{Nu_t} = a + b \cdot \theta_g$ = average Nusselt number
$a = -8.605 - 9.372 \log Q - 2.972(\log Q)^2 - 0.5229(\log Q)^3$
$b = 1.547 + 0.5623 \log Q + 1.213(\log Q)^2$
$\mathrm{Pr} = \nu\rho C_p/k$ = Prandtl number $\simeq 0.72$
$\rho$ = density of air
$C_p$ = heat capacity of air
k = thermal conductivity of air

$$Q = \nu \mathrm{Gr}/q \tag{108}$$

The mixed mean air temperature exiting the channel is:

$$\overline{\theta_f} = \dot{H}_L/Q \tag{109}$$

where
$\theta_f = (T_f - T_o)/(T_m - T_o)$
$T_f$ = air temperature

To predict the performance of a Trombe wall under given climatological conditions, first calculate the wall and inside glazing surface temperatures assuming a stagnant air gap. Then calculate the flowrate, heat collected and average exit temperature using Equations 106 to 109. The effect of this convective heat removal is then included in the energy balance equation to recalculate the wall and inner-glass temperatures, and new values of flowrate, heat collected and exit temperature are determined. Simulation programs incorporating these equations would calculate pertinent parameters at regular time intervals using a weather data file.

### *Pratt Method for Calculating Free Convective Flowrate*

The Akbari model for free convective flow between parallel plates does not account for the important effect of the vents at the top and bottom of the Trombe wall. This problem has been examined by Pratt and Karaki [1979] who solved the simultaneous momentum, energy and continuity equations (as did Akbari), but with external frictional effects modeled as head losses of the form $0.5k\bar{u}^2$ where:

$$K = (\{B(0.872 - 0.015t/d - 0.08d/t)(1 - B^{3.3})B^{4.3}[1 + 0.134(t/d)^{1/2}]^{-1}\}^{-1} - 1)^2 \quad (110)$$

for fully reattached flows in the range $0.8 \geq t/d$. For $t/d < 0.8$ the flow in the orifice is fully separated, and the correlation is

$$K = \left[\frac{1}{0.608B(1 - B^{2.6})(1 + (t/d)^{3.5}) + B^{3.6}} - 1\right]^2 \quad (111)$$

where B = area of vent/area of duct
t = thickness of Trombe wall
d = hydraulic radius of the vent

There are two limiting cases of air flow in a Trombe wall duct [Pratt and Karaki 1979] as illustrated by Figure 59: case A, where the average wall temperature is much greater than room temperature, so that flow is upward everywhere in the duct; and case B, where the wall is hotter than room temperature, but the inner glazing is colder. These two cases are represented in Figure 60. In the latter case, a convection loop exists within the wall duct transferring heat from the wall to the inner glass, with no net heat transfer to the building.

Figure 61 shows type A dimensionless velocity and temperature profiles calculated for an 8-ft-high Trombe wall with a 6-in. wide duct with $B = 0.75$, $d/t = 1.25$, $T_t = 120°F$, $T_g = 75°F$ and $T_b = 70°F$. Here, y is the distance from the wall and b is the gap width. The total vent loss is twice the duct inlet velocity head. The temperatures and velocity profiles are

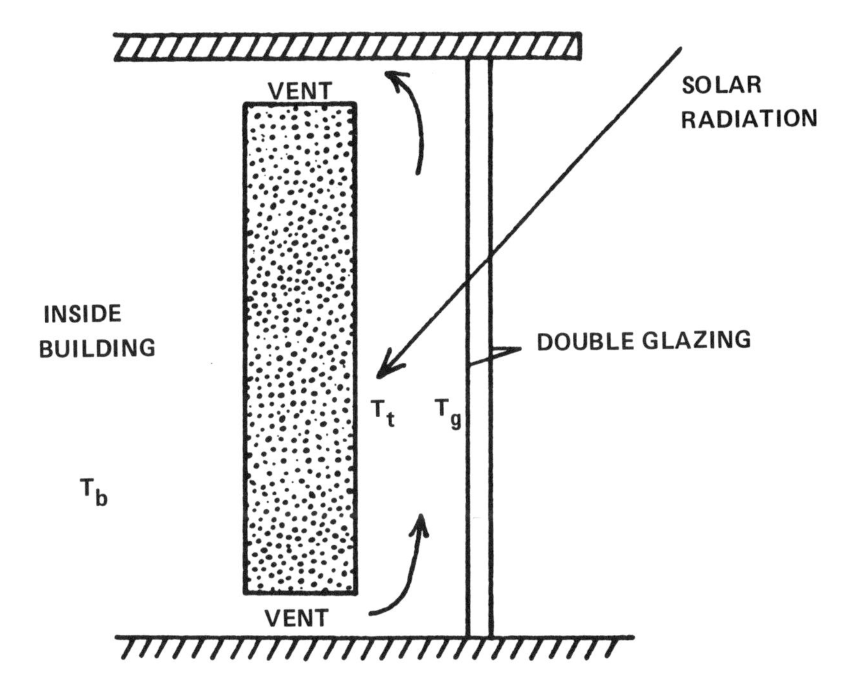


**Figure 59.** Trombe wall with vents.

given near the entrance (x = distance from the bottom of the duct divided by its height), halfway up and at the top of the duct. Figure 62 illustrates case B, where the Trombe wall surface temperature $T_t$ is 86°F, the inner glass temperature $T_g$ is 54°F, and the temperature inside the building $T_b$ remains 70°F.

This type of model was applied to a 130-$m^2$ Trombe wall which heats a 4500-$m^2$ industrial building in San Francisco [Bagshaw and Whitehouse 1978]. The concrete Trombe wall is 14 cm thick with vents on 2.7-m (9-ft) centers with a vertical separation of 2.7 m (9 ft). The problem was solved using a finite number of temperature nodes as illustrated by Figure 63. The nodes within the wall have thermal capacity and the other nodes do not. The node spacing was 4.6 cm in the horizontal direction through the wall and 30.5 cm in the vertical direction. Solving the energy balance equation results in an algebraic equation describing a node on the inside face of the wall:

$$TN_i = \frac{\dfrac{2T_{i,3}}{R_1} + \dfrac{T_{\infty,i}}{R_c}}{(2/R_1 + 1/R_c)} \tag{112}$$

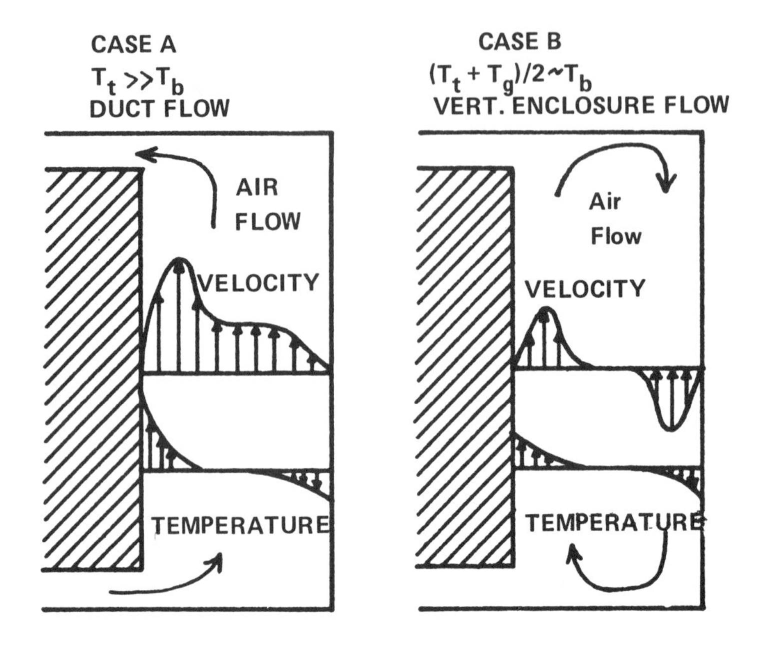


**Figure 60.** Two types of Trombe wall flow.

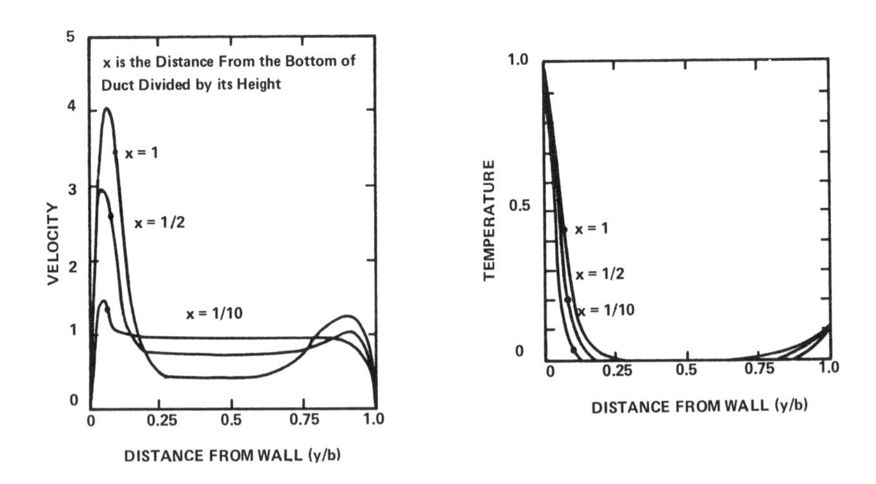


**Figure 61.** Velocity and temperature profiles for $T_t = 120°F$, $T_g = 75°F$, $T_b = 70°F$.

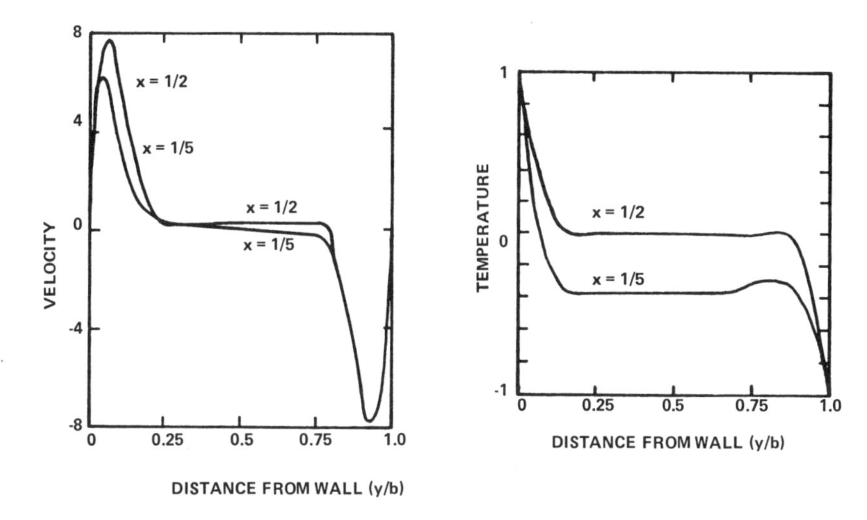


**Figure 62.** Velocity and temperature profiles for $T_t = 86°F$, $T_g = 54°F$, $T_b = 70°F$.

where $T_{i,3}$ = the adjacent wall node
$T_{\infty,i}$ = the inside air temperature

The equation for a typical node on the outer wall surface is:

$$TW_i = \frac{Q_S + \dfrac{2T_{i,1}}{R_1} + h_c \cdot TA_i + h_r \cdot TG_i}{\left(\dfrac{2}{R_1} + h_c + h_r\right)} \tag{113}$$

where $Q_s$ = insolation absorbed by the wall surface
$TG_i$ = temperature of the inside surface of the glazing
$h$ = convective coefficient of the adjacent boundary layer formed by the moving air in the flow passage
$TA_i$ = bulk temperature of the adjacent air
$T_{i,1}$ = temperature of the adjacent region on the concrete wall
$h_r$ = linearized coefficient describing infrared radiation transfer between the wall surface and the interior glass surface given by
$\epsilon_g, \epsilon_w$ = emissivities of the glass and wall surfaces, respectively
$\sigma$ = Stefan-Boltzmann constant

$$h_r = \left[\frac{\sigma(TW^4 - TG^4)}{1/\epsilon_g + 1/\epsilon_w - 1}\right] \Bigg/ (TW - TG) \tag{114}$$

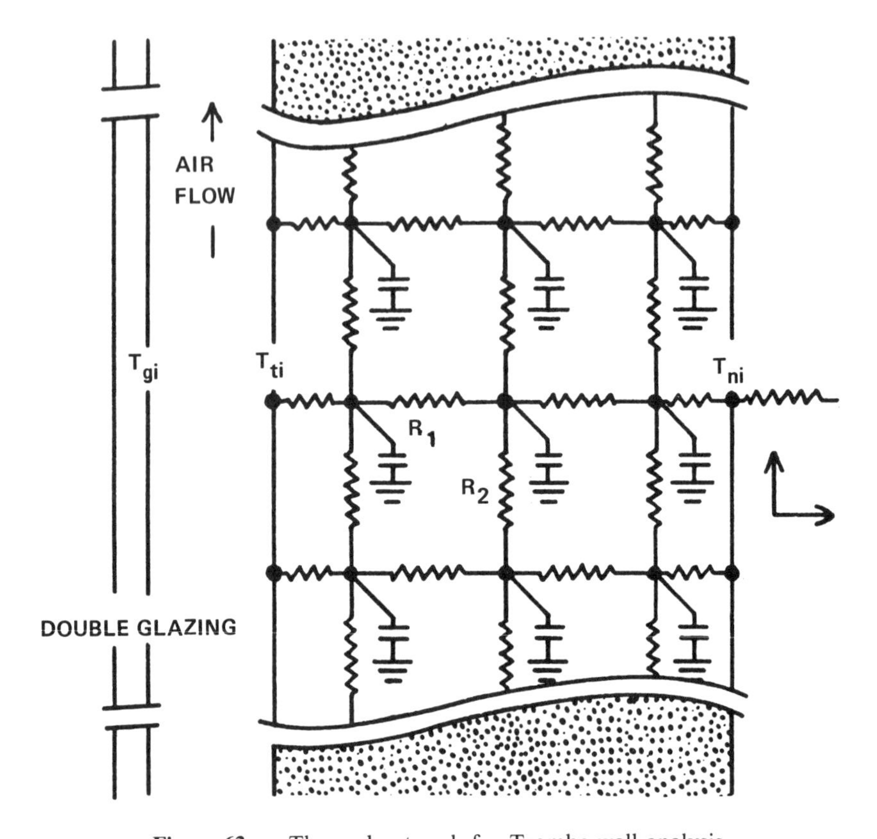


**Figure 63.** Thermal network for Trombe wall analysis.

Denoting the entering and exiting air temperature as TI and TO, the average nodal air temperature TA is:

$$TA_i \equiv (TI_i + TO_i)/2 \tag{115}$$

The energy balance equation is:

$$\dot{m}C_p(TO_i - TI_i) + h_c(TA_i - TG_i) - h_c(TW_i - TA_i) = 0 \tag{116}$$

where $\dot{m}$ = mass flowrate of air

Combining Equations 115 and 116 results in the outlet temperature:

$$TO_i = \frac{TW_i + TG_i + TO_{i-1}(C - 1)}{1 + C} \tag{117}$$

where

$$C = \dot{m}C_p/h_c \tag{118}$$

Also, the inner glass temperature is

$$TG_i = (h_c \cdot TA_i + h_r \cdot TW_i + T_{\infty,o}/R_3) \Bigg/ \left(h_c + h_r + \frac{1}{R_3}\right) \tag{119}$$

where $R_3$ = total heat transfer resistance from the inner glass surface to the outside air
$T_{\infty,o}$ = outside temperature
$h_c, h_r$ = radiative and convection heat transfer coefficients

The calculation for January used a convection heat transfer coefficient of 28.4 W/m²-°C (5 Btu/ft²-hr-°F) and time steps of 0.1 hr. Figure 64 shows the amount of heat transferred to air flowing through the wall and into the building, the heat lost through the glazing, and the heat conducted through the wall and subsequently transmitted inside by convection from the inner wall surface and by radiation into the heated space. The heat transferred to the air circulating by natural convection through

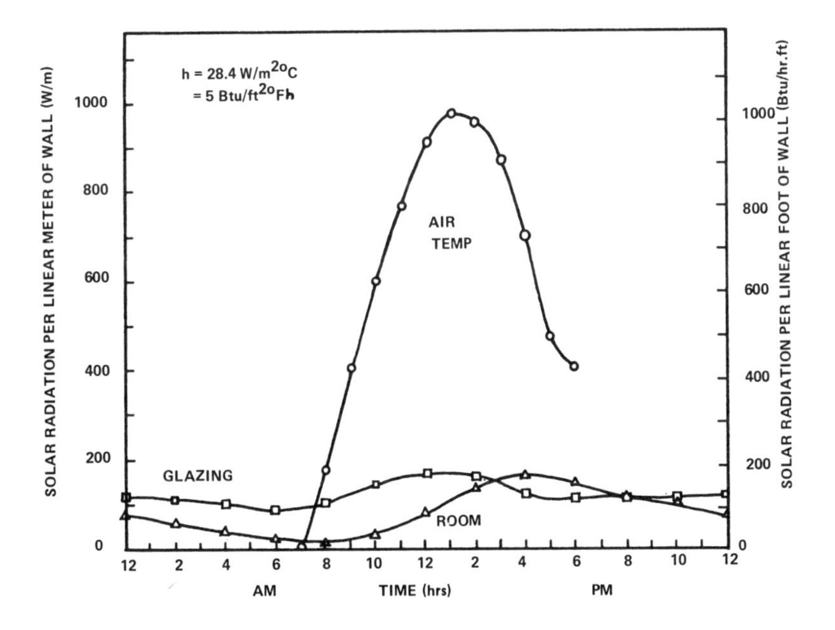


**Figure 64.** Results of Trombe wall analysis.

the gap between the wall and inner glazing follows the solar radiation curve and peaks at 1 p.m. at about 1000 W/linear meter (not per $m^2$) of wall. The heat conducted through the wall and then added to the room peaks several hours later.

### *Calculating Heat Transfer Characteristics of the Trombe Wall*

Three-dimensional heat transfer characteristics of both conventional and composite thermal storage walls were examined by Connolly et al. [1980] using a 152-node thermal network of the type shown in Figure 63, but extending in three dimensions. Three-minute time steps were used to compare the performance of uniformly and nonuniformly (shadowed) irradiated storage walls. It was concluded that the simpler two-dimensional models were adequate for uniformly irradiated storage walls, but not if the solar radiation falling on the aperture is nonuniform. The use of $\epsilon = 0.2$ selective surface on the Trombe wall was found to increase its performance by 13%, which is consistent with the findings of Ortega et al. [1980].

## Further Calculations of the Free Convective Flowrate

Casperson and Hocevar [1979a,b] instrumented a Trombe wall constructed of 11-9/16-in.-thick solid concrete blocks with a double-glazed fiber-reinforced plastic Kalwall® cover. The effect of the air gap was investigated by varying the gap between 1 and 8 in. The Trombe wall was 8 ft high × 10 ft wide. Temperature measurements were made at numerous locations in the wall, glazing and the building envelope. The velocity profile across the gap between the wall and inner glazing also was measured as a function of height, and the solar radiation intensity on the wall was recorded along with the other data. The wall outside surface temperature was found to be highly nonuniform because of partial shading during parts of the day and the convection flow processes. The temperature and velocity profiles observed were found to be consistent with the predictions of Akbari and Borgers [1978a,b] (Figures 61 and 62). The efficiency of the Trombe wall for 2-, 4- and 6-in. gaps was found to be:

$$\eta = 0.663 - 1.370 \frac{T_i - T_a}{H_T} \qquad \text{(2-in. gap)} \tag{120}$$

$$\eta = 0.594 - 1.038 \frac{T_i - T_a}{H_T} \qquad \text{(4-in. gap)} \tag{121}$$

$$\eta = 0.638 - 1.574 \frac{T_i - T_a}{H_T} \qquad \text{(6-in. gap)} \qquad (122)$$

where $\eta$ = efficiency = (energy collected)/(energy incident)
$T_i$ = inlet temperature
$T_a$ = outside ambient temperature
$H_T$ = instantaneous solar radiation intensity on the aperture

It was concluded that laminar flow is the usual situation in Trombe walls, not turbulent flow as previous analytical studies had anticipated, except that high up the wall, turbulence is frequently encountered. The optimum time to cover the outside of the wall with insulation was found to be between one and two hours before the solar intensity on the wall fell to zero.

## Trombe Walls vs Direct-Gain Systems

Several studies [Noll and Thayer 1979; Noll et al. 1979; Wray and Balcomb 1979] have compared Trombe walls with direct-gain systems. Noll concluded that with night insulation the direct-gain system tends to be more cost-effective than Trombe wall systems. Without night insulation, the direct-gain system has the edge in most cases. In most of the United States, night insulation is cost-effective for Trombe walls, whereas for direct-gain systems, night insulation is cost-effective in the North but not the South. Wray concluded that Trombe walls offer a higher solar heating fraction if the total thermal storage mass is about $\leq$175 lb/ft$^2$ of aperture. If more storage mass is used, and the mass is distributed and direct-coupled, the direct-gain system performance tends to be better than that of a Trombe wall of equal aperture. This occurs because a Trombe wall reaches its peak performance at a thickness of 12–16 in. of 150-lb/ft$^3$ high-density concrete, while the performance of a direct-gain system continues to increase as the surface area of the thermal storage mass is increased.

A small fan to increase air flow through a Trombe wall can significantly increase its performance [Sebald et al. 1979] and permits a 6-in.-thick wall with a fan to outperform a 12- to 16-in. wall.

Telkes [1978] has proposed the use of Glauber salt (sodium sulfate decahydrate) for Trombe walls, since such a heat-of-fusion salt hydrate wall only 2.5 cm (1 in.) thick can store as much heat as a 50-cm (20-in.)-thick concrete wall. A 1-in. salt-hydrate–impregnated wall weighing about 58.6 kg/m$^2$ (12 lb/ft$^2$) of aperture can store 3.78 kWh/m$^2$ (1200 Btu/ft$^2$), which is typically the amount of solar radiation transmitted through the wall on a clear day. Glauber salt undergoes its phase change at 32°C (89°F).

## OTHER THERMAL STORAGE WALLS

Thermal storage walls have been developed in a variety of configurations other than the conventional Trombe wall. The most popular storage wall medium, other than concrete, is water stored in drums, tanks or cylinders. Thermal storage walls incorporating water as the primary heat storage medium are commonly referred to as water walls. Other heat storage media that have been used include mixtures of metal and concrete and phase-change materials.

### Baer Water Drum House

One of the first solar houses incorporating a water wall for heating was the drum wall house constructed by Baer [1973]. He chose water as the storage medium because of the higher heat transfer rates associated with convection within the drums and the higher heat capacity of water relative to concrete [Anderson 1976]. His home used about one hundred 55-gal drums filled with water and painted black, stacked adjacent to the south-facing aperture. His system is illustrated in Figures 3 and 65. The insulating shutter lies flat on the ground during the day, and its reflective upper surface reflects additional solar radiation onto the black surface of the drums. The insulating shutters are raised at night to cover the wall and reduce heat loss. On clear December days, this drum wall provides about 1430 Btu/ft$^2$ of solar aperture to the heated space. With the outside insulation in place, the drum wall can also moderate temperature fluctuations within the heated space due to heating from other sources such as a wood stove. In some climates the drum wall can provide effective cooling in the summer if the insulating shutter is lowered at night and closed during the day. In addition, windows may be opened at night to allow cool air to enter and chill the drums. The chilled water in the drums helps to maintain comfortable indoor temperatures during hot days. South-facing drum walls of this type are effective at latitudes greater than about 30°.

### Gunderson Water Wall and Shaded Roof House

The Gunderson house in Santa Fe, New Mexico [Figure 66], uses a combination of water wall and shaded roof aperture to heat the 2200-ft$^2$

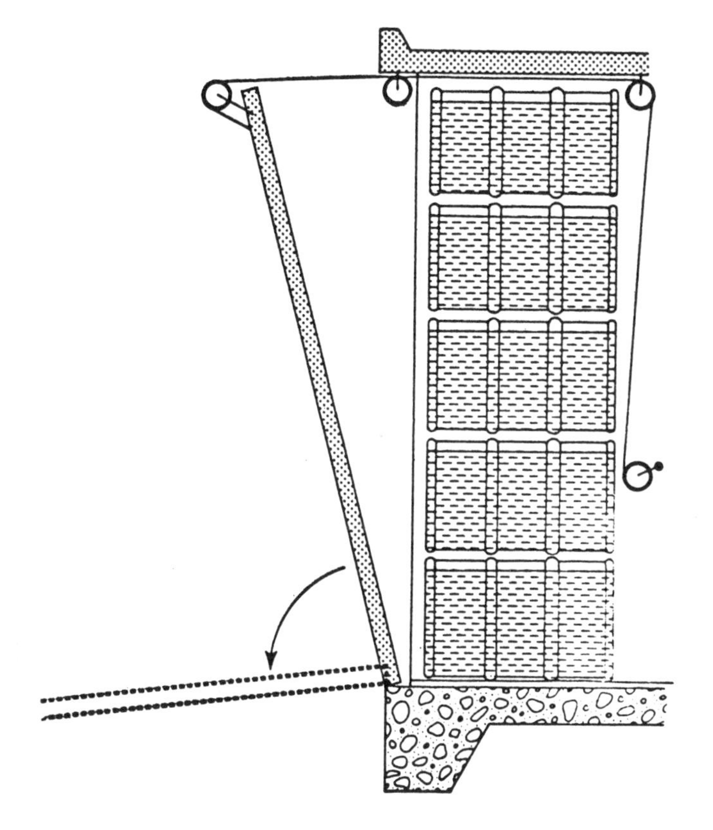

**Figure 65.** Drum wall of Baer house [Anderson 1976].

home [Sandia 1979]. The house is passively heated by the double-glazed shaded roof aperture and the south-facing double-glazed water wall. Both the shaded roof aperture and water wall incorporate movable insulation. Thermal storage is provided by the water wall, the masonry interior wall, the masonry north wall and tile on concrete floors. Auxiliary heating is by electric baseboard heaters. Movable shutters permit thermal control of solar and heat gains from the water wall systems. Vents at the top of the south wall also permit ventilation to reject excess heat. Figure 67 illustrates the floor plan of the house with the water wall providing heating for the two bedrooms on the south side. The kitchen, master bedroom and bath on the north side of the house are heated by direct-gain through large clerestory windows.

The water walls are constructed of precast concrete sections with a 6-in.-thick cavity lined with a plastic bag filled with water. The exterior south surface is painted black and double-glazed. Insulating shutters hinged at the bottom are lowered during the day to concentrate sunlight

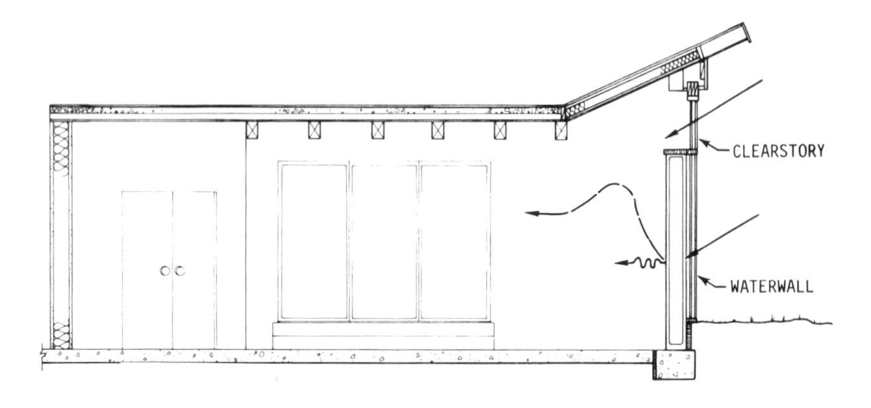


**Figure 66.** Water wall of Gunderson house [Sandia 1979].

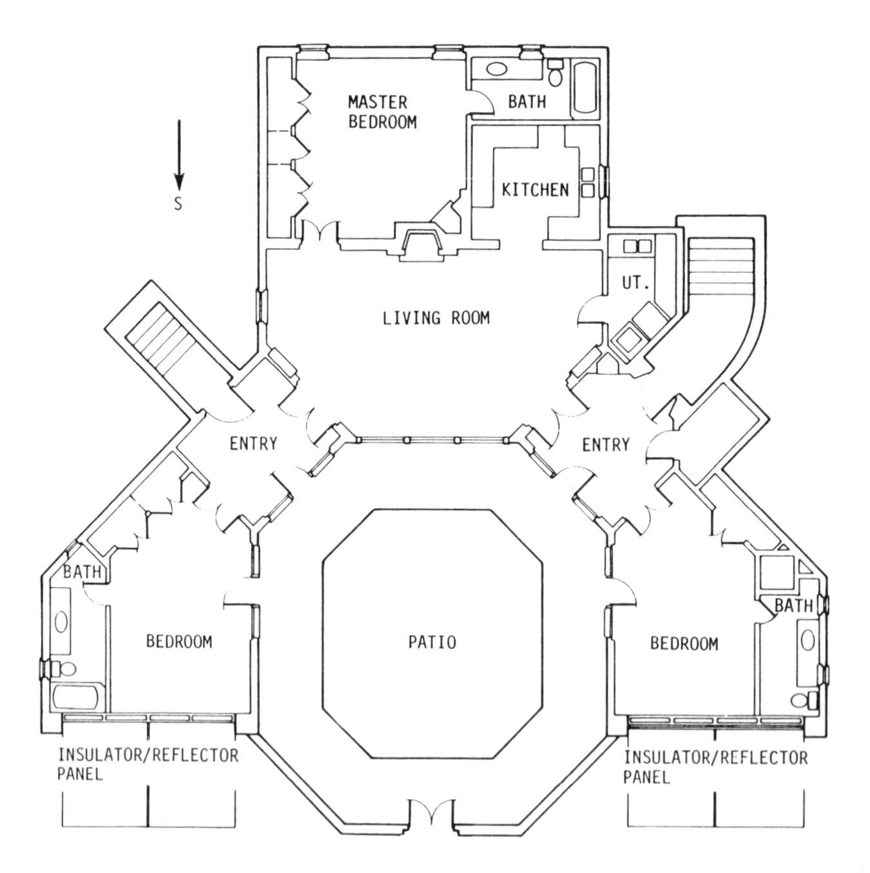


**Figure 67.** Floor plan of Gunderson house with water wall [Sandia 1979].

onto the water wall by reflection from its polished aluminum surface. A cable and crank system, as illustrated by Figure 3, is used to raise the insulating shutters. The northern 12-in. concrete block wall is filled with concrete. In addition, an 8-in.-thick concrete block wall with filled voids is incorporated into some of the inner walls to provide some of the additional thermal storage mass. Exterior concrete walls are insulated on the outside with 2 in. of styrofoam. These concrete walls and the 4-in.-thick concrete slab floor provide additional thermal storage mass.

Underground perimeter heat loss is reduced by an 18-in.-wide strip of 2-in.-thick styrofoam. The combination of south-facing water walls and direct-gain aperture with a large amount of direct-coupled distributed storage mass results in a high solar-heating fraction and moderate interior temperature fluctuations. The insulating shutters on the water wall can be operated in the winter for heating and in the summer for cooling, as described previously.

Figure 68 illustrates recorded data from this home during a two-week period in the winter from 1978–1979. During this period, several sunny days were followed by a period of cloudy weather. Ambient temperatures were usually below freezing, ranging from a high of 40°F during the day to as low as 5°F at night. The temperature of the inner surface of the water wall is close to the average temperature of water within the wall, typically ranging from a peak of about 90°F during the day and dropping to about 70°F at night. Interior temperatures range from about 55 to 75°F. During this period of cold weather, the home was heated entirely from solar energy. Day/night temperatures fluctuated only by about 10°F during the summer; peak temperatures inside remained below 75°F, even though outside temperatures may have exceeded 100°F. The minimum temperature experienced in the house during a full year of occupancy was 55°F. The building loss coefficient for the house was calculated to be 24,887 Btu/dd, or 11.31 Btu/ft$^2$-dd. The annual solar heating fraction is 72%.

## Star Tannery Water Wall House

A home in Star Tannery, Virginia, uses a 400-ft$^2$ vertical south-facing water wall to heat 1250 ft$^2$. This home also combines direct-gain through a shaded roof aperture and direct-coupled storage mass in the north wall with the water wall heating system. Thermal storage is provided by 4000 gal of water in the wall, a solid masonry north wall, and the concrete floor. A cross section of this home is shown in Figure 69, and the floor plan in Figure 70. The water wall is triple-glazed with upper glazing of

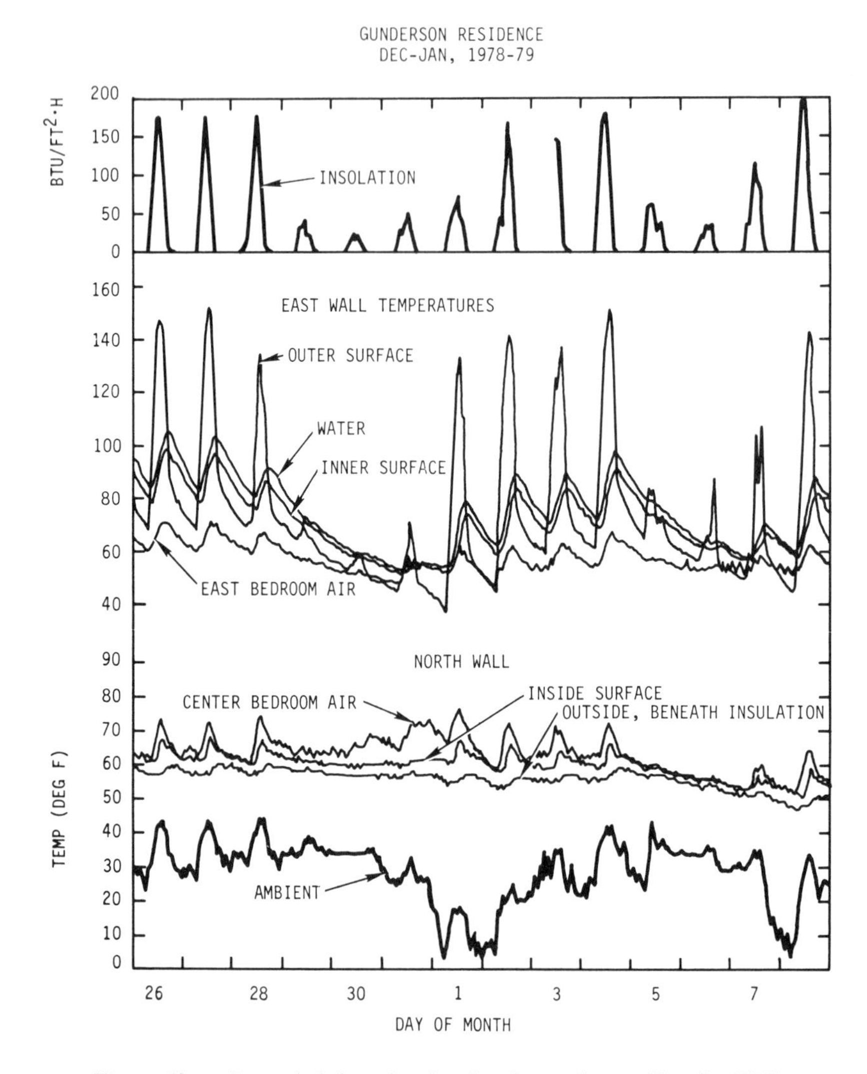


**Figure 68.** Recorded data for the Gunderson house [Sandia 1979].

1/8-in.-thick low-iron glass and two layers of extruded polycarbonate plastic sheeting. The exterior surface of the water wall is of corrugated aluminum against which are stacked vinyl plastic bags of water. A standard $2 \times 4$ stud partition is located inside the water wall so that the bags of water are not visible from the interior. The 147-ft$^2$ direct-gain aperture is double-glazed with extruded polycarbonate plastic sheeting.

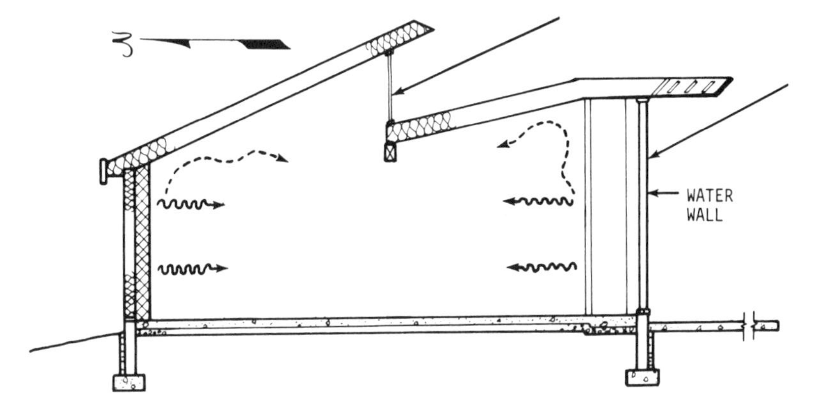


**Figure 69.** Heat flow in Star Tannery house [Sandia 1979].

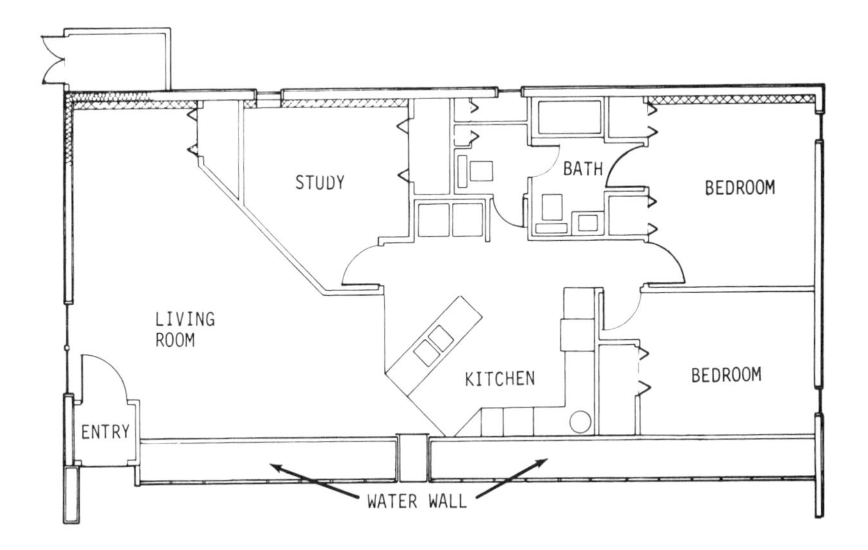


**Figure 70.** Floor plan of Star Tannery house [Sandia 1979].

Heat is transferred to the interior space through vents at the top and bottom of the interior partition, as well as by radiation.

Because the plastic bags leaked, they were replaced with rigid containers. Also, the two layers of plastic glazing proved unsatisfactory and were replaced with Teflon® film. The building loss coefficient was estimated at 9200 Btu/dd and the solar heating fraction at about 80%.

## Dove Publications Drum Wall Warehouse

The Dove Publications warehouse and office building in Pecos, New Mexico, uses a 413-ft$^2$ south-facing drum wall in conjunction with 908 ft$^2$ of direct-gain aperture to heat the 7700-ft$^2$ building. Figure 71 illustrates the location of the drum wall on the south side of the offices and the direct-gain aperture for the office and warehouse. Temperatures within the warehouse do not have to be maintained as high as those in the offices. Auxiliary heating in the offices is by electric radiant panels. There is no back-up heating in the warehouse area. Baer, who first developed the drum wall for his home, was involved in the design of this building.

The solar apertures are double glazed and thermal storage is provided by the 138 drums (55 gal) of water in the drum wall, the concrete slab floor, the interior sand-filled concrete block wall between the offices and the warehouse, and the contents of the warehouse. Vents in the interior concrete block wall can be opened to permit heat transfer by natural convection from the office space into the warehouse.

Figure 72 illustrates typical temperature profiles within the office and warehouse. During a few days in February 1977, outside ambient temperatures ranged from 50 to 10°F. Without any auxiliary heat, the temperature inside the offices ranged from 62°F at night to 78°F during the day, while warehouse temperatures ranged from about 50 to 70°F. The lowest temperature inside the warehouse during the winter was 48°F. It is significant to note that the lowest temperatures in the offices (55°F) occur only during nonworking hours. During the winter of 1977, while data were taken, no back-up heating was used.

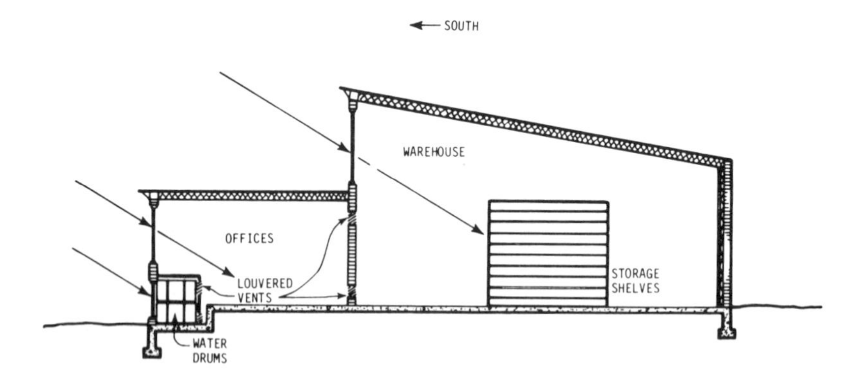


**Figure 71.** Cross section of Dove Publications warehouse.

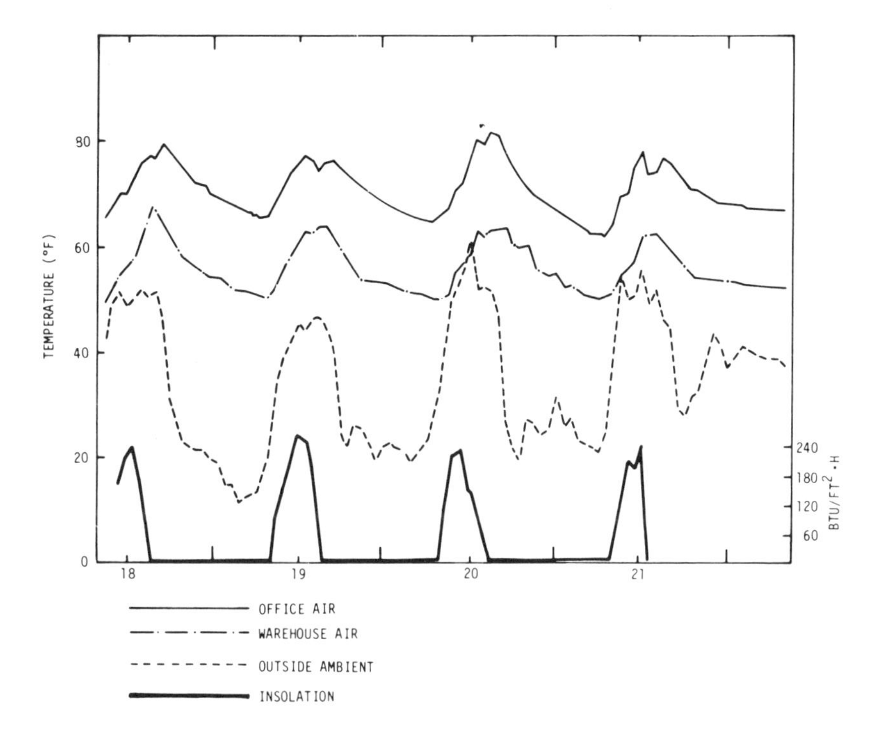


**Figure 72.** Data for the Dove Publications warehouse.

Figure 73 is a floor plan for this building showing the offices, a small apartment on the west side and the warehouse space. The building is basically rectangular, 100-ft long × 150-ft wide, with the long axis east and west. The loss coefficient for the office area only is 24,652 Btu/dd. The solar heating fraction for the office area has been estimated at about 80%, whereas the solar heating fraction for the warehouse is essentially 100%.

## Other Water Walls

Several solar homes with different types of water walls have been built in Davis, California [Bainbridge 1979]. These houses have achieved solar heating fractions of 80–90% as well as substantial cooling during the summer. Three types of containers were used for water storage: rectangular tanks, drums and culverts.

The steel rectangular tank provides an attractive storage unit that can be located just inside the south-facing windows. The uninsulated rec-

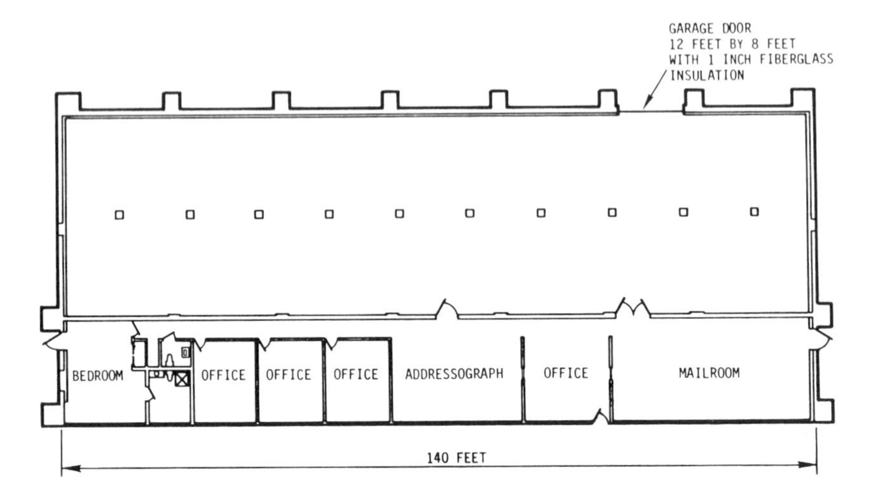


**Figure 73.** Floor plan of the Dove Publications warehouse [Sandia 1979].

tangular tank serves as a room divider as well as direct-couple storage mass. Fiberglass modular tanks have also been used. Evaporative cooling using a spray fountain may be integrated with a water wall in the summer. Drums are less expensive than tanks, but are less attractive, and therefore are generally more appropriate for farm, commercial, and industrial uses where cost rather than esthetics is the primary factor. For residential applications, the drums may be screened with a wood lattice. The water inside metal tanks or drums must be treated, preferably with an antifreeze solution containing a rust inhibitor. An air void should be included in the containers to accommodate thermal expansion and contraction of the water. Standard metal culverts standing vertically on end can be attractive and durable. Translucent fiberglass tubes also have been used.

A fiberglass water wall module has been developed [Maloney 1978,1979; Maloney and Habib 1979] consisting of nested units, which can be stacked to construct a thermal storage wall (Figure 74). A single horizontal rectilinear unit is 95 in. long, 24.5 in. tall and 14 in. wide. When installed in a building (Figure 75) this wall provides 52 lb of water storage per net $ft^2$ of south-facing aperture area. Since a single unit weighs only 33 lb empty, shipping and installation are simplified. Tight thermal plastic lids seal each unit to prevent evaporation. These one-design thermal storage modules (Figures 74 and 75) and other types of water storage containers are compared in Table XII [Bainbridge 1979].

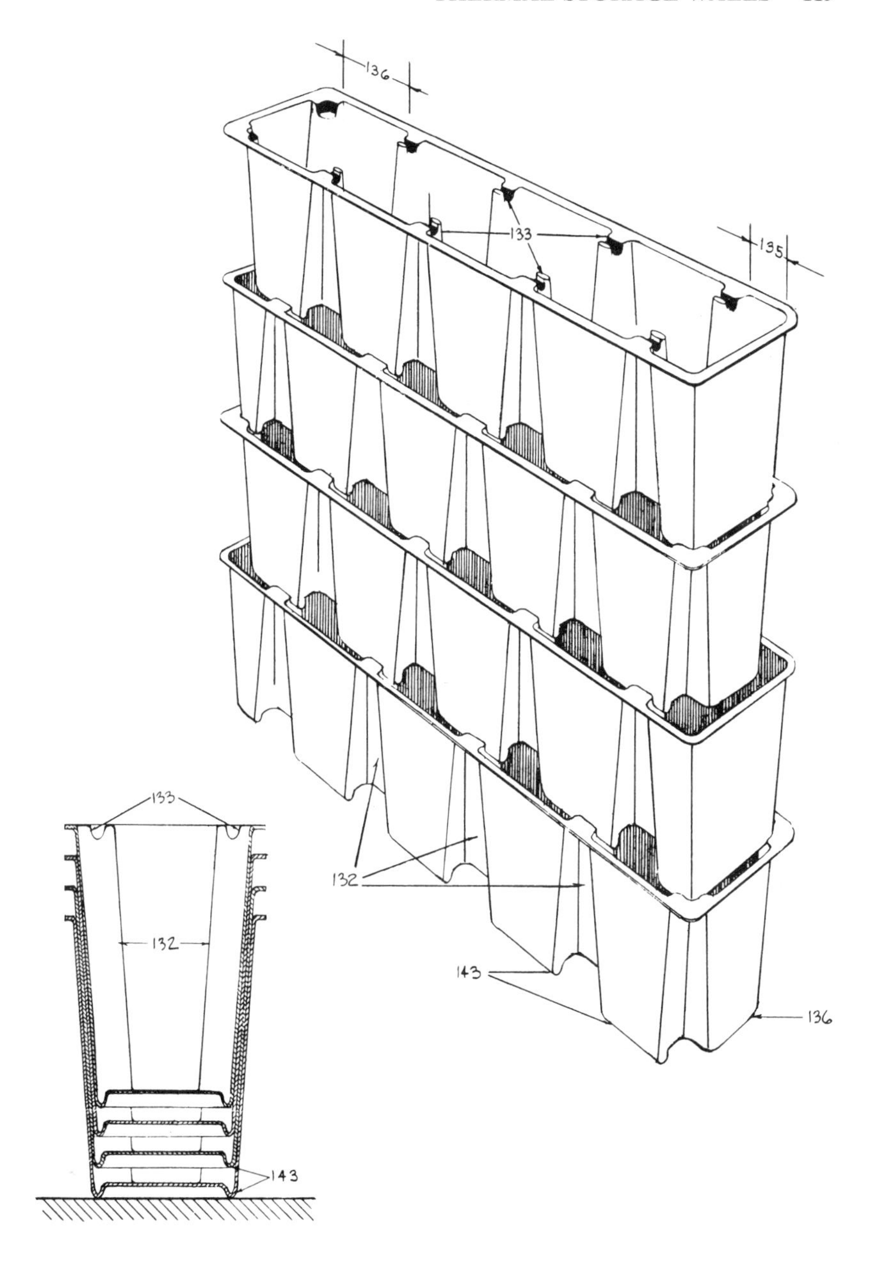


**Figure 74.** Nested fiberglass water-well units [Maloney 1979; Maloney and Habib 1979].

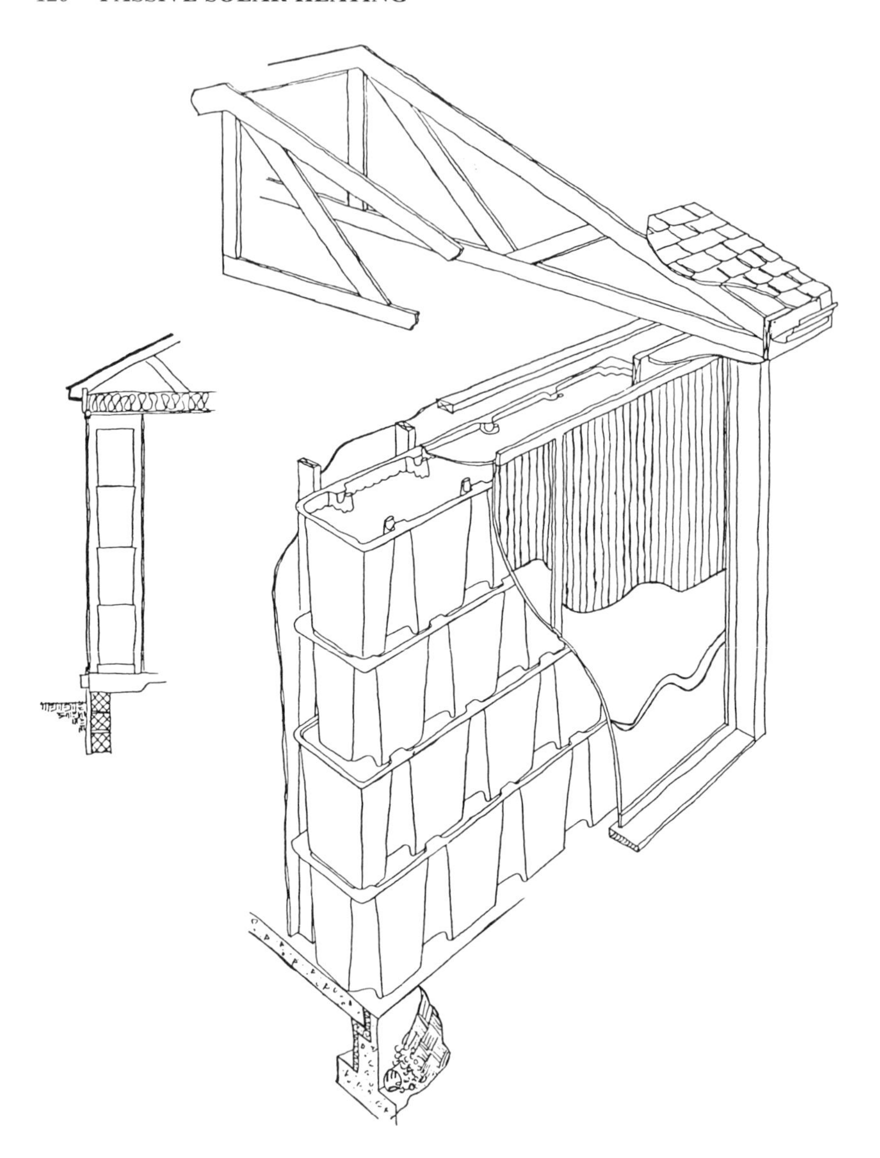

**Figure 75.** Nested fiberglass water wall installation.

## Phase-Change Materials

Although the most popular storage mass materials for thermal storage walls are concrete and encapsulated water, considerable interest has developed in phase-change materials because of their much greater ability to store and release heat when they undergo a change of phase

**Table XII. Comparison of Water Wall Containers (1979 $) [Bainbridge 1979]**

| Type | Size | Volume | Cost per gal ($) | Installed Cost ($) | Notes |
|---|---|---|---|---|---|
| Tank | Any 1.5 × 3 × 6 ft | Any | $0.30–1.50 | $0.50–1.50 | Esthetic, easy to install, effective |
| Drums | | 30 or 50 gal | $0.10–0.45 | $0.20–1.00 | Cheap, readily available, hard to clean, must be stacked carefully |
| Culverts | ≥12 in. diam | Depends on length | $0.40–0.50 | $0.50–1.70 | Tough, attractive to some, helps where floor space is tight; make sure installation is seismically safe |
| KalWall Cylinders | 12 & 18 in. | Depends on length | $0.40–1.45 | $0.50–1.70 | Translucent, easy to install and move, easy to damage; best where traffic is light |
| PVC Pipe | 6 & 12 in. | Varies | $0.10–0.20 | $0.30–1.20 | Light, durable, heat transfer not as good, must rack or brace to mount |
| Glass Bottles | Varies | Up to 10 gal | | | Cheap, readily available, must seal carefully, moving difficult |
| Metal Cans | Varies | To 5 gal[a] | $0–1.00 | | Good for furniture modules, slow to fill, would need bracing for tall stacks |
| Steel or Al Pipe | 6–12 in. | Varies | $0.10–0.50 | $0.30–1.50 | Readily available, time-consuming to build racks, hard to clean |
| Plastic Bottles & Drums | 1–5 gal | 1–5 gal | $0.10–0.50 | $0.15–1.00 | Cheap, may provide pleasant light, no rust; slow to fill and install; weak |

**Table XII, continued**

| Type | Size | Volume | Cost per gal ($) | Installed Cost ($) | Notes |
|---|---|---|---|---|---|
| One Design | Module[b] | | $1.00 | $1.50 | Easy to install and ship; good potential for cooling |
| Tabline Tanks | 36 in. × 4 ft × 16 in. | 90 gal | ≥$1.00 | $1.50 | Easy retrofit, good interface with stud construction |

[a] Price ranges to $0.60/gal for 5-gal can.
[b] See Figure 74.

between liquid and solid. The two most common phase-change materials presently considered are hydrated salts and hydrocarbons. Hydrated salts are inexpensive and store more heat than hydrocarbon materials such as paraffin, but may suffer long-term degradation due to irreversible phase-change processes. The hydrated salts are also corrosive and tend to degrade plastics. A disadvantage of hydrocarbons is their flammability. Table XIII lists several phase-change materials that could be incorporated into thermal storage walls [Collier and Grinmer 1979].

Because of the relatively low thermal conductivity of phase-change materials, encapsulation is necessary so that heat can be transferred into and out of the material. Since, for a given amount of heat storage, phase-change units are much lighter in weight and take up less space than water walls or Trombe walls, they may offer a considerable advantage in retrofit applications and for the incorporation of thermal storage walls into conventional structures which are not designed to carry the weight of massive thermal storage materials.

Paraffin wax has been used for moderating temperature fluctuations in spacecraft and in constant-temperature shipping containers [Askew 1978]. It has also been proposed for moderating temperature variations in buildings. Paraffin absorbs and releases 104.7 Btu/lb when it changes phase at a temperature of 83.7°F. Its density is 47.2 $lb/m^2$. A storage wall containing paraffin typically would have a thickness between 1 and 2 in. Askew [1978] estimated the overall thermal efficiency of such a wall to be about 35%. The efficiency could be increased with a selective coating.

Hauer et al. [1978] used 0.22-in.-thick plastic sheets filled with a mixture of stearic acid, paraffin and mineral oil to construct a solar storage

**Table XIII. Comparison of Phase-Change Materials (PCM) [Collier and Grimmer 1979]**

| PCM | Chemical Formula | Generic Type | Phase-Change Temp. (°C) | Thermal Conductivity (W/m-°C) | Latent Heat Capacity ($10^3$ $kJ/m^3$) |
|---|---|---|---|---|---|
| Octadecane | $C_{18}H_{38}$ | Paraffin | 28 | 0.15 | 188 |
| Eicosane | $C_{20}H_{42}$ | Paraffin | 37 | 0.15 | 192 |
| Eicosene | $C_{20}H_{40}$ | Olefin | 27 | | |
| Calcium Chloride Hexahydrate | $CaCl_2 \cdot 6H_2O$ | Hydrated salt | 30 | 1.1 | 285<br>323 |

wall. Dye was added to this mixture to absorb solar radiation. The paraffin content was about 80%. Without the dye, transmission is about 34% when solid and 81% when the wax is melted. While the wax is melted and optically transparent, the storage wall becomes a window.

A thermal storage wall incorporating sodium decahydrate (Figure 76) was developed at the University of Delaware [Faunce et al. 1978]. Sodium decahydrate changes phase at a temperature of 32°C (89°F). The test wall had an aperture area of 2 $m^2$ (21.6 $ft^2$) and a total storage capability of 6.6 kWh (22,500 Btu). Movable insulation was used to improve overall collection efficiency and reduce heat loss at night. The amount of sodium decahydrate was 55 kg/$m^2$ of aperture (10 lb/$ft^2$ of aperture), as compared to a water wall, which would require 220 kg/$m^2$ (45 lb/$ft^2$) and a concrete wall, which would require 11,000 kg/$m^2$ (225 lb/$ft^2$) to store

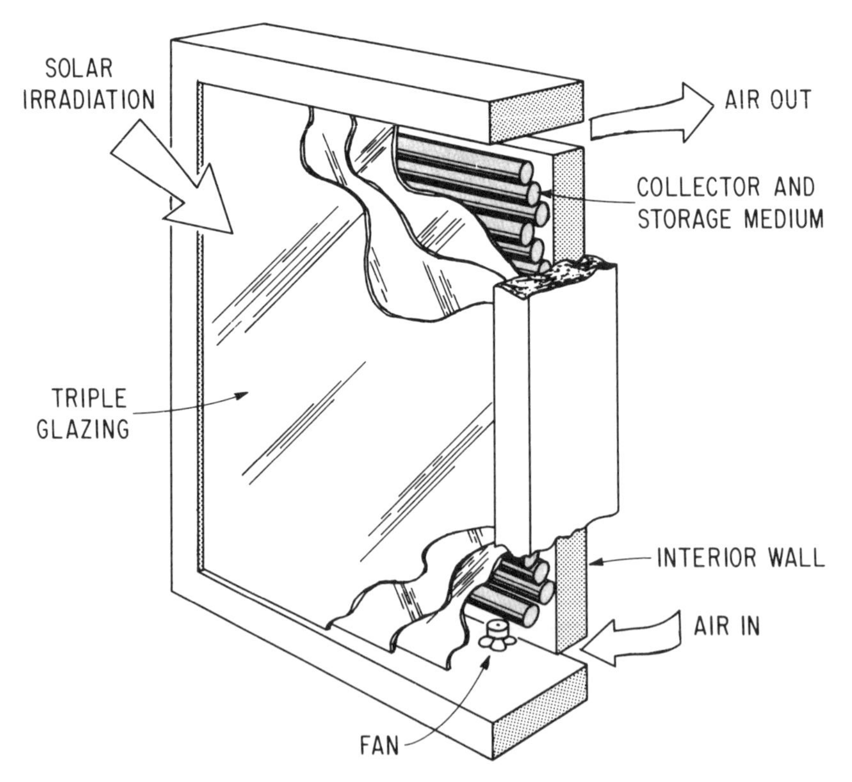


**Figure 76.** Thermal storage wall with sodium decahydrate phase-change material.

0.255 kWh/m$^2$-°C (45 Btu/ft$^2$-°F). The sodium decahydrate was contained in horizontal tubes behind the triple-glazed aperture. The movable insulation consisted of 2.5 cm (1 in.) of ridged urethane foam, which was inserted between the glazing and the phase-change tubes at night. The insulation R-factor was 3.5 during the day and 8.5 at night.

The sodium decahydrate was encapsulated in 57 polyethylene tubes 1.2 m long and 4 cm in diameter (48 in. long × 1.5 in. in diameter). Each tube contained 1.8 kg (4 lb) of sodium sulfate decahydrate providing a latent heat storage capability of 3.2 kWh/m$^2$ (1000 Btu/ft$^2$). It was shown that a panel of this type can provide 20–50% more heating than a conventional Trombe wall.

# CHAPTER 4

# THERMAL STORAGE ROOFS

## ATASCADERO, CALIFORNIA, ROOF POND HOUSE

The concept of using the thermal storage roof in modern residential construction was pioneered by Hay [1973a,b,c], who constructed a test building, and later a house that demonstrated the effectiveness of the thermal storage roof in maintaining comfortable indoor temperatures throughout the year. A three-bedroom, two-bath house with a roof pond was completed in 1973 in Atascadero, California. This house used black plastic bags of water on the roof for thermal storage. During the winter, the black bags of water were exposed to solar radiation during the day and then covered with insulation at night (Figure 4). Heat radiated into the interior space from the ceiling heated the home. During the summer, the process was reversed; the black bags of water were exposed to the night sky and then covered with insulation during the day, as illustrated in Figure 4. This system maintained interior temperatures of 62–79°F without any backup heating or cooling, even though outside temperatures ranged from 26 to 100°F [Hay 1975a,b].

The experimental house in Atascadero had an overall heat-transfer coefficient of about 9500 Btu/dd, excluding the roof. The collector area was about 1100 $ft^2$, essentially the same as the floor space. The average water depth of the roof pond was about 8.5 in., corresponding to about 6000 gal of water. Niles [1975] found the daily collector efficiency to be 60% for a horizontal solar radiation intensity of 1100 Btu/$ft^2$. About 20% of the incident solar radiation was actually delivered to the conditioned space. During the summer the cooling rate of the roof pond was typically 5 Btu/hr-$ft^2$-°F.

Figure 77 is a cross-sectional view of the roof pond and movable insulation system used on the Atascadero house, and Figure 78 illustrates

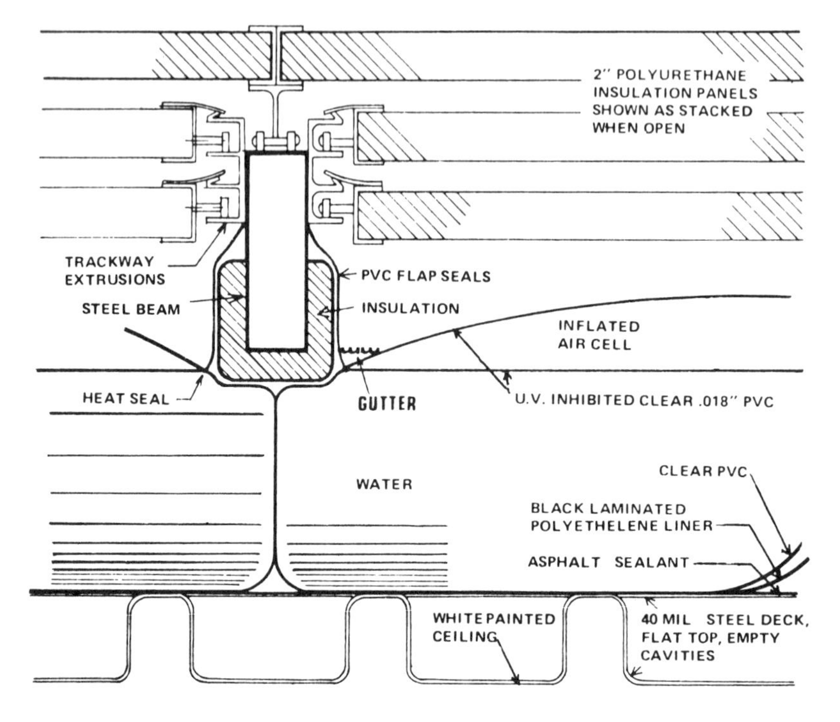


**Figure 77.** Details of thermal storage roof of Atascadero house [DOE 1980].

some performance data. The water is sealed in clear ultraviolet (UV)-inhibited 20-ml-thick polyvinyl chloride (PVC) water bags about 8 in. thick. An inflated air cell reduces heat loss. Underneath the 53,600 lb of water is a layer of black polyethylene plastic to absorb solar radiation transmitted through the water to the bottom of the bags. To reduce heat loss, the air cell is inflated during the winter; during the summer, to enhance radiant cooling, it is not inflated. The roof deck of 40-mil steel provides good support for the weight of the water and good heat transfer to and from the conditioned space. The movable insulating panels above the bags are mounted on horizontal steel tracks. These insulating panels are of 2-in.-thick rigid polyurethane faced on both sides with aluminum foil to reduce radiative heat transfer. The panels are moved into position in about 10 min by a 1-hp electric motor.

A thermal storage roof of this type is most effective at lower latitudes and in dry climates. Summer cooling can be enhanced by spraying additional water on the roof to cool by evaporation as well as by night sky radiation. Performance data for the Atascadero house reported by Niles [1975] are illustrated in Figure 78. It is seen that the indoor temperature

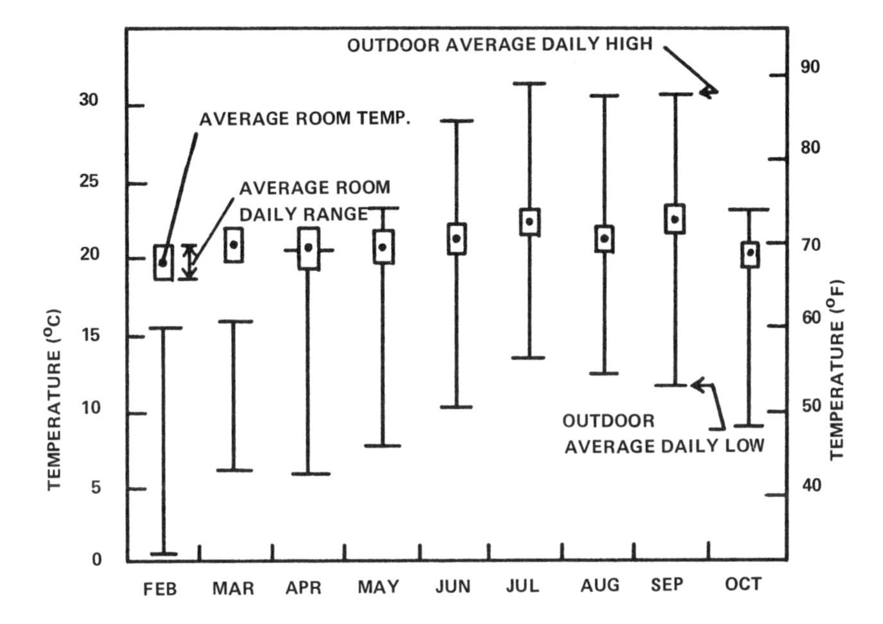


**Figure 78.** Monthly ranges of average daily indoor and outdoor temperatures of the Atascadero house [DOE 1980].

underwent only small variations, although outdoor temperatures varied from freezing to about 90°F. The occupants reported uniform comfortable indoor temperatures year around, even though there was no backup system.

The selection of the plastic liner for a roof pond is an important consideration. The upper part of the water bags and the inflated cover, if any, should be transparent to ensure that as much solar radiation as possible will penetrate the water to the lower surfaces of the bags. This will prevent stratification from degrading thermal performance as a result of increased heat loss from the hotter water at the top of the bag. The bottom portion of the bag should be black, to absorb the solar radiation transmitted through the water, rather than to reflect it. The plastic must also be resistant to UV degradation.

## SKYTHERM® SYSTEM

Although roof ponds were used during the 1930s as a means of passive cooling, they did not take advantage of insulating covers. The concept of black bags with movable insulation, as introduced by Hay, is known as the Skytherm system. The movable insulating panels not only improve cooling performance in the summer but also protect the plastic film from UV degradation during the summer, so that the transparent plastic bags are exposed to direct solar radiation only during the winter, when the UV component is substantially reduced [Hay 1978a,b]. Since the movement of the insulating panels can be manual as well as automatic, the system can be fully operational during a power outage. Except for when the insulating panels are moved, this space heating and cooling is completely noiseless.

## MODEL FOR PREDICTING THE PERFORMANCE OF THE ATASCADERO HOUSE

A steady periodic sinusoidal model for predicting steady-state temperatures and the magnitude of the temperature swing was developed by Niles [1975]. This model was applied to Hay's Atascadero house with good results. The temperature on both sides of the walls were assumed to vary sinusoidally, so:

$$T_1 = |T_1| \cos(\omega t + \phi_1) \tag{123}$$

$$T_2 = |T_2| \cos(\omega t + \phi_2) \tag{124}$$

where $T_1$ = inside wall temperature
$|T_1|$ = average inside wall temperature
$T_2$ = outside wall temperature
$|T_2|$ = average outside wall temperature
$\omega$ = 0.2618/hr
$\phi_1$ = phase angle for inside of wall
$\phi_2$ = phase angle for outside of wall

If the temperature variations are sinusoidal, then the heat flow must be also, so:

$$Q_1 = |Q_1| \cos(\omega t + \phi_1') \tag{125}$$

$$Q_2 = |Q_2| \cos(\omega t + \phi_2') \tag{126}$$

where $Q_1$ = heat flow at the inside surface
$|Q_1|$ = average heat flow at inside surface
$Q_2$ = heat flow at the outside surface
$|Q_2|$ = average heat flow at outside surface
$\phi_1'$ = phase angle for heat flow on inside surface
$\phi_2'$ = phase angle for heat flow on outside surface

The sinusoidal components of the inside temperatures and heat flow can be represented in terms of the outside sinusoidal components by:

$$\dot{T}_1 = \dot{T}_2 \cosh\sqrt{j\omega CR} + \dot{Q}_2\sqrt{R/j\omega C}\ \sinh\sqrt{j\omega CR} = |\dot{T}_1| \angle\phi_1 \quad (127)$$

$$\dot{Q}_1 = \dot{Q}_2 \cosh\sqrt{j\omega CR} + \dot{T}_2\sqrt{j\omega C/R}\ \sinh\sqrt{j\omega CR} = |\dot{Q}_1| \angle\phi_2 \quad (128)$$

where $C$ = heat capacity of the wall (J/m$^2$-°C)
$R$ = thermal resistance of the wall (m$^2$-°C/W)

If $\dot{Q}_2 = 0$, meaning that the exterior surface of the wall is perfectly insulated, then:

$$\dot{A}_1 = \frac{\dot{Q}_1}{\dot{T}_1} = \frac{\sqrt{j\omega C/R}\ \sinh\sqrt{j\omega CR}}{\cosh\sqrt{j\omega CR}} \quad (129)$$

where $\dot{A}_1$ = thermal admittance

If $\dot{Q}_2$ is not 0, then Equations 127 and 128 may be solved for $Q_1$ in terms of $T_1^{\cdot}$ and $T_2^{\cdot}$, so:

$$\dot{Q}_1 = (j\omega C/RA_1)(\dot{T}_1 - \dot{T}_2/\cosh\sqrt{j\omega CR}\ ) \quad (130)$$

If thermal resistances $R_1$ and $R_2$ are added to the inside and outside surfaces to represent surface and/or insulation resistance, then:

$$\dot{Q}_1 = \dot{C}_1\dot{T}_r + \dot{C}_2\dot{T}_0 \quad (131)$$

where $\dot{T}_r$ = sinusoidal component of room temperature change
$\dot{T}_0$ = sinusoidal component of outside temperature change

$$\dot{C}_1 = j\omega C/A_1^{\cdot}R\dot{C}_D \quad (132)$$

$$\dot{C}_2 = -j\omega C/[R\dot{C}_D(1 + R_2\dot{A}_1)\sqrt{j\omega C/R}\ \sinh\sqrt{j\omega CR}\ ] \quad (133)$$

$$\dot{C}_D = 1 + jC(R_1 + R_2/[(1 + R_2\dot{A}_1)\cosh^2\sqrt{j\omega CR}\ ])/R\dot{A}_1 \quad (134)$$

Applying this model to the Atascadero house and solving for the amplitude of the room temperature variation results in

$$T_r = \frac{\dot{Q}_s/(1 + \dot{A}_1R_1) + \dot{Q}_m + \dot{T}_0(1/R_3 - a_3\dot{C}_2) + \dot{T}_p/R_p}{\dfrac{1}{R_3} + \dfrac{1}{R_p} + \dfrac{a_1}{\dfrac{1}{A_1} + R_i} + \dfrac{a_2}{\dfrac{1}{A_2} + R_i} + a_3C_1} \quad (135)$$

where $\dot{Q}_s$ = solar gain through windows sinusoidal amplitude
$\dot{Q}_m$ = internal heat generation sinusoidal amplitude
$\dot{T}_0$ = outside air temperature sinusoidal amplitude
$\dot{T}_p$ = temperature of water on roof
$\dot{A}_1$ = admittance of direct-coupled surfaces
$a_1$ = area of sunlit surfaces
$\dot{A}_2$ = admittance of nonsunlit surfaces
$a_2$ = area of nonsunlit surfaces
$R_i$ = internal surface resistance of both sunlit and nonsunlit surfaces
$R_3$ = resistance to heat transfer by conduction through windows, infiltration, conduction through frame walls, and other low-heat capacity paths
$R_p$ = thermal resistance from water bags to room

Niles applied his model to the Atascadero house with $\dot{Q}_s = 1087 \angle 0$ W

$$a_1 = 5.57\,m^2 \text{ (the average sunlit window area)}$$

$$\dot{Q}_m = 0 \text{ (no fluctuations in internal heat generation)}$$

$$\dot{T}_o = 6.9 \angle -45^\circ \quad {}^\circ C$$

$$\dot{T}_p = 1.7 \angle -60^\circ \quad {}^\circ C$$

$$R_p = 0.00312\,{}^\circ C/W$$

$$R_i = 0.12\ m^2\,{}^\circ C/W$$

$$\dot{A}_1 = 5.3 \angle 70.62 \quad W/m^2\text{-}{}^\circ C$$

$$\dot{A}_2 = 5.2 \angle 70.62 \quad W/m^2\text{-}{}^\circ C$$

$$a_2 = 223\ m^2$$

$$R_3 = 0.0080 \quad {}^\circ C/W$$

$$\dot{C}_1 = 3.475 \angle 28.6 \quad W/m^2\text{-}{}^\circ C$$

$$\dot{C}_2 = 0.661 \angle 74.7 \quad W/m^2\text{-}{}^\circ C$$

$$a_3 = 37.2\ m^2$$

$$\dot{T}_r = \{1087/[1+(0.12)5.3\ \underline{\angle 70.6}] + 0 + 6.9\ \underline{\angle -45}\,[1/0.008 - (37.2)0.661\ \underline{\angle 74.7}]$$

$$+1.7\ \underline{\angle -60}/0.00312\}/\{1/0.008+1/0.00312$$

$$+(5.6+233)/(1/5.3\ \underline{\angle 70.6}+0.12)+(37.2)3.475\ \underline{\angle 28.6}\}$$

$$= 1.5\ \underline{\angle -76.1^\circ C}$$

This corresponds to a 3°C temperature fluctuation. The phase angle of −76.1° represents a room temperature peak at 5:06 p.m. The room temperature is therefore

$$T_r = 20.6 + 1.5\cos(\omega t - 76.1) \quad ^\circ C \tag{136}$$

where t = time in hours from solar noon

## VARIATIONS ON THE ROOF POND SYSTEM

The performance of a thermal storage roof heating system may be improved, at high latitudes, by including a south-facing water wall and/or vertical reflectors on the roof to concentrate more solar radiation onto the bags of water [Haggard 1976]. Another approach [Pittinger et al. 1978] involves moving the water instead of the insulation, in which case the insulation floats on the roof and the water is stored in an insulated tank. During the winter, stored water is warmed during the day by spraying it over the upper surface of the floating insulation and underneath a clear plastic film which prevents evaporation. This concept was tested at Arizona State University between 1976 and 1977, and it was shown that the temperature rise of the stored water during a clear winter day was about 8°F. When a second clear plastic film was placed over the absorbing insulation, supported by air from a small blower, the heat collected increased by 20%. This warmed water is circulated beneath the insulation at night to heat the interior space.

Operation of the system is reversed during the cooling season. In this case, water is sprayed across the roof at night so that heat is lost by radiation and evaporation. About 0.1 kg/hr (0.2 lb/hr) of water is consumed by evaporation on the hottest days.

### Performance Test of the Arizona State Building

The Arizona State test building was 24 ft long (east/west), 12 ft wide, and 9 ft high inside. The ceiling was of type N corrugated steel decking with a 1-in.-thick layer of urethane foam insulation fastened to the upper surface of this deck. A small pump is turned on by the room thermostat to transfer water from storage to the channels in the roof when heat is needed. The overall collector efficiency is typically 30%. This system was found to be capable of providing 100% of the heating and cooling requirements of the building from solar energy.

## Performance Test of the Skytherm System

The thermal performance, comfortable conditions and supplementary cooling requirements of roof pond houses of the Skytherm design were examined for 11 American cities utilizing computer modeling techniques [Clark and Allen 1979]. It was concluded that the Skytherm passive cooling technique could provide effective heating and cooling for residential applications in humid as well as dry climates; however, the latent cooling load cannot be satisfied by such a purely passive technique. According to Yellott [1976], evaporation does most of the cooling during the summer. During the spring and fall, when the dew point falls below 30°F, radiation and convection become more important, and evaporation may not be needed. Cooling capability of the Skytherm system, therefore, is, tied closely to the atmospheric dew-point temperature, and its heating capability depends primarily on the amount of horizontal solar radiation.

# CHAPTER 5

# CONVECTIVE LOOPS

A convective loop uses a solar air heating collector somewhat similar to conventional flat-plate solar air heaters, except that airflow is by natural rather than forced convection. In a typical loop, one or two layers of glass or plastic are placed over a black absorber. The air may flow above, beneath or through the absorber if the absorber contains air passages. Insulation on the back of the collector reduces heat loss. Since airflow is by natural convection, air passages must be large so as not unduly to restrict the flow of air.

## JONES HOUSE THERMOSIPHONING LOOP

An example of a convective loop with rock bed storage is the 2650-$ft^2$ Jones house in Santa Fe County, New Mexico. Figure 79 illustrates the operation of the thermosiphoning loop. The collector is single-glazed with a 45° slope and a total aperture area of 532 $ft^2$. Solar radiation striking the collector causes air between the collector surface and glazing to be warmed, and this warm air rises into the upper plenum over the rock bin. The rock bin contains 500 $ft^3$ (30 tons) of washed river rock of 2–4 in. diameter. The cross section of the rock bin is 4 ft high × 4 ft deep, and its length along the upper part of the collector is 32 ft. Hot air is supplied to the house from the collector and/or rock bin by a conventional forced-air distribution system. Auxiliary heating is provided by an electric furnace. The collector array on the south side of the house is below the upper floor level, as shown in Figure 80. The exterior walls of the house are a double layer wood frame with a 2- × 6-in. stud wall on the outside, an additional 2- × 4-in. stud wall on the inside and a 2-in. dead air space between the inner and outer walls. Fiberglass batt insulation is placed

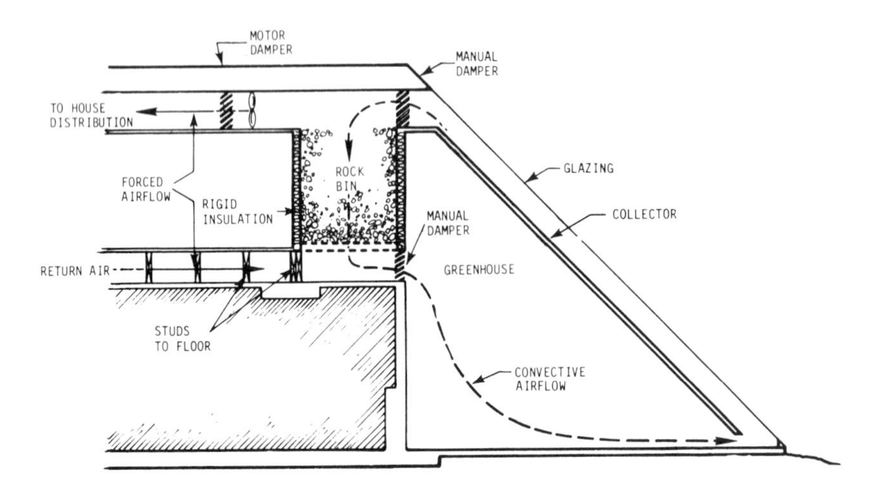


**Figure 79.** Thermosiphoning heating system for Jones house.

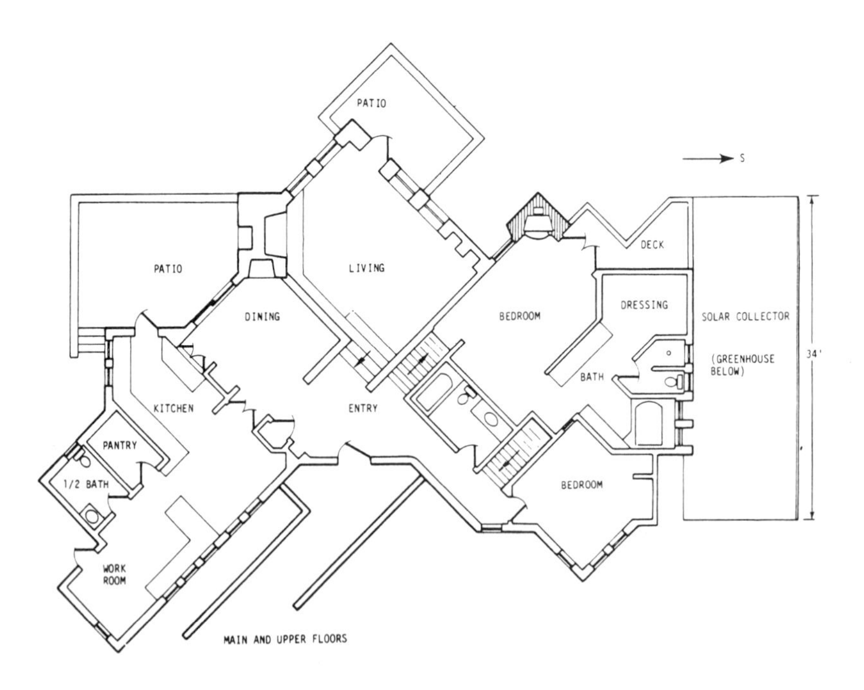


**Figure 80.** Floor plan of Jones house [Sandia 1979].

between the studs in both the outer and inner walls. The roof is insulated with 10 in. of fiberglass batts. Both the walls and roof have a rated R-value of 30.

The solar collector aperture measures 18.5 ft high × 34 ft long. It is single glazed with KalWall® fiberglass-reinforced plastic sheeting. Three layers of meshed wire beneath the Kalwall form the absorbing surface. The mesh wire is sprayed flat black, as is the pan beneath the wire. As long as the rocks in the rock bin are cooler than the air rising from the collector, the air will be cooled by the rocks, causing it to flow downward through the rock bin and back into the collector. When solar radiation is no longer available, the collector cools below the temperature of the rock bed, causing the thermosiphoning flow to reverse. Dampers in the upper and lower plenums block this reverse flow to prevent heat loss. Whenever the thermostat on the livingroom wall turns on the furnace fan, air is drawn in from the upper rock bed plenum to the furnace for distribution. If the air exiting the rock bed is not hot enough to heat the house, electric coils are turned on in the furnace to provide auxiliary heat.

## Performance Data for the Jones House

This solar heating system was instrumented with 28 thermocouples in the collector, rock bin and other locations to determine system performance. The highest temperature monitored in the solar collector while the collector was operating was 194°F during February. Figure 81 shows recorded data for two weeks during the winter. These data illustrate a period of cloudy weather followed by a period of sunny weather. It is seen that the temperature at the top of the rock bin fluctuates much more than at the bottom, reaching temperatures as high as 150°F. As is to be expected, the temperature in the rock bin increases with distance from the bottom. Air temperatures exiting the collector reached as high as 170°F, even though entering air temperatures dropped below 40°F. Temperatures in the house were continually maintained in the 65–70°F range during a major part of the heating season without auxiliary heat. The building loss coefficient for this house is 20,105 Btu/dd, or 7.5 Btu/ft$^2$-dd. The overall collector efficiency for the thermosiphoning system is 31%. The overall solar heating fraction is 84%, of which 74% is provided by the collector and rock bed system. According to Morris [1979] this system had been operating successfully with essentially no backup heat requirements since it was completed in February 1978.

In systems of this type, the rock should be as uniform in size as

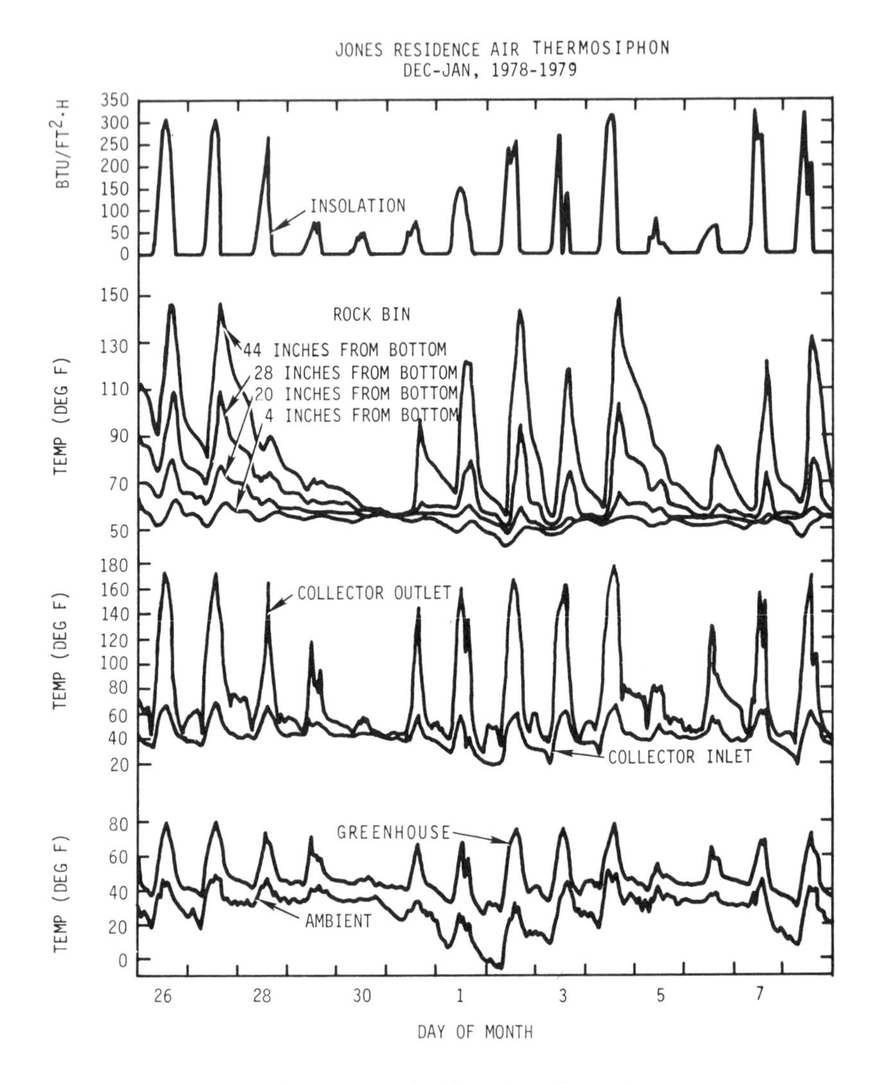


**Figure 81.** Recorded data from Jones house.

possible to permit adequate airflow in the spaces between the rocks. The warm air from the collector should always flow downward through the rocks, and the supply air to the house should flow upward to take advantage of stratification effects. The optimum rock size depends on the depth of the rock bed. Bed depth should be at least 40 rock diameters thick, which would require that the rock diameter for a 4-ft-deep bed should not exceed 2 in.

## OTHER EXAMPLES OF THERMOSIPHONING LOOPS

### Collector Placed Below the Rock Bed

A variety of solar heating systems use thermosiphoning loops of the types shown in Figure 6 through 8. A small pottery studio in La Cienega, New Mexico, uses a vertical, south-facing thermosiphoning collector located entirely below the rock bed storage. In this case, no dampers are needed for the collector to prevent reverse convection at night. The rock storage underlies the entire floor area. The single-glazed vertical collector is 5 ft 4 in. high × 26 ft wide. The absorber surface consists of four layers of black metal lath over a sheet metal pan. The rock bed beneath the floor is 16 ft wide × 2.5 ft deep, and contains 700 lb of rock per $ft^2$ of collector. Much of the heat transfer from storage into the building is by conduction through the floor, but heat is also transferred by convection through dampers. Overhangs and permanent shading devices are used to keep collectors of this type from providing unwanted heating during the summer months.

Morris [1979] recommends that, for systems of this type, the flow channel depth of the collector should be about 1/16 of the collector's length. If a diagonal mesh screen is used for the absorbing surface, the depth should be 1/20 of the length. The rock bed storage should have at least 200 lb rock/$ft^2$ of collector and should be located at as high an elevation as practicable, relative to the collector. Flow restrictions in the system must be avoided, and all vents and ducts must have at least the same cross-sectional flow area as the flow channels in the solar collector. Systems of this type should exhibit an overall collection efficiency of about 30% in cold climates.

### Simple U-Tube Collector

A simple U-tube collector, either vertically integrated, as shown in Figure 6, or attached to the bottom of a window, as shown in Figure 82, provides additional heat during the day. These collectors are simple thermosiphoning units that do not in themselves incorporate thermal storage. Thus, if collectors of this type are used to provide a substantial solar-heating fraction for a building, indirect-coupled storage mass may be needed within the heated space to moderate day/night temperature fluctuations. Such collectors are particularly useful in office buildings, warehouses and other structures that are used primarily during the day. In this case, simple U-tube thermosiphoning collectors on the east side

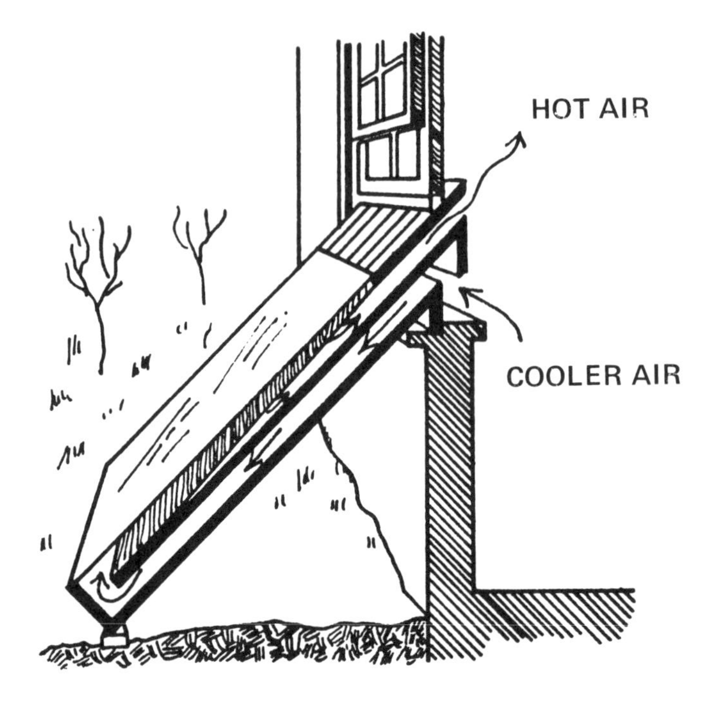


**Figure 82.** Window box convective loop air heater [Morris 1979].

(in the northern hemisphere) can help warm the building in the early morning, while south-facing collectors can provide more heat during the middle and later part of the day. Figure 83 illustrates a possible arrangement for using vertical U-tube thermosiphoning collectors, indirectly coupled with masonry or concrete floors that serve as thermal storage mass, for heating a multistory building [Morris 1978]. Figure 84 illustrates a similar approach for a single-story building using a tilted U-tube collector.

## Window Boxes and Thermosiphoning Walls

The simple window box (Figure 82) can be expected to last at least 10 years [Tukel 1979] if it is maintained properly and stored during the summer. The window box unit must be kept well sealed and the insulation maintained to retain an adequate collection efficiency. The seal between the window box and the house is also important. The vertical thermosiphoning wall, or panels in a wall, if properly designed and installed, should last the life of the building. For new construction,

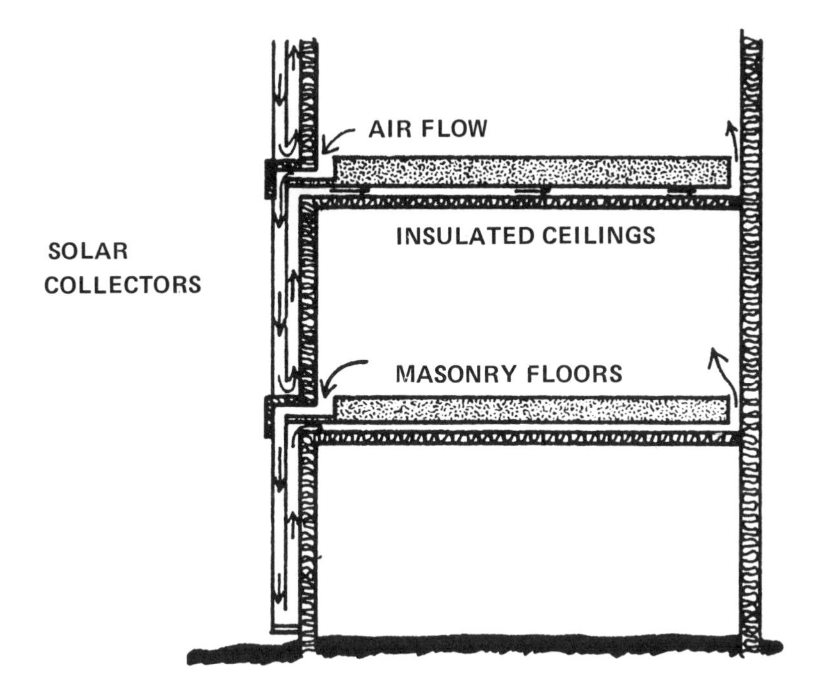


**Figure 83.** Multi-story convective loop heaters [Morris 1979].

integrated panels of this type (Figures 6, 83) are more cost-effective than the window box type, since they are incorporated into the wall of the structure (thereby reducing the incremental cost per square foot of area) and tend to be more efficient. The window box has the decided advantage of retrofitting easily to any south-facing unshaded window and does not require modification to the existing structure; nor does it require electrical wiring or electronic controls. Its disadvantage is that it tends to be less efficient than active collectors because of the lower flowrate of air and higher absorber plate operating temperature and the absence of direct-coupled thermal storage.

## Thermic Diode Collector

A novel approach to utilizing a thermosiphoning loop for solar heating was developed by Buckley [1974, 1975, 1976] at the Massachusetts Institute of Technology (MIT). The particular collector-storage configuration is called a "thermic diode." The principle of the thermic diode is

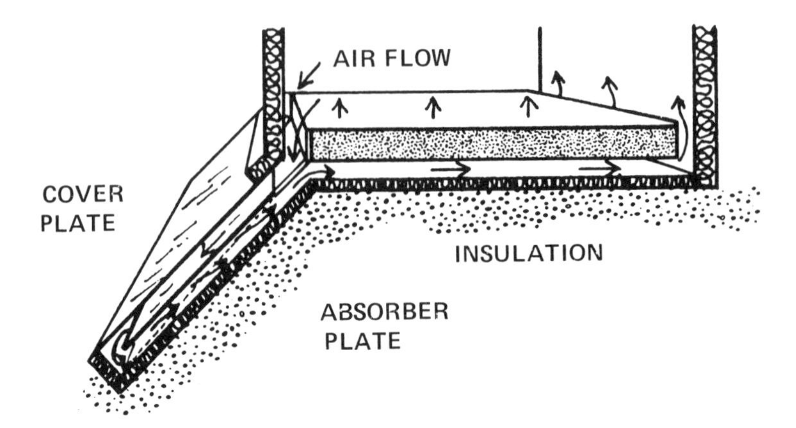


**Figure 84.** Tilted U-tube collector with indirect-coupled thermal storage mass [Morris 1979].

illustrated in Figure 85. Solar radiation during the day heats the collector absorber plate, and hot fluid from the absorber plate flows by natural convection into a storage unit inside the building. A check valve prevents reverse thermosiphoning at night. Since relatively small pipes connect the collector on the outside to the storage unit inside the heated space, the wall on which the collector is mounted can be well insulated. The panel is mounted so that the storage layer is located on the inner surface of the wall opposite the solar collector on the outside. Thus, the thermic diode panel can be installed as a single unit in a south-facing wall, which permits fairly efficient collection of solar heat whenever it is available, and, at the same time, the panel has a high insulating value. Since the processes are all passive, no control devices are needed. A full-flow, manually closed globe or gate valve in the pipe connecting the collector to the panel can terminate the flow of heat when it is not needed. Thus, a single 4-$\times$8-ft panel can contain all the elements of a complete solar energy system: collector, controls, storage, heat exchangers and ducting [Buckley 1978].

If a thermic diode panel forms an integral part of a roof or wall, it must have structural strength as well as a high insulating value. Prototype panels under development are designed to insulate and carry structural loads, and can be installed at any slope greater than about 30°. The collector and storage unit are filled with water with tubing connecting them at the top and bottom. Heat is transferred then by natural convection of the heated water. The check valve in the upper connecting tube

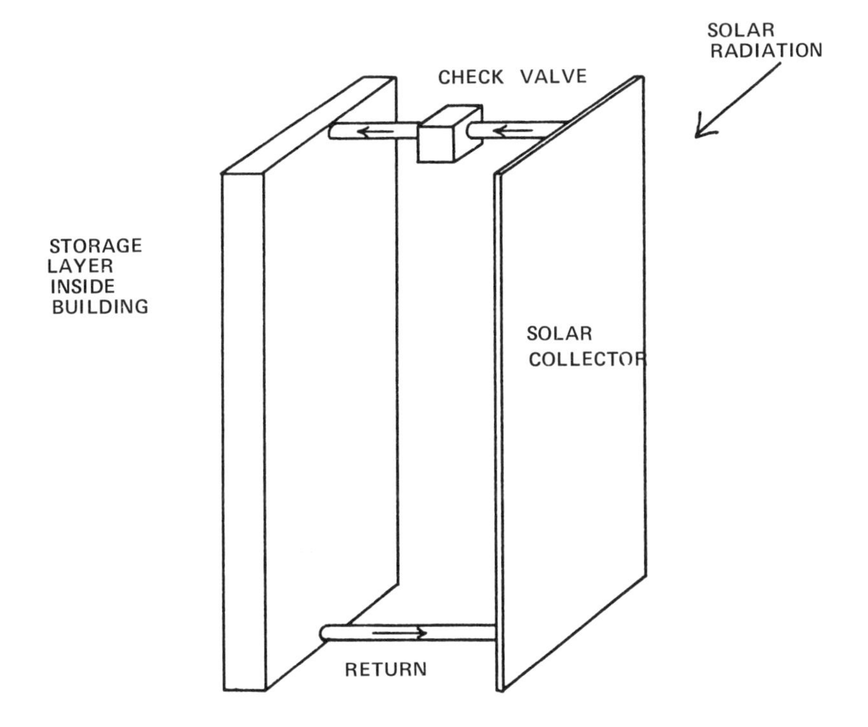


**Figure 85.** Thermic diode panel schematic [Buckeley 1978].

provides the diode action by preventing reverse thermosiphoning. This is similar to an operation of a thermosiphoning domestic hot water system, except that the storage is not located above the collector.

Since the check valve must respond to very small pressure differences—permitting free flow in the forward direction, but completely blocking reverse thermosiphoning—the valve developed for this device (Figure 86) has been shown to be very effective. A riser tube is inserted a small distance through the interface of the upper oil layer floating on the water in the valve. A pressure of only 0.001 psi is needed to initiate the water flow in the forward direction. However, when cooling of the outside collector surface at night causes a reverse thermosiphoning pressure gradient to be created, oil is drawn down into the riser tube until a sufficient counterbalancing pressure head is created to prevent reverse flow from occurring. The depth of penetration of the riser tube into the oil layer and the thickness of the oil layer obviously are important parameters here.

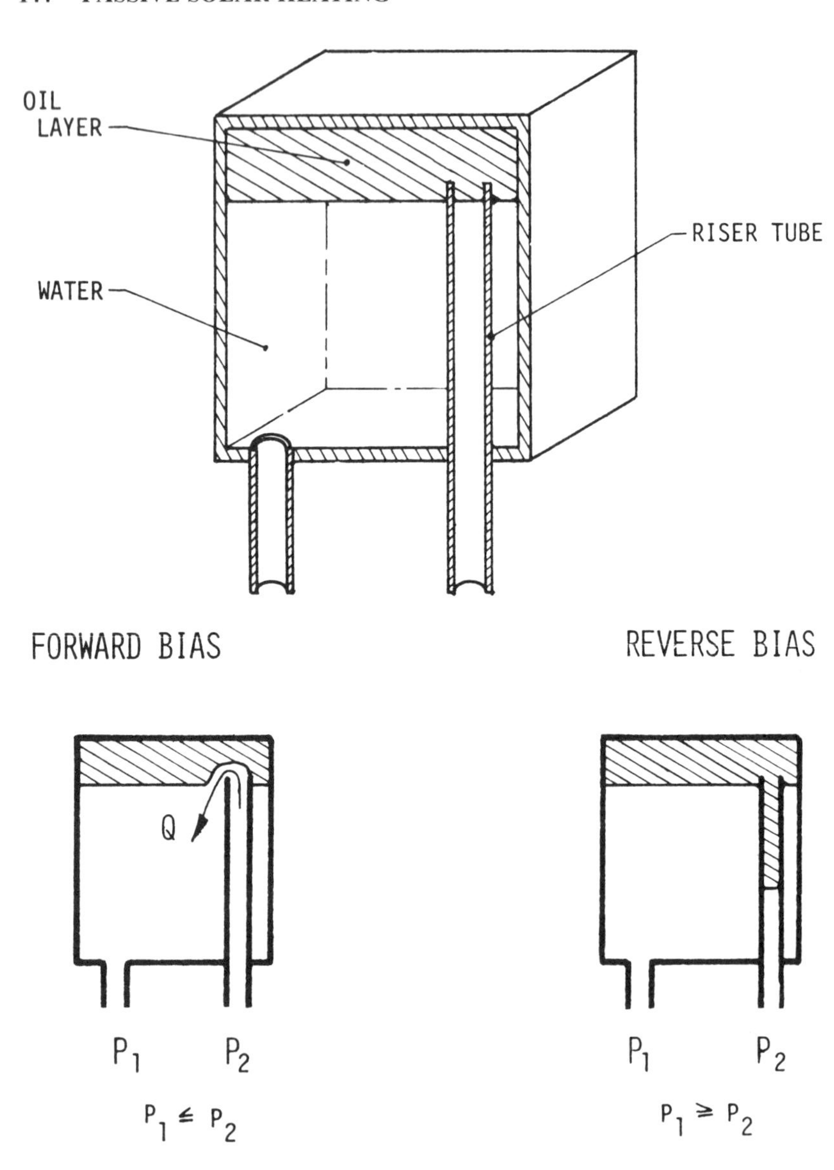


**Figure 86.** Check valve in thermic diode panel [Buckeley 1978].

## *Prototype Thermic Diode Collector*

A manufacturing prototype thermic diode thermosiphoning collector panel is illustrated in Figure 87. This panel has a stamped aluminum collector skin backed by a plastic membrane, which forms the water passages for the collector. Elastic stretching of the plastic permits freezing of

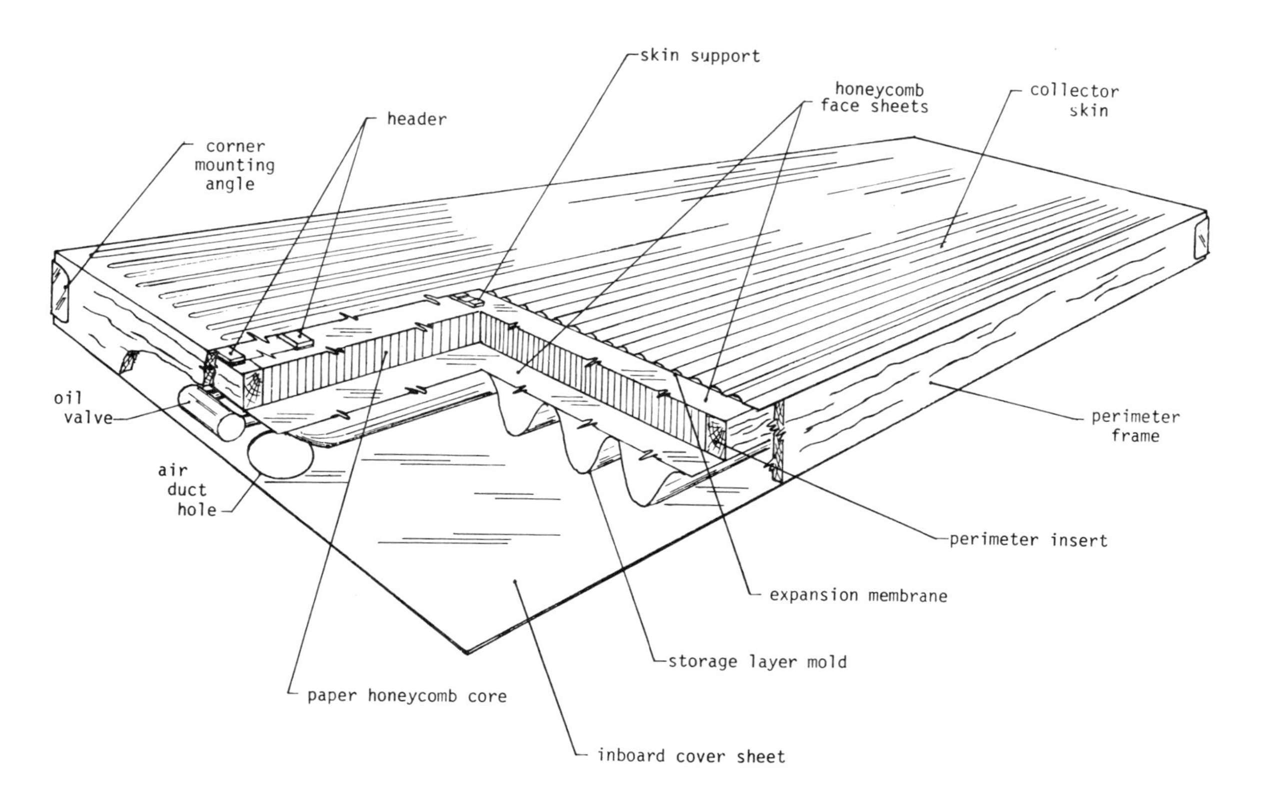


**Figure 87.** Prototype thermic diode panel [Buckeley 1978].

the water without collector damage. A foam-filled paper honeycomb core provides structural rigidity and insulation. The glazing is not shown in Figure 87. The wooden perimeter frame provides the structural support normally required of a wall section. The oil check valve is shown at the top of the collector. The absorber plate is a stamped sheet consisting of 24 beaded channels with a closed end, painted black on the outside. The thermic diode panel is a thermosiphoning collector that behaves similarly to a thermal storage wall in that the collected solar energy heats the storage mass in the wall or sloping roof of the structure, which, in turn, heats the interior space by convection and radiation.

### *Thermic Diode Summer Check Valve*

A thermic diode panel may also incorporate a separate "summer check valve" that is put into operation by closing off the tube to the winter check valve and opening a tube to the summer check valve. The summer check valve includes an oil layer penetrated by a riser as illustrated in Figure 86, except that the flow direction is reversed: reversed thermosiphoning is permitted while the heating convection loop is blocked. During a hot summer day, solar heating of the water causes the oil to be forced down the inlet riser, thus preventing the convection loop that would otherwise transmit solar heat into the interior space. However, at night, water in the collector absorber plate is cooled by convection and radiation to the ambient air and night sky so that warmer water from inside the room flows through the diode and into the collector absorber plate and is replaced by cooler water from the outside absorber. The result is that the storage layer on the inside surface of the wall and roof panels helps cool the interior space during the day. A simple three-way valve switches from the winter check valve to the summer check valve, thereby permitting the thermic diode panel to be operated in either the heating or cooling mode. Thermic diode panels have also been proposed for radiant heating and passive cooling of industrial buildings [Buckley 1975].

## HEAT PIPE TRANSFERENCE SYSTEM

The heat pipe was originally developed in 1963 as a passive means of transferring heat nearly isothermically from one point to another. It consists of a sealed container, usually a tube, which is evacuated and contains a suitable working fluid such as water or a refrigerant. Heat is transferred by the closed-cycle processes of evaporation and condensation. When heat is supplied to one portion of the pipe, some of the fluid evaporates, and vapor flows to the unheated sections, where it condenses and releases the latent heat of condensation. Since the latent heat of all these fluids is quite large, a relatively small mass transport can result in a fairly large transport of heat. If the vapor is condensing at a location lower than the evaporator section, a wick can be incorporated in the heat pipe so that liquid is returned to the evaporator section by capillary action. Thus, the heat pipe is completely passive. Corliss et al. [1978] investigated the possibility of incorporating heat pipes into passive solar heating systems. Most heat pipes applied to solar systems use gravity instead of a wick to return the working fluid. This has an advantage in that the heat flow is unidirectional; heat is conducted normally as long as it is applied to the lower evaporator section, and the heat that is transported is released at the condenser. However, little heat is transferred in the opposite direction. Thus, when the heat input to the evaporator is insufficient to raise the evaporator temperature above the condenser temperature, the heat pipe becomes inactive. In this regard, the heat pipe's operation is somewhat similar to that of a thermic diode, except the heat is transferred by the vapor phase of the fluid rather than by its liquid phase, and no check valve is needed. This ensures that any individual collector within an array that does not receive sufficient solar radiation to provide energy to the system will shut off automatically. Heat pipes can also be extremely reliable due to the lack of any moving mechanical parts.

Corliss et al. [1978] proposed integrating heat pipes into a water wall to transfer heat from the absorber surface of the south-facing wall into the water thermal storage. This would result in an effect similar to that achieved with the thermic diode, except that heat pipes incorporated in the wall, rather than the check valves, would provide the diode action. The heat pipe is inherently more reliable since its operation is not dependent on maintaining a precise oil level in the check valve. Corliss et al. showed that heat pipe–augmented passive heating systems should outperform the conventional water wall by as much as a factor of 2.

## BUBBLE PUMP HEAT CIRCULATING SYSTEM

Most passive heating techniques require that the thermal storage unit be located at about the same elevation as the solar collectors or higher. Wachtell [1978a,b] proposed a bubble pump that would permit the solar collectors to be located on the roof and the thermal storage in the basement. The result is a passive system designed very much like an active system, except that the bubble pump provides circulation, and no electrical devices are required. Figure 88 is a schematic representation of a solar system using a vapor bubble pump. Gravity flow occurs in two paths. Path one is from the vapor separator, which must be above the solar collectors, through the thermal energy storage and through the condenser where the cooler liquid condenses the vapor in the separator. This

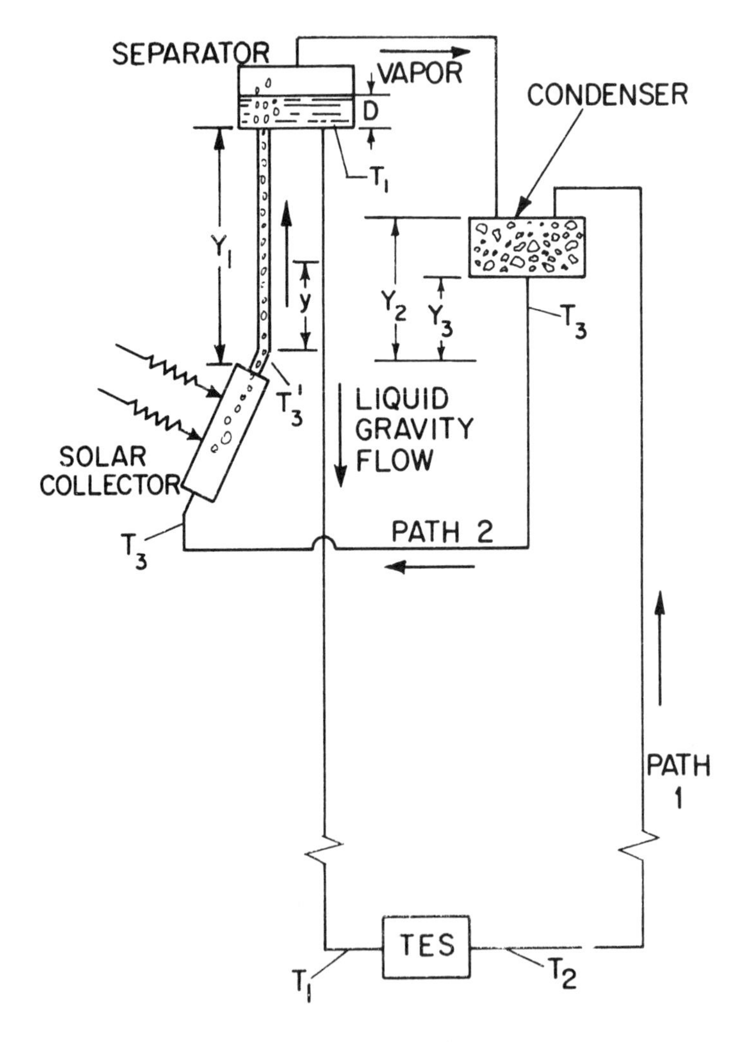


**Figure 88.** Solar heating system with vapor bubble pump [Wachtell 1978].

leads to a mixture, at a temperature $T_3$, which is intermediate between $T_1$ and $T_2$, flowing back to the solar collectors. Vapor bubbles that have warmed in the collector cause a two-phase mixture to flow up the tube at height $Y_1$ and into the separator. Although the volume flowrate of vapor is much greater than that of liquid, the mass flowrate is much smaller. The separator should be located above the collector to produce the gravity head needed to drive the fluid around the loops. The result is energy collection and the necessary fluid flows to operate the solar system. When the solar radiation density is insufficient to create the two-phase mixture in the collector, the flow stops and the system shuts down. Thus, no pumps, valves or controls are needed.

## VAPOR EXPANSION AND STRATIFIED STORAGE SELF-PUMPING SYSTEMS

Figures 89 and 90 illustrate two additional schemes, in which the expansion of vapor generated as the circulating liquid is vaporized provides the pressure differential needed to drive the fluid through the energy storage device and other system components. In Figure 89, with

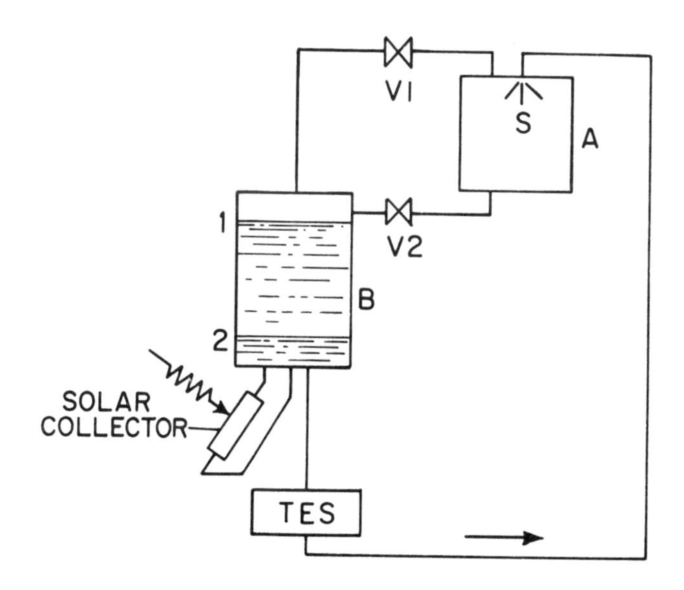


**Figure 89.** System with vapor expansion self-pumping [Wachtell 1978].

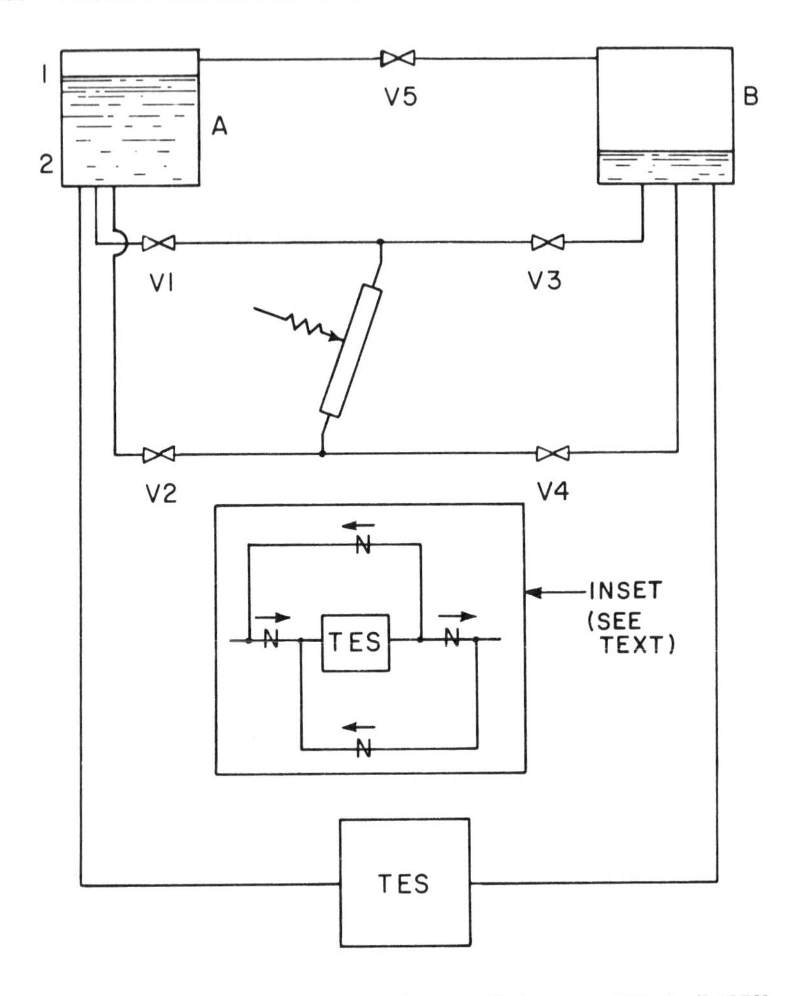


**Figure 90.** Self-pumping system with stratified storage [Wachtell 1978].

valves V1 and V2 closed, the two-phase mixture rising into vessel B will drive liquid from vessel B through the energy storage system into vessel A. This cooler fluid exiting the energy storage system is sprayed in vessel A thereby condensing vapor in A, which causes the vapor pressure in A to drop below B. When the level of liquid in vessel B falls to point 2, valves V1 and V2 are opened by a liquid level sensor in vessel B, and the condensed liquid in vessel A will flow into vessel B. When the liquid level in B again rises to point 1, the valve is closed and the cycle resumes. The problem with this scheme is that the flow through the thermal storage energy system is intermittent.

## SELF-PUMPING SYSTEM WITH STRATIFIED STORAGE

A similar scheme, illustrated in Figure 92, exhibits almost continuous flow. In this case, when valves V1 and V2 are opened and V3, V4 and V5 are closed, this system operates as in Figure 89, removing liquid from vessel A to vessel B. However, when the level A falls to point 2, valves V1 and V2 are closed while V3 and V4 are opened. V5 is also opened briefly to equalize the pressures in the two vessels. Thus, flow through the energy storage system is almost immediately resumed, in the opposite direction. The check valves shown in the figure may be used in conjunction with the energy storage subsystem to maintain flow in one direction through the storage unit, thereby avoiding a disruption of thermal stratification.

## LATENT HEAT WITH CONDENSATE RETURN SYSTEM

Figure 91 illustrates how vapor expansion can also be used for condensate return in a latent heat transport system. The condensate is lifted in several steps as shown in the figure. V1, V2, V3 and V4 are operated so that either all are open or one is closed. If they are all opened, vapor will flow through all four valves in series into chambers B and C, where it condenses. Condensate then flows back through check valve CV5 into chamber D4. The floating insulator in D4 inhibits vapor condensation. If only valve V1 is closed, then the expansion of vapor in chamber A forces liquid from D1 into B. Valve V1 is closed first, then valve V2, followed by valves V3 and V4, only one being closed at a given time. This causes liquid to be lifted in turn from D1 into B, from D2 into D1, from D3 into D2, and from D4 into D3. Then all the valves are opened and the cycle resumes. With the valves all open, liquid flows through the check valve from chamber B into A. Thus, latent heat is transported into chamber C continuously. The complexity of such a system borders on that of an active solar heating system. The electric power requirement, however, is much less. The electric power required to operate the motorized valves is considerably less than the electric power needed to run a pump. This power might be supplied by a few photovoltaic panels. Thus, it would be possible to operate such a solar heating system without auxiliary electric power.

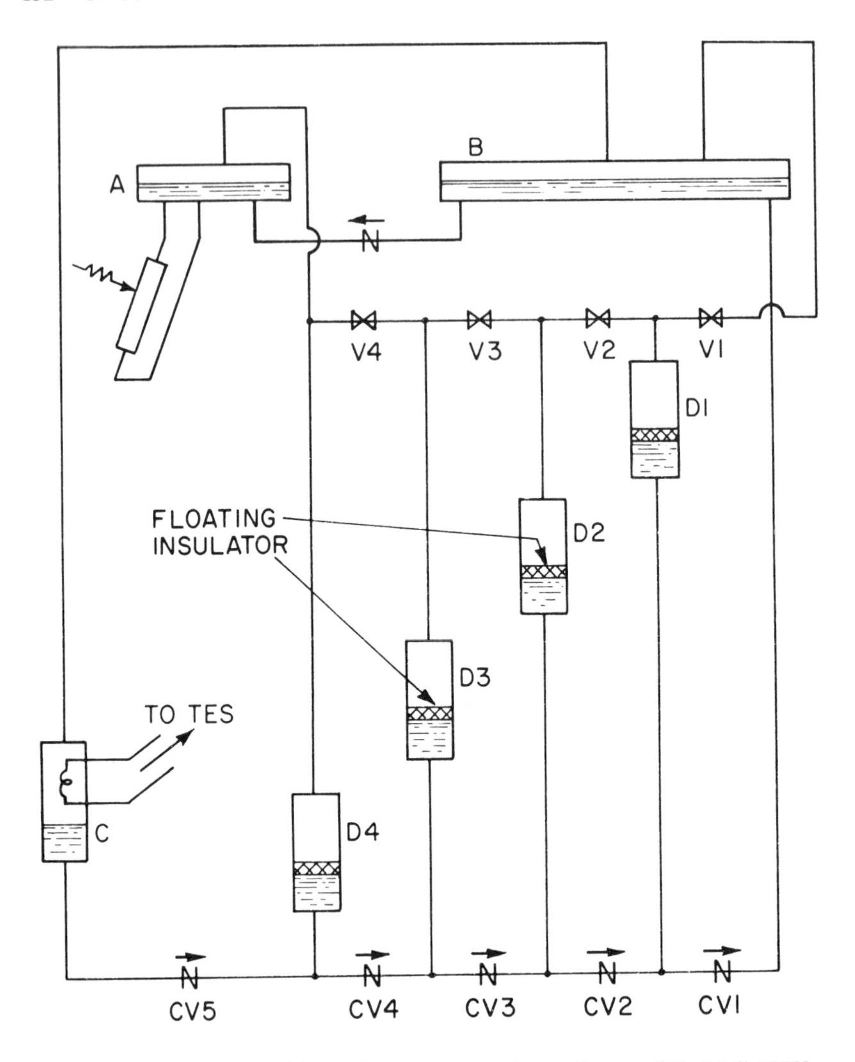


**Figure 91.** System with condensate return in small steps [Wachtell 1978].

## SYSTEM WITH CONDENSATE RETURN IN SMALL STEPS

Figure 92 illustrates an extension of this concept that provides the effect of an infinite number of stages. Vapor circulates downward from separator A and entrains condensate which overflows the trap. The condensate droplets are delivered to chamber B, and condensation occurs in C. This scheme is proposed to function over a wide range of

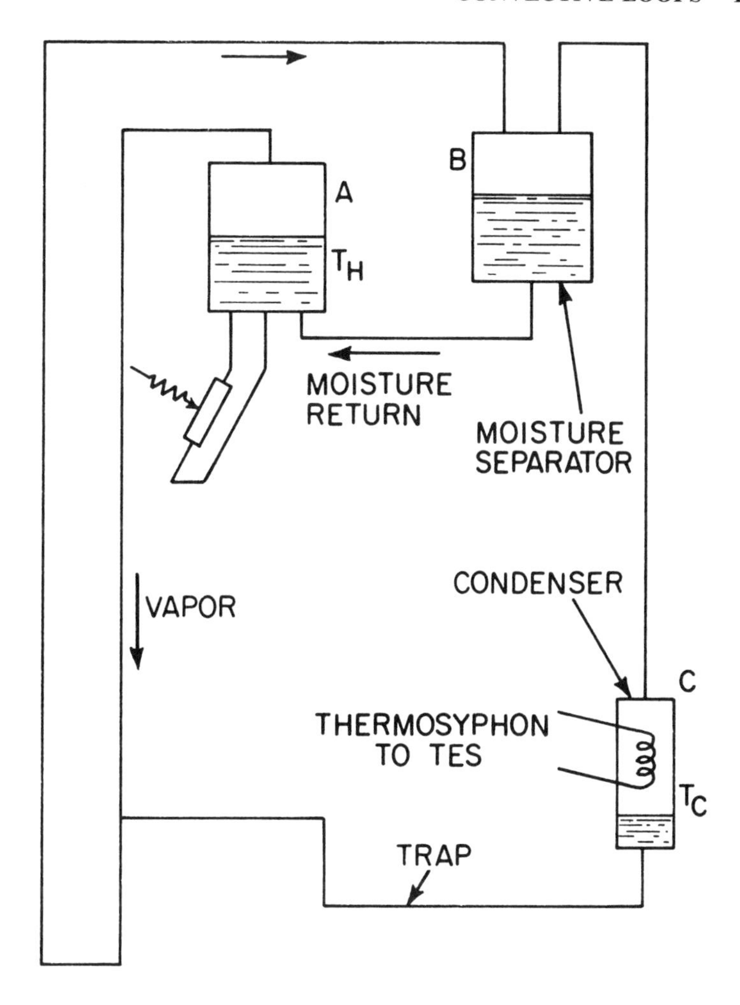


**Figure 92.** Latent heat system with condensate return [Wachtell 1978].

heat transfer rates, but requires that the vapor flowing upward into chamber B be sufficient to transport the condensate droplets.

These systems described by Wachtell [1978a,b] illustrate approaches that might be used to provide the benefits of passive solar heating without the necessity of locating the solar collectors below the thermal storage subsystem. They all rely on using vapor generated in the collector to drive the circulating fluids in the solar system.

# CHAPTER 6

# SUNSPACES

Probably the single greatest disadvantage of direct-gain solar systems is their tendency to cause fairly large fluctuations in indoor temperatures. The attached sunspace, or greenhouse, is in effect a direct-gain solar system with thermal storage mass that is located in a part of the structure that can tolerate large temperature fluctuations. Examples include greenhouses, atria, sun porches and garages. Such systems are referred to as attached sunspaces rather than direct-gain systems, since the space allowed wide temperature fluctuations is separated from the main portion of the building. Thus, extra heat available from this sunspace can be used to augment the heating of the rest of the building, or the sunspace can be isolated when heat is not needed. A well designed attached sunspace will also hold considerable heat into the evening hours, which can be used to continue to augment building heat needs. Attached sunspaces not only supply solar heat but reduce heat loss from buildings by acting as buffers between the main parts of buildings and the outside.

## BALCOMB ATTACHED SUNSPACE HOUSE

A well known example of a passively heated solar house utilizing an attached sunspace is the Balcomb home in Santa Fe, New Mexico. This 2300-$ft^2$ house uses a south-facing greenhouse with an aperture of 412 $ft^2$. Thermal storage is in an adobe mass wall that separates the greenhouse from the main portion of the house, and in the floor of the greenhouse. Two small fans circulate air from the top of the sunspace through two rock storage bins beneath the floor, and the exhaust air is returned to the greenhouse as illustrated in Figure 93. This direct-coupled storage mass in turn distributes heat by radiation and convection from the floor and the brick walls. Auxiliary heating is provided by electric baseboard heaters and a wood stove.

## Balcomb House and Sunspace Design

The floor plan of the two-story house (Figure 94) illustrates the L-shaped structure enclosing the solar greenhouse. The first floor includes the living room, dining room and kitchen, which are open to permit free circulation of air. The living and dining rooms open into the greenhouse, and the kitchen has a window into the greenhouse. A circular staircase at the center of the L leads from the greenhouse to the second-floor balcony overlooking the greenhouse area and providing access to each of the three bedrooms on the second floor. Most of the lower floor of the house is below grade, since the lot slopes to the south.

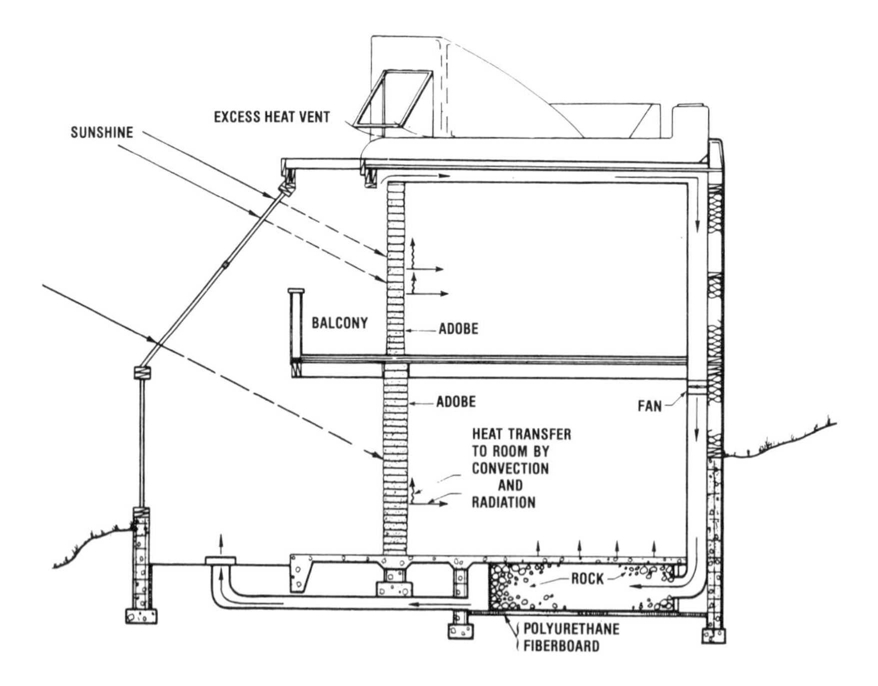


**Figure 93.** Cross section of Balcomb house with attached sunspace [Sandia 1979].

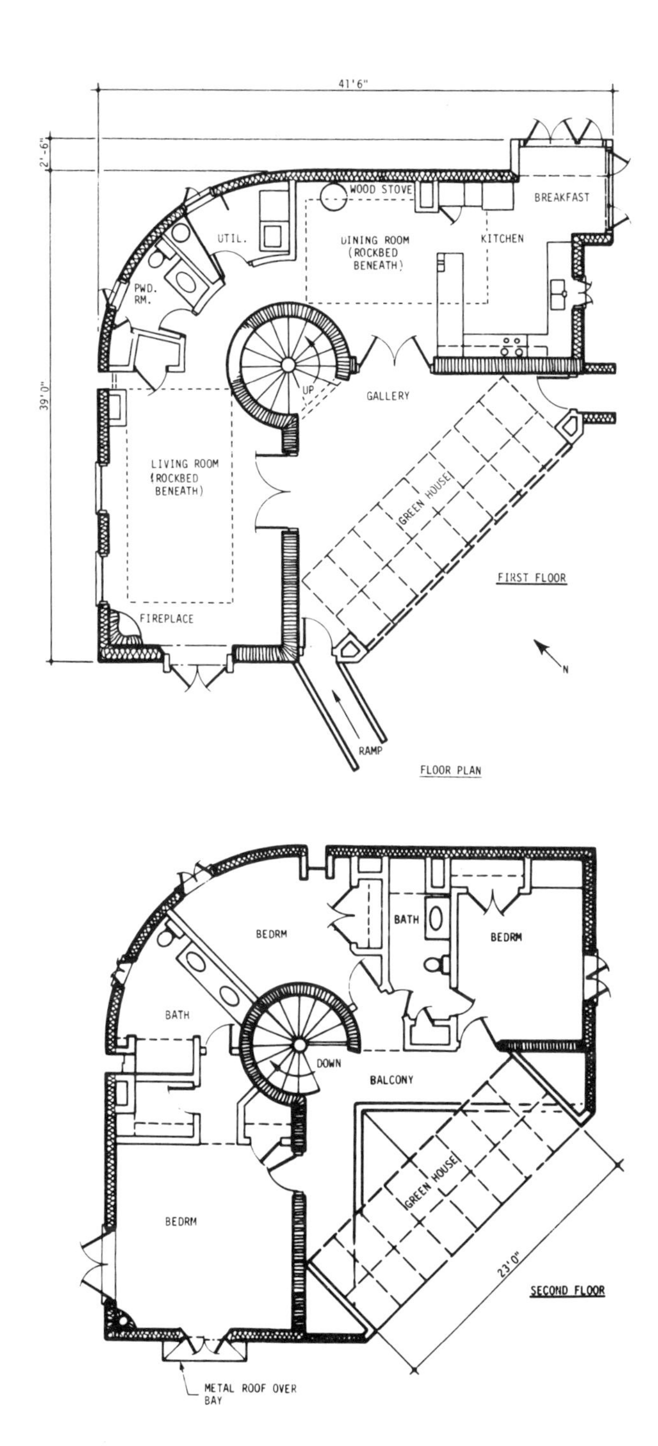


**Figure 94.** Floor plan of Balcomb house with attached sunspace [Sandia 1979].

The south wall of the greenhouse is constructed of eight tempered, double-glazed, sealed, thermal glass units, each 34 in. wide × 74 in. long. The roof of the greenhouse has a slope of 50° and is composed of 16 panels of double-glazed thermal glass units each also measuring 34 in. wide × 76 in. high. This provides a total of 276 $ft^2$ of aperture on the sloping roof, plus 136 $ft^2$ on the vertical south wall. The adobe walls at the rear of the greenhouse are 14-in. thick on the first floor and 10 in. on the second. This direct-coupled thermal storage wall is supplemented by thermal storage in the floor and 25 $yd^3$ of 3- to 5-in. diameter round riverbed stones. Air is circulated from the top of the greenhouse through the rock bed by two ⅓-hp fans. The outer walls of the house are framed by 2- × 8-in. studs with the spacing between insulated with 1.5-in. rigid fiberglass over a 6-in. fiberglass batt with a vapor barrier on the inside.

The fans coupled to the rock beds are quite effective in moderating temperature fluctuations within the greenhouse. These fans are controlled by a differential thermostat that senses the temperature of the air at the top of the greenhouse and the rock bed. Whenever this temperature differential exceeds 15°F, the fans will go on. The fans can also be turned on or manually disabled as desired. Heat flow from the greenhouse into the living space is controlled primarily by the opening and closing of doors and windows of rooms which open into the greenhouse. Two of the glass panels on the south wall in both access doors can be opened to allow outside air to ventilate the greenhouse to prevent overheating. During summer nights these vents are left open.

## Performance of the Balcomb House

Figure 95 illustrates data taken from the Balcomb house between December 26, 1978, and January 8, 1979. This illustrates a winter period in which several sunny days are followed by a period of cloudy weather. The second pair of traces from the top, below the solar radiation data, are the temperatures near the inside and outside surfaces of the adobe wall in the greenhouse. As shown, this wall temperature rises to as high as 120°F on sunny days. The temperature of the floor above the rock bed ranges from about 60 to 75°F. The ambient temperature during this period is generally below freezing and reached as low as −12°F. But in spite of the below-zero temperatures outside, the temperature inside the house, as represented by the dinining room temperature, remains in the 60s and low 70s. Temperature swings in the dining room moderated to about 8°F. Temperature fluctuations in the greenhouse were about 30°F.

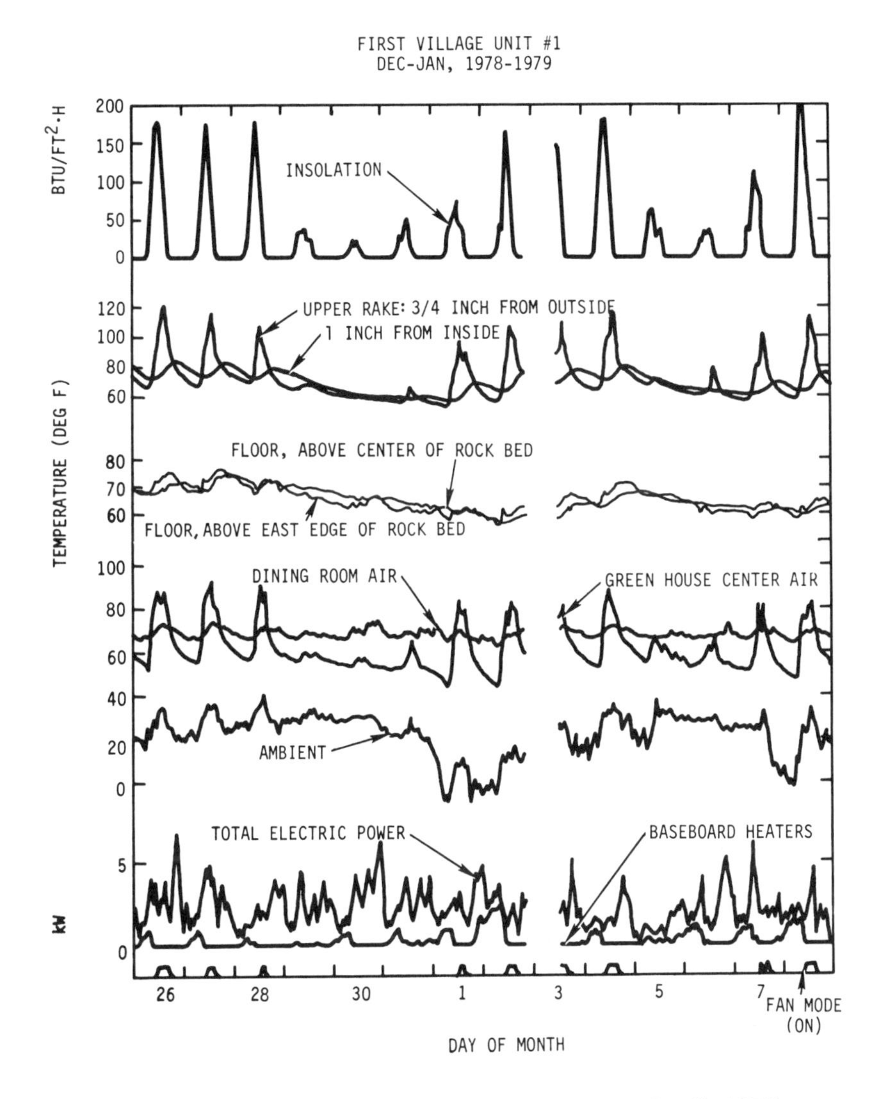


**Figure 95.** Performance data from Balcomb house [Sandia 1979].

A standard heat loss analysis for this house indicates that the total building loss coefficient is 15,920 Btu/dd, or 8.64 Btu/dd-ft$^2$. The annual solar-heating fraction was estimated to be 84%. Data taken during the first years of operation indicate that this solar heating fraction is probably being realized.

## ANTON CHICO GREENHOUSE

A small 896-$ft^2$ house of traditional design in Anton Chico, New Mexico, is heated by a greenhouse along the south side of the house. The 420-$ft^2$ solar aperture is double glazed with fiberglass panels, as illustrated in Figure 96. The direct-coupled thermal storage mass consists of the thick adobe wall of the house plus additional water drums located along the wall, as shown in Figure 97. A wood stove provides auxiliary heat. The building loss coefficient is about 13,500 Btu/dd, and the solar-heating fraction is about 73%. Since the greenhouse is used for growing food, some problems were encountered with high humidity in the greenhouse during parts of the year.

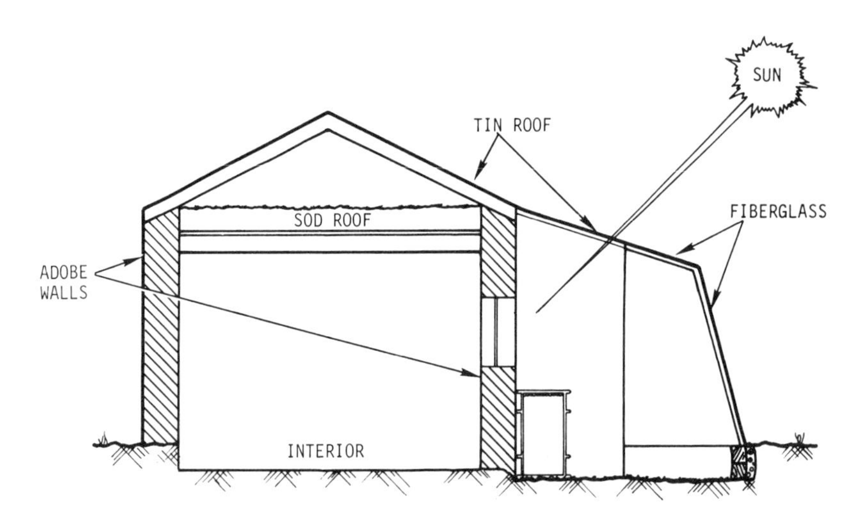


**Figure 96.** Cross section of Anton Chico house.

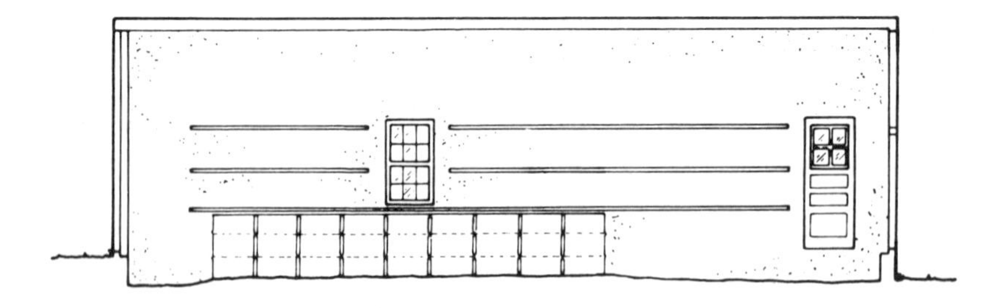

**Figure 97.** South wall of Anton Chico house.

## HOLDRIDGE RESIDENCE GREENHOUSE

The attached greenhouse at the Holdridge residence in Hinesberg, Vermont, incorporates four water drums for thermal storage and fans to circulate heat into the interior of the home when it is needed. This simple attached sunspace is illustrated in Figures 98 and 99. The south-facing wall of the greenhouse is glazed with translucent fiberglass panels at a slope of 60%. The three $4 \times 8$ panels provide a total of 96 $ft^2$ of aperture. The four 55-gal drums are painted black and filled with water for thermal storage. Since this 90-$ft^2$ aperture solar greenhouse was attached to a much larger 1800-$ft^2$ home, the solar-heating fraction was quite small. This is an example of the type of simple sunspace which has become quite popular. It provides the advantages of a greenhouse for growing plants, plus some space heating. Such an attached sunspace can also increase humidity in the house in the winter.

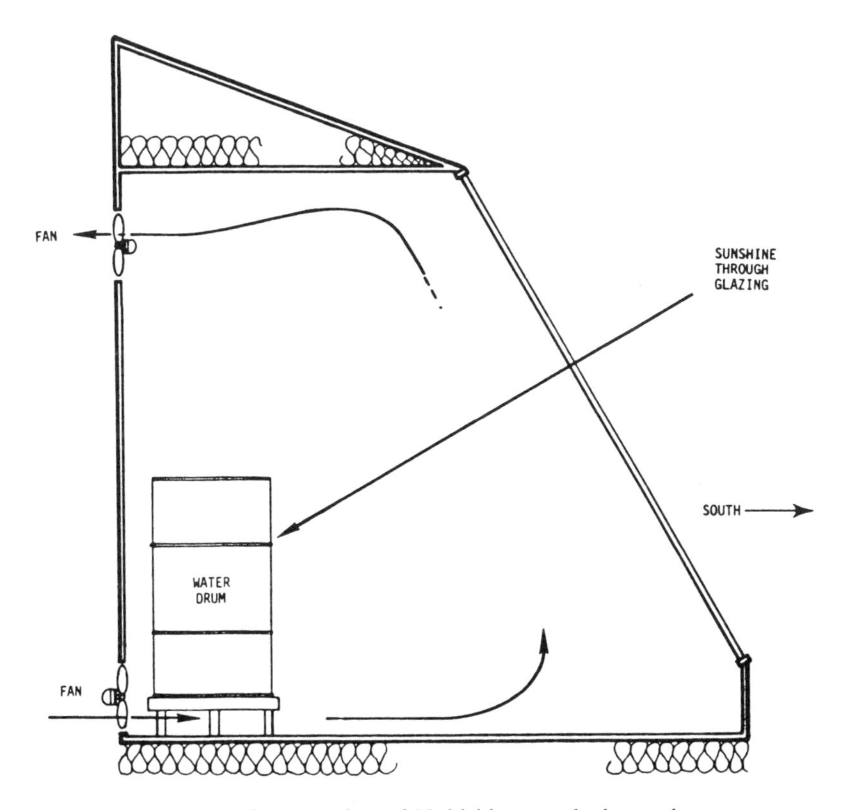


**Figure 98.** Cross section of Holdridge attached greenhouse.

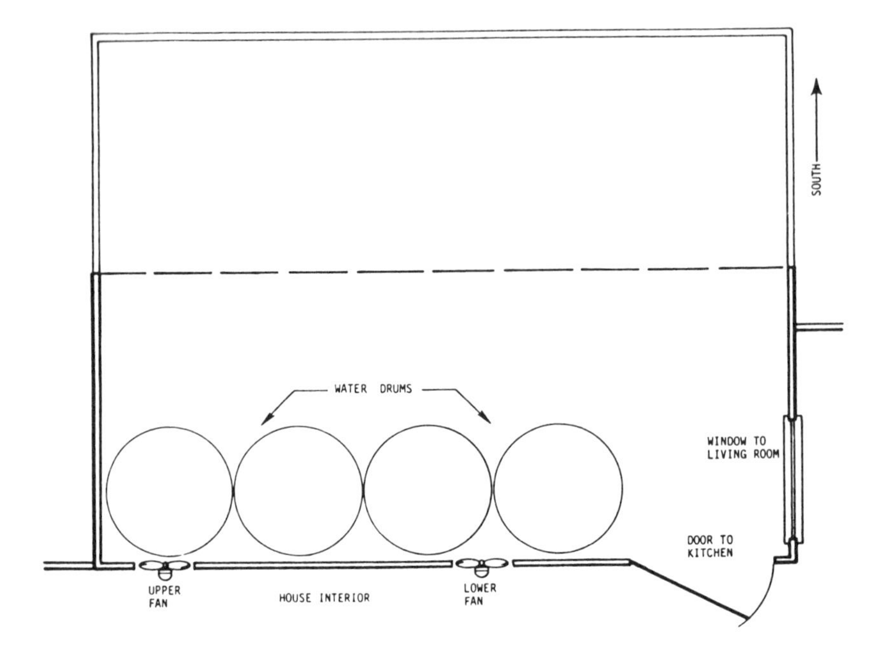


**Figure 99.** Floor plan of the Holdridge attached greenhouse.

## SELECTING AN ATTACHED SUNSPACE

### Commercial Units

Attached sunspaces of this type are relatively simple to build, but the cost of matching the quality and durability of the house's construction may be fairly high. Commercial units now available provide a simple and attractive lightweight frame that attaches to the house to support plastic glazing. Such a double-glazed enclosure can be an economical and effective sunspace for growing plants and providing a significant amount of heat to the building in the winter. However, in general, it is more economical to construct a quality sunspace that will enhance the appraised value of the building rather than an inexpensive unit with a poor appearance and short usable lifetime. In addition, zoning regulations may effectively inhibit installation of inexpensive units.

### Sunspaces for Growing Plants

Sunspaces used for growing plants can tolerate fairly large temperature fluctuations, as long as the temperature does not drop significantly below freezing within the sunspace. An attached sunspace may also require auxiliary heating during extended cloudy periods in winter to prevent the plants from being damaged. In northern climates, three layers of glazing may be appropriate. Movable insulation can also be effective in reducing auxiliary energy requirements. If extensive horticulture is undertaken within a sunspace, the occupants must be aware that potential insect and plant disease problems may be encountered. Plants should also be selected based on expected temperature, solar radiation and humidity conditions and fluctuations within the greenhouse.

## Selecting the Number of Glazing Panels

The selection of the number of glazing panels for an attached sunspace involves some fairly complicated tradeoffs. Clearly, single-glazed panels will transmit more solar radiation for plant growth and solar heating than multiple-glazed panels, but heat losses are greater. Single-glazed sunspaces are most appropriate in southern climates where temperatures rarely drop below 0°F. In northern climates, double, or even triple glazing is usually needed. A properly designed and constructed double-glazed sunspace will remain above freezing without auxiliary heat in most of the United States. In climates of greater than 6000 dd/year, either movable insulation or additional glazing layers may be required. Since light transmission is important for sunspaces, when triple or quadruple glazing is used, highly transmitting plastic film or low-iron glass should be used for some of the glazing layers. The U-value for triple glazing is typically 0.35 Btu/ft$^2$-°F; for quadruple glazing it is 0.24 Btu/ft$^2$-°F. It is important that moisture be kept from between layers of multiple glazing, since condensation will reduce the transmission of solar radiation.

There are advantages to wrapping the building around the sunspace as was done in the case of the Balcomb house. This reduces heat loss from the sunspace and building and improves transmission of heat from the sunspace to the building. It permits substantial natural lighting from the sunspace, makes the sunspace more usable, and may reduce cost.

Thermal storage may be provided by walls, containers of water, circulation of hot air from the top of the sunspace through gravel beds and soil for growing plants. Thermal storage mass within the sunspace may not be required if the excess heat during the day will be needed by the building.

## COOK HOME SUNSPACE WITH MOVABLE INSULATION

Movable insulation can considerably improve the performance of an attached sunspace. An example is the 1950-$ft^2$ four-bedroom Cook home on a south-sloping hill above Lake George in Ticonderoga, New York. The double-glazed attached sunspace is to the south of the main floor. As shown in Figure 100, 12-in.-diameter tubes of water stand in front of the single-glazed glass sliding doors separating the interior of the house from the sunspace. Two sets of movable insulating panels cover the exterior glazing at night, as shown in the figure. These panels are of 1-in. polystyrene foam insulation with ⅛-in. masonite on both sides. The panels for the upper glazing are riveted at the top, as shown, and the panels for the vertical glass are mounted in tracks. A large overhang reduces unwanted direct solar radiation in the summer. Scully [1978] modeled the Cook house over a period of two winter days and arrived at a solar-heating fraction of 55%.

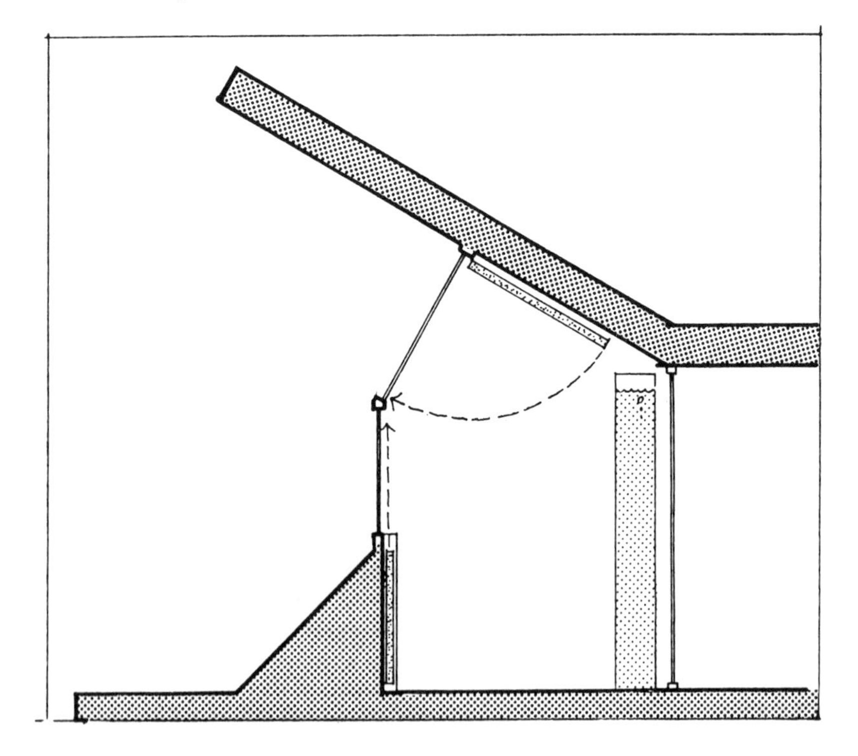

**Figure 100.** Cook house sunspace with movable insulation.

## COLORADO STATE UNIVERSITY SUNSPACE SYSTEM

Colorado State University constructed a solar heating residence with an attached sunspace with a total floor area of 1208 $ft^2$. The greenhouse has a glazed area of 47 $m^2$ (507 $ft^2$) with thermal storage in the rear wall and rock bin. The system combines active air heating with passive heating from the sunspace. The solar-heating fraction during a recent winter was 78% [Farrer et al. 1978].

## EXAMPLES OF ATTACHED GREENHOUSES

Skiles [1979] reported on three homes in northwest Arkansas with attached greenhouses. These greenhouses continued to produce food crops through severe winter conditions and supplied a minor but significant fraction of the heating requirements for the homes. Three residences for a wildlife biologist and his staff on Ossabawi, off the coast of Savannah, Georgia, use passive solar heating augmented by a wood stove [Mickelson 1979]. The 1248-$ft^2$ home incorporated a 320-$ft^2$ sun room on the south side glazed with Tedlar-coated fiberglass panels. The solar-heating fraction is estimated at 80%.

# CHAPTER 7

# SOLAR RADIATION

The earth follows an elliptical orbit about the sun, with its closest approach (perihelion) of $1.47 \times 10^{11}$ m occurring January 3. The earth is at its greatest distance from the sun ($1.52 \times 10^{11}$ m) about July 5. The mean solar distance of $1.495 \times 10^{11}$ m is referred to as the astronomical unit. At this distance the earth receives $1.7 \times 10^{17}$ W of energy from the sun; the average intensity of solar radiation reaching the earth before it becomes attenuated by the earth's atmosphere is called the solar constant. Although the solar output varies slightly over a sunspot cycle, the solar constant remains within one percent of 1353 W/$m^2$ (429.2 Btu/hr-$ft^2$, 4871 kJ/$m^2$-hr) [Eddy 1975]. The only correction that usually need be made to the solar constant is the intensity correction due to the variation in the earth's distance from the sun during the year (Figure 101). The correction factor may be calculated from

$$f = 1 + 0.034\cos[0.9863(n - 5)] \tag{137}$$

where n, the number of the day of the year ($n = 1$ on January 1, $n = 2$ on January 2, etc.), may be found from Table XIV, where x is the day of the month. For leap years, 1 must be added to x for all months after February.

The influence of solar radiation on a particular solar energy system depends both on the intensity and the direction from which the solar radiation is received. In the Northern Hemisphere, the altitude of the sun is much greater in the summer than in the winter, and the days are longer. The angles shown in Figure 102 are for an elevation of 40° N latitude.

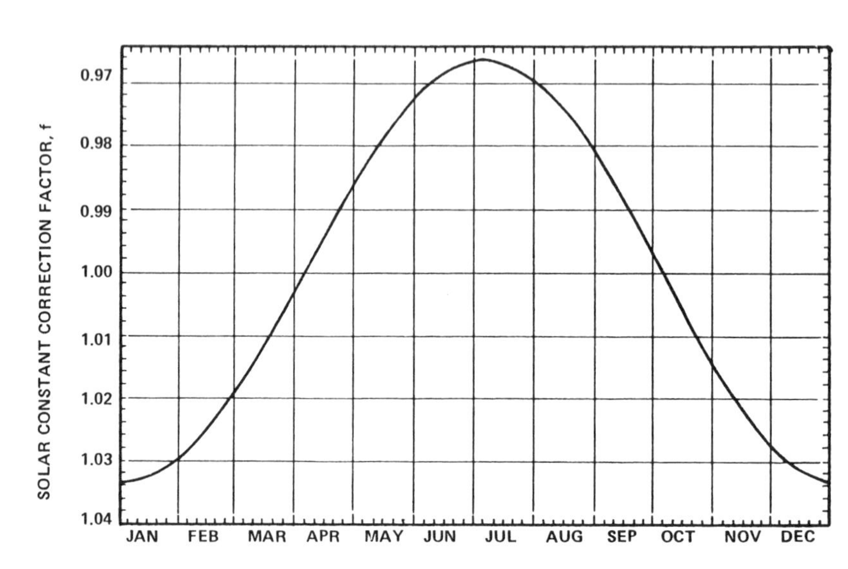


**Figure 101.** Intensity correction factor, f.

**Table XIV. Date to Day of Year Conversion**

| Month | n |
|---|---|
| January | x |
| February | x + 31 |
| March | x + 59 |
| April | x + 90 |
| May | x + 120 |
| June | x + 151 |
| July | x + 181 |
| August | x + 212 |
| September | x + 243 |
| October | x + 273 |
| November | x + 304 |
| December | x + 334 |

## SOLAR ANGLES

In performing calculations involving the solar radiation input to solar collectors, one must know the latitude, the hour angle of the sun, and the solar declination angle. These angles are defined by Figure 103. Imagine an observer standing on a horizontal surface aware of the directions east,

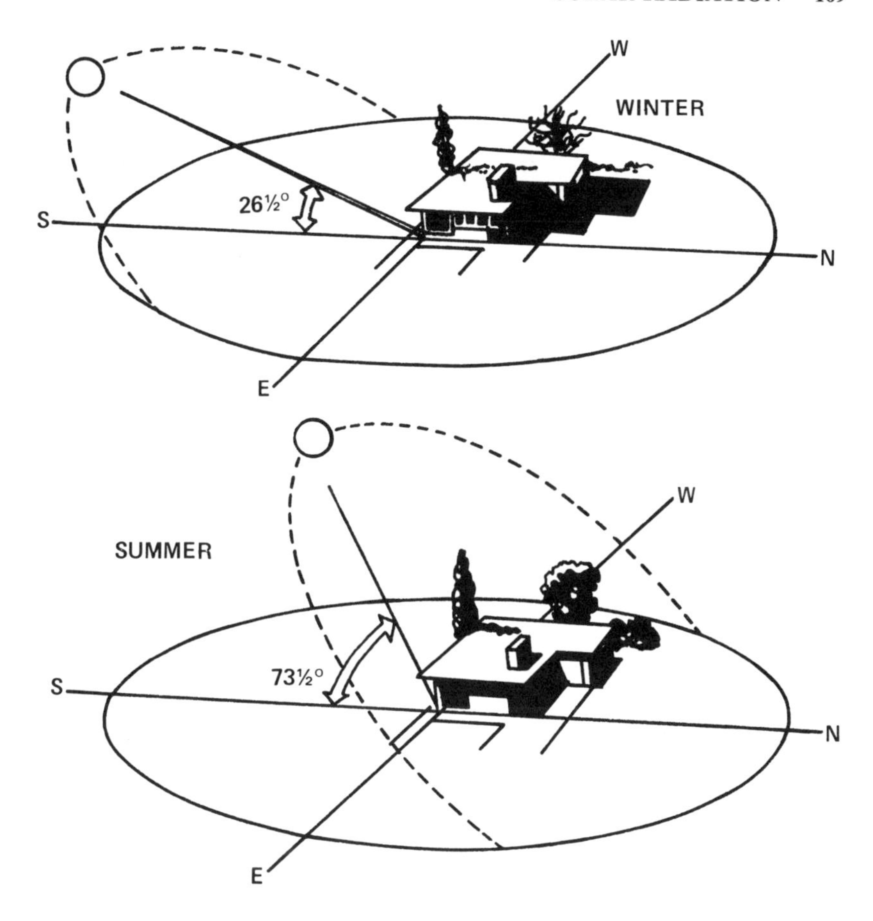


**Figure 102.** Altitude of the sun in summer and winter [Buffer 1978].

west, north, and south. He is also aware of the zenith, which is a vertical line extending from the horizontal surface at the point where the east-west and north-south axes intersect. Consider now a ray of sunlight directly from the sun which strikes the origin of this coordinate system. The angle that ray makes with the zenith is called the zenith angle, $\theta$. The elevation angle of the sun, which is the angle the sun's ray makes with the horizontal plane, is then 90° minus $\theta$. The plane containing the zenith and the ray of sunlight that strikes the origin is therefore vertical to the horizontal plane since it contains the zenith. This plane intersects the horizontal plane at an angle of $\gamma$ from the south-pointing axis. Gamma ($\gamma$) is known as the azimuthal angle. Imagine another plane containing the line parallel to the polar axis and the east-west axis; this plane is

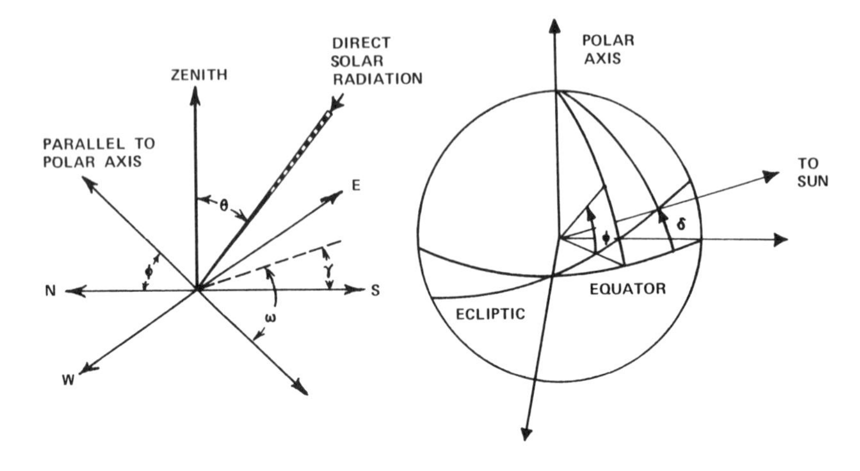


**Figure 103.** Solar angles.

referred to as the latitude plane. The longitude plane contains the zenith and north-south axis. The angle in the latitude plane between the intersection of the plane containing the zenith and ray of sunlight and the longitude plane is referred to as the hour angle. The hour angle of the sun changes by 15° each hour.

## Calculating the Zenith Angle

If one knows the latitude $\phi$, the solar declination angle $\delta$, and the hour angle $\omega$ one may calculate the zenith angle $\theta$ from

$$\cos\theta = \cos\phi\cos\delta\cos\omega + \sin\phi\sin\delta \tag{138}$$

where $\theta$ = the solar zenith angle
$\phi$ = the latitude
$\delta$ = the solar declination angle
$\omega$ = the hour angle (in degrees)

$\omega$ is positive before solar noon and negative after solar noon. The declination angle is the angle that incoming solar radiation makes with the plane of the earth's equator. The hour angle may be calculated from

$$\omega = 15(12 - T_s) \tag{139}$$

where $T_s$ is the true solar time in hours (24-hour clock).

Solar time is usually different from the local standard time. The sun reaches its highest point in the sky at solar noon. Solar time is related to local standard time by

$$T_s = T_{ls} + E + 4(L_{sm} - L_l) \tag{140}$$

where $T_{ls}$ = the local standard time in hours and minutes
$E$ = the equation of time in minutes
$L_{sm}$ = the longitude (in degrees) of the standard meridian for the local time zone (75° for Eastern Standard, 90° for Central Standard, 105° for Mountain Standard, 120° for Pacific Standard, 135° for Yukon Standard, 150° for Alaska-Hawaii Standard)
$L_l$ = local meridian

If daylight savings time is in effect, it must be converted to standard time before Equation 140 is used.

## The Analemma

The analemma (Figure 104) allows both the sun's declination angle $\delta$ and the equation of time E to be estimated for any day of the year [Watt 1980]. The declination angle varies from year to year because the earth actually requires 365.25 days to complete its orbit. For precise values of $\delta$, one must consult an ephemeris or almanac. The declination angle $\delta$ and equation of time E may be calculated to an accuracy of 1 minute for nonleap years by

$$\begin{aligned}\delta = 0.36 - 22.96\cos(0.9856n) - 0.37\cos(2 \times 0.9856n) \\ - 0.15\cos(3 \times 0.9856n) + 4\sin(0.9856n)\end{aligned} \tag{141}$$

and

$$\begin{aligned}
E &= -14.2\sin\left[(n + 7)\left(\frac{180}{111}\right)\right] && \text{for n between 1 and 106} \\
E &= 4\sin\left[(n - 106)\left(\frac{180}{59}\right)\right] && \text{for n between 107 and 166} \\
E &= -6.5\sin\left[(n - 166)\left(\frac{180}{80}\right)\right] && \text{for n between 167 and 246}
\end{aligned} \tag{142}$$

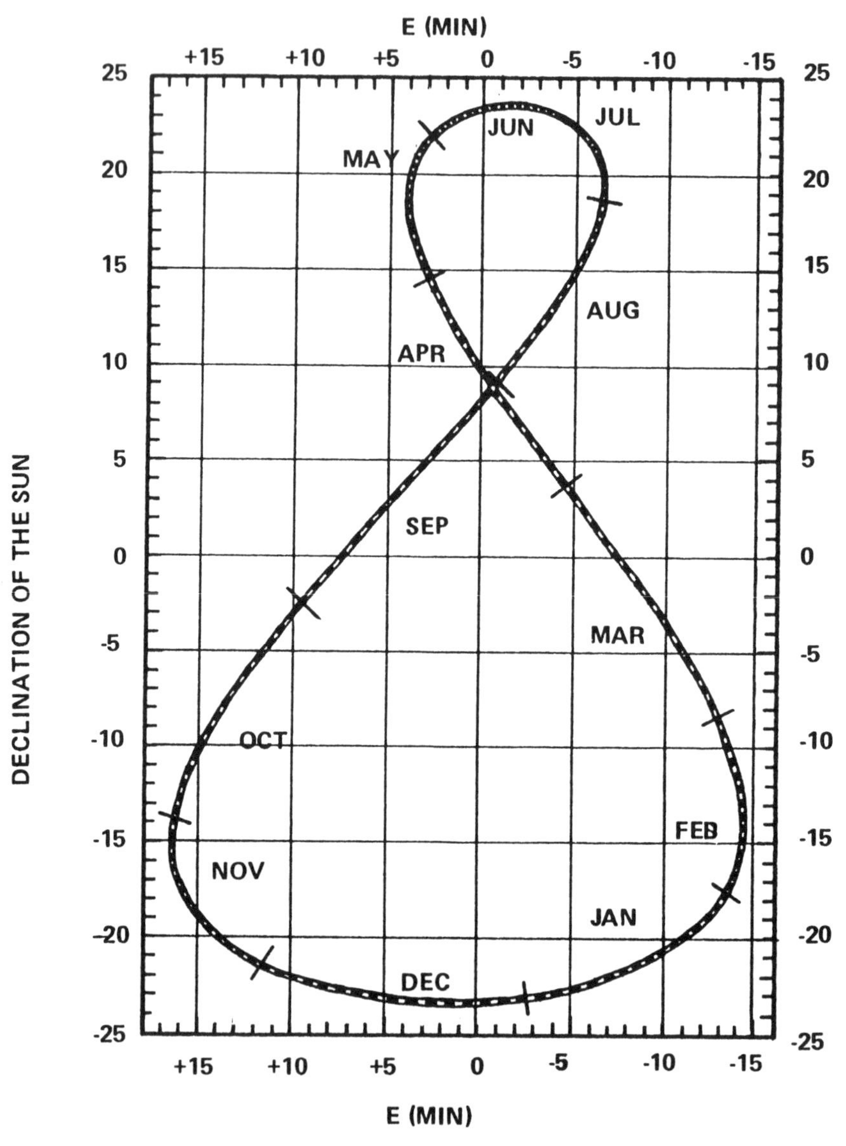


**Figure 104.** Analemma for determining $\delta$ and E [Watt 1980].

$$E = 16.4 \sin\left[(n - 247)\left(\frac{180}{113}\right)\right] \qquad \text{for n between 247 and 365}$$

Table XV lists weekly values of the solar constant correction factor f and the declination angle $\delta$.

Table XV. Solar Declination δ and the Ratio f of Solar Radiation Intensity at Normal Incidence Outside Earth's Atmosphere to Solar Constant

| | Day of Month | | | | | | | |
|---|---|---|---|---|---|---|---|---|
| | 1 | | 8 | | 15 | | 22 | |
| **Month** | δ | f | δ | f | δ | f | δ | f |
| Jan | −23°04′ | 1.0335 | −22°21′ | 1.0325 | −21°16′ | 1.0315 | −19°51′ | 1.0300 |
| Feb | −17°19′ | 1.0288 | −15°14′ | 1.0263 | −12°56′ | 1.0235 | −10°28′ | 1.0207 |
| Mar | −7°53′ | 1.0173 | −5°11′ | 1.0140 | −2°26′ | 1.0103 | 0°20′ | 1.0057 |
| Apr | 4°15′ | 1.0009 | 6°55′ | 0.9963 | 9°30′ | 0.9913 | 11°56′ | 0.9875 |
| May | 14°51′ | 0.9841 | 16°53′ | 0.9792 | 18°41′ | 0.9757 | 20°14′ | 0.9727 |
| Jun | 21°57′ | 0.9714 | 22°47′ | 0.9692 | 23°17′ | 0.9680 | 23°27′ | 0.9670 |
| Jul | 23°10′ | 0.9666 | 22°34′ | 0.9670 | 21°39′ | 0.9680 | 20°26′ | 0.9692 |
| Aug | 18°13′ | 0.9709 | 16°22′ | 0.9727 | 14°18′ | 0.9757 | 12°03′ | 0.9785 |
| Sep | 8°34′ | 0.9828 | 5°59′ | 0.9862 | 3°20′ | 0.9898 | 0°37′ | 0.9945 |
| Oct | −2°54′ | 0.9995 | −5°36′ | 1.0042 | −8°14′ | 1.0087 | −10°47′ | 1.0133 |
| Nov | −14°11′ | 1.0164 | −16°21′ | 1.0207 | −18°18′ | 1.0238 | −19°58′ | 1.0267 |
| Dec | −21°41′ | 1.0288 | −22°39′ | 1.0305 | −23°14′ | 1.0318 | −23°27′ | 1.0327 |

## Example 1: Calculating Solar Time and Hour Angle

What is the solar time, $T_s$, and the hour angle, $\omega$, in Washington, DC (Longitude = 77°) at 4:30 p.m. on July 4?

### *Solution*

According to Table XIV on July 4 the day number n is 185. Using Equation 142, E = −4.4 minutes. Thus, the local solar time is found from Equation 140

$$\begin{aligned} T_s &= T_{ls} + E + 4(L_{sm} - L_1) \\ &= 4{:}30 - 4 + 4(75 - 77) = 4{:}14\,\text{p.m.} \end{aligned} \tag{140}$$

The hour angle is found from Equation 139 after first converting 4:14 p.m. to 16:14 hr (24-hr clock time) and then into fractional hours (16 + 14/60 = 16.23 hr)

$$\begin{aligned} \omega &= 15(12 - T_s) \\ &= 15(12 - 16.23) = -63.5° \end{aligned} \tag{139}$$

The azimuthal angle $\gamma$ may be calculated from

$$\sin(\gamma - 180) = \frac{\cos\delta \sin\omega}{\sin\theta} \tag{143}$$

or

$$\cos\gamma = \frac{\sin\delta - \sin\phi\cos\theta}{\cos\phi\sin\theta} \tag{144}$$

Equation 138 can be solved for the sunset hour angle $\omega_s$ that is, the value of $\omega$ at sunset when $\theta = 90°$. The result is

$$\cos\omega_s = -\frac{\sin\phi\sin\delta}{\cos\phi\cos\delta} = -\tan\phi\tan\delta \tag{145}$$

or

$$\omega_s = \cos^{-1}(-\tan\phi\tan\delta) \tag{146}$$

Since the number of hours of daylight is equal $(2/15)\omega_s$, the day length, DL, is given by

$$\mathrm{DL} = \frac{2}{15}\cos^{-1}(-\tan\phi\tan\delta) \tag{147}$$

## The Simple Nomogram

A simple nomogram (Figure 105) may be used to determine the hour of sunrise and sunset in solar time [Whillier 1965]. A straight line drawn from the latitude through the declination angle intersects the time of sunrise and sunset (solar time). This solar time can then be converted to local standard time using Equation 140.

## Example 2: Calculating Zenith Angle and Azimuth

What is the zenith angle and azimuth of the sun on July 4 at 4:30 p.m. EST in Washington, DC (Latitude = 38° 51′)?

### *Solution*

From the previous example, the true solar time at 4:30 p.m. EST is 4:14 p.m., or 16:14 hours. The hour angle $\omega$ is $-63.5°$. The declination angle is found from Equation 141 to be

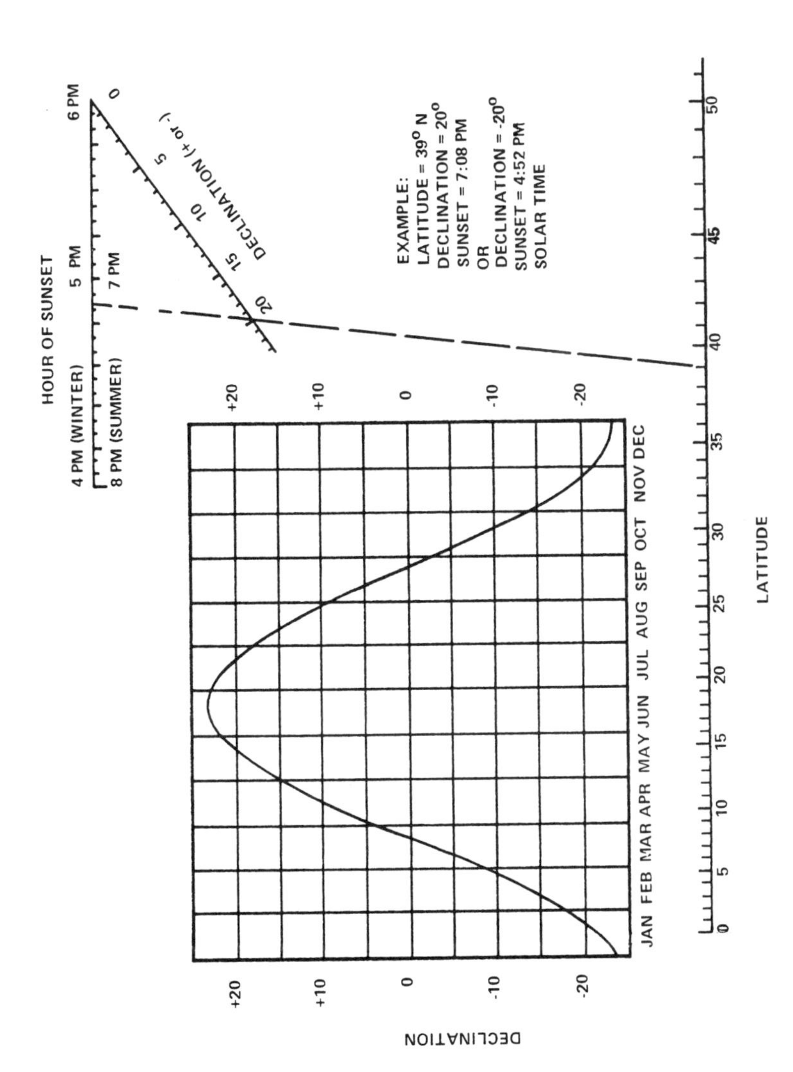


**Figure 105.** Nomogram to determine $\delta$ and hour of sunrise/sunset in solar time [Whillier 1965].

$$\delta = 0.36 + 22.94 - 0.37 + 0.15 - 0.16 = 22.92°$$

Interpolating from Table XV yields $\delta = 22.91$.

$$\phi = 38° 51' = 38 + 51/60 \text{ degrees} = 38.85°$$

So, from Equation 138,

$$\theta = \cos^{-1}[\cos(38.85)\cos(22.92)\cos(-63.5) + \sin(38.85)\sin(22.92)]$$

$$= \cos^{-1}[0.320 + 0.244] = 55.64° = 55° 39'$$

And from Equation 144,

$$\gamma = \cos^{-1}[(\sin(22.92) - \sin(38.85)\cos(55.64))/(\cos(38.85)\sin(55.64))]$$

$$= \cos^{-1}[(0.389 - 0.354)/0.643] = 86.88° = 86° 53'$$

## TERRESTRIAL SOLAR RADIATION

The solar radiation intensity reaching the earth varies from about 75% of the solar constant to zero. The solar radiation from the sun interacts with the atmosphere causing some of it to be reflected by clouds and scattered by dust. The ozone layer in the upper atmosphere absorbs most of the ultraviolet radiation. Much of the infrared spectrum is absorbed by carbon dioxide, water vapor, and other gases in the earth's atmosphere.

The solar radiation reaching the earth is characterized as direct and diffuse. Direct radiation is that solar radiation which reaches us directly from the sun without being scattered or reflected. The diffuse radiation has been scattered or reflected at least once. On a clear day, the solar radiation reaching the earth is typically about 90% direct and 10% diffuse. On cloudy days, all of the solar radiation reaching the ground may be diffuse. Figure 106 illustrates the various interactions of solar energy inside the earth's atmosphere.

The scattering of solar radiation in the atmosphere is a wavelength-dependent phenomenon, with shorter wavelength radiation tending to be scattered more frequently by suspended atmospheric particulates than longer wavelengths. The selective reduction of the shorter wavelength components of the solar spectrum is illustrated in Figure 107 which shows measured values of direct (nonscattered) solar radiation intensity

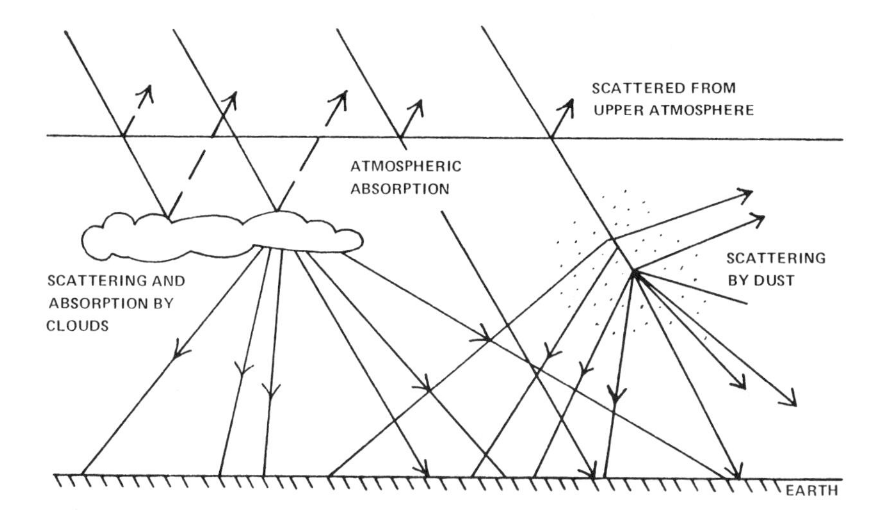


**Figure 106.** Interactions of solar radiation with the earth's atmosphere.

as a function of wavelength from 0.32 to 0.88 $\mu$m. These measurements were made in Golden, Colorado, on October 21, 1980. The air mass 1.57 data in this figure were taken when the sun was near its highest point in the sky. The air mass 6.08 data were taken with the sun much lower in the sky, and the air mass 13.13 data represent the spectrum of direct solar radiation near sunset. The air mass refers to the length of passage of the solar radiation through the atmosphere as compared with the length traversed if the sun were directly overhead. The air mass is related to the air mass with the sun directly overhead ($m = m_o$ at $\theta = 0$) by

$$m \simeq m_o / \cos\theta \tag{148}$$

Figure 108 illustrates solar spectral measurements for 5 air mass values over the range of 0.3 to 2.3 $\mu$m, covering both the visible and near infrared regions of the spectrum. The absorption bands in the near infrared due to water vapor and carbon dioxide in the atmosphere are quite prominent. It is also seen that, except for these absorption bands, the shorter wavelength radiation tends to be absorbed and scattered more strongly than the longer wavelength radiation. This, of course, is the reason that the setting sun appears red and the sky blue.

Since the shorter wavelength radiation is scattered preferentially, the diffuse component of solar radiation tends to consist primarily of shorter wavelength radiation toward the blue end of the spectrum. Figure 109

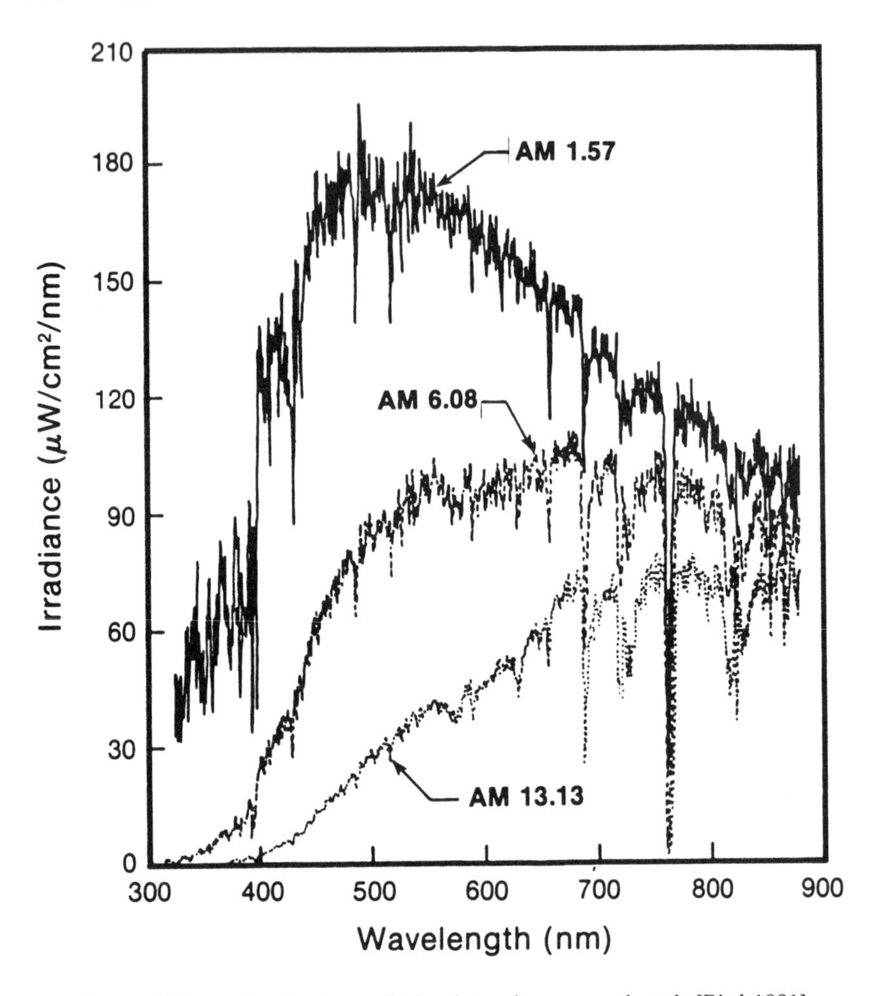


**Figure 107.** Direct solar radiation intensity vs wavelength [Bird 1981].

shows the global solar radiation intensity in Golden, Colorado, as well as the diffuse component. The global value is the sum of both the diffuse and the direct components.

The major factor depleting the solar radiation in the atmosphere is usually cloudiness. Various attempts have been made, beginning with Ångstrom [1924], to estimate the effect of cloudiness on the long-term value of solar radiation received. Ångstrom assumed the following linear relationship:

$$\bar{H} = \bar{H}'\left(a' + b'\frac{S}{S_o}\right) \tag{149}$$

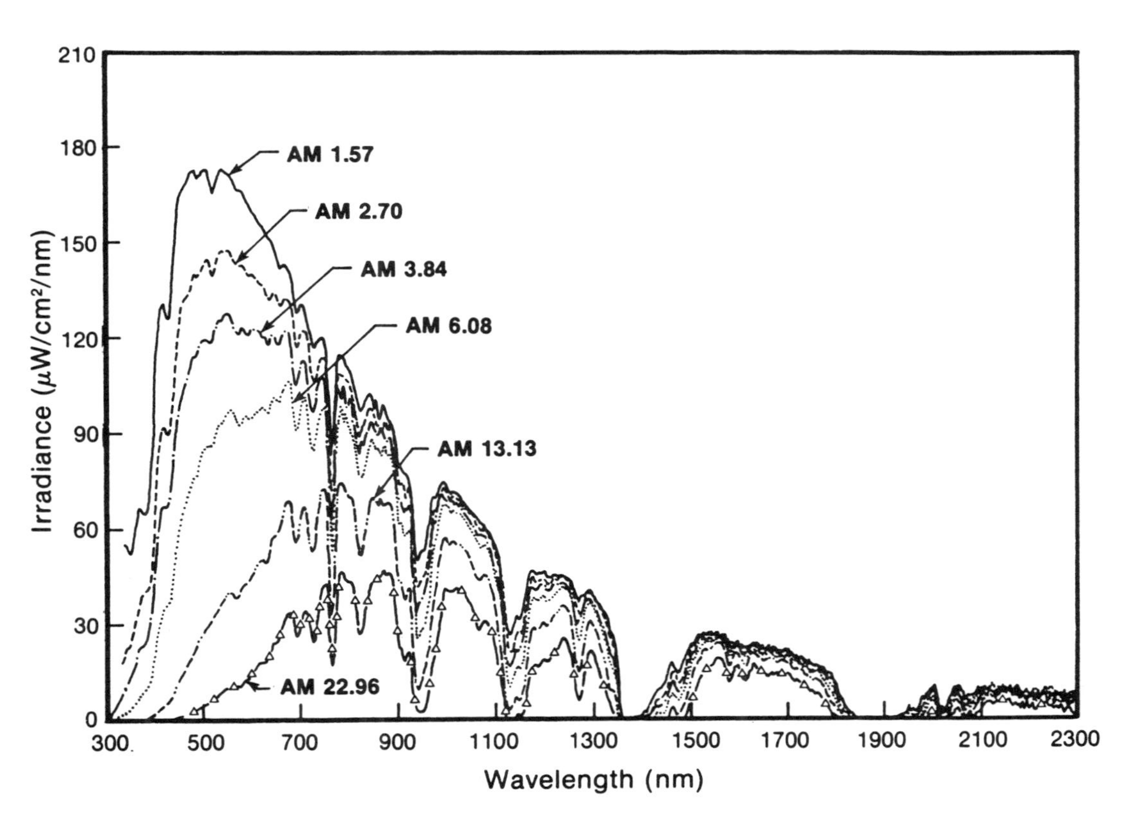


**Figure 108.** Terrestrial solar spectrum vs air mass [Bird 1981].

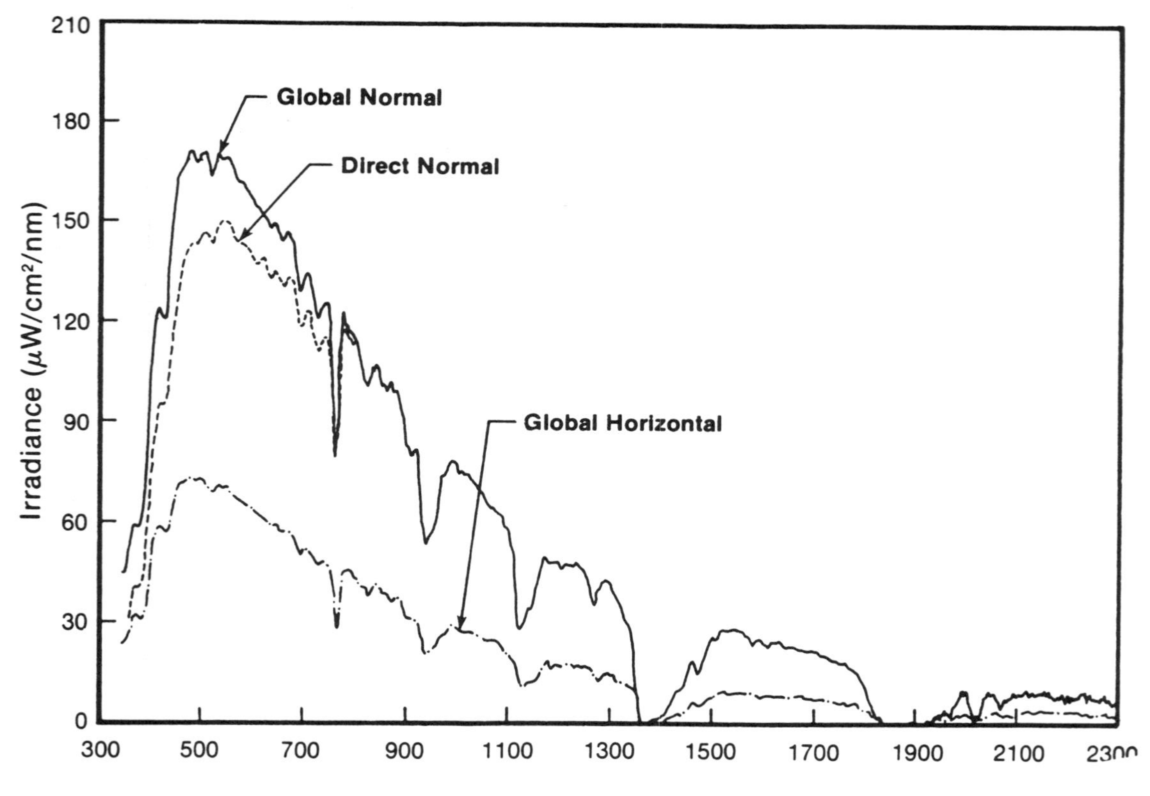


**Figure 109.** Spectrum of solar radiation in Golden, Colorado [Bird 1981].

where $\bar{H}$ = average horizontal solar radiation received during a certain period
$\bar{H}'$ = clear day horizontal solar radiation for the same period
$S$ = average daily hours of bright sunshine for the same period
$S_o$ = maximum daily hours of bright sunshine for the same period
$a', b'$ = constants used with clear day horizontal solar radiation

Table XVI lists monthly values of a′ and b′ for several locations around the world. $\bar{H}'$ may be obtained from Figure 110, and $S_o$ is found by summing the day length (Equation 147) for each day in the period. If the period is a month, then

$$S_o = (\overline{DL})N \tag{150}$$

**Table XVI. Some Values of a′ and b′**

| Country (City) | | Jan | Feb | Mar | Apr | May | Jun | Jul | Aug | Sep | Oct | Nov | Dec | Annual Mean |
|---|---|---|---|---|---|---|---|---|---|---|---|---|---|---|
| Australia | | | | | | | | | | | | | | |
| (Aspendale) | a′= | .36 | .36 | .36 | .40 | .40 | .40 | .40 | .40 | .40 | .36 | .36 | .36 | .38 |
| | b′= | .64 | .64 | .64 | .60 | .60 | .60 | .60 | .60 | .60 | .64 | .64 | .64 | .62 |
| (Deniliquin) | a′= | .32 | .32 | .32 | .37 | .37 | .37 | .37 | .37 | .37 | .32 | .32 | .32 | .345 |
| | b′= | .68 | .68 | .63 | .63 | .63 | .63 | .63 | .63 | .63 | .68 | .68 | .68 | .655 |
| Greece | | | | | | | | | | | | | | |
| (Athens) | a′= | .39 | .39 | .29 | .37 | .34 | .29 | .29 | .25 | .32 | .30 | .41 | .44 | .34 |
| | b′= | .60 | .67 | .65 | .68 | .63 | .63 | .63 | .63 | .58 | .60 | .64 | .58 | .63 |
| India | | | | | | | | | | | | | | |
| (Calcutta) | a′= | .32 | .32 | .32 | .32 | .32 | .32 | .35 | .35 | .35 | .32 | .32 | .32 | .33 |
| | b′= | .49 | .49 | .49 | .49 | .49 | .49 | .54 | .54 | .54 | .49 | .49 | .49 | .48 |
| (Delhi) | a′= | .47 | .47 | .47 | .47 | .47 | .47 | .29 | .29 | .29 | .47 | .47 | .47 | .38 |
| | b′= | .45 | .45 | .45 | .45 | .45 | .45 | .71 | .71 | .71 | .45 | .45 | .45 | .57 |
| (Madras) | a′= | .37 | .37 | .37 | .37 | .37 | .37 | .39 | .39 | .39 | .37 | .37 | .37 | .37 |
| | b′= | .49 | .49 | .49 | .49 | .49 | .49 | .49 | .49 | .49 | .49 | .49 | .49 | .49 |
| (Poona) | a′= | .42 | .42 | .42 | .42 | .42 | .42 | .42 | .42 | .42 | .42 | .42 | .42 | .42 |
| | b′= | .52 | .52 | .52 | .52 | .52 | .52 | .61 | .61 | .61 | .52 | .52 | .52 | .54 |
| Indonesia | | | | | | | | | | | | | | |
| (Bandung) | a′= | .40 | .40 | .37 | .34 | .32 | .29 | .29 | .29 | .32 | .35 | .38 | .40 | .35 |
| | b′= | .60 | .60 | .63 | .66 | .68 | .71 | .71 | .71 | .68 | .65 | .62 | .60 | .65 |
| Netherlands | | | | | | | | | | | | | | |
| (DeBilt) | a′= | .23 | .30 | .31 | .31 | .32 | .33 | .31 | .32 | .31 | .27 | .28 | .24 | .32 |
| | b′= | .77 | .70 | .69 | .69 | .18 | .67 | .69 | .68 | .69 | .73 | .72 | .76 | .68 |
| Sweden | | | | | | | | | | | | | | |
| (Stockholm) | a′= | .27 | .27 | .25 | .25 | .25 | .23 | .23 | .23 | .25 | .25 | .25 | .27 | .25 |
| | b′= | .73 | .73 | .75 | .75 | .75 | .77 | .77 | .77 | .75 | .75 | .75 | .73 | .75 |

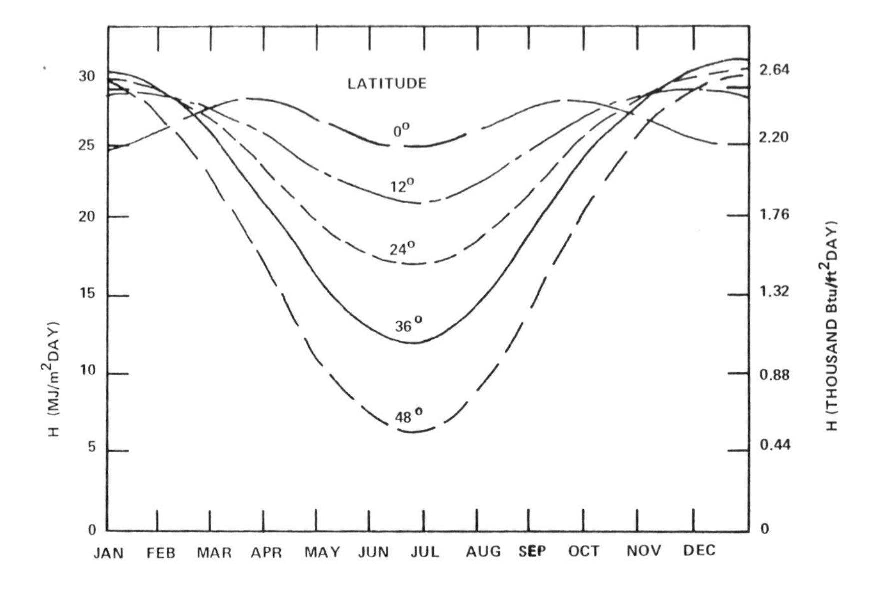


**Figure 110.** Clear day horizontal solar radiation vs latitude.

where $\overline{DL}$ = average day length for the month
$N$ = number of days in the month

The day length may also be found from Figure 105 as the length of time from sunrise to sunset.

Page [1961,1975] modified this method by basing it on extraterrestrial radiation on a horizontal surface:

$$\bar{H} = \overline{H_o}\left(a + b\,\frac{S}{S_o}\right) \tag{151}$$

where $\overline{H_o}$ = horizontal extraterrestrial radiation for the same period and location in question
$a, b$ = constants used with horizontal extraterrestrial radiation, where:

$$a = \frac{\bar{H}'}{\overline{H_o}}\,a' \quad \text{and} \quad b = \frac{\bar{H}'}{\overline{H_o}}\,b' \tag{152}$$

Some annual values of a and b are given in Table XVII. $\overline{H_o}$ can be obtained from Figure 111 or 112. Lof et al. [1966] developed Table XVI, as suggested by Kimball [1954]. Figures 111 and 112 depict extraterrestrial

**Table XVII. Constants a and b and Average Percent Possible Sunshine $\bar{S}/\bar{S}_0$ for Various Locations and Climate Types [Lof 1966]**

| Location | Type of Climate | a | b | $\bar{S}/\bar{S}_0$ |
|---|---|---|---|---|
| Miami, FL | Tropical rainy, winter dry | 0.42 | 0.22 | 0.65 |
| Honolulu, HI | Tropical rainy, no dry season | 0.14 | 0.73 | 0.65 |
| Stanleyville, Congo | Tropical rainy, no dry season | 0.28 | 0.39 | 0.48 |
| Poona, India | Tropical rainy, no dry season | 0.30 | 0.51 | 0.37 |
| Malange, Angola | Tropical rainy, winter dry | 0.34 | 0.34 | 0.58 |
| Ely, NV | Dry, arid (desert) | 0.54 | 0.18 | 0.77 |
| Tamanrasset, Sahara | Dry, arid (desert) | 0.30 | 0.43 | 0.83 |
| El Paso, TX | Dry, arid (desert) | 0.54 | 0.20 | 0.84 |
| Albuquerque, NM | Dry, arid (desert) | 0.41 | 0.37 | 0.78 |
| Brownsville, TX | Dry, semiarid (steppe) | 0.35 | 0.31 | 0.62 |
| Charleston, SC | Humid mesothermal, no dry season | 0.48 | 0.09 | 0.67 |
| Atlanta, GA | Humid mesothermal, no dry season | 0.38 | 0.26 | 0.59 |
| Buenos Aires, Argentina | Humid mesothermal, no dry season | 0.26 | 0.50 | 0.59 |
| Hamburg, Germany | Humid mesothermal, no dry season | 0.22 | 0.57 | 0.36 |
| Nice, France | Humid mesothermal, dry summer | 0.17 | 0.63 | 0.61 |
| Madison, WI | Humid continental, no dry season | 0.30 | 0.34 | 0.58 |
| Blue Hill, MA | Humid continental, no dry season | 0.22 | 0.50 | 0.52 |
| Dairen, Manchuria | Humid continental, dry winter | 0.36 | 0.23 | 0.67 |

daily solar radiation on a horizontal surface for the middle of each month as a function of latitude.

## SOLAR RADIATION ESTIMATION TECHNIQUES

One of the earlier efforts numerically to model solar radiation [Liu and Jordan 1960] considers the absorption and scattering processes in the atmosphere to arrive at estimates of global, direct and diffuse radiation. They defined the transmission coefficient for direct solar radiation $\tau_D$ to be the ratio of the intensity of the direct component reaching the earth to the intensity just outside the earth's atmosphere, and the transmission coefficient for diffuse radiation on a horizontal surface $\tau_{dh}$ to be the ratio of the intensity of diffuse radiation on a horizontal surface on the earth to the intensity of diffuse radiation on a parallel surface just outside the earth's atmosphere. $\tau_D$ is independent of surface orientation, as long as

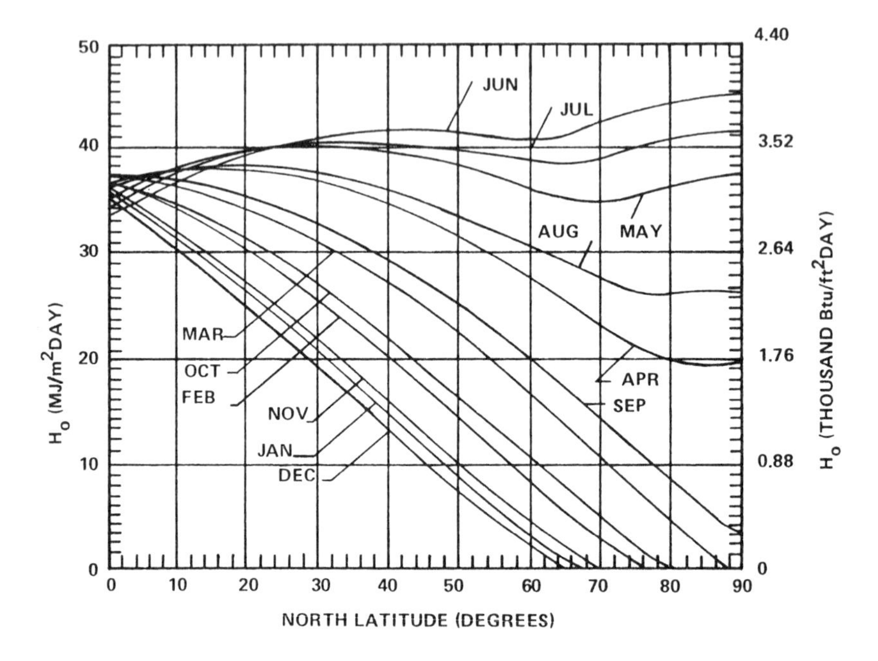


**Figure 111.** Extraterrestrial solar radiation vs north latitude at midmonth.

the surface does not face away from the sun, and is defined in the normal manner for a transmission coefficient. $\tau_{dh}$ is merely the ratio of the intensity of diffuse radiation on a horizontal surface on the ground to the total solar intensity outside the atmosphere. These transmission coefficients depend on the altitude of the sun, the amount of water vapor and dust in the atmosphere, cloudiness, and other factors such as man-made air pollution. In the absence of air pollution, daily variations in these coefficients at a fixed solar altitude are primarily due to changes in the water vapor content of the atmosphere.

The four upper curves in Figure 113 are calculated relationships between $\tau_D$ and $\tau_{dh}$ using $\tau$ values computed by Kimball [1948] for air masses 1 through 4 for a cloudless and dust-free atmosphere [Liu 1960]; these curves represent an upper limit to the intensity of diffuse radiation at ground level. The lower curve is the best fit to experimental data [Moore 1920] taken at Hump Mountain, NC (latitude 36° 08′ N, elevation 4800 ft), for which $\tau_{dh} = 0.271 - 0.2939\tau_D$, which may be considered independent of air mass (or solar altitude) for altitude angles greater than about 10°. Liu and Jordan [1960] showed that this relationship is also valid for Minneapolis, Minnesota (Figure 114) and other locations.

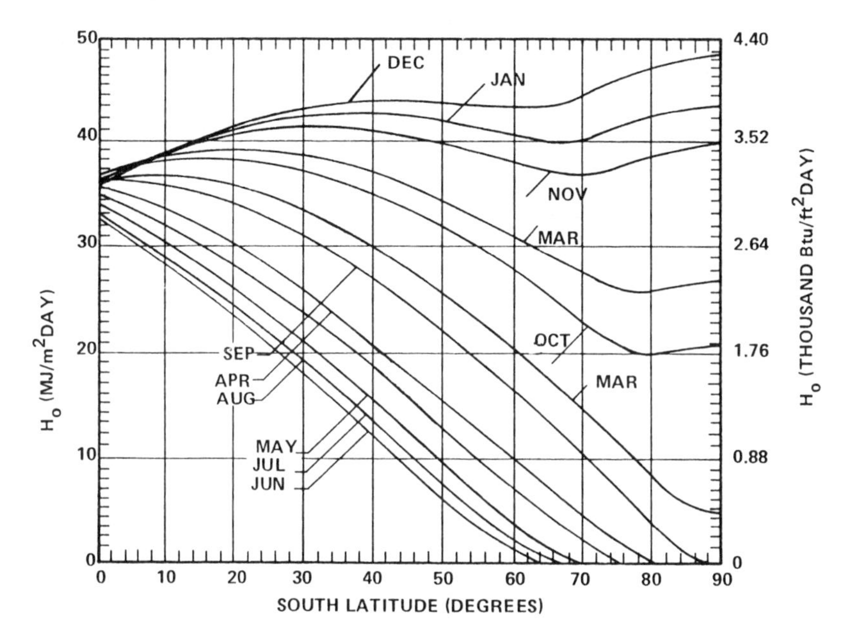


**Figure 112.** Extraterrestrial solar radiation vs south latitude at midmonth.

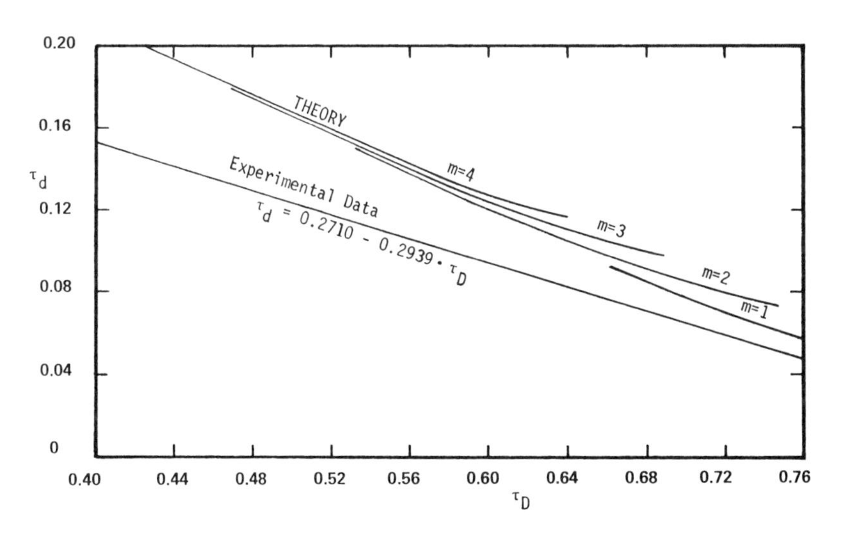


**Figure 113.** Theoretical and experimental correlation between diffuse and direct solar radiation on a horizontal surface for a cloudless atmosphere at 4800 ft elevation [Liu 1960].

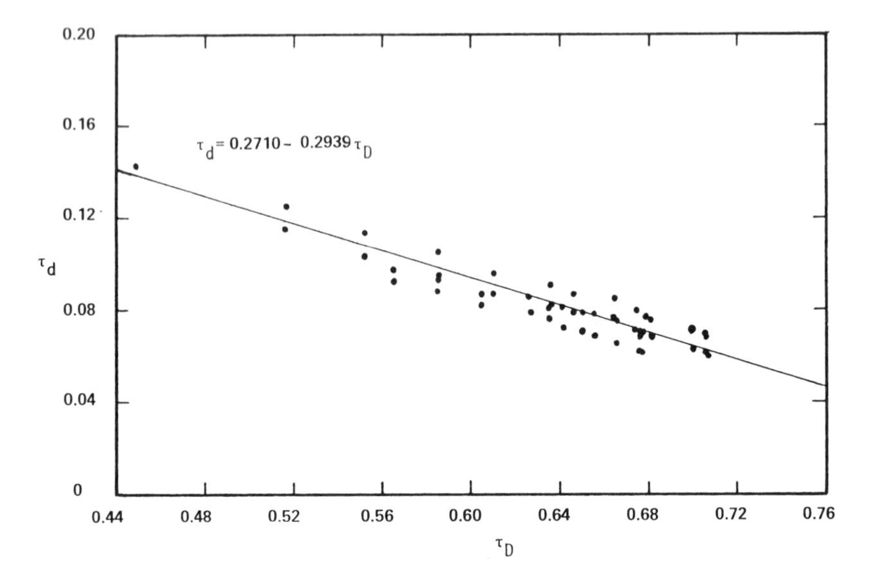


**Figure 114.** Empirical relation between diffuse and direct radiation on a horizontal surface [Liu 1960].

Since $\tau_{dh} + \tau_D = \tau_{Th}$ (the ratio of the total radiation on a horizontal surface on the ground to that on a parallel surface just outside the earth's atmosphere), the expression becomes

$$\tau_{dh} = 0.338 - 0.4151 \times \tau_{Th} \tag{153}$$

This provides a means of estimating $\tau_{dh}$ if $\tau_{Th}$ is known.

One cannot predict the instantaneous relationship between $\tau_{dh}$ and $\tau_{Th}$ (or $\tau_D$) during partly cloudy or cloudy weather, since the values are extremely variable. However, if one compares the global solar radiation received during a whole day to the diffuse radiation received during that day, the data for the different days of a month tend to fall on a smooth curve (Figure 115).

The day-to-day variation of daily global radiation and the daily diffuse radiation received on a horizontal surface is primarily due to the day-to-day variation of cloudiness. The differences in radiation received from month to month result from differences in weather and from the monthly differences in the horizontal component of extraterrestrial solar radiation at that location. Thus, by dividing the daily global H and diffuse D radiation on a horizontal surface by the horizontal component of the extraterrestrial daily radiation, $H_o$ (Figure 116), a correlation is found

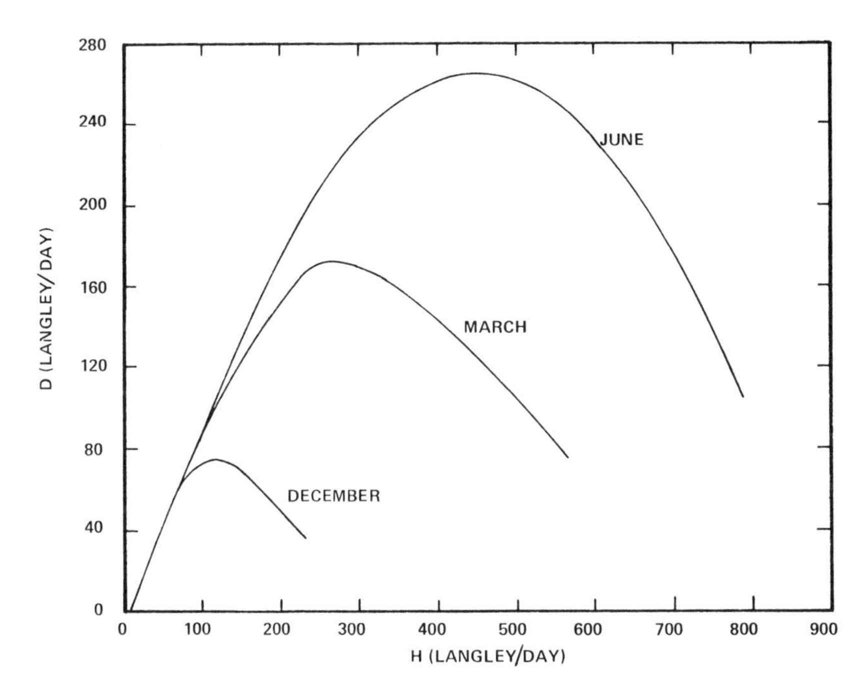


**Figure 115.** Daily diffuse vs daily total radiation [Liu 1960]. (Multiply by 3.6866 to convert Langleys to Btu/ft$^2$, or by 41,840 to convert Langleys to Joules/m$^2$.)

between H and D which is valid for all months (Figure 117). The normalized parameters $K_d$ and $K_T$ (the cloudiness index) are:

$$K_d = \frac{D}{H_o} \quad \text{and} \quad K_T = \frac{H}{H_o} \tag{154}$$

where $H_o$ may be taken from Figures 111, 112 or 116 or Table XVIII or calculated from

$$H_o = \frac{24}{\pi} fI_{sc}[\cos\phi\cos\delta\sin\omega_s + (\pi/180)\omega_s\sin\phi\sin\delta] \tag{155}$$

where f is the ratio of the solar radiation intensity at normal incidence outside the atmosphere to the solar constant (Figure 101), $I_{sc}$ is the solar constant, $\phi$ is the latitude, $\delta$ is the declination, and $\omega_s$ is the hour angle at which the sun sets in the west, as calculated from Equation 146.

As seen from Figure 117, the daily horizontal diffuse radiation is higher for partly cloudy or lightly overcast days than on either clear days

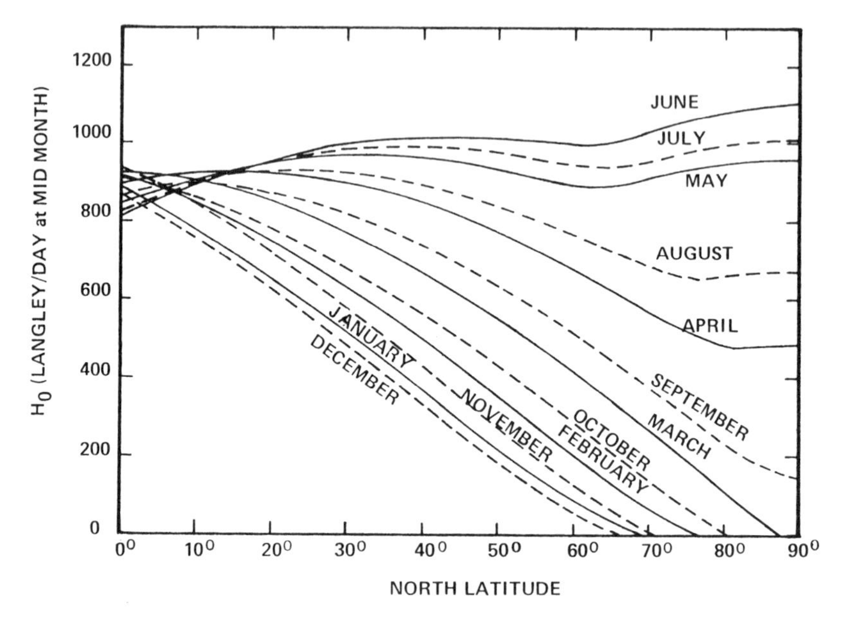


**Figure 116.** Extraterrestrial daily solar radiation on a horizontal surface in Langleys/day at midmonth.

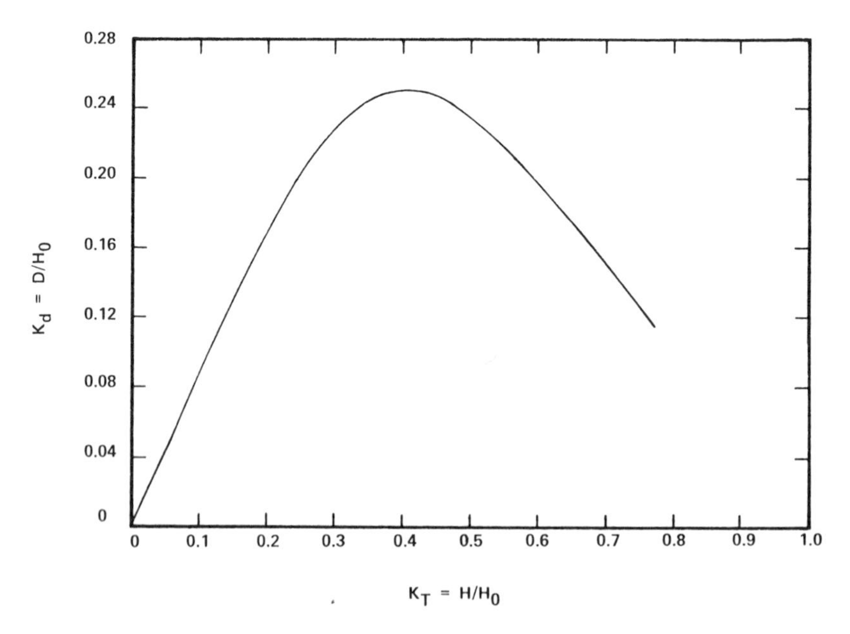


**Figure 117.** $K_d$ vs cloudiness index $K_T$ [Liu 1960].

Table XVIII. Monthly Average Daily Extraterrestrial Radiation ($\bar{H}_o$)

(Btu/ft$^2$) and (kJ/m$^2$)

| Lat | Jan | Feb | Mar | Apr | May | Jun | Jul | Aug | Sep | Oct | Nov | Dec |
|---|---|---|---|---|---|---|---|---|---|---|---|---|
| 20° | 2,349 | 2,676 | 3,024 | 3,307 | 3,428 | 3,451 | 3,425 | 3,338 | 3,112 | 2,768 | 2,425 | 2,250 |
| | 26,644 | 30,359 | 34,307 | 37,515 | 38,884 | 39,144 | 38,893 | 37,864 | 35,300 | 31,402 | 27,512 | 25,519 |
| 25° | 2,107 | 2,478 | 2,896 | 3,271 | 3,496 | 3,530 | 3,491 | 3,335 | 3,018 | 2,593 | 2,196 | 1,998 |
| | 23,902 | 28,115 | 32,848 | 37,111 | 39,356 | 40,046 | 39,606 | 37,832 | 34,238 | 29,413 | 24,909 | 22,669 |
| 30° | 1,854 | 2,264 | 2,745 | 3,212 | 3,488 | 3,588 | 3,532 | 3,307 | 2,902 | 2,399 | 1,953 | 1,738 |
| | 21,034 | 25,679 | 31,141 | 36,436 | 39,569 | 40,706 | 40,071 | 37,534 | 32,917 | 27,213 | 22,161 | 19,714 |
| 35° | 1,593 | 2,034 | 2,574 | 3,129 | 3,489 | 3,625 | 3,551 | 3,259 | 2,763 | 2,188 | 1,701 | 1,471 |
| | 18,069 | 23,072 | 29,200 | 35,497 | 39,530 | 41,129 | 40,292 | 36,976 | 31,348 | 24,820 | 19,296 | 16,687 |
| 40° | 1,326 | 1,791 | 2,384 | 3,024 | 3,460 | 3,643 | 3,551 | 3,188 | 2,604 | 1,962 | 1,441 | 1,201 |
| | 15,043 | 20,319 | 27,040 | 34,303 | 39,247 | 41,328 | 40,281 | 36,166 | 29,542 | 22,255 | 16,344 | 13,626 |
| 45° | 1,058 | 1,538 | 2,175 | 2,897 | 3,415 | 3,643 | 3,531 | 3,096 | 2,425 | 1,723 | 1,176 | 933 |
| | 11,998 | 17,448 | 24,677 | 32,869 | 38,737 | 41,322 | 40,055 | 35,118 | 27,515 | 19,541 | 13,344 | 10,579 |
| 50° | 792 | 1,277 | 1,951 | 2,751 | 3,352 | 3,627 | 3,495 | 2,984 | 2,229 | 1,472 | 912 | 670 |
| | 8,987 | 14,490 | 22,131 | 31,209 | 38,025 | 41,147 | 39,644 | 33,851 | 25,283 | 16,705 | 10,342 | 7,605 |
| 55° | 536 | 1,013 | 1,712 | 2,587 | 3,275 | 3,602 | 3,447 | 2,855 | 2,015 | 1,214 | 652 | 422 |
| | 6,082 | 11,486 | 19,423 | 29,345 | 37,152 | 40,863 | 39,100 | 32,391 | 22,863 | 13,778 | 7,396 | 4,791 |
| 60° | 299 | 748 | 1,461 | 2,407 | 3,190 | 3,578 | 3,395 | 2,713 | 1,787 | 952 | 405 | 201 |
| | 3,395 | 8,486 | 16,576 | 27,308 | 36,188 | 40,584 | 38,513 | 30,779 | 20,277 | 10,798 | 4,598 | 2,277 |

($K_T \simeq 0.75$) or heavily overcast days ($K_T < 0.1$). Figure 117 was developed using data from Blue Hill, Massachusetts, at a latitude of 42°13′N, but may be used for estimating the daily diffuse solar radiation at other locations between latitudes of about 25 and 60°. Figure 118 is a plot of D/H as a function of $H/H_o$ (or $K_T$).

Correlations relating the average hourly to the daily total and diffuse radiation are given in Figures 119 and 120. These relationships, originally developed by Liu and Jordan, provide a simple means of estimating average daily values of diffuse, direct (=global − diffuse), and global solar radiation on a horizontal surface if monthly values of total daily global horizontal radiation are known. Table XIX lists long-term average values of daily global horizontal solar radiation by month for various locations around the United States and Canada.

## Example 3: Calculating Extraterrestrial Daily Solar Radiation

Calculate the extraterrestrial daily horizontal solar radiation intensity at a latitude of 38° 51′ and longitude of 77° (Washington, DC) on July 4. Compare with Figures 111 and 116.

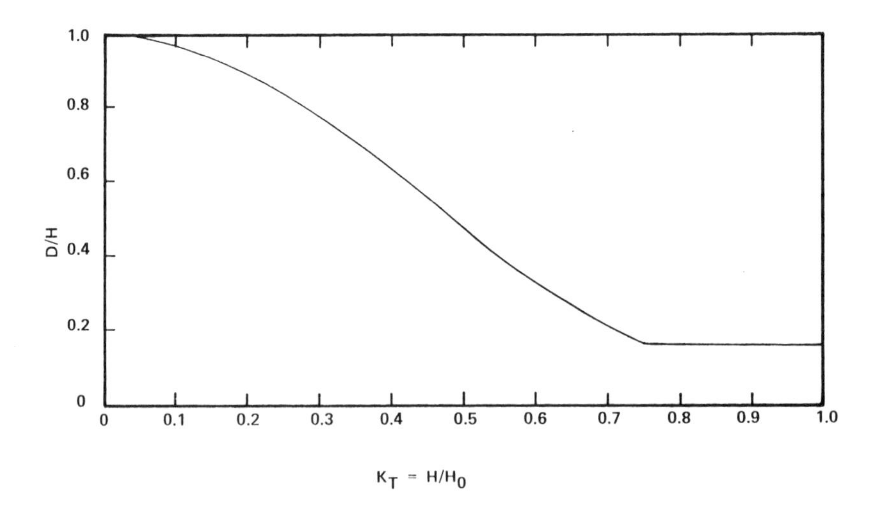


**Figure 118.** Ratio of daily diffuse to global horizontal radiation vs $K_T$ [Liu 1960].

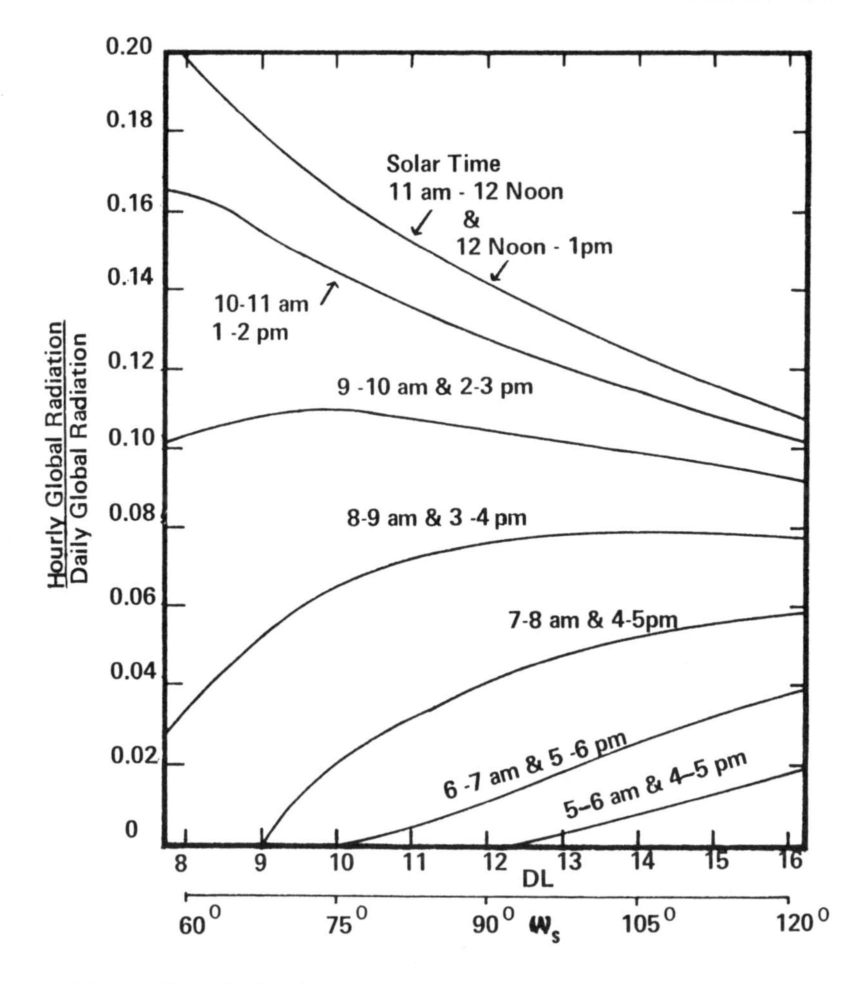


**Figure 119.** Ratio of hourly total to daily total radiation [Liu 1960].

*Solution*

From Examples 1 and 2, we have

$$\delta = \text{declination} = 22.92°$$

$$\phi = \text{latitude} = 38.85°$$

The sunset hour angle $\omega_s$ is found from Equation 146 to be

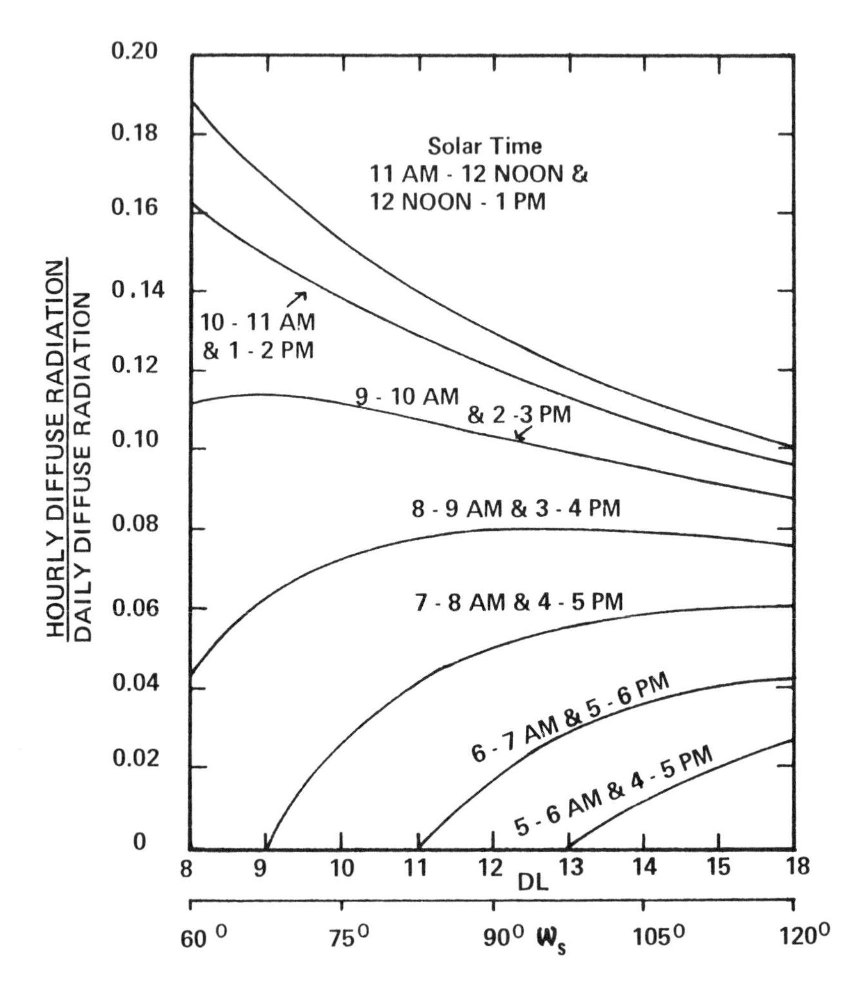


**Figure 120.** Ratio of hourly diffuse to daily diffuse radiation [Liu 1960].

$$\omega_s = \cos^{-1}[-\tan(38.85)\tan(22.92)] = 109.9°$$

Figure 105 yields a value of 110°.

The solar constant correction factor f is given by Equation 137

$$f = 1 + 0.034\cos[0.9863(180)] = 0.966$$

Interpolating Table XV yields f = 0.9668. Now $H_o$ can be calculated from Equation 155

**Table XIX. Monthly Average Daily Global Radiation on a Horizontal Surface ($\bar{H}$) in Btu/ft$^2$-day and Monthly Average Cloudiness Index, $\overline{K_T}$ [Liu 1963] (To convert Btu/ft$^2$-day to kJ/m$^2$-day, multiply by 11.35653)**

| Latitude; Elevation | Jan | Feb | Mar | Apr | May | Jun | Jul | Aug | Sep | Oct | Nov | Dec |
|---|---|---|---|---|---|---|---|---|---|---|---|---|
| Albuquerque, NM | 1151 | 1454 | 1925 | 2344 | 2561 | 2758 | 2561 | 2388 | 2120 | 1640 | 1274 | 1052 |
| $\phi = 35°3'$; 5314 ft | 0.704 | 0.691 | 0.719 | 0.722 | 0.713 | 0.737 | 0.695 | 0.708 | 0.728 | 0.711 | 0.684 | 0.704 |
| Annette I., AK | 237 | 428 | 883 | 1357 | 1635 | 1639 | 1632 | 1269 | 962 | 455 | 220 | 152 |
| $\phi = 55°2'$; 110 ft | 0.427 | 0.415 | 0.492 | 0.507 | 0.484 | 0.441 | 0.454 | 0.427 | 0.449 | 0.347 | 0.304 | 0.361 |
| Apalachicola, FL | 1107 | 1378 | 1654 | 2041 | 2269 | 2196 | 1979 | 1913 | 1703 | 1545 | 1243 | 982 |
| $\phi = 29°45'$; 35 ft | 0.577 | 0.584 | 0.576 | 0.612 | 0.630 | 0.594 | 0.542 | 0.558 | 0.559 | 0.608 | 0.574 | 0.543 |
| Astoria, OR | 338 | 607 | 1009 | 1402 | 1839 | 1754 | 2008 | 1721 | 1323 | 780 | 414 | 295 |
| $\phi = 46°12'$; 8 ft | 0.330 | 0.397 | 0.454 | 0.471 | 0.524 | 0.466 | 0.551 | 0.538 | 0.526 | 0.435 | 0.336 | 0.332 |
| Atlanta, GA | 848 | 1080 | 1427 | 1807 | 2018 | 2103 | 2003 | 1898 | 1519 | 1291 | 998 | 752 |
| $\phi = 33°39'$; 976 ft | 0.493 | 0.496 | 0.522 | 0.551 | 0.561 | 0.564 | 0.545 | 0.559 | 0.515 | 0.543 | 0.510 | 0.474 |
| Barrow, AK | 13 | 143 | 713 | 1492 | 1883 | 2055 | 1602 | 954 | 428 | 152 | 23 | 3 |
| $\phi = 71°20'$; 22 ft | 0.3 | 0.776 | 0.773 | 0.726 | 0.553 | 0.533 | 0.448 | 0.337 | 0.315 | 0.35 | 0.3 | 0.3 |
| Bismarck, ND | 587 | 934 | 1328 | 1668 | 2056 | 2174 | 2306 | 1929 | 1441 | 1018 | 600 | 464 |
| $\phi = 46°47'$; 1660 ft | 0.594 | 0.628 | 0.605 | 0.565 | 0.588 | 0.579 | 0.634 | 0.606 | 0.581 | 0.584 | 0.510 | 0.547 |
| Blue Hill, MA | 555 | 797 | 1144 | 1438 | 1776 | 1944 | 1882 | 1622 | 1314 | 941 | 592 | 482 |
| $\phi = 42°13'$; 629 ft | 0.445 | 0.458 | 0.477 | 0.464 | 0.501 | 0.516 | 0.513 | 0.495 | 0.492 | 0.472 | 0.406 | 0.436 |
| Boise, ID | 519 | 885 | 1280 | 1814 | 2189 | 2377 | 2500 | 2149 | 1718 | 1128 | 679 | 457 |
| $\phi = 43°34'$; 2844 ft | 0.446 | 0.533 | 0.548 | 0.594 | 0.619 | 0.631 | 0.684 | 0.660 | 0.656 | 0.588 | 0.494 | 0.442 |
| Boston, MA | 506 | 738 | 1067 | 1355 | 1769 | 1864 | 1861 | 1570 | 1268 | 897 | 636 | 443 |
| $\phi = 42°22'$; 29 ft | 0.410 | 0.426 | 0.445 | 0.438 | 0.499 | 0.495 | 0.507 | 0.480 | 0.477 | 0.453 | 0.372 | 0.400 |
| Brownsville, TX | 1106 | 1263 | 1506 | 1714 | 2092 | 2289 | 2345 | 2124 | 1775 | 1536 | 1105 | 982 |
| $\phi = 25°55'$; 20 ft | 0.517 | 0.500 | 0.505 | 0.509 | 0.584 | 0.627 | 0.650 | 0.617 | 0.566 | 0.570 | 0.468 | 0.488 |

Table XIX, continued

| Latitude, Elevation | Jan | Feb | Mar | Apr | May | June | Jul | Aug | Sep | Oct | Nov | Dec |
|---|---|---|---|---|---|---|---|---|---|---|---|---|
| Caribou, ME | 497 | 862 | 1360 | 1496 | 1780 | 1780 | 1898 | 1676 | 1255 | 793 | 416 | 399 |
| $\phi = 46°52'$; 628 ft | 0.504 | 0.579 | 0.619 | 0.507 | 0.509 | 0.473 | 0.522 | 0.527 | 0.506 | 0.455 | 0.352 | 0.470 |
| Charleston, SC | 946 | 1153 | 1352 | 1919 | 2063 | 2113 | 1649 | 1934 | 1557 | 1332 | 1074 | 952 |
| $\phi = 32°54'$; 46 ft | 0.541 | 0.521 | 0.491 | 0.584 | 0.574 | 0.567 | 0.454 | 0.569 | 0.525 | 0.554 | 0.539 | 0.586 |
| Cleveland, OH | 467 | 682 | 1207 | 1444 | 1928 | 2103 | 2094 | 1841 | 1410 | 997 | 527 | 427 |
| $\phi = 41°24'$; 805 ft | 0.361 | 0.383 | 0.497 | 0.464 | 0.543 | 0.559 | 0.571 | 0.559 | 0.524 | 0.491 | 0.351 | 0.371 |
| Columbia, MO | 651 | 941 | 1316 | 1631 | 2000 | 2129 | 2149 | 1953 | 1690 | 1203 | 840 | 590 |
| $\phi = 38°58'$; 785 ft | 0.458 | 0.492 | 0.520 | 0.514 | 0.559 | 0.566 | 0.585 | 0.588 | 0.606 | 0.562 | 0.510 | 0.457 |
| Davis, CA | 599 | 945 | 1504 | 1959 | 2369 | 2619 | 2566 | 2288 | 1857 | 1289 | 796 | 551 |
| $\phi = 38°33'$; 51 ft | 0.416 | 0.490 | 0.591 | 0.617 | 0.662 | 0.697 | 0.697 | 0.687 | 0.664 | 0.598 | 0.477 | 0.421 |
| Dodge City, KS | 953 | 1186 | 1566 | 1976 | 2127 | 2460 | 2401 | 2211 | 1842 | 1421 | 1065 | 874 |
| $\phi = 37°46'$; 2592 ft | 0.639 | 0.598 | 0.606 | 0.618 | 0.594 | 0.655 | 0.652 | 0.663 | 0.654 | 0.650 | 0.625 | 0.652 |
| East Lansing, MI | 426 | 739 | 1086 | 1250 | 1733 | 1914 | 1885 | 1628 | 1303 | 892 | 473 | 380 |
| $\phi = 42°44'$; 856 ft | 0.35 | 0.431 | 0.456 | 0.406 | 0.489 | 0.508 | 0.514 | 0.498 | 0.493 | 0.456 | 0.333 | 0.349 |
| East Wareham, MA | 504 | 762 | 1132 | 1393 | 1705 | 1958 | 1874 | 1607 | 1364 | 997 | 636 | 521 |
| $\phi = 41°46'$; 18 ft | 0.398 | 0.431 | 0.469 | 0.449 | 0.480 | 0.520 | 0.511 | 0.489 | 0.508 | 0.496 | 0.431 | 0.461 |
| Edmonton, Alberta | 332 | 652 | 1165 | 1542 | 1900 | 1914 | 1965 | 1528 | 1113 | 704 | 414 | 245 |
| $\phi = 53°35'$; 2219 ft | 0.529 | 0.585 | 0.624 | 0.504 | 0.558 | 0.514 | 0.549 | 0.506 | 0.506 | 0.504 | 0.510 | 0.492 |
| El Paso, TX | 1248 | 1613 | 2049 | 2447 | 2673 | 2731 | 2391 | 2351 | 2078 | 1705 | 1325 | 1052 |
| $\phi = 31°48'$; 3916 ft | 0.686 | 0.714 | 0.730 | 0.741 | 0.743 | 0.733 | 0.652 | 0.669 | 0.693 | 0.695 | 0.647 | 0.626 |
| Ely, NV | 872 | 1255 | 1750 | 2103 | 2322 | 2649 | 2417 | 2308 | 1935 | 1473 | 1079 | 815 |
| $\phi = 39°17'$; 6262 ft | 0.618 | 0.660 | 0.692 | 0.664 | 0.649 | 0.704 | 0.656 | 0.695 | 0.696 | 0.691 | 0.658 | 0.64 |

| | | | | | | | | | | | | |
|---|---|---|---|---|---|---|---|---|---|---|---|---|
| Fairbanks, AK | 66 | 283 | 861 | 1481 | 1806 | 1971 | 1703 | 1248 | 700 | 324 | 104 | 20 |
| $\phi = 64°49'$; 436 ft | 0.639 | 0.556 | 0.674 | 0.647 | 0.546 | 0.529 | 0.485 | 0.463 | 0.419 | 0.416 | 0.47 | 0.458 |
| Fort Worth, TX | 936 | 1199 | 1598 | 1829 | 2105 | 2438 | 2293 | 2217 | 1881 | 1476 | 1148 | 914 |
| $\phi = 32°50'$; 544 ft | 0.530 | 0.541 | 0.577 | 0.556 | 0.585 | 0.654 | 0.624 | 0.653 | 0.634 | 0.612 | 0.576 | 0.563 |
| Fresno, CA | 713 | 1117 | 1653 | 2049 | 2409 | 2642 | 2512 | 2301 | 1898 | 1416 | 907 | 617 |
| $\phi = 36°46'$; 331 ft | 0.462 | 0.551 | 0.632 | 0.638 | 0.672 | 0.703 | 0.682 | 0.686 | 0.665 | 0.635 | 0.512 | 0.44 |
| Gainsville, FL | 1037 | 1325 | 1635 | 1956 | 1935 | 1961 | 1896 | 1874 | 1615 | 1312 | 1170 | 920 |
| $\phi = 29°39'$; 165 ft | 0.535 | 0.56 | 0.568 | 0.587 | 0.538 | 0.531 | 0.519 | 0.547 | 0.529 | 0.515 | 0.537 | 0.508 |
| Glasgow, MT | 573 | 966 | 1438 | 1741 | 2127 | 2262 | 2415 | 1985 | 1531 | 997 | 575 | 428 |
| $\phi = 48°13'$; 2277 ft | 0.621 | 0.678 | 0.672 | 0.597 | 0.611 | 0.602 | 0.666 | 0.630 | 0.629 | 0.593 | 0.516 | 0.548 |
| Grand Junction, CO | 848 | 1211 | 1623 | 2002 | 2300 | 2645 | 2518 | 2157 | 1958 | 1395 | 970 | 793 |
| $\phi = 39°07'$; 4849 ft | 0.597 | 0.633 | 0.643 | 0.632 | 0.643 | 0.704 | 0.690 | 0.65 | 0.705 | 0.654 | 0.59 | 0.621 |
| Grand Lake, CO | 735 | 1135 | 1579 | 1877 | 1975 | 2370 | 2103 | 1709 | 1716 | 1212 | 776 | 661 |
| $\phi = 40°15'$; 8389 ft | 0.541 | 0.615 | 0.637 | 0.597 | 0.553 | 0.63 | 0.572 | 0.516 | 0.626 | 0.583 | 0.494 | 0.542 |
| Great Falls, MT | 524 | 869 | 1370 | 1621 | 1971 | 2179 | 2383 | 1986 | 1537 | 985 | 575 | 421 |
| $\phi = 47°29'$; 3664 ft | 0.552 | 0.596 | 0.631 | 0.551 | 0.565 | 0.580 | 0.656 | 0.627 | 0.626 | 0.574 | 0.503 | 0.518 |
| Greensboro, NC | 744 | 1032 | 1323 | 1755 | 1989 | 2111 | 2034 | 1810 | 1517 | 1203 | 908 | 691 |
| $\phi = 36°05'$; 891 ft | 0.469 | 0.499 | 0.499 | 0.543 | 0.554 | 0.563 | 0.552 | 0.538 | 0.527 | 0.531 | 0.501 | 0.479 |
| Griffin, GA | 890 | 1136 | 1451 | 1924 | 2163 | 2176 | 2065 | 1961 | 1606 | 1352 | 1074 | 782 |
| $\phi = 33°15'$; 980 ft | 0.513 | 0.517 | 0.528 | 0.586 | 0.601 | 0.583 | 0.562 | 0.578 | 0.543 | 0.565 | 0.545 | 0.487 |
| Hatteras, NC | 892 | 1184 | 1590 | 2128 | 2376 | 2438 | 2334 | 2086 | 1758 | 1338 | 1054 | 798 |
| $\phi = 35°13'$; 7 ft | 0.546 | 0.563 | 0.593 | 0.655 | 0.661 | 0.652 | 0.634 | 0.619 | 0.605 | 0.58 | 0.566 | 0.535 |
| Indianapolis, IN | 526 | 797 | 1184 | 1481 | 1828 | 2042 | 2040 | 1832 | 1513 | 1094 | 662 | 491 |
| $\phi = 39°44'$; 793 ft | 0.380 | 0.424 | 0.472 | 0.47 | 0.511 | 0.543 | 0.554 | 0.552 | 0.549 | 0.520 | 0.413 | 0.391 |
| Inyokern, CA | 1149 | 1554 | 2137 | 2595 | 2925 | 3109 | 2909 | 2759 | 2409 | 1819 | 1370 | 1094 |
| $\phi = 35°39'$; 2440 ft | 0.716 | 0.745 | 0.803 | 0.80 | 0.815 | 0.830 | 0.790 | 0.820 | 0.834 | 0.795 | 0.743 | 0.742 |

Table XIX, continued

| Latitude, Elevation | Jan | Feb | Mar | Apr | May | June | Jul | Aug | Sep | Oct | Nov | Dec |
|---|---|---|---|---|---|---|---|---|---|---|---|---|
| Ithaca, NY | 434 | 755 | 1075 | 1323 | 1779 | 2026 | 2031 | 1736 | 1320 | 918 | 466 | 371 |
| $\phi = 42°27'$; 950 ft | 0.351 | 0.435 | 0.45 | 0.428 | 0.502 | 0.538 | 0.554 | 0.530 | 0.497 | 0.465 | 0.324 | 0.337 |
| Lake Charles, LA | 899 | 1146 | 1487 | 1802 | 2080 | 2213 | 1968 | 1910 | 1678 | 1506 | 1122 | 876 |
| $\phi = 30°13'$; 12 ft | 0.473 | 0.492 | 0.521 | 0.542 | 0.578 | 0.597 | 0.538 | 0.558 | 0.553 | 0.597 | 0.524 | 0.494 |
| Lander, WY | 786 | 1146 | 1638 | 1989 | 2114 | 2492 | 2438 | 2121 | 1713 | 1302 | 837 | 695 |
| $\phi = 42°48'$; 5370 ft | 0.65 | 0.672 | 0.691 | 0.647 | 0.597 | 0.662 | 0.665 | 0.649 | 0.647 | 0.666 | 0.589 | 0.643 |
| Las Vegas, NV | 1036 | 1438 | 1926 | 2323 | 2630 | 2799 | 2524 | 2342 | 2062 | 1603 | 1190 | 964 |
| $\phi = 36°5'$; 2162 ft | 0.654 | 0.697 | 0.728 | 0.719 | 0.732 | 0.746 | 0.685 | 0.697 | 0.716 | 0.704 | 0.657 | 0.668 |
| Lemont, IL | 590 | 879 | 1256 | 1482 | 1866 | 2042 | 1991 | 1837 | 1469 | 1016 | 639 | 531 |
| $\phi = 41°40'$; 595 ft | 0.464 | 0.496 | 0.520 | 0.477 | 0.525 | 0.542 | 0.542 | 0.559 | 0.547 | 0.506 | 0.433 | 0.467 |
| Lexington, KY | 624 | 969 | 1316 | 1835 | 2171 | 2315 | 2247 | 2065 | 1776 | 1316 | 903 | 682 |
| $\phi = 38°2'$; 979 ft | 0.52 | 0.54 | 0.56 | 0.575 | 0.606 | 0.61 | 0.610 | 0.619 | 0.631 | 0.604 | 0.55 | 0.513 |
| Lincoln, NE | 713 | 956 | 1300 | 1588 | 1856 | 2041 | 2011 | 1903 | 1544 | 1216 | 774 | 643 |
| $\phi = 40°51'$; 1189 ft | 0.542 | 0.528 | 0.532 | 0.507 | 0.522 | 0.542 | 0.547 | 0.577 | 0.568 | 0.596 | 0.508 | 0.545 |
| Little Rock, AR | 704 | 974 | 1336 | 1669 | 1960 | 2092 | 2081 | 1939 | 1641 | 1283 | 914 | 701 |
| $\phi = 34°44'$; 265 ft | 0.424 | 0.458 | 0.496 | 0.513 | 0.545 | 0.559 | 0.566 | 0.574 | 0.561 | 0.552 | 0.484 | 0.463 |
| Los Angeles, CA | 931 | 1284 | 1730 | 1948 | 2197 | 2272 | 2414 | 2155 | 1898 | 1373 | 1082 | 901 |
| $\phi = 33°56'$; 99 ft | 0.547 | 0.596 | 0.635 | 0.595 | 0.610 | 0.608 | 0.657 | 0.635 | 0.641 | 0.574 | 0.551 | 0.566 |
| Los Angeles, CA | 912 | 1224 | 1641 | 1867 | 2061 | 2259 | 2428 | 2199 | 1892 | 1362 | 1053 | 878 |
| $\phi = 34°3'$ | 0.538 | 0.568 | 0.602 | 0.571 | 0.573 | 0.605 | 0.66 | 0.648 | 0.643 | 0.578 | 0.548 | 0.566 |
| Madison, WI | 565 | 812 | 1232 | 1455 | 1745 | 2032 | 2047 | 1740 | 1444 | 993 | 556 | 496 |
| $\phi = 43°8'$; 866 ft | 0.49 | 0.478 | 0.522 | 0.474 | 0.493 | 0.540 | 0.559 | 0.534 | 0.549 | 0.510 | 0.396 | 0.467 |

| | | | | | | | | | | | | |
|---|---|---|---|---|---|---|---|---|---|---|---|---|
| Matanuska, AK | 119 | 345 | 892 | 1328 | 1628 | 1728 | 1527 | 1169 | 737 | 374 | 143 | 56 |
| $\phi = 61°30'$; 180 ft | 0.513 | 0.503 | 0.52 | 0.545 | 0.494 | 0.466 | 0.434 | 0.419 | 0.401 | 0.390 | 0.372 | 0.364 |
| Medford, OR | 435 | 804 | 1260 | 1807 | 2216 | 2441 | 2607 | 2262 | 1672 | 1044 | 559 | 347 |
| $\phi = 42°23'$; 1329 ft | 0.353 | 0.464 | 0.527 | 0.584 | 0.625 | 0.648 | 0.710 | 0.689 | 0.628 | 0.526 | 0.384 | 0.313 |
| Miami, FL | 1292 | 1555 | 1829 | 2021 | 2069 | 1992 | 1993 | 1891 | 1647 | 1437 | 1321 | 1183 |
| $\phi = 25°47'$; 9 ft | 0.604 | 0.616 | 0.612 | 0.600 | 0.578 | 0.545 | 0.552 | 0.549 | 0.525 | 0.534 | 0.559 | 0.588 |
| Midland, TX | 1066 | 1346 | 1785 | 2036 | 2301 | 2318 | 2302 | 2193 | 1922 | 1471 | 1244 | 1023 |
| $\phi = 31°56'$; 2854 ft | 0.587 | 0.596 | 0.638 | 0.617 | 0.639 | 0.622 | 0.628 | 0.643 | 0.642 | 0.600 | 0.609 | 0.611 |
| Nashville, TN | 590 | 907 | 1247 | 1662 | 1997 | 2149 | 2080 | 1863 | 1601 | 1224 | 823 | 614 |
| $\phi = 36°07'$; 605 ft | 0.373 | 0.440 | 0.472 | 0.514 | 0.556 | 0.573 | 0.565 | 0.554 | 0.556 | 0.540 | 0.454 | 0.426 |
| Newport, RI | 566 | 856 | 1232 | 1485 | 1849 | 2019 | 1943 | 1687 | 1411 | 1035 | 656 | 528 |
| $\phi = 41°29'$; 60 ft | 0.438 | 0.482 | 0.507 | 0.477 | 0.520 | 0.536 | 0.529 | 0.513 | 0.524 | 0.512 | 0.44 | 0.460 |
| New York, NY | 540 | 791 | 1180 | 1426 | 1738 | 1994 | 1939 | 1606 | 1349 | 978 | 598 | 476 |
| $\phi = 40°46'$; 52 ft | 0.406 | 0.435 | 0.480 | 0.455 | 0.488 | 0.53 | 0.528 | 0.486 | 0.500 | 0.475 | 0.397 | 0.403 |
| Oak Ridge, TN | 604 | 896 | 1242 | 1690 | 1943 | 2066 | 1972 | 1796 | 1560 | 1195 | 796 | 610 |
| $\phi = 36°01'$; 905 ft | 0.382 | 0.435 | 0.471 | 0.524 | 0.541 | 0.551 | 0.536 | 0.534 | 0.542 | 0.527 | 0.438 | 0.422 |
| Oklahoma City, OK | 938 | 1193 | 1534 | 1849 | 2005 | 2355 | 2274 | 2211 | 1819 | 1410 | 1086 | 897 |
| $\phi = 35°24'$; 1304 ft | 0.580 | 0.571 | 0.576 | 0.570 | 0.558 | 0.629 | 0.618 | 0.656 | 0.628 | 0.614 | 0.588 | 0.608 |
| Ottawa, ONT | 539 | 852 | 1251 | 1507 | 1857 | 2085 | 2045 | 1752 | 1327 | 827 | 459 | 409 |
| $\phi = 45°20'$; 339 ft | 0.499 | 0.540 | 0.554 | 0.502 | 0.529 | 0.554 | 0.560 | 0.546 | 0.521 | 0.450 | 0.359 | 0.436 |
| Phoenix, AZ | 1127 | 1515 | 1967 | 2388 | 2710 | 2782 | 2451 | 2300 | 2131 | 1689 | 1290 | 1041 |
| $\phi = 33°26'$; 1112 ft | 0.65 | 0.691 | 0.716 | 0.728 | 0.753 | 0.745 | 0.667 | 0.677 | 0.722 | 0.708 | 0.657 | 0.652 |
| Portland, ME | 566 | 875 | 1330 | 1528 | 1923 | 2017 | 2096 | 1799 | 1429 | 1035 | 592 | 508 |
| $\phi = 43°39'$; 63 ft | 0.482 | 0.524 | 0.569 | 0.500 | 0.544 | 0.536 | 0.572 | 0.554 | 0.546 | 0.539 | 0.431 | 0.491 |
| Rapid City, SD | 688 | 1033 | 1504 | 1807 | 2028 | 2194 | 2236 | 2020 | 1628 | 1179 | 763 | 590 |
| $\phi = 44°09'$; 3218 ft | 0.601 | 0.627 | 0.649 | 0.594 | 0.574 | 0.583 | 0.612 | 0.622 | 0.628 | 0.624 | 0.566 | 0.588 |

**Table XIX, continued**

| Latitude, Elevation | Jan | Feb | Mar | Apr | May | June | Jul | Aug | Sep | Oct | Nov | Dec |
|---|---|---|---|---|---|---|---|---|---|---|---|---|
| Riverside, CA<br>$\phi = 33°57'$; 1020 ft | 1000<br>0.589 | 1335<br>0.617 | 1751<br>0.643 | 1943<br>0.594 | 2282<br>0.635 | 2493<br>0.667 | 2444<br>0.665 | 2264<br>0.668 | 1955<br>0.665 | 1510<br>0.639 | 1169<br>0.606 | 980<br>0.626 |
| Saint Cloud, MN<br>$\phi = 45°35'$; 1034 ft | 633<br>0.595 | 977<br>0.629 | 1383<br>0.614 | 1598<br>0.534 | 1859<br>0.530 | 2003<br>0.533 | 2088<br>0.573 | 1828<br>0.570 | 1369<br>0.539 | 890<br>0.490 | 545<br>0.435 | 463<br>0.504 |
| Salt Lake City, UT<br>$\phi = 40°46'$; 4227 ft | 622<br>0.468 | 986<br>0.509 | 1301<br>0.529 | 1813<br>0.578 | 2101<br>0.60 | 2289<br>0.64 | 2286<br>0.64 | 2031<br>0.64 | 1689<br>0.621 | 1250<br>0.610 | 807<br>0.55 | 553<br>0.467 |
| San Antonio, TX<br>$\phi = 29°32'$; 794 ft | 1045<br>0.541 | 1299<br>0.550 | 1560<br>0.542 | 1665<br>0.500 | 2025<br>0.563 | 815<br>0.220 | 2364<br>0.647 | 2185<br>0.637 | 1845<br>0.603 | 1487<br>0.584 | 1104<br>0.507 | 955<br>0.528 |
| Santa Maria, CA<br>$\phi = 34°54'$; 238 ft | 984<br>0.595 | 1296<br>0.613 | 1806<br>0.671 | 2068<br>0.636 | 2376<br>0.661 | 2600<br>0.695 | 2541<br>0.690 | 2293<br>0.678 | 1966<br>0.674 | 1566<br>0.676 | 1169<br>0.624 | 944<br>0.627 |
| Sault Ste. Marie, MI<br>$\phi = 46°28'$; 724 ft | 489<br>0.490 | 844<br>0.560 | 1337<br>0.606 | 1559<br>0.526 | 1962<br>0.560 | 2064<br>0.549 | 2149<br>0.590 | 1768<br>0.554 | 1207<br>0.481 | 809<br>0.457 | 392<br>0.323 | 360<br>0.408 |
| Sayville, NY<br>$\phi = 40°30'$; 20 ft | 603<br>0.453 | 936<br>0.511 | 1259<br>0.510 | 1561<br>0.498 | 1857<br>0.522 | 2123<br>0.564 | 2041<br>0.555 | 1735<br>0.525 | 1447<br>0.530 | 1087<br>0.527 | 698<br>0.450 | 534<br>0.447 |
| Schenectady, NY<br>$\phi = 42°50'$; 217 ft | 488<br>0.406 | 754<br>0.441 | 1027<br>0.443 | 1272<br>0.413 | 1553<br>0.438 | 1688<br>0.448 | 1662<br>0.454 | 1495<br>0.458 | 1125<br>0.426 | 821<br>0.420 | 436<br>0.309 | 357<br>0.331 |
| Seattle, WA<br>$\phi = 47°27'$; 386 ft | 283<br>0.296 | 521<br>0.355 | 992<br>0.456 | 1507<br>0.510 | 1882<br>0.538 | 1910<br>0.508 | 2111<br>0.581 | 1689<br>0.533 | 1212<br>0.492 | 702<br>0.407 | 386<br>0.336 | 240<br>0.292 |
| Seattle, WA<br>$\phi = 47°36'$; 14 ft | 252<br>0.266 | 472<br>0.324 | 917<br>0.423 | 1376<br>0.468 | 1665<br>0.477 | 1724<br>0.459 | 1805<br>0.498 | 1617<br>0.511 | 1129<br>0.459 | 638<br>0.372 | 326<br>0.284 | 218<br>0.269 |
| Seabrook, NJ<br>$\phi = 39°30'$; 100 ft | 592<br>0.426 | 854<br>0.453 | 1196<br>0.476 | 1519<br>0.481 | 1801<br>0.504 | 1965<br>0.522 | 1950<br>0.530 | 1715<br>0.517 | 1446<br>0.524 | 1072<br>0.508 | 722<br>0.449 | 523<br>0.416 |

| | | | | | | | | | | | | |
|---|---|---|---|---|---|---|---|---|---|---|---|---|
| Spokane, WA | 446 | 838 | 1200 | 1765 | 2104 | 2227 | 2480 | 2076 | 1511 | 845 | 486 | 279 |
| $\phi = 47°40'$; 1968 ft | 0.478 | 0.579 | 0.556 | 0.602 | 0.603 | 0.593 | 0.684 | 0.656 | 0.616 | 0.494 | 0.428 | 0.345 |
| State College, PA | 502 | 749 | 1107 | 1399 | 1755 | 2028 | 1968 | 1690 | 1336 | 1017 | 580 | 444 |
| $\phi = 40°48'$; 1175 ft | 0.381 | 0.413 | 0.451 | 0.448 | 0.493 | 0.539 | 0.536 | 0.512 | 0.492 | 0.496 | 0.379 | 0.376 |
| Stillwater, OK | 764 | 1082 | 1464 | 1703 | 1879 | 2236 | 2224 | 2039 | 1724 | 1314 | 992 | 783 |
| $\phi = 36°09'$; 910 ft | 0.484 | 0.527 | 0.555 | 0.528 | 0.523 | 0.596 | 0.604 | 0.607 | 0.599 | 0.581 | 0.548 | 0.544 |
| Tampa, FL | 1224 | 1461 | 1772 | 2016 | 2228 | 2147 | 1992 | 1845 | 1688 | 1493 | 1328 | 1120 |
| $\phi = 27°55'$; 11 ft | 0.605 | 0.600 | 0.606 | 0.602 | 0.620 | 0.583 | 0.548 | 0.537 | 0.546 | 0.572 | 0.590 | 0.589 |
| Toronto, ONT | 451 | 675 | 1089 | 1388 | 1785 | 1942 | 1967 | 1623 | 1284 | 835 | 458 | 353 |
| $\phi = 43°41'$; 379 ft | 0.388 | 0.406 | 0.467 | 0.455 | 0.506 | 0.516 | 0.539 | 0.500 | 0.493 | 0.438 | 0.336 | 0.346 |
| Tucson, AZ | 1172 | 1454 | 1991 | 2435 | 2687 | 2602 | 2292 | 2180 | 2123 | 1641 | 1322 | 1132 |
| $\phi = 32°07'$; 2556 ft | 0.648 | 0.646 | 0.70 | 0.738 | 0.72 | 0.698 | 0.625 | 0.640 | 0.710 | 0.672 | 0.650 | 0.679 |
| Upton, NY | 583 | 873 | 1280 | 1610 | 1892 | 2159 | 2045 | 1790 | 1473 | 1103 | 687 | 551 |
| $\phi = 40°52'$; 75 ft | 0.444 | 0.483 | 0.522 | 0.514 | 0.532 | 0.574 | 0.557 | 0.542 | 0.542 | 0.538 | 0.448 | 0.467 |
| Washington, DC | 632 | 902 | 1255 | 1600 | 1847 | 2081 | 1930 | 1712 | 1446 | 1083 | 764 | 594 |
| $\phi = 38°51'$; 64 ft | 0.445 | 0.470 | 0.496 | 0.504 | 0.516 | 0.553 | 0.524 | 0.516 | 0.520 | 0.506 | 0.464 | 0.460 |
| Winnipeg, Manitoba | 488 | 835 | 1354 | 1641 | 1904 | 1962 | 2124 | 1761 | 1190 | 768 | 445 | 345 |
| $\phi = 49°54'$; 786 ft | 0.601 | 0.636 | 0.661 | 0.574 | 0.550 | 0.524 | 0.587 | 0.567 | 0.504 | 0.482 | 0.436 | 0.503 |

$$H_o = ((24\ \text{hr/d})/\pi)(0.9668)(1353\ \text{W/m}^2)(3600\ \text{sec/hr})[\cos(38.85)$$

$$\cdot \cos(22.92)\sin(109.9) + (\pi/180)(109.9)\sin(38.85)\sin(22.92)]$$

$$= 35.97\ \text{MJ/m}^2 \cdot [0.6745 + 0.4686] = 41.1\ \text{MJ/m}^2\text{-d}$$

Interpolating between the mid-June and mid-July curves of Figure 111 yields $H_o = 41$ MJ/m$^2$-day. Converting to Langleys/day, 41.1/0.04181 = 982 La/d, which is in agreement with Figure 116.

## SOLAR RADIATION MODELS FOR SYSTEMS ANALYSIS

### Existing Models

In order to calculate the performance of any solar energy system, a reasonable model of the expected variations in solar radiation and other meteorological parameters is required for the period of time over which the system is expected to operate. The simplest model consists of the long-term average of daily solar radiation on a horizontal surface for each month of the year, and the maximum, mean, and minimum temperature for each month. Such a model is useful only in obtaining gross estimates of solar system performance. The best models currently available consist of hourly or even more frequent values of horizontal global radiation, direct normal solar radiation, wet bulb and dry bulb temperature, wind speed, wind direction, and other parameters of interest. Regardless which type of model is used, the global radiation values are presented almost always in terms of the global radiation intensity on a horizontal surface.

### Solar Year Model for Predicting Performance of a Solar Energy System

In order to predict more accurately the performance of a solar energy system, a solar year model is needed which contains hourly (or more frequent) measurements of solar radiation and pertinent meteorological parameters for a typical year. A model for a specific solar energy project is given as an example.

The project under consideration was a solar power and process heat facility employing several acres of parabolic dish concentrators. The existing solar radiation data base consisted of 23 years of daily global solar radiation records from the local airport. The recording instrument at the airport produced a circular chart of instantaneous horizontal global radiation each day, as well as a digital readout of the daily horizontal global radiation. The digital readouts were made part of the permanent record, and the circular charts were stored at the National Climatic Center (NCC).

### *Step One in Building Solar Year Model*

The first step in developing the solar year model was to examine the charts at NCC to determine the quality of the data. The 23 years of charts (over 700) were examined in one man-day, when defects or gaps in the data were verbally noted using a microcassette transcriber. Subsequently, this information was transcribed into a logbook for future reference.

The daily values of horizontal global radiation were averaged for each month of each year. Also, the standard deviation of the daily values from the month's mean was calculated for each month of each year. The model year was then made up of those months for which the mean and the standard deviation were both the closest to the long-term average mean and standard deviation for that month, and for which a complete or nearly complete set of circular charts were available. For example, January 1953 was chosen because the average daily radiation was close to the average daily radiation for all Januarys over the 23-year period, the standard deviation of the daily values from the monthly mean was close to the average of the standard deviation for all Januarys over the 23-year period, and the circular charts were complete for each day in January 1953. Likewise, the months of February 1971, March 1969, April 1965, May 1957, June 1957, July 1970, August 1959, September 1963, October 1967, November 1967, and December 1970 were chosen for the model year. Thus, the model year was made up of actual measurements of horizontal global radiation which were most typical of what had occurred over the 23-year period. Data from different years, of course, cannot be averaged together, since realistic fluctuations in radiation intensity would be smoothed out.

Having selected the months for the model year, the circular charts for those months were manually digitized at 15-minute intervals by two people in one and one half days. The digitized data were recorded into a computer data file and the data then were used to reconstruct the circular charts on a graphics terminal to compare with the original charts for data verification. The daily totals were summed and compared with the previously recorded values for further verification.

### *Step Two in Building Solar Year Model*

The next step was data rehabilitation to correct for long-term instrument degradation due to dust accumulation and other factors. This was done by considering the day with the highest daily global radiation out of each 40-day interval to be a clear day. The annual means of these clear day data were compiled to determine the long-term degradation over each year of operation, which can be expressed as

$$A = C_1 T + C_2 \tag{156}$$

where $A$ = annual mean percent of possible daily global radiation
$T$ = time since instrument installation or calibration
$C_1, C_2$ = regression coefficients

The correction factor F for adjusting measured values to actual values is then given by

$$F = 1 + \frac{C_2}{C_1 T} \tag{157}$$

## U.S. Department of Energy Solar Year Data

The U.S. Department of Energy has developed similar Typical Meteorological Years (TMY) for each of the 26 U.S. cities that have about 23 years of meteorological data [Freeman 1979]. These rehabilitated data are available on computer tape from the National Climatic Center and are known as the SOLMET [SOLMET 1977] data. The SOLMET data were used for developing the TMY. The selection of the typical months out of the 23 years of data was based on weighting 13 indices: the daily global horizontal radiation, and the average daily maximum, mean, minimum and range of the dry bulb temperature, dew point and wind speed. The solar radiation data were assigned as much weight as the other indices combined; all other parameters were assigned equal weight.

## Hoyt Model

Hoyt [1978] reported a model to calculate directly the instantaneous global radiation; this model was used to rehabilitate the National Weather Service solar radiation data from 26 sites by comparing measured values on clear days at solar noon with the theoretical value at solar noon. His model is a refinement of models developed earlier by Katayama [1966], Sasamori [1972] and Hoyt [1976]. In his model, the direct solar radiation is given by

$$I_D = I_{sc} f \cos\theta \left(1 - \sum_{i=1}^{5} \alpha_i\right)(1 - S_a)(1 - S_d) \tag{158}$$

and the diffuse solar radiation is

$$I_d = I_{sc} f \cos\theta \left(1 - \sum_{i=1}^{5} \alpha_i\right)(0.5S_a + 0.75S_d) \tag{159}$$

where $I_{sc}$ = solar constant (1353 $W/m^2$)
$f$ = factor to correct for changes in the earth's distance from the sun (Figure 101)
$\theta$ = zenith angle
$\alpha_1$ = absorption ratio of water vapor given by:

$$\alpha_1 = 0.110(u_1 + 0.000631)^{0.3} - 0.0121 \tag{160}$$

where $u_1$ = total pressure-corrected precipitable water (cm) in the path
$\alpha_2$ = absorption ratio of carbon dioxide given by:

$$\alpha_2 = 0.00235(u_2 + 0.0129)^{0.26} - 0.00075 \tag{161}$$

where $u_2$ = pressure-corrected path length of carbon dioxide (cm at STP; for air mass = 1, $u_2$ = 126 cm)

$$\alpha_3 = 0.045(u_3 + 0.000834)^{0.38} - 0.0031 \tag{162}$$

where $u_3$ = ozone path length (cm at STP)

$$\alpha_4 = 0.0075 m^{0.875} \tag{163}$$

where $m$ = pressure-corrected air mass

$$\alpha_5 = (1 - A) g(\beta)^m \tag{164}$$

where $A$ = albedo for single scattering $\simeq 0.95$
$\beta$ = Ångstrom turbidity coefficient, which is related here to optical depth, $\tau$, and wavelength, $\lambda$, by $\lambda = \beta/\tau$, $g(\beta)$ is a function calculated using the solar spectrum (see Table XX)

The scattering ratio for pure air $S_a$ is given by:

$$S_a = 1 - f(m)^m \tag{165}$$

where $f(m)$ = given by Table XXI

**Table XX.** $g(\beta)$ vs $\beta$

| $\beta$ | $g(\beta)$ |
|---|---|
| 0.00 | 1.000 |
| 0.02 | 0.972 |
| 0.04 | 0.945 |
| 0.06 | 0.919 |
| 0.08 | 0.894 |
| 0.10 | 0.870 |
| 0.12 | 0.846 |
| 0.14 | 0.824 |
| 0.16 | 0.802 |
| 0.18 | 0.780 |
| 0.20 | 0.758 |
| 0.24 | 0.714 |
| 0.28 | 0.670 |
| 0.32 | 0.626 |

**Table XXI.** f(m) vs m.

| m | f(m) |
|---|---|
| 0.0 | 1.000 |
| 0.5 | 0.909 |
| 1.0 | 0.917 |
| 1.5 | 0.921 |
| 2.0 | 0.925 |
| 2.5 | 0.929 |
| 3.0 | 0.932 |
| 3.5 | 0.935 |
| 4.0 | 0.937 |

The air mass m may be approximated by:

$$m \simeq \frac{P/P_o}{\cos\theta}$$

where $P$ = the total atmosphere pressure
$P_o$ = 1013.25 mb = 760 mm Hg
$\theta$ = zenith angle

f(m) first decreases rapidly due to the depletion of shorter wavelength radiation and then increases because of increased scattering at longer path lengths.

$S_d$ = scattering ratio for dust given by

$$S_d = 1 - g(\beta)^m \tag{166}$$

In order to calculate precisely the global radiation, the solar radiation (101.32 kPa, 29.92 in. Hg, 760.0 mm Hg). R is the averaged instantaneous intensity of solar radiation reflected from the earth into the atmosphere given by

$$R' = R\left(1 - \sum_{i=1}^{5} \alpha_i'\right)(0.5S_a' + 0.75S_d') \tag{167}$$

where $S_a'$ and $S_d'$ are evaluated for an optical air mass of 1.66 $P/P_o$ and the $\alpha$s are evaluated for air mass $m + 1.66P/P_o$, where P is the local surface pressure and $P_o$ is the sea level surface pressure of 1013.25 mb (101.32 kPa, 29.92 in. Hg, 760.0 mm Hg). R is the averaged instantaneous intensity of solar radiation reflected from the earth into the atmosphere given by

$$R = a(I_D + I_d) \tag{168}$$

where a is the ground reflectivity (albedo) of Table XXII.

The instantaneous global radiation on a horizontal surface, $I_g$ is

$$I_g = I_D + I_d + R' \tag{169}$$

In this model, $I_d$ is the diffuse component from the sky, excluding the radiation from the ground and scattered back down from the sky, which is R′. When calculating radiation intensity on surfaces, the usual practice is to include R′ in the diffuse component. The accuracy of this model is within a few percent, and comparisons with experimental data are usually within the ±5% accuracy claim for the pyranometers.

To calculate the daily global radiation on a horizontal surface, Equation 169 is summed in 15-minute increments from sunrise to sunset.

## Example 4: Calculating Solar Radiation at Sea Level

Calculate the global horizontal solar radiation at sea level for 2.383 cm of pressure-corrected precipitable water, 126 cm of $CO_2$, 0.318 cm of ozone, air mass 1 (pressure corrected), surface albedo of 0.2, zenith angle 0, and $\beta = 0.04$. How much would the global solar radiation intensity increase if the surface albedo were increased 0.8?

**Table XXII. Ground Reflectivity [Riches 1980]**

| Nature of Surface | Reflectivity (%) | References |
|---|---|---|
| Land | | |
| Desert | 26.0 | List 1968 |
| Sand, Dry | 18.0 | List 1968 |
| Sand, Wet | 9.0 | List 1968 |
| Fields, Dry Plowed | 22.0 | List 1968 |
| Fields, Green | 12.0 | List 1968 |
| Fields, Wheat | 7.0 | List 1968 |
| Field, Moist Plowed | 14.0 | Robinson 1966; Kondratiev 1969 |
| Grass, Green | 26.0 | Robinson 1966 |
| Grass, Dried in Sun | 19.0 | Robinson 1966; Kondratiev 1969 |
| Grass, Tall and Dry | 32.0 | List 1968 |
| Grass, Tall and Wet | 22.0 | List 1968 |
| Bare Ground | 15.0 | List 1968 |
| Snow, Fresh | 81.0 | List 1968 |
| Snow, Several Days Old, White & Smooth | 70.0 | List 1968 |
| Snow, White Field | 78.0 | List 1968 |
| Urban Developments | | |
| Downtown, City | 14.0 | Peterson 1980 |
| Outer City, Established Suburbs | 19.0 | Peterson 1980 |
| Old Residential | 13.0 | Peterson 1980; Dabberdt and Davis 1974 |
| Old Residential, Some Light Commercial | 12.0 | Dabberdt and Davis 1974 |
| Old Residential, Commercial/Industrial | 14.0 | Dabberdt and Davis 1974 |
| New Residential | 21.0 | Peterson 1980 |
| Urban Surfaces | | |
| Cement Streets | 28.0 | Dirmhirn 1964 |
| Granite Pavement | 19.0 | Dirmhirn 1964 |
| Asphalt | 14.0 | Dirmhirn 1964 |
| Crushed Stone Pavement | 10.0 | Dirmhirn 1964 |
| Woodlands | | |
| Forest, Green | 12.0 | List 1968 |
| Forest, Snow-Covered Ground | 18.0 | List 1968 |
| Water (Direct Beam Only) | | |
| Zenith Angle, 0–40° | 2.5 | Kondratiev 1969 |
| Zenith Angle, 0–50° | 3.5 | Kondratiev 1969 |
| 60° | 6.2 | Kondratiev 1969 |
| 70° | 13.6 | Kondratiev 1969 |
| 80° | 35.0 | Kondratiev 1969 |
| 90° | 100.0 | Kondratiev 1969 |

*Solution*

$$\alpha_1 = 0.110(2.383)^{0.3} - 0.0121 = 0.131$$

$$\alpha_2 = 0.00235(126)^{0.26} - 0.00075 = 0.0075$$

$$\alpha_3 = 0.045(0.318)^{0.38} - 0.0031 = 0.0419$$

$$\alpha_4 = 0.0075$$

$$\alpha_5 = 0.05(0.945) = 0.04725$$

$$S_a = 1 - 0.917 = 0.083$$

$$S_d = 1 - 0.945 = 0.055$$

$$I_{sc} \cos\theta = 1353 \text{ W/m}^2$$

$$1 - \sum_{i=1}^{5} \alpha_i = 1 - 0.131 - 0.0075 - 0.0419 - 0.0075 - 0.04725 = 0.765$$

$$I_D = 1353(.765)(.917)(.945) = 896.9 \text{ W/m}^2$$

$$I_d = 1353(0.765)(0.0415 + 0.0412) = 85.6 \text{ W/m}^2$$

$$R = 0.2(896.9 + 85.6) = 196.5 \text{ W/m}^2$$

$$\alpha_1' = 0.110(2.66 \times 2.383)^{.3} - 0.0121 = 0.179$$

$$\alpha_2' = 0.00235(2.66 \times 126)^{.26} - .00075 = 0.010$$

$$\alpha_3' = 0.045(2.66 \times 0.318)^{.38} - .0031 = 0.039$$

$$\alpha_4' = 0.0075(2.66)^{.875} = 0.018$$

$$\alpha_5' = 0.05(0.945)^{2.66} = 0.043$$

$$\sum_{i=1}^{5} \alpha_i = 0.289$$

$$S_a' = 1 - 0.922^{1.66} = 0.126$$

$$S'_d = 1 - 0.945^{1.66} = 0.090$$

$$R' = 196.5(1 - 0.289)(0.5 \times 0.126 + 0.75 \times 0.09)$$

$$= 196.5(0.711)(0.1305) = 18.2 \text{ W/m}^2$$

$$I_g = I_D + I_d + R'$$

$$= 896.9 + 85.6 + 18.2 = 1000.7 \frac{\text{W}}{\text{m}^2}$$

If the surface albedo were increased to 0.8,

$$R' = 0.8(896.9 + 85.6)(0.711)(0.1305)$$

$$= 72.9 \text{ W/m}^2$$

$$I_g = I_D + I_d + R'$$

$$= 896.9 + 85.6 + 72.9 = 1055 \frac{\text{W}}{\text{m}^2}$$

a 5.4% increase.

## SOLAR RADIATION ON TILTED SURFACES

Solar collectors are usually not horizontal, but oriented at a tilt and toward the south (in the Northern Hemisphere). Thus, in order to calculate the solar radiation falling on a collector at any given time, one must be able to determine from the horizontal global radiation values what the intensity would be on a surface of arbitrary orientation. If I is the intensity of the direct component, then the intensity of the component on a surface is $I \cos \psi$, where $\psi$ is the incident angle. Figure 121 is similar to Figure 103, except it includes a surface with azimuthal angle $\alpha$ slope and $\beta$. Alpha ($\alpha$) is the angle between the south axis and the intersection of a plane containing the zenith and surface normal with the horizontal plane. This angle is zero if the surface faces toward the south, positive if it faces west of south (90° if it faces west), and negative if it faces east of south (−90° if it faces east). Beta ($\beta$) is simply the slope of the surface as compared to a horizontal plane, that is, $\beta = 0°$ for a horizontal surface, and $\beta = 90°$ for a vertical surface. Using the angles and those defined in Figure 121, the equation for the angle of incidence, $\psi$, of the direct component of solar radiation on the surface is

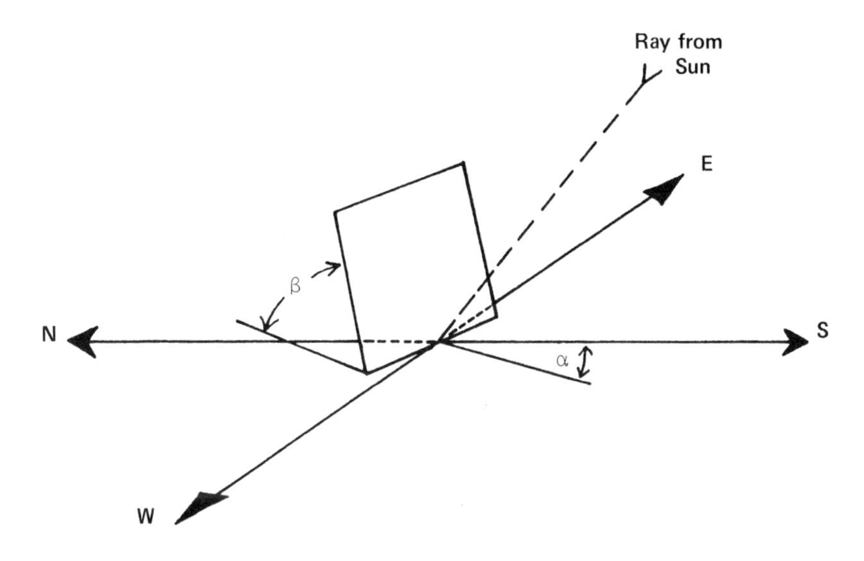


**Figure 121.** Surface azimuth angle and slope defined.

$$\cos\psi = \sin\beta(\cos\delta(\sin\phi\cos\alpha\cos\omega + \sin\alpha\sin\omega) - \sin\delta\cos\phi\cos\alpha) + \cos\beta(\cos\delta\cos\phi\cos\omega + \sin\delta\sin\phi) \tag{170}$$

where $\psi$ = angle between the ray of sunlight and the surface normal
$\beta$ = slope of the surface relative to the horizontal
$\delta$ = declination angle
$\phi$ = latitude (see Figure 103)
$\alpha$ = azimuth angle for the surface
$\omega$ = hour angle of the sun (see Figure 103)

This equation is only valid for values of $\psi < 90°$, $\beta < 90°$, and $\theta < 90°$; that is, the sun should not be behind the surface, the surface should not face downward, and the sun should not be below the horizon.

If the surface is horizontal ($\beta = 0°$), this equation reduces to

$$\cos\psi = \cos\delta\cos\phi\cos\omega + \sin\delta\sin\phi \tag{171}$$

which is the same as Equation 138, since for this case $\phi = \theta$. For a vertical surface ($\beta = 90°$) Equation 169 becomes

$$\cos\psi = \cos\delta(\sin\phi\cos\alpha\cos\omega + \sin\alpha\sin\omega) - \sin\delta\cos\phi\cos\alpha \tag{172}$$

If the vertical surface faces due east ($\alpha = -90°$)

$$\cos\psi = -\sin\omega\cos\delta \tag{173}$$

If it faces due south ($\alpha = 0°$)

$$\cos\psi = \cos\delta\sin\phi\cos\omega - \sin\delta\cos\phi \tag{174}$$

If it faces due west ($\alpha = 90°$)

$$\cos\psi = \sin\omega\cos\delta \tag{175}$$

And if it faces due north ($\alpha = 180°$)

$$\cos\psi = \sin\delta\cos\phi - \cos\delta\sin\phi\cos\omega \tag{176}$$

Whenever these equations are used in a computer program, one must be careful to set the intensity of the beam radiation on the surface to zero if $\psi$ is greater than 90° (the sun is behind the surface), or if the solar zenith angle $\theta$ (Equation 138) exceeds 90° (the sun is below the horizon). Additional restrictions must be placed frequently on the angles for which direct solar radiation reaches the surface because of shadowing by nearby structures, trees, and so forth.

## Calculating Solar Radiation for a South-facing Collector at a Tilt

A common orientation for a solar collector is south facing at some tilt ($\alpha = 0°$). In this case, Equation 169 reduces to

$$\cos\psi = \sin(\phi - \beta)\sin\delta + \cos(\phi - \beta)\cos\delta\cos\omega \tag{177}$$

or a tilted surface facing in a different direction

$$\cos\psi = \cos(\gamma - \alpha)\cos(90 - \theta)\sin\beta + \sin(90 - \theta)\cos\beta \tag{178}$$

The average angle of incidence on a cylindrical surface is given by

$$\cos\psi = \{1 - (\sin(\beta - \theta)\cos\delta\cos\omega + \cos(\beta - \theta)\sin\delta^2\}^{0.5} \tag{179}$$

if the axis of the cylinder is in the longitude plane at an angle $\beta$ to the horizontal plane.

The amount of solar radiation intercepted during the day is substantially increased if the surface tracks the sun. This is generally done with concentrating solar collectors, since tracking is usually necessary to focus the incoming solar radiation on the receiver. Double-axis tracking collectors remain pointed directly at the sun from sunrise to sunset, and the incidence angle $\psi$ remains zero. Single-axis tracking collectors are usually mounted with the axis horizontal, either east-west or north-south. The incidence angle for a tracking collector with a north-south horizontal axis is

$$\cos\psi = \{(\sin\phi\sin\delta + \cos\phi\cos\delta\cos\omega)^2 + \cos^2\delta\sin^2\omega\}^{0.5} \tag{180}$$

and if the horizontal axis is east-west, this becomes

$$\cos\psi = (1 - \cos^2\delta\sin^2\omega)^{0.5} \tag{181}$$

Single-axis tracking collectors are sometimes mounted with their north-south axis tilted at the latitude angle in order to intercept more solar radiation during the course of the year. In this case, the axis of the collector is parallel to the earth's axis, and as long as the collector is tracking the sun,

$$\psi = \delta \tag{182}$$

The extraterrestrial daily solar radiation on a horizontal surface is given by Equation 155, or Figures 111, 112 and 116. Values of daily solar radiation on a horizontal surface on the ground are tabulated in Table XIX and elsewhere, or, for reasonably clear days, may be calculated by summing Equation 169 in 15-minute increments from sunrise to sunset. The ratio $H/H_o$ is $K_T$ (Figures 117 and 118).

## Calculating Daily Diffuse Radiation on a Horizontal Surface on the Ground

Knowing $K_T$ and either $H_o$ or H, the daily diffuse component of solar radiation on a horizontal surface on the ground, $H_d$, may be found from the following [Erbs 1981]:

If $\omega_s < 81.4°$ then

$$H_d/H = 1.0 - 0.2727K_T + 2.4495K_T^2 - 11.9514K_T^3 + 9.3879K_T^4 \quad \text{for } K_T < 0.715 \tag{183}$$

$$H_d/H = 0.143 \quad \text{for } K_T > 0.715$$

If, on the other hand, $\omega_s > 81.4°$ then

$$H_d/H = 1.0 + 0.2832K_T - 2.5557K_T^2 + 0.8448K_T^3 \qquad \text{for } K_T < 0.722$$
$$H_d/H = 0.175 \qquad \text{for } K_T > 0.722 \tag{184}$$

where $\omega_s$ is the sunset hour angle (Equation 146).

If H represents the daily global radiation on a horizontal surface on the ground, and $H_d$ the diffuse component of this radiation, then the daily direct, or beam, solar radiation on the horizontal surface $H_D$ is $H - H_d$.

A tilted surface receives solar radiation from three sources, directly from the sun, scattered from the sky, and reflected from the ground or other objects on the earth. Let $I_D$ represent the instantaneous direct (or beam) component of solar radiation on a horizontal surface, then the direct normal solar radiation is

$$I_b = \frac{I_D}{\cos\theta} \tag{185}$$

and, since the intensity of the direct component of solar radiation on a surface is

$$I_{Ds} = I\cos\psi \tag{186}$$

then the instantaneous direct (beam) solar radiation on the surface is

$$I_{Ds} = I\left(\frac{\cos\psi}{\cos\theta}\right) \tag{187}$$

The ratio $\cos\psi/\cos\theta$ is called the tilt factor for beam radiation $F_D$ since it is the ratio of beam radiation on a surface to the horizontal beam radiation.

$$F_D = \frac{\cos\psi}{\cos\theta} \tag{188}$$

The tilt factor for diffuse radiation from the sky is given by

$$F_d = \cos^2\left(\frac{\beta}{2}\right) = (1 + \cos\beta)/2 \tag{189}$$

under the assumption that the sky is a uniform source of diffuse radiation.

The radiation reflected from the ground which falls on the surface $I_{rs}$ equal to $a(I_D + I_d)$, where a is the albedo (fraction of incident radiation reflected by the ground) or ground reflectance (Table XXII). A tilt factor can be defined for the reflected radiation as

$$F_r = a.\sin^2\left(\frac{\beta}{2}\right) = a[(1 - \cos\beta)/2] \tag{190}$$

under the assumption that the ground is a uniform reflector of radiation. The total diffuse and reflected radiation falling on the surface is

$$I_{ds} + I_{rs} = I_d \cos^2\left(\frac{\beta}{2}\right) + a(I_D + I_d)\sin^2\left(\frac{\beta}{2}\right) \tag{191}$$

and the total global radiation on the surface is

$$I_{gs} = I_{Ds} + I_{ds} + I_{rs} \tag{192}$$

In calculating daily solar radiation on a surface, the daily average value of $F_D$ may be estimated for a southward-facing surface ($\alpha = 0$), by taking the average value of $\cos\psi$ and dividing it by the average value of $\cos\theta$ [Liu 1961]. This leads to:

$$\overline{F_D} = \frac{\cos(\phi - \beta)\cos\delta\sin\omega_s' + (\pi/180)\omega_s'\sin(\phi - \beta)\sin\delta}{\cos\phi\cos\delta\sin\omega_s + (\pi/180)\,\omega_s\sin\phi\sin\delta} \tag{193}$$

when $\omega_s$ is the lesser of $\cos^{-1}(-\tan\phi\tan\delta)$ (the value of $\omega_s$ for which $\theta = 90°$) or $\cos^{-1}(-\tan(\phi - \beta)\tan\delta)$ (the value of $\omega_s$ for which $\psi = 90°$). In the case of the diffuse and reflected components, the daily average tilt factors in this model are the same as the instantaneous tilt factors.

$$\overline{F_d} = F_d \qquad \text{and} \qquad \overline{F_r} = F_r \tag{194}$$

Thus, the daily solar radiation on a tilted surface $H_T$ is given by

$$H_T = \overline{F_D}H_D + \overline{F_d}H_d + \overline{F_r}H \tag{195}$$

An overall tilt factor F can be expressed as

$$\bar{F} = \frac{H_T}{H} + \left(1 - \frac{H_d}{H}\right)\overline{F_D} + \frac{H_d}{H}\cos^2\left(\frac{\beta}{2}\right) + a.\sin^2\left(\frac{\beta}{2}\right) \tag{196}$$

where $\overline{F_D}$ is given by Equation 193. The daily total radiation falling on the tilted surface is

$$H_T = \bar{F}H \tag{197}$$

Table XXIII lists monthly values of the tilt factor $\bar{F}$ for average cloudiness index, $\overline{K_T}$, values from 0.3 to 0.6, latitudes, $\phi$, from 20° to 60° N, and south-facing solar aperture tilts, $\beta$, of $\phi$-15°, $\phi$, $\phi + 15°$ and vertical. $\overline{H_T}$, the monthly average daily global radiation on a tilted surface, is tabulated in Table XXIV, over the same range of $\phi$, $\beta$ and $\overline{K_T}$.

## Example 5: Estimating Amount of Solar Radiation on a Tilted Surface

Estimate the amount of solar radiation falling on a 10 m$^2$ south-facing surface with a 45° slope in Washington, DC, on July 4.

### *Solution*

First determine the overall tilt factor $\bar{F}$ from Equations 193 and 196. From Examples 2 and 3,

$$\phi = 38.85°$$

$$\beta = 45°$$

$$\delta = 22.92°$$

$$\omega_s = 109.9°$$

$$H_o = 41.1 \text{ MJ/m}^2\text{-day}$$

$$\omega_s' = \cos^{-1}(-\tan(-6.15)\tan(22.92)) = 87.4°$$

Now $\overline{F_D}$ is calculated from Equation 193

$$\overline{F_D} = \frac{\cos(-6.15)\cos(22.92)\sin(87.4) + (\pi/180)(87.4)\sin(-6.15)\sin(22.92)}{\cos(38.85)\cos(22.92)\sin(109.9) + (\pi/180)(109.9)\sin(38.85)\sin(22.92)}$$

$$= \frac{0.9148 - 0.0636}{0.6745 + 0.4686} = 0.745$$

**Table XXIII. Average Tilt Factor $\bar{F}$ vs Latitude $\phi$, Slope $\beta$ and Average Cloudiness Index ($\overline{K_T}$)**

| $\phi$ | $\beta$ | $\overline{K_T}$ | Jan | Feb | Mar | Apr | May | Jun | Jul | Aug | Sep | Oct | Nov | Dec |
|---|---|---|---|---|---|---|---|---|---|---|---|---|---|---|
| 20 | 5 | 0.3 | 1.06 | 1.05 | 1.03 | 1.01 | 1.01 | 1.00 | 1.01 | 1.01 | 1.02 | 1.04 | 1.06 | 1.07 |
| 25 | 10 | 0.3 | 1.12 | 1.08 | 1.05 | 1.02 | 1.00 | 0.99 | 1.00 | 1.01 | 1.03 | 1.07 | 1.11 | 1.09 |
| 30 | 15 | 0.3 | 1.14 | 1.13 | 1.07 | 1.03 | 1.00 | 0.98 | 0.99 | 1.02 | 1.05 | 1.11 | 1.12 | 1.16 |
| 35 | 20 | 0.3 | 1.23 | 1.19 | 1.10 | 1.04 | 0.99 | 0.97 | 0.98 | 1.02 | 1.07 | 1.15 | 1.20 | 1.26 |
| 40 | 25 | 0.3 | 1.35 | 1.28 | 1.14 | 1.05 | 0.99 | 0.97 | 0.98 | 1.02 | 1.09 | 1.22 | 1.31 | 1.40 |
| 45 | 30 | 0.3 | 1.53 | 1.31 | 1.18 | 1.07 | 1.00 | 0.97 | 0.98 | 1.03 | 1.13 | 1.31 | 1.46 | 1.68 |
| 50 | 35 | 0.3 | 1.71 | 1.45 | 1.25 | 1.09 | 1.00 | 0.97 | 0.98 | 1.04 | 1.17 | 1.36 | 1.73 | 1.88 |
| 55 | 40 | 0.3 | 2.27 | 1.67 | 1.34 | 1.11 | 1.01 | 0.96 | 0.98 | 1.06 | 1.23 | 1.52 | 1.99 | 2.74 |
| 60 | 45 | 0.3 | 3.09 | 2.07 | 1.47 | 1.15 | 1.01 | 0.96 | 0.98 | 1.09 | 1.31 | 1.77 | 2.92 | 4.41 |
| 20 | 20 | 0.3 | 1.15 | 1.10 | 1.04 | 0.99 | 0.96 | 0.94 | 0.95 | 0.98 | 1.02 | 1.08 | 1.14 | 1.17 |
| 25 | 25 | 0.3 | 1.22 | 1.13 | 1.06 | 0.99 | 0.95 | 0.93 | 0.94 | 0.98 | 1.03 | 1.11 | 1.19 | 1.18 |
| 30 | 30 | 0.3 | 1.23 | 1.18 | 1.08 | 1.00 | 0.94 | 0.92 | 0.93 | 0.97 | 1.04 | 1.14 | 1.20 | 1.26 |
| 35 | 35 | 0.3 | 1.33 | 1.25 | 1.10 | 1.00 | 0.94 | 0.90 | 0.92 | 0.97 | 1.06 | 1.19 | 1.29 | 1.38 |
| 40 | 40 | 0.3 | 1.47 | 1.36 | 1.14 | 1.01 | 0.93 | 0.90 | 0.91 | 0.97 | 1.08 | 1.26 | 1.41 | 1.54 |
| 45 | 45 | 0.3 | 1.68 | 1.38 | 1.19 | 1.02 | 0.93 | 0.89 | 0.91 | 0.98 | 1.11 | 1.36 | 1.58 | 1.88 |
| 50 | 50 | 0.3 | 1.88 | 1.53 | 1.26 | 1.04 | 0.93 | 0.88 | 0.90 | 0.98 | 1.15 | 1.41 | 1.89 | 2.10 |
| 55 | 55 | 0.3 | 2.53 | 1.77 | 1.35 | 1.06 | 0.93 | 0.87 | 0.90 | 1.00 | 1.21 | 1.58 | 2.18 | 3.12 |
| 60 | 60 | 0.3 | 3.48 | 2.21 | 1.48 | 1.09 | 0.93 | 0.87 | 0.89 | 1.02 | 1.29 | 1.85 | 3.26 | 5.07 |
| 20 | 35 | 0.3 | 1.19 | 1.10 | 1.01 | 0.92 | 0.88 | 0.85 | 0.86 | 0.91 | 0.98 | 1.07 | 1.16 | 1.22 |
| 25 | 40 | 0.3 | 1.27 | 1.13 | 1.02 | 0.93 | 0.87 | 0.84 | 0.85 | 0.90 | 0.98 | 1.09 | 1.22 | 1.22 |
| 30 | 45 | 0.3 | 1.26 | 1.18 | 1.04 | 0.93 | 0.85 | 0.82 | 0.83 | 0.89 | 0.99 | 1.13 | 1.22 | 1.31 |
| 35 | 50 | 0.3 | 1.37 | 1.25 | 1.06 | 0.93 | 0.84 | 0.80 | 0.82 | 0.89 | 1.00 | 1.18 | 1.31 | 1.43 |
| 40 | 55 | 0.3 | 1.51 | 1.37 | 1.09 | 0.93 | 0.83 | 0.80 | 0.81 | 0.89 | 1.02 | 1.25 | 1.43 | 1.61 |
| 45 | 60 | 0.3 | 1.74 | 1.37 | 1.14 | 0.94 | 0.83 | 0.78 | 0.80 | 0.89 | 1.05 | 1.35 | 1.62 | 1.99 |
| 50 | 65 | 0.3 | 1.95 | 1.53 | 1.20 | 0.95 | 0.82 | 0.77 | 0.79 | 0.89 | 1.08 | 1.38 | 1.95 | 2.21 |
| 55 | 70 | 0.3 | 2.65 | 1.78 | 1.29 | 0.97 | 0.82 | 0.76 | 0.78 | 0.90 | 1.14 | 1.56 | 2.25 | 3.32 |
| 60 | 75 | 0.3 | 3.66 | 2.23 | 1.42 | 0.99 | 0.81 | 0.75 | 0.77 | 0.91 | 1.21 | 1.84 | 3.39 | 5.41 |
| 20 | 90 | 0.3 | 0.88 | 0.72 | 0.58 | 0.44 | 0.39 | 0.38 | 0.38 | 0.42 | 0.52 | 0.67 | 0.83 | 0.93 |
| 25 | 90 | 0.3 | 1.00 | 0.79 | 0.63 | 0.49 | 0.41 | 0.39 | 0.40 | 0.45 | 0.57 | 0.73 | 0.93 | 0.95 |
| 30 | 90 | 0.3 | 1.01 | 0.88 | 0.68 | 0.53 | 0.44 | 0.41 | 0.42 | 0.49 | 0.61 | 0.80 | 0.95 | 1.07 |
| 35 | 90 | 0.3 | 1.14 | 0.98 | 0.74 | 0.57 | 0.47 | 0.44 | 0.45 | 0.53 | 0.66 | 0.89 | 1.07 | 1.22 |
| 40 | 90 | 0.3 | 1.32 | 1.13 | 0.81 | 0.62 | 0.51 | 0.47 | 0.49 | 0.56 | 0.72 | 0.99 | 1.23 | 1.44 |
| 45 | 90 | 0.3 | 1.59 | 1.17 | 0.89 | 0.66 | 0.55 | 0.50 | 0.52 | 0.61 | 0.79 | 1.13 | 1.45 | 1.87 |
| 50 | 90 | 0.3 | 1.83 | 1.36 | 0.99 | 0.72 | 0.59 | 0.54 | 0.56 | 0.65 | 0.87 | 1.20 | 1.82 | 2.10 |
| 55 | 90 | 0.3 | 2.56 | 1.64 | 1.12 | 0.78 | 0.62 | 0.57 | 0.59 | 0.71 | 0.96 | 1.41 | 2.14 | 3.27 |
| 20 | 5 | 0.4 | 1.07 | 1.05 | 1.03 | 1.01 | 1.01 | 1.00 | 1.00 | 1.01 | 1.02 | 1.05 | 1.07 | 1.08 |
| 25 | 10 | 0.4 | 1.15 | 1.10 | 1.05 | 1.02 | 1.00 | 0.99 | 0.99 | 1.01 | 1.04 | 1.08 | 1.13 | 1.11 |
| 30 | 15 | 0.4 | 1.18 | 1.16 | 1.08 | 1.03 | 1.00 | 0.98 | 0.98 | 1.02 | 1.06 | 1.13 | 1.16 | 1.20 |
| 35 | 20 | 0.4 | 1.29 | 1.23 | 1.12 | 1.05 | 0.99 | 0.97 | 0.98 | 1.02 | 1.09 | 1.19 | 1.26 | 1.33 |
| 40 | 25 | 0.4 | 1.44 | 1.35 | 1.17 | 1.06 | 0.99 | 0.97 | 0.98 | 1.03 | 1.12 | 1.27 | 1.39 | 1.51 |
| 45 | 30 | 0.4 | 1.68 | 1.40 | 1.24 | 1.09 | 1.00 | 0.97 | 0.98 | 1.05 | 1.17 | 1.39 | 1.58 | 1.85 |
| 50 | 35 | 0.4 | 1.90 | 1.58 | 1.32 | 1.12 | 1.01 | 0.97 | 0.99 | 1.06 | 1.23 | 1.46 | 1.92 | 2.11 |
| 55 | 40 | 0.4 | 2.60 | 1.86 | 1.44 | 1.16 | 1.02 | 0.97 | 0.99 | 1.09 | 1.30 | 1.66 | 2.25 | 3.16 |
| 60 | 45 | 0.4 | 3.59 | 2.36 | 1.61 | 1.21 | 1.03 | 0.97 | 1.00 | 1.13 | 1.41 | 1.99 | 3.40 | 5.16 |
| 20 | 20 | 0.4 | 1.19 | 1.12 | 1.05 | 0.99 | 0.95 | 0.93 | 0.94 | 0.97 | 1.03 | 1.10 | 1.17 | 1.21 |

Table XXIII, continued

| $\phi$ | $\beta$ | $\overline{K_T}$ | Jan | Feb | Mar | Apr | May | Jun | Jul | Aug | Sep | Oct | Nov | Dec |
|---|---|---|---|---|---|---|---|---|---|---|---|---|---|---|
| 25 | 25 | 0.4 | 1.28 | 1.17 | 1.08 | 1.00 | 0.94 | 0.92 | 0.93 | 0.97 | 1.04 | 1.14 | 1.24 | 1.23 |
| 30 | 30 | 0.4 | 1.30 | 1.23 | 1.11 | 1.00 | 0.94 | 0.91 | 0.92 | 0.97 | 1.06 | 1.19 | 1.26 | 1.34 |
| 35 | 35 | 0.4 | 1.43 | 1.32 | 1.14 | 1.01 | 0.93 | 0.89 | 0.91 | 0.98 | 1.09 | 1.25 | 1.37 | 1.49 |
| 40 | 40 | 0.4 | 1.61 | 1.45 | 1.19 | 1.03 | 0.93 | 0.89 | 0.91 | 0.98 | 1.12 | 1.34 | 1.53 | 1.70 |
| 45 | 45 | 0.4 | 1.88 | 1.49 | 1.26 | 1.05 | 0.93 | 0.89 | 0.91 | 0.99 | 1.16 | 1.47 | 1.75 | 2.12 |
| 50 | 50 | 0.4 | 2.13 | 1.69 | 1.35 | 1.08 | 0.94 | 0.88 | 0.90 | 1.01 | 1.22 | 1.54 | 2.14 | 2.40 |
| 55 | 55 | 0.4 | 2.94 | 2.00 | 1.47 | 1.11 | 0.94 | 0.88 | 0.90 | 1.03 | 1.30 | 1.76 | 2.50 | 3.66 |
| 60 | 60 | 0.4 | 4.09 | 2.56 | 1.64 | 1.16 | 0.95 | 0.88 | 0.91 | 1.06 | 1.41 | 2.11 | 3.84 | 5.98 |
| 20 | 35 | 0.4 | 1.25 | 1.14 | 1.03 | 0.92 | 0.86 | 0.83 | 0.84 | 0.90 | 0.98 | 1.10 | 1.22 | 1.29 |
| 25 | 40 | 0.4 | 1.35 | 1.19 | 1.05 | 0.93 | 0.85 | 0.81 | 0.83 | 0.89 | 1.00 | 1.14 | 1.30 | 1.30 |
| 30 | 45 | 0.4 | 1.36 | 1.25 | 1.07 | 0.93 | 0.84 | 0.80 | 0.82 | 0.89 | 1.01 | 1.19 | 1.30 | 1.41 |
| 35 | 50 | 0.4 | 1.49 | 1.34 | 1.11 | 0.94 | 0.83 | 0.79 | 0.81 | 0.89 | 1.03 | 1.25 | 1.42 | 1.57 |
| 40 | 55 | 0.4 | 1.68 | 1.48 | 1.15 | 0.95 | 0.83 | 0.78 | 0.80 | 0.89 | 1.06 | 1.34 | 1.58 | 1.80 |
| 45 | 60 | 0.4 | 1.98 | 1.51 | 1.22 | 0.96 | 0.83 | 0.77 | 0.80 | 0.90 | 1.10 | 1.47 | 1.82 | 2.27 |
| 50 | 65 | 0.4 | 2.24 | 1.72 | 1.30 | 0.99 | 0.83 | 0.76 | 0.79 | 0.91 | 1.16 | 1.53 | 2.24 | 2.56 |
| 55 | 70 | 0.4 | 3.11 | 2.03 | 1.42 | 1.01 | 0.83 | 0.76 | 0.79 | 0.93 | 1.23 | 1.76 | 2.61 | 3.92 |
| 60 | 75 | 0.4 | 4.32 | 2.61 | 1.59 | 1.05 | 0.83 | 0.75 | 0.78 | 0.95 | 1.33 | 2.11 | 4.03 | 6.42 |
| 20 | 90 | 0.4 | 0.95 | 0.76 | 0.57 | 0.40 | 0.34 | 0.33 | 0.33 | 0.37 | 0.50 | 0.69 | 0.89 | 1.01 |
| 25 | 90 | 0.4 | 1.09 | 0.84 | 0.63 | 0.46 | 0.36 | 0.34 | 0.35 | 0.41 | 0.56 | 0.77 | 1.01 | 1.04 |
| 30 | 90 | 0.4 | 1.11 | 0.94 | 0.70 | 0.50 | 0.40 | 0.36 | 0.38 | 0.46 | 0.61 | 0.85 | 1.04 | 1.18 |
| 35 | 90 | 0.4 | 1.28 | 1.07 | 0.77 | 0.56 | 0.44 | 0.40 | 0.41 | 0.50 | 0.68 | 0.95 | 1.19 | 1.38 |
| 40 | 90 | 0.4 | 1.51 | 1.25 | 0.86 | 0.61 | 0.48 | 0.44 | 0.46 | 0.55 | 0.75 | 1.08 | 1.39 | 1.65 |
| 45 | 90 | 0.4 | 1.84 | 1.30 | 0.96 | 0.67 | 0.53 | 0.48 | 0.50 | 0.60 | 0.83 | 1.25 | 1.66 | 2.17 |
| 50 | 90 | 0.4 | 2.13 | 1.54 | 1.08 | 0.74 | 0.58 | 0.52 | 0.54 | 0.66 | 0.93 | 1.34 | 2.12 | 2.47 |
| 55 | 90 | 0.4 | 3.04 | 1.90 | 1.24 | 0.82 | 0.62 | 0.55 | 0.58 | 0.73 | 1.04 | 1.60 | 2.51 | 3.90 |
| 20 | 5 | 0.5 | 1.08 | 1.06 | 1.03 | 1.01 | 1.01 | 1.00 | 1.00 | 1.01 | 1.02 | 1.05 | 1.08 | 1.09 |
| 25 | 10 | 0.5 | 1.17 | 1.11 | 1.06 | 1.03 | 1.00 | 0.98 | 0.99 | 1.01 | 1.04 | 1.09 | 1.15 | 1.13 |
| 30 | 15 | 0.5 | 1.21 | 1.18 | 1.10 | 1.04 | 0.99 | 0.97 | 0.98 | 1.02 | 1.07 | 1.15 | 1.19 | 1.24 |
| 35 | 20 | 0.5 | 1.34 | 1.27 | 1.14 | 1.05 | 0.99 | 0.97 | 0.98 | 1.03 | 1.10 | 1.22 | 1.30 | 1.38 |
| 40 | 25 | 0.5 | 1.52 | 1.40 | 1.20 | 1.08 | 1.00 | 0.97 | 0.98 | 1.04 | 1.14 | 1.32 | 1.46 | 1.60 |
| 45 | 30 | 0.5 | 1.80 | 1.47 | 1.28 | 1.11 | 1.01 | 0.97 | 0.98 | 1.06 | 1.20 | 1.45 | 1.69 | 1.99 |
| 50 | 35 | 0.5 | 2.06 | 1.68 | 1.38 | 1.14 | 1.02 | 0.97 | 0.99 | 1.08 | 1.27 | 1.54 | 2.08 | 2.30 |
| 55 | 40 | 0.5 | 2.87 | 2.01 | 1.52 | 1.19 | 1.03 | 0.97 | 1.00 | 1.12 | 1.36 | 1.78 | 2.46 | 3.51 |
| 60 | 45 | 0.5 | 4.01 | 2.60 | 1.72 | 1.25 | 1.05 | 0.98 | 1.01 | 1.16 | 1.49 | 2.16 | 3.80 | 5.78 |
| 20 | 20 | 0.5 | 1.22 | 1.14 | 1.06 | 0.99 | 0.94 | 0.92 | 0.93 | 0.97 | 1.03 | 1.12 | 1.20 | 1.25 |
| 25 | 25 | 0.5 | 1.33 | 1.20 | 1.09 | 1.00 | 0.94 | 0.91 | 0.92 | 0.97 | 1.05 | 1.16 | 1.29 | 1.28 |
| 30 | 30 | 0.5 | 1.36 | 1.28 | 1.13 | 1.01 | 0.93 | 0.89 | 0.91 | 0.97 | 1.08 | 1.22 | 1.31 | 1.40 |
| 35 | 35 | 0.5 | 1.51 | 1.38 | 1.18 | 1.02 | 0.93 | 0.89 | 0.90 | 0.98 | 1.11 | 1.30 | 1.45 | 1.58 |
| 40 | 40 | 0.5 | 1.72 | 1.53 | 1.24 | 1.04 | 0.93 | 0.88 | 0.90 | 0.99 | 1.15 | 1.41 | 1.63 | 1.83 |
| 45 | 45 | 0.5 | 2.05 | 1.59 | 1.32 | 1.07 | 0.93 | 0.88 | 0.90 | 1.01 | 1.20 | 1.56 | 1.89 | 2.31 |
| 50 | 50 | 0.5 | 2.34 | 1.83 | 1.42 | 1.10 | 0.94 | 0.88 | 0.91 | 1.03 | 1.28 | 1.64 | 2.35 | 2.65 |
| 55 | 55 | 0.5 | 3.28 | 2.19 | 1.57 | 1.15 | 0.95 | 0.88 | 0.91 | 1.06 | 1.37 | 1.91 | 2.77 | 4.09 |
| 60 | 60 | 0.5 | 4.59 | 2.85 | 1.77 | 1.21 | 0.97 | 0.88 | 0.92 | 1.09 | 1.50 | 2.32 | 4.31 | 6.74 |
| 20 | 35 | 0.5 | 1.30 | 1.17 | 1.04 | 0.92 | 0.85 | 0.81 | 0.82 | 0.89 | 0.99 | 1.12 | 1.26 | 1.34 |
| 25 | 40 | 0.5 | 1.42 | 1.23 | 1.07 | 0.93 | 0.84 | 0.79 | 0.81 | 0.89 | 1.01 | 1.17 | 1.36 | 1.36 |
| 30 | 45 | 0.5 | 1.43 | 1.31 | 1.10 | 0.93 | 0.83 | 0.78 | 0.80 | 0.89 | 1.03 | 1.23 | 1.37 | 1.50 |

Table XXIII, continued

| | | | | | | | | | | | | | | |
|---|---|---|---|---|---|---|---|---|---|---|---|---|---|---|
| 35 | 50 | 0.5 | 1.59 | 1.42 | 1.15 | 0.95 | 0.82 | 0.77 | 0.79 | 0.89 | 1.06 | 1.31 | 1.51 | 1.69 |
| 40 | 55 | 0.5 | 1.82 | 1.58 | 1.20 | 0.96 | 0.82 | 0.77 | 0.79 | 0.90 | 1.10 | 1.42 | 1.71 | 1.96 |
| 45 | 60 | 0.5 | 2.18 | 1.62 | 1.28 | 0.98 | 0.83 | 0.76 | 0.79 | 0.91 | 1.15 | 1.57 | 1.99 | 2.50 |
| 50 | 65 | 0.5 | 2.48 | 1.87 | 1.38 | 1.01 | 0.83 | 0.76 | 0.79 | 0.93 | 1.21 | 1.65 | 2.48 | 2.84 |
| 55 | 70 | 0.5 | 3.49 | 2.25 | 1.52 | 1.05 | 0.84 | 0.75 | 0.79 | 0.95 | 1.30 | 1.92 | 2.91 | 4.42 |
| 60 | 75 | 0.5 | 4.88 | 2.93 | 1.73 | 1.10 | 0.84 | 0.75 | 0.79 | 0.98 | 1.43 | 2.34 | 4.56 | 7.26 |
| 20 | 90 | 0.5 | 1.00 | 0.78 | 0.57 | 0.37 | 0.29 | 0.29 | 0.29 | 0.33 | 0.49 | 0.71 | 0.94 | 1.08 |
| 25 | 90 | 0.5 | 1.17 | 0.88 | 0.64 | 0.43 | 0.32 | 0.29 | 0.31 | 0.38 | 0.55 | 0.79 | 1.07 | 1.11 |
| 30 | 90 | 0.5 | 1.19 | 1.00 | 0.71 | 0.49 | 0.37 | 0.32 | 0.34 | 0.43 | 0.62 | 0.89 | 1.11 | 1.28 |
| 35 | 90 | 0.5 | 1.39 | 1.15 | 0.80 | 0.55 | 0.41 | 0.36 | 0.38 | 0.48 | 0.69 | 1.01 | 1.28 | 1.51 |
| 40 | 90 | 0.5 | 1.66 | 1.35 | 0.90 | 0.61 | 0.46 | 0.41 | 0.43 | 0.54 | 0.77 | 1.16 | 1.51 | 1.83 |
| 45 | 90 | 0.5 | 2.05 | 1.42 | 1.01 | 0.68 | 0.52 | 0.45 | 0.48 | 0.60 | 0.86 | 1.35 | 1.83 | 2.42 |
| 50 | 90 | 0.5 | 2.37 | 1.70 | 1.16 | 0.76 | 0.57 | 0.50 | 0.53 | 0.67 | 0.97 | 1.46 | 2.37 | 2.77 |
| 20 | 5 | 0.6 | 1.09 | 1.06 | 1.04 | 1.01 | 1.00 | 1.00 | 1.00 | 1.01 | 1.03 | 1.06 | 1.08 | 1.10 |
| 25 | 10 | 0.6 | 1.19 | 1.13 | 1.07 | 1.03 | 1.00 | 0.98 | 0.99 | 1.01 | 1.05 | 1.11 | 1.17 | 1.15 |
| 30 | 15 | 0.6 | 1.24 | 1.20 | 1.11 | 1.04 | 0.99 | 0.97 | 0.98 | 1.02 | 1.08 | 1.17 | 1.21 | 1.27 |
| 35 | 20 | 0.6 | 1.39 | 1.31 | 1.17 | 1.06 | 0.99 | 0.96 | 0.98 | 1.03 | 1.12 | 1.25 | 1.35 | 1.44 |
| 40 | 25 | 0.6 | 1.60 | 1.46 | 1.23 | 1.09 | 1.00 | 0.96 | 0.98 | 1.05 | 1.17 | 1.37 | 1.53 | 1.68 |
| 45 | 30 | 0.6 | 1.92 | 1.54 | 1.32 | 1.12 | 1.01 | 0.97 | 0.99 | 1.07 | 1.23 | 1.52 | 1.79 | 2.13 |
| 50 | 35 | 0.6 | 2.22 | 1.79 | 1.44 | 1.17 | 1.03 | 0.97 | 0.99 | 1.10 | 1.32 | 1.63 | 2.24 | 2.49 |
| 55 | 40 | 0.6 | 3.13 | 2.17 | 1.60 | 1.23 | 1.05 | 0.98 | 1.01 | 1.14 | 1.42 | 1.90 | 2.68 | 3.85 |
| 60 | 45 | 0.6 | 4.41 | 2.83 | 1.83 | 1.30 | 1.07 | 0.99 | 1.02 | 1.19 | 1.57 | 2.34 | 4.19 | 6.39 |
| 20 | 20 | 0.6 | 1.25 | 1.16 | 1.07 | 0.99 | 0.94 | 0.91 | 0.92 | 0.97 | 1.04 | 1.13 | 1.23 | 1.28 |
| 25 | 25 | 0.6 | 1.37 | 1.23 | 1.11 | 1.00 | 0.93 | 0.89 | 0.91 | 0.97 | 1.06 | 1.19 | 1.33 | 1.32 |
| 30 | 30 | 0.6 | 1.41 | 1.32 | 1.15 | 1.01 | 0.92 | 0.88 | 0.90 | 0.97 | 1.09 | 1.26 | 1.37 | 1.47 |
| 35 | 35 | 0.6 | 1.59 | 1.44 | 1.21 | 1.03 | 0.92 | 0.88 | 0.90 | 0.98 | 1.13 | 1.35 | 1.52 | 1.67 |
| 40 | 40 | 0.6 | 1.84 | 1.61 | 1.28 | 1.06 | 0.93 | 0.88 | 0.90 | 1.00 | 1.18 | 1.47 | 1.73 | 1.96 |
| 45 | 45 | 0.6 | 2.21 | 1.69 | 1.37 | 1.09 | 0.94 | 0.88 | 0.90 | 1.02 | 1.25 | 1.65 | 2.03 | 2.50 |
| 50 | 50 | 0.6 | 2.54 | 1.96 | 1.50 | 1.13 | 0.95 | 0.88 | 0.91 | 1.05 | 1.33 | 1.75 | 2.55 | 2.90 |
| 55 | 55 | 0.6 | 3.61 | 2.38 | 1.66 | 1.19 | 0.96 | 0.88 | 0.92 | 1.08 | 1.44 | 2.05 | 3.04 | 4.53 |
| 60 | 60 | 0.6 | 5.08 | 3.13 | 1.90 | 1.26 | 0.98 | 0.89 | 0.93 | 1.13 | 1.59 | 2.53 | 4.79 | 7.48 |
| 20 | 35 | 0.6 | 1.35 | 1.20 | 1.05 | 0.92 | 0.83 | 0.79 | 0.81 | 0.88 | 1.00 | 1.15 | 1.30 | 1.40 |
| 25 | 40 | 0.6 | 1.48 | 1.27 | 1.09 | 0.93 | 0.82 | 0.78 | 0.80 | 0.88 | 1.02 | 1.21 | 1.41 | 1.42 |
| 30 | 45 | 0.6 | 1.51 | 1.36 | 1.13 | 0.94 | 0.82 | 0.77 | 0.79 | 0.88 | 1.05 | 1.28 | 1.44 | 1.58 |
| 35 | 50 | 0.6 | 1.70 | 1.49 | 1.18 | 0.95 | 0.82 | 0.76 | 0.78 | 0.89 | 1.08 | 1.37 | 1.60 | 1.80 |
| 40 | 55 | 0.6 | 1.96 | 1.68 | 1.25 | 0.98 | 0.82 | 0.76 | 0.78 | 0.90 | 1.13 | 1.50 | 1.83 | 2.12 |
| 45 | 60 | 0.6 | 2.37 | 1.73 | 1.34 | 1.01 | 0.83 | 0.75 | 0.78 | 0.92 | 1.19 | 1.68 | 2.16 | 2.73 |
| 50 | 65 | 0.6 | 2.71 | 2.07 | 1.46 | 1.04 | 0.83 | 0.75 | 0.79 | 0.94 | 1.27 | 1.77 | 2.72 | 3.13 |
| 55 | 70 | 0.6 | 3.87 | 2.46 | 1.63 | 1.09 | 0.85 | 0.75 | 0.79 | 0.97 | 1.38 | 2.08 | 3.21 | 4.91 |
| 60 | 75 | 0.6 | 5.42 | 3.24 | 1.86 | 1.15 | 0.86 | 0.76 | 0.80 | 1.01 | 1.52 | 2.56 | 5.08 | 8.08 |
| 20 | 90 | 0.6 | 1.06 | 0.81 | 0.56 | 0.34 | 0.25 | 0.25 | 0.25 | 0.29 | 0.47 | 0.72 | 0.98 | 1.15 |
| 25 | 90 | 0.6 | 1.24 | 0.92 | 0.64 | 0.41 | 0.29 | 0.25 | 0.26 | 0.35 | 0.54 | 0.82 | 1.14 | 1.18 |
| 30 | 90 | 0.6 | 1.27 | 1.05 | 0.73 | 0.47 | 0.33 | 0.29 | 0.30 | 0.41 | 0.62 | 0.93 | 1.18 | 1.38 |
| 35 | 90 | 0.6 | 1.50 | 1.22 | 0.82 | 0.54 | 0.38 | 0.33 | 0.35 | 0.47 | 0.70 | 1.07 | 1.38 | 1.64 |
| 40 | 90 | 0.6 | 1.81 | 1.45 | 0.94 | 0.61 | 0.44 | 0.38 | 0.40 | 0.53 | 0.79 | 1.23 | 1.64 | 2.00 |
| 45 | 90 | 0.6 | 2.26 | 1.53 | 1.07 | 0.69 | 0.50 | 0.43 | 0.46 | 0.60 | 0.90 | 1.45 | 2.01 | 2.66 |
| 50 | 90 | 0.6 | 2.62 | 1.85 | 1.23 | 0.78 | 0.56 | 0.48 | 0.52 | 0.67 | 1.02 | 1.58 | 2.61 | 3.07 |

**Table XXIV. Monthly Average Daily Solar Radiation on a Tilted Surface ($\overline{H}_T$) vs Latitude ($\phi$), Slope ($\beta$) and Average Cloudiness Index ($\overline{K}_T$) in Btu/ft$^2$ (To convert from Btu/ft$^2$ to kJ/m$^2$, multiply by 11.35653)**

| $\phi$ | $\beta$ | $\overline{K}_T$ | Jan | Feb | Mar | Apr | May | Jun | Jul | Aug | Sep | Oct | Nov | Dec |
|---|---|---|---|---|---|---|---|---|---|---|---|---|---|---|
| 20 | 5 | 0.3 | 746 | 842 | 933 | 1011 | 1037 | 1034 | 1038 | 1010 | 951 | 863 | 770 | 721 |
| 25 | 10 | 0.3 | 707 | 802 | 911 | 1000 | 1040 | 1047 | 1046 | 1009 | 931 | 831 | 730 | 653 |
| 30 | 15 | 0.3 | 633 | 767 | 880 | 991 | 1045 | 1054 | 1048 | 1011 | 913 | 798 | 656 | 604 |
| 35 | 20 | 0.3 | 587 | 725 | 848 | 975 | 1034 | 1054 | 1043 | 996 | 886 | 754 | 611 | 555 |
| 40 | 25 | 0.3 | 536 | 687 | 814 | 951 | 1026 | 1058 | 1043 | 974 | 851 | 717 | 566 | 504 |
| 45 | 30 | 0.3 | 485 | 604 | 769 | 929 | 1023 | 1058 | 1037 | 956 | 821 | 676 | 515 | 470 |
| 50 | 35 | 0.3 | 406 | 555 | 731 | 899 | 1004 | 1054 | 1026 | 930 | 781 | 600 | 472 | 378 |
| 55 | 40 | 0.3 | 365 | 507 | 688 | 860 | 991 | 1036 | 1012 | 907 | 743 | 553 | 389 | 347 |
| 60 | 45 | 0.3 | 301 | 464 | 644 | 830 | 965 | 1029 | 997 | 886 | 702 | 505 | 354 | 265 |
| 20 | 20 | 0.3 | 809 | 882 | 942 | 981 | 986 | 972 | 976 | 980 | 951 | 896 | 829 | 789 |
| 25 | 25 | 0.3 | 770 | 839 | 920 | 970 | 988 | 984 | 983 | 979 | 932 | 862 | 783 | 706 |
| 30 | 30 | 0.3 | 683 | 800 | 888 | 962 | 982 | 989 | 984 | 962 | 904 | 819 | 702 | 656 |
| 35 | 35 | 0.3 | 635 | 762 | 848 | 938 | 982 | 978 | 979 | 948 | 878 | 780 | 658 | 608 |
| 40 | 40 | 0.3 | 584 | 730 | 814 | 915 | 964 | 982 | 968 | 927 | 843 | 741 | 609 | 554 |
| 45 | 45 | 0.3 | 532 | 636 | 776 | 886 | 952 | 971 | 963 | 909 | 807 | 702 | 557 | 525 |
| 50 | 50 | 0.3 | 446 | 586 | 737 | 857 | 934 | 956 | 942 | 876 | 768 | 622 | 516 | 422 |
| 55 | 55 | 0.3 | 406 | 537 | 693 | 822 | 913 | 939 | 930 | 856 | 731 | 575 | 426 | 395 |
| 60 | 60 | 0.3 | 309 | 495 | 648 | 786 | 889 | 933 | 905 | 829 | 691 | 527 | 396 | 305 |
| 20 | 35 | 0.3 | 838 | 882 | 915 | 912 | 903 | 879 | 884 | 910 | 913 | 888 | 843 | 822 |
| 25 | 40 | 0.3 | 802 | 839 | 885 | 912 | 904 | 889 | 889 | 890 | 886 | 847 | 803 | 731 |
| 30 | 45 | 0.3 | 700 | 800 | 856 | 895 | 888 | 882 | 879 | 883 | 861 | 812 | 714 | 682 |
| 35 | 50 | 0.3 | 654 | 762 | 818 | 872 | 877 | 869 | 873 | 870 | 828 | 774 | 668 | 630 |
| 40 | 55 | 0.3 | 600 | 735 | 779 | 843 | 860 | 873 | 862 | 850 | 796 | 735 | 617 | 580 |
| 45 | 60 | 0.3 | 551 | 631 | 743 | 816 | 849 | 851 | 825 | 826 | 763 | 697 | 571 | 556 |
| 50 | 65 | 0.3 | 463 | 586 | 701 | 783 | 824 | 837 | 827 | 796 | 721 | 609 | 533 | 444 |
| 55 | 70 | 0.3 | 426 | 540 | 662 | 752 | 805 | 820 | 806 | 770 | 688 | 568 | 440 | 420 |
| 60 | 75 | 0.3 | 328 | 500 | 622 | 714 | 774 | 804 | 783 | 740 | 648 | 525 | 412 | 325 |
| 20 | 90 | 0.3 | 619 | 577 | 525 | 436 | 401 | 392 | 390 | 420 | 485 | 556 | 603 | 627 |
| 25 | 90 | 0.3 | 631 | 587 | 547 | 480 | 426 | 413 | 418 | 450 | 516 | 567 | 612 | 569 |
| 30 | 90 | 0.3 | 561 | 597 | 559 | 510 | 460 | 441 | 445 | 485 | 530 | 575 | 556 | 557 |
| 35 | 90 | 0.3 | 544 | 597 | 571 | 534 | 491 | 478 | 479 | 518 | 547 | 584 | 545 | 538 |
| 40 | 90 | 0.3 | 524 | 606 | 578 | 562 | 528 | 513 | 521 | 535 | 562 | 582 | 530 | 518 |
| 45 | 90 | 0.3 | 504 | 539 | 580 | 573 | 563 | 546 | 550 | 557 | 574 | 583 | 511 | 523 |
| 20 | 5 | 0.4 | 1004 | 1122 | 1245 | 1335 | 1383 | 1378 | 1370 | 1347 | 1268 | 1161 | 1037 | 971 |
| 25 | 10 | 0.4 | 968 | 1089 | 1215 | 1333 | 1386 | 1396 | 1381 | 1346 | 1254 | 1118 | 991 | 886 |
| 30 | 15 | 0.4 | 874 | 1049 | 1185 | 1322 | 1394 | 1405 | 1397 | 1349 | 1229 | 1083 | 905 | 833 |
| 35 | 20 | 0.4 | 821 | 999 | 1152 | 1313 | 1378 | 1405 | 1391 | 1328 | 1203 | 1040 | 855 | 782 |
| 40 | 25 | 0.4 | 763 | 966 | 1114 | 1281 | 1369 | 1412 | 1388 | 1312 | 1165 | 995 | 800 | 725 |
| 45 | 30 | 0.4 | 710 | 860 | 1078 | 1262 | 1364 | 1412 | 1383 | 1299 | 1139 | 957 | 743 | 684 |
| 50 | 35 | 0.4 | 601 | 806 | 1029 | 1231 | 1353 | 1406 | 1382 | 1264 | 1095 | 859 | 699 | 565 |
| 55 | 40 | 0.4 | 557 | 752 | 985 | 1199 | 1335 | 1396 | 1363 | 1244 | 1047 | 806 | 586 | 533 |
| 60 | 45 | 0.4 | 429 | 705 | 940 | 1164 | 1313 | 1387 | 1357 | 1225 | 1007 | 757 | 551 | 414 |
| 20 | 20 | 0.4 | 1117 | 1198 | 1269 | 1308 | 1301 | 1282 | 1288 | 1294 | 1281 | 1217 | 1134 | 1088 |

**Table XXIV, continued**

| | | | | | | | | | | | | | | |
|---|---|---|---|---|---|---|---|---|---|---|---|---|---|---|
| 25 | 25 | 0.4 | 1078 | 1159 | 1250 | 1307 | 1303 | 1298 | 1297 | 1292 | 1254 | 1181 | 1088 | 982 |
| 30 | 30 | 0.4 | 963 | 1113 | 1215 | 1283 | 1310 | 1305 | 1298 | 1282 | 1229 | 1208 | 984 | 930 |
| 35 | 35 | 0.4 | 910 | 1073 | 1172 | 1263 | 1294 | 1289 | 1291 | 1276 | 1203 | 1093 | 931 | 876 |
| 40 | 40 | 0.4 | 853 | 1038 | 1134 | 1245 | 1285 | 1296 | 1291 | 1248 | 1165 | 1050 | 881 | 816 |
| 45 | 45 | 0.4 | 794 | 915 | 1095 | 1215 | 1269 | 1295 | 1255 | 1224 | 1124 | 1018 | 822 | 790 |
| 50 | 50 | 0.4 | 674 | 862 | 1052 | 1187 | 1259 | 1275 | 1257 | 1204 | 1086 | 906 | 780 | 642 |
| 55 | 55 | 0.4 | 630 | 809 | 1006 | 1147 | 1230 | 1267 | 1239 | 1175 | 1047 | 854 | 651 | 618 |
| 60 | 60 | 0.4 | 489 | 765 | 957 | 1116 | 1211 | 1258 | 1234 | 1149 | 1007 | 802 | 621 | 480 |
| 20 | 35 | 0.4 | 1173 | 1219 | 1245 | 1215 | 1178 | 1144 | 1151 | 1200 | 1219 | 1217 | 1182 | 1160 |
| 25 | 40 | 0.4 | 1136 | 1178 | 1215 | 1215 | 1178 | 1143 | 1158 | 1186 | 1206 | 1181 | 1141 | 1038 |
| 30 | 45 | 0.4 | 1008 | 1130 | 1173 | 1193 | 1171 | 1147 | 1157 | 1177 | 1171 | 1141 | 1015 | 979 |
| 35 | 50 | 0.4 | 948 | 1089 | 1142 | 1175 | 1156 | 1144 | 1149 | 1159 | 1137 | 1093 | 965 | 923 |
| 40 | 55 | 0.4 | 890 | 1059 | 1095 | 1148 | 1147 | 1135 | 1135 | 1134 | 1103 | 1050 | 909 | 863 |
| 45 | 60 | 0.4 | 837 | 928 | 1060 | 1111 | 1132 | 1121 | 1129 | 1113 | 1066 | 1012 | 855 | 846 |
| 50 | 65 | 0.4 | 709 | 878 | 1013 | 1088 | 1117 | 1102 | 1103 | 1085 | 1033 | 900 | 816 | 686 |
| 55 | 70 | 0.4 | 666 | 821 | 971 | 1044 | 1086 | 1094 | 1088 | 1061 | 990 | 854 | 680 | 661 |
| 60 | 75 | 0.4 | 516 | 780 | 928 | 1009 | 1058 | 1072 | 1058 | 1030 | 950 | 802 | 652 | 515 |
| 20 | 90 | 0.4 | 892 | 813 | 688 | 530 | 466 | 455 | 452 | 493 | 662 | 763 | 862 | 980 |
| 25 | 90 | 0.4 | 918 | 832 | 728 | 601 | 499 | 480 | 488 | 546 | 675 | 798 | 886 | 830 |
| 30 | 90 | 0.4 | 822 | 850 | 768 | 642 | 557 | 516 | 536 | 608 | 707 | 815 | 812 | 819 |
| 35 | 90 | 0.4 | 814 | 869 | 792 | 700 | 613 | 579 | 582 | 651 | 751 | 830 | 809 | 811 |
| 40 | 90 | 0.4 | 800 | 894 | 819 | 737 | 664 | 640 | 653 | 701 | 780 | 847 | 800 | 792 |
| 45 | 90 | 0.4 | 778 | 799 | 834 | 776 | 723 | 699 | 705 | 742 | 804 | 860 | 780 | 809 |
| 50 | 90 | 0.4 | 674 | 786 | 842 | 813 | 777 | 754 | 754 | 787 | 828 | 788 | 772 | 661 |
| 20 | 5 | 0.5 | 1267 | 1417 | 1564 | 1668 | 1729 | 1723 | 1712 | 1684 | 1585 | 1452 | 1308 | 1224 |
| 25 | 10 | 0.5 | 1231 | 1374 | 1532 | 1683 | 1733 | 1728 | 1726 | 1682 | 1568 | 1411 | 1261 | 1128 |
| 30 | 15 | 0.5 | 1120 | 1334 | 1508 | 1668 | 1725 | 1738 | 1729 | 1686 | 1551 | 1377 | 1161 | 1076 |
| 35 | 20 | 0.5 | 1066 | 1290 | 1466 | 1641 | 1723 | 1756 | 1739 | 1679 | 1518 | 1333 | 1194 | 1014 |
| 40 | 25 | 0.5 | 1007 | 1252 | 1429 | 1631 | 1728 | 1765 | 1738 | 1656 | 1483 | 1293 | 1051 | 960 |
| 45 | 30 | 0.5 | 951 | 1129 | 1391 | 1606 | 1722 | 1764 | 1728 | 1639 | 1454 | 1247 | 993 | 927 |
| 50 | 35 | 0.5 | 815 | 1072 | 1345 | 1566 | 1701 | 1757 | 1728 | 1609 | 1414 | 1132 | 947 | 770 |
| 55 | 40 | 0.5 | 769 | 1016 | 1300 | 1537 | 1685 | 1745 | 1722 | 1597 | 1369 | 1078 | 801 | 740 |
| 60 | 45 | 0.5 | 599 | 971 | 1255 | 1503 | 1673 | 1751 | 1713 | 1572 | 1330 | 1026 | 769 | 579 |
| 20 | 20 | 0.5 | 1413 | 1533 | 1601 | 1635 | 1609 | 1622 | 1593 | 1617 | 1601 | 1548 | 1454 | 1404 |
| 25 | 25 | 0.5 | 1400 | 1485 | 1576 | 1634 | 1629 | 1604 | 1604 | 1615 | 1583 | 1502 | 1415 | 1278 |
| 30 | 30 | 0.5 | 1259 | 1447 | 1549 | 1620 | 1620 | 1595 | 1605 | 1602 | 1565 | 1462 | 1278 | 1215 |
| 35 | 35 | 0.5 | 1201 | 1402 | 1517 | 1594 | 1619 | 1612 | 1597 | 1595 | 1532 | 1421 | 1232 | 1161 |
| 40 | 40 | 0.5 | 1139 | 1369 | 1476 | 1571 | 1606 | 1601 | 1596 | 1576 | 1496 | 1382 | 1173 | 1098 |
| 45 | 45 | 0.5 | 1083 | 1221 | 1434 | 1548 | 1586 | 1601 | 1587 | 1562 | 1454 | 1342 | 1110 | 1076 |
| 50 | 50 | 0.5 | 926 | 1167 | 1384 | 1511 | 1574 | 1594 | 1588 | 1535 | 1424 | 1206 | 1070 | 887 |
| 55 | 55 | 0.5 | 878 | 1107 | 1343 | 1486 | 1554 | 1583 | 1567 | 1512 | 1379 | 1158 | 902 | 863 |
| 60 | 60 | 0.5 | 686 | 1065 | 1292 | 1455 | 1545 | 1572 | 1560 | 1477 | 1339 | 1103 | 873 | 676 |
| 20 | 35 | 0.5 | 1527 | 1566 | 1572 | 1521 | 1457 | 1397 | 1406 | 1485 | 1540 | 1550 | 1528 | 1507 |
| 25 | 40 | 0.5 | 1496 | 1524 | 1580 | 1521 | 1457 | 1394 | 1414 | 1484 | 1524 | 1517 | 1493 | 1359 |
| 30 | 45 | 0.5 | 1326 | 1482 | 1509 | 1493 | 1448 | 1399 | 1413 | 1472 | 1494 | 1475 | 1338 | 1303 |
| 35 | 50 | 0.5 | 1272 | 1444 | 1480 | 1486 | 1429 | 1396 | 1403 | 1450 | 1465 | 1433 | 1284 | 1243 |
| 40 | 55 | 0.5 | 1207 | 1415 | 1430 | 1451 | 1418 | 1402 | 1403 | 1437 | 1432 | 1393 | 1232 | 1177 |
| 45 | 60 | 0.5 | 1152 | 1246 | 1392 | 1420 | 1417 | 1384 | 1395 | 1409 | 1395 | 1352 | 1170 | 1166 |

**Table XXIV, continued**

| $\phi$ | $\beta$ | $\overline{K_T}$ | Jan | Feb | Mar | Apr | May | Jun | Jul | Aug | Sep | Oct | Nov | Dec |
|---|---|---|---|---|---|---|---|---|---|---|---|---|---|---|
| 50 | 65 | 0.5 | 982 | 1194 | 1346 | 1389 | 1391 | 1378 | 1380 | 1388 | 1348 | 1215 | 1130 | 952 |
| 55 | 70 | 0.5 | 935 | 1139 | 1301 | 1358 | 1375 | 1350 | 1361 | 1356 | 1310 | 1166 | 949 | 933 |
| 60 | 75 | 0.5 | 730 | 1096 | 1264 | 1324 | 1340 | 1342 | 1341 | 1329 | 1278 | 1114 | 924 | 729 |
| 20 | 90 | 0.5 | 1174 | 1044 | 862 | 612 | 496 | 500 | 497 | 550 | 762 | 983 | 1140 | 1215 |
| 25 | 90 | 0.5 | 1232 | 1090 | 927 | 703 | 555 | 512 | 541 | 634 | 830 | 1024 | 1175 | 1109 |
| 30 | 90 | 0.5 | 1103 | 1132 | 975 | 787 | 645 | 574 | 600 | 711 | 899 | 1068 | 1084 | 1112 |
| 35 | 90 | 0.5 | 1107 | 1169 | 1030 | 860 | 714 | 652 | 675 | 782 | 953 | 1105 | 1089 | 1110 |
| 40 | 90 | 0.5 | 1100 | 1209 | 1072 | 922 | 796 | 747 | 763 | 861 | 1003 | 1138 | 1088 | 1099 |
| 45 | 90 | 0.5 | 1084 | 1092 | 1099 | 985 | 888 | 819 | 847 | 929 | 1043 | 1163 | 1070 | 1028 |
| 20 | 5 | 0.6 | 1536 | 1702 | 1887 | 2004 | 2057 | 2070 | 2052 | 2023 | 1923 | 1760 | 1572 | 1485 |
| 25 | 10 | 0.6 | 1504 | 1680 | 1859 | 2022 | 2082 | 2076 | 2074 | 2021 | 1901 | 1727 | 1541 | 1379 |
| 30 | 15 | 0.6 | 1379 | 1630 | 1828 | 2004 | 2072 | 2088 | 2077 | 2025 | 1880 | 1684 | 1418 | 1324 |
| 35 | 20 | 0.6 | 1107 | 1598 | 1807 | 1990 | 2070 | 2088 | 2088 | 2014 | 1857 | 1641 | 1378 | 1271 |
| 40 | 25 | 0.6 | 1273 | 1569 | 1759 | 1977 | 2076 | 2098 | 2087 | 2008 | 1828 | 1613 | 1323 | 1211 |
| 45 | 30 | 0.6 | 1218 | 1421 | 1723 | 1947 | 2069 | 2120 | 2097 | 1987 | 1790 | 1571 | 1263 | 1192 |
| 50 | 35 | 0.6 | 1055 | 1372 | 1685 | 1931 | 2071 | 2110 | 2076 | 1969 | 1765 | 1440 | 1225 | 1002 |
| 55 | 40 | 0.6 | 1007 | 1318 | 1644 | 1909 | 2063 | 2118 | 2089 | 1953 | 1717 | 1384 | 1048 | 976 |
| 60 | 45 | 0.6 | 792 | 1270 | 1604 | 1877 | 2048 | 2125 | 2078 | 1937 | 1683 | 1336 | 1019 | 770 |
| 20 | 20 | 0.6 | 1761 | 1862 | 1941 | 1964 | 1933 | 1884 | 1892 | 1942 | 1942 | 1876 | 1790 | 1727 |
| 25 | 25 | 0.6 | 1732 | 1829 | 1928 | 1963 | 1936 | 1885 | 1906 | 1941 | 1920 | 1851 | 1752 | 1582 |
| 30 | 30 | 0.6 | 1568 | 1793 | 1894 | 1946 | 1925 | 1894 | 1907 | 1926 | 1898 | 1814 | 1606 | 1532 |
| 35 | 35 | 0.6 | 1520 | 1757 | 1869 | 1934 | 1923 | 1914 | 1918 | 1916 | 1874 | 1772 | 1551 | 1474 |
| 40 | 40 | 0.6 | 1463 | 1730 | 1831 | 1923 | 1930 | 1923 | 1917 | 1913 | 1843 | 1730 | 1495 | 1413 |
| 45 | 45 | 0.6 | 1402 | 1560 | 1788 | 1895 | 1926 | 1923 | 1907 | 1895 | 1819 | 1705 | 1424 | 1399 |
| 50 | 50 | 0.6 | 1207 | 1502 | 1756 | 1865 | 1911 | 1915 | 1906 | 1880 | 1778 | 1546 | 1395 | 1166 |
| 55 | 55 | 0.6 | 1161 | 1446 | 1705 | 1847 | 1886 | 1902 | 1902 | 1850 | 1741 | 1493 | 1189 | 1148 |
| 60 | 60 | 0.6 | 912 | 1405 | 1666 | 1820 | 1875 | 1910 | 1894 | 1839 | 1705 | 1445 | 1165 | 900 |
| 20 | 35 | 0.6 | 1092 | 1927 | 1905 | 1825 | 1707 | 1636 | 1666 | 1762 | 1867 | 1910 | 1891 | 1890 |
| 25 | 40 | 0.6 | 1870 | 1888 | 1894 | 1825 | 1707 | 1652 | 1676 | 1761 | 1847 | 1882 | 1858 | 1702 |
| 30 | 45 | 0.6 | 1680 | 1847 | 1861 | 1811 | 1716 | 1658 | 1674 | 1747 | 1828 | 1842 | 1688 | 1647 |
| 35 | 50 | 0.6 | 1625 | 1818 | 1822 | 1784 | 1714 | 1653 | 1662 | 1758 | 1791 | 1798 | 1633 | 1589 |
| 40 | 55 | 0.6 | 1560 | 1805 | 1787 | 1778 | 1702 | 1661 | 1662 | 1719 | 1766 | 1765 | 1582 | 1528 |
| 45 | 60 | 0.6 | 1504 | 1597 | 1749 | 1756 | 1701 | 1639 | 1652 | 1709 | 1732 | 1736 | 1524 | 1527 |
| 50 | 65 | 0.6 | 1288 | 1548 | 1709 | 1717 | 1669 | 1632 | 1656 | 1583 | 1698 | 1563 | 1488 | 1259 |
| 55 | 70 | 0.6 | 1245 | 1494 | 1674 | 1692 | 1670 | 1621 | 1634 | 1662 | 1669 | 1516 | 1256 | 1244 |
| 60 | 75 | 0.6 | 973 | 1454 | 1631 | 1661 | 1646 | 1631 | 1629 | 1644 | 1630 | 1462 | 1235 | 973 |
| 20 | 90 | 0.6 | 1494 | 1300 | 1016 | 674 | 514 | 517 | 514 | 581 | 877 | 781 | 1426 | 1552 |
| 25 | 90 | 0.6 | 1567 | 1368 | 1112 | 805 | 604 | 530 | 545 | 700 | 978 | 1276 | 1502 | 1415 |
| 30 | 90 | 0.6 | 1413 | 1426 | 1202 | 906 | 690 | 624 | 636 | 814 | 1079 | 1338 | 1383 | 1439 |
| 35 | 90 | 0.6 | 1434 | 1489 | 1266 | 1014 | 794 | 718 | 746 | 919 | 1160 | 1404 | 1408 | 1447 |
| 40 | 90 | 0.6 | 1440 | 1558 | 1344 | 1107 | 913 | 830 | 852 | 1013 | 1234 | 1448 | 1417 | 1441 |
| 45 | 90 | 0.6 | 1434 | 1412 | 1396 | 1199 | 1024 | 939 | 974 | 1114 | 1310 | 1499 | 1419 | 1488 |

From Table XIX one may interpolate between the mid-June and mid-July values given to arrive at the following for July

$$\bar{H} = 1984 \text{ Btu/day}$$

$$\overline{K_T} = 0.534$$

Using Equation 184

$$H_d/H = 1.0 + 0.2832(0.534) - 2.5557(0.534)^2 + 0.8448(0.534)^3$$

$$= 1.0 + 0.1512 - 0.7288 + 0.1286 = 0.551$$

Now $\bar{F}$ may be calculated from Equation 196

$$\bar{F} = (1 - 0.551)(0.745) + 0.551 \cos^2(22.5) + 0.14 \sin^2(22.5)$$

$$= 0.3345 + 0.4703 + 0.0205 = 0.825$$

So $H_T = (0.825)(1984 \text{ Btu/ft}^2\text{/day}) = 1637 \text{ Btu/ft}^2\text{/day}$. Since $A_c = 10 \text{ m}^2 = 107.6 \text{ ft}^2$, the amount of solar radiation striking the surface on an average July 4 will be 1637(107.6) = 0.176 MBtu or 186 MJ.

Erbs [1981] utilized hourly data from Raleigh, NC, Livermore, Ca, Ford Hood, TX, and Maynard, MA, to develop the following correlations for $I_d/I_g$, the ratio of the hourly diffuse horizontal radiation to the hourly global radiation, with the cloudiness index $K_T$.

$$I_d I_g = 1.0 - 0.09K_T \qquad \text{for } K_T < 0.22 \tag{198}$$

$$I_d/I_g = 0.9511 - 0.1604K_T + 4.388K_T^2 - 16.638K_T^3 + 12.336K_T^4 \qquad \text{for } 0.22 < K_T < 0.8 \tag{199}$$

$$I_d I_g = 0.165 \qquad \text{for } K_T > 0.8 \tag{200}$$

The direct hourly component is then

$$I_D = I_g - I_d \tag{201}$$

So, if the hourly global horizontal solar radiation and corresponding values of $K_T$ are known, this correlation can be used to determine typical values of the hourly direct and diffuse components. Similarly, the following correlation was developed to estimate the diffuse fraction of monthly average horizontal solar radiation if $0.3 < \overline{K}_T < 0.8$.

If $\omega_s < 81.4°$

$$\overline{H}_d/\overline{H} = 1.391 - 3.560\overline{K}_T + 4.189\overline{K}_T^2 - 2.137\overline{K}_T^3 \tag{202}$$

If, on the other hand, $\omega_s > 81.4°$

$$\overline{H}_d/\overline{H} = 1.311 - 3.022\overline{K}_T + 3.427\overline{K}_T^2 - 1.821\overline{K}_T^3 \tag{203}$$

The monthly average direct component of the horizontal solar radiation is

$$\overline{H}_D = \overline{H} - \overline{H}_d \tag{204}$$

So, if the horizontal monthly average radiation is known, the monthly average diffuse and direct components can be estimated.

Hogan [1981] compared the Liu and Jordan [1960] technique of estimating the solar radiation on a tilted surface with two more recent models by Hay and Klucher [1978]. All three models break the instantaneous global solar radiation on the surface, $I_{gs}$, into three components:

$I_{Ds}$ = the direct beam component on the surface

$I_{ds}$ = the diffuse component on the surface

$I_{rs}$ = the reflected component on the surface

So, the instantaneous global radiation on the tilted surface is

$$I_{gs} = I_{Ds} + I_{ds} + I_{rs} \tag{205}$$

The direct component on a tilted surface, $I_{Ds}$, is given by

$$I_{Ds} = I \cos \psi \tag{186}$$

where $I$ = the direct normal solar radiation
$\psi$ = the angle of incidence

The direct normal component can always be calculated if the horizontal direct component, $I_D$, is known for

$$I = I_D/\cos\theta \tag{185}$$

where $\theta$ is the zenith angle. The reflected component is assumed to be the result of a diffuse, isotropically reflecting ground surface, and is given by

$$I_{rs} = a[(1 - \cos\beta)/2]I_g \tag{206}$$

where
- $a$ = the albedo (reflectance) from Table XIX
- $\beta$ = slope of surface
- $I_g$ = instantaneous horizontal global solar radiation

The difference between the Liu, Hay and Klucher models is their handling of the diffuse component.

Liu's isotropic model assumes that the source of diffuse radiation from the slope is uniform, so

$$I_{ds} = [(1 + \cos\beta)/2]I_d \tag{207}$$

Hay's anisotropic model treats the diffuse component on the surface as the sum of a circumsolar component (from the general direction of the sun) and an isotropic component. This is more realistic since the sky tends to be brighter closer to the apparent location of the sun. Thus

$$I_{ds} = I_{ds}^{cs} + I_{ds}^{iso} \tag{208}$$

where

$$I_{ds}^{cs} = [(I\cos\psi)/(I_{sc}\cos\theta)]I_d \tag{209}$$

and

$$I_{ds}^{iso} = [1 - I/I_{sc}][(1 + \cos\beta)/2]I_d \tag{210}$$

where $I_{sc}$ is the solar constant (1353 W/m$^2$, 429.2 Btu/ft$^2$-hr).

Klucher's all-sky anisotropic model is a revision of the Temps-Coulson clear sky model [Temps 1977] and represents the diffuse component by

$$I_{ds} = [(1+\cos\beta)/2][1+\{1-(I_d/I_g)^2\}\sin^2(\beta/2)][1+\{1-(I_d/I_g)^2\cos^2\psi\cdot\sin\theta]I_d \tag{211}$$

On heavily overcast days, ($I_d = I_g$), this equation reduces to the isotropic equation (207).

Table XXV compares errors between predicted (with global and diffuse horizontal solar radiation as inputs) and measured values of solar

**Table XXV. Percent Errors in Model Predictions [Hogan 1981]**

| Direction of Surface | Tilt of Surface | Liu Model | Hay Model | Klucher Model |
|---|---|---|---|---|
| North | 90° | 3.1 | 2.4 | 1.8 |
| East | 90° | 3.5 | 3.4 | 2.7 |
| West | 90° | 3.4 | 3.2 | 2.8 |
| South | 90° | 4.1 | 3.9 | 3.6 |
| South | 40° | 3.9 | 4.1 | 4.3 |
| South | 30° | 3.8 | 4.0 | 4.2 |
| South | 20° | 3.7 | 4.0 | 4.0 |

radiation on tilted surfaces, using each of the three models. There does not appear to be much difference in accuracy between the models, except that the Klucher model appears to be more accurate for vertical surfaces facing east, west or north.

# REFERENCES

Aihara, T. (1963) "Heat Transfer Due to Natural Convection from Parallel Vertical Plates," *Trans. Japan Soc. Mech. Eng.* 29:903.

Aihara, T. (1973) "Effects of Inlet Boundary-Conditions on Numerical Solutions of Free Convection Between Vertical Parallel Plates," Report of the Institute of High Speed Mechanics, Tohaka University 28:1–27.

Akbari, H., and T. R. Borgers (1978a) "Correlations for Several Important Design Parameters of Laminar-Free Convective Flow Within the Trombe Wall Channel," in *Proceedings of the Second National Passive Solar Conference, Passive Solar State of the Arts, Vol. 2* (Newark, DE: American Section, International Solar Energy Society), pp. 570–574.

Akbari, H., and T. R. Borgers (1978b) "Free Convective Laminar Flow Within the Trombe Wall Channel," Lawrence Berkeley Laboratory Report LBL-7802.

Allen, R. B. (1978) "Controlled Experiments Using Passive Solar Techniques in the Pacific Northwest," in *Proceedings of the Second National Passive Solar Conference, Passive Solar State of the Arts, Vol. 2* (Newark, DE: American Section, International Solar Energy Society), pp. 431–434.

Anderson, B. (1976) "Heat Transfer Mechanisms, the 1967 Odeillo House, Integrated Collection and Storage Systems," in *Proceedings of the Passive Solar Heating and Cooling Conference and Workshop,* ERDA Report LA-6637-L, pp. 23–28.

Ångstrom, A. K. (1924) "Solar and Terrestrial Radiation," *Quart. J. Roy. Meterol. Soc.* (50):121–125.

Askew, G. L. (1978) "Solar Heating Utilizing a Paraffin Phase Change Material," in *Proceedings of the Second National Passive Solar Conference, Passive Solar State of the Arts, Vol. 2* (Newark, DE: American Section, International Solar Energy Society), pp. 509–513.

Aung, F., and S. Aung (1972) "Developing Laminar Free Convection Between Vertical Flat Plates with Asymmetric Heating," *Int. J. Heat Mass Transfer* Vol. 15.

Baer, S. (1973) "The Drum Wall," in *Proceedings of the Solar Heating and Cooling for Buildings Workshop* (Washington, DC: National Science Foundation), pp. 186–187.

Bagshaw, D. P., and H. T. Whitehouse (1978) "A South-Wall Heating System for a Commercial Building Employing Tilt-up Concrete Construction," in *Proceedings of the Second National Passive Solar Conference, Passive Solar State of the Arts, Vol. 1* (Newark, DE: American Section, International Solar Energy Society), pp. 94–101.

Bainbridge, D. A. (1979) "Water Wall Passive Systems for New and Retrofit Construction," in *Proceedings of the Third National Passive Solar Conference, Vol. 3* (Newark, DE: American Section, International Solar Energy Society), pp. 473–478.

Balcomb, J. D., and R. D. McFarland (1978) "A Simple Empirical Method for Estimating the Performance of a Passive Solar Heated Building of the Thermal Storage Wall Type," in *Proceedings of the Second National Passive Solar Conference, Passive Solar State of the Arts, Vol. 2* (Newark, DE: American Section, International Solar Energy Society), pp. 377–389.

Bier, J. (1978) "Vertical Solar Louvers: A System for Tempering and Storing Solar Energy," in *Proceedings of the Second National Passive Solar Conference, Passive Solar State of the Arts, Vol. 1* (Newark, DE: American Section, International Solar Energy Society), pp. 209–213.

Bird, R. E., and R. L. Hulstrom (1981) "Solar Spectral Measurements and Modeling," SERI Report SERI/TR-642-1013.

Block, D. A., and L. Hodges (1979) "Earth-Integrated Direct Gain Residence Using Concrete Cored Slab," in *Proceedings of the Third National Passive Solar Conference* (Newark, DE: American Section, International Solar Energy Society), pp. 771–778.

Bodoia, J. R., and J. F. Osterle (1962) "The Development of Free Convection Between Heated Vertical Plates," *J. Heat Transfer, Trans. Am. Soc. Mech. Eng.,* Ser. C 84:40.

Buckley, S. (1974) "Thermic Diode Solar Panels," in *Proceedings of the Workshop on Solar Collectors for Heating and Cooling of Buildings,* NSF-RANN-74-109 (Washington, DC: National Science Foundation), pp. 267–274.

Buckley, S. (1975) "Application of Thermic Diode Solar Panels," in *Application of Solar Energy* (Huntsville, AL: University of Alabama—Huntsville Press), pp. 249–268.

Buckley, S. (1976) "Thermic Diode Solar Panels: Passive and Modular," in *Proceedings of the Passive Solar Heating and Cooling Conference and Workshop,* ERDA Report LA-6637-C, pp. 293–299.

Buckley, S. (1978) "Development and Evaluation of Thermic Diode Solar Panels for Building Heating and Cooling," DOE Report COO-2854-1.

Buffer, J. L., Jr. (1978) "Fundamental of Solar Heating," DOE Report NCP-M4038-01 (Rev).

Casperson, R. L., and C. J. Hocevar (1970a) "Experimental Investigation of the Trombe Wall Passive Solar Energy System," in *Proceedings of the Third National Passive Solar Conference, Vol. 3* (Newark, DE: American Section, International Solar Energy Society), pp. 231–235.

Casperson, R. L., and C. J. Hocevar (1979b) "Experimental Investigation of the Trombe Wall," DOE Report DOE/CS/34145-1.

CCB/Cumali Associates (1979) "Passive Solar Calculation Methods," DOE Report DSE-5221-T2.

Clark, G., and C. P. Allen (1979) "Supplemental Cooling Requirements of Passively Cooled Buildings in Selected American Cities," in *Proceedings of the Third National Passive Solar Conference, Vol. 3* (Newark, DE: American Section, International Solar Energy Society), pp. 344-349.

Collier, R. K., and D. P. Grimmer (1979) "The Experimental Evaluation of Phase Change Material Building Walls Using Passive Test Boxes," in *Proceedings of the Third National Passive Solar Conference, Vol. 3* (Newark, DE: American Section, International Solar Energy Society), pp. 547-552.

Connolly, J., C. E. Bingham and J. K. E. Ortega (1980) "Computer Modeling of Thermal Storage Walls," SERI Report SERI/TP-721-610.

Corliss, J. M., et al. (1978) "An Analytical Evaluation of Heat Pipe Augmented Passive Solar Heating Systems," in *Proceedings of the Second National Passive Solar Conference, Passive Solar State of the Arts, Vol. 1* (Newark, DE: American Section, International Solar Energy Society), pp. 106-110.

Corsin, B. A. (1978) "An Energy Efficient Office Building for the State of California," in *Proceedings of the Second National Passive Solar Conference, Passive Solar State of the Arts, Vol. 1* (Newark, DE: American Section, International Solar Energy Society), pp. 233-239.

Dabberdt, W., and P. A. Davis (1974) "Determination of Energetic Characteristics of Urban-Rural Surfaces in the Greater St. Louis Area," paper presented at the Symposium on Atmospheric Diffusion and Air Pollution, Santa Barbara, CA, September 9-13.

Dirmhirn, I. (1964) *Das Strahlungsfeld im Lebensraum* (Frankfurt, FRG: Akademisches Verlag), p. 426.

Dobrovolny, P. (1979) "Passive Solar Architecture," in *Proceedings of the Third National Passive Solar Conference, Vol. 3* (Newark, DE: American Section, International Solar Energy Society), pp. 757-761.

DOE (1979) "Interim Report: National Program Plan for Passive and Hybrid Solar Heating and Cooling," DOE Report DOE/CS-0089.

DOE (1980) "Passive Solar Design Concepts, Vol. 1, Passive Solar Design Handbook," DOE Report DOE/CS/0127.

Eddy, J. A. (1975) "The Last 500 Years of the Sun," Proceedings of the California Institute of Technology Solar Constant Workshop, Big Bear Observatory, CA, May 19-21.

Elenbass, W. (1942) "Heat Dissipation of Parallel Plates by Free Convection," *Physica* 9(1).

Engle, R. K., and W. K. Mueller (1967) "An Analytical Investigation of Natural Convection in Vertical Channels," American Society of Mechanical Engineers Paper 67-HT-16.

Erbs, D. G., J. A. Duffie and S. A. Klein (1981) "Relationships for Estimation of the Diffuse Fraction of Hourly Daily and Monthly-Average Global Radiation," in *Proceedings of the 1981 Meeting of the American Section, International Solar Energy Society* (Newark, DE: American Section, International Solar Energy Society).

Farrer, R. G., et al. (1978) "Solar Space and Soil Heating in the Colorado State University Combined Residence-Greenhouse," in *Proceedings of the 1978 Meeting of the American Section of the International Solar Energy Society,*

*Vol. 2.1* (Newark, DE: American Section, International Solar Energy Society), pp. 742–749.

Faunce, S. F., et al. (1978) "Application of Phase Change Materials in a Passive Solar System," in *Proceedings of the Second National Passive Solar Conference, Passive Solar State of the Arts, Vol. 2* (Newark, DE: American Section, International Solar Energy Society), pp. 475–480.

Freeman, T. L. (1979) "Investigation of the SOLMET Typical Meteorological Year," in *Proceedings of the International Solar Energy Society Silver Jubilee Congress, Vol. 3* (Parkville, Victoria, Australia: International Solar Energy Society), pp. 2183–2187.

Haggard, K. (1976) "An Investigation of Architectural Adaptations of Thermal Ponds and Movable Insulation," in *Proceedings of the Passive Solar Heating and Cooling Conference and Workshop,* ERDA Report LA-6637-C, pp. 307–325.

Hauer, C. R., R. V. Remillard and L. Nichols (1978) "Passive Solar Collector Wall Incorporating Phase Change," in *Proceedings of the Second National Passive Solar Conference, Passive Solar State of the Arts, Vol. 2* (Newark, DE: American Section, International Solar Energy Society), pp. 485–488.

Hay, H. R. (1973a) "Building for Energy Conservation: Use of Natural Radiation Balance," *Solar Energy Data Workshop Proceedings* (Washington, DC: National Science Foundation), pp. 115–116.

Hay, H. R. (1973b) "Energy, Technology and Solarchitecture," *Mech. Eng.* (November), pp. 18–22.

Hay, H. R. (1973c) "Evaluation of Proven Natural Radiation Flux Heating and Cooling," in *Proceedings of the Solar Heating and Cooling for Buildings Workshop* (Washington, DC: National Science Foundation), p. 185.

Hay, H. R. (1975a) "A Naturally Air Conditioned Building," Skytherm Processes & Engineering, Los Angeles, CA.

Hay, H. R. (1975b) "Passive Thermal Control Systems: Philosophy and Reality," in *Transactions of the 1975 International Solar Energy Congress* (Parkville, Victoria, Australia: International Solar Energy Society), pp. 48–49.

Hay, H. R. (1978a) "Roof Mass and Comfort," in *Proceedings of the Second National Passive Solar Conference, Passive Solar State of the Arts, Vol. 1* (Newark, DE: American Section, International Solar Energy Society), pp. 23–27.

Hay, H. R. (1978b) "Skytherm Natural Air Conditioning for a Texas Factory," in *Proceedings of the Second National Passive Solar Conference, Passive Solar State of the Arts, Vol. 1* (Newark, DE: American Section, International Solar Energy Society), pp. 214–217.

Hogan, W. D., and F. M. Loxsom (1981) "Preliminary Validation of Models Predicting Insolation on Tilted Surfaces," in *Proceedings of the 1981 Meeting of the American Section of the International Solar Energy Society* (Newark, DE: American Section, International Solar Energy Society).

Hoyt, D. V. (1976) "The Radiation and Energy Budgets of the Earth Using Both Ground-Based and Satellite-Derived Values of Total Cloud Cover," NOAA Report ERL-362.

Hoyt, D. V. (1978) "A Model for the Calculation of Solar Global Insolation," *Solar Energy* 21:27–35.

Jakob, M. (1957) *Heat Transfer* (New York: John Wiley & Sons, Inc.).

Johnson, T. (1978) "Preliminary Performance of the MIT Solar Building 5," in *Proceedings of the Second National Passive Solar Conference, Passive Solar State of the Arts, Vol. 2* (Newark, DE: American Section, International Solar Society), pp. 610–616.

Katayama, A. (1966) "On the Radiation Budget of the Troposphere over the Northern Hemisphere," *J. Met. Soc. Japan* 45:26.

Kelbaugh, D. (1976) "Kelbaugh House," in *Proceedings of the Passive Solar Heating and Cooling Conference and Workshop,* ERDA Report LA-6637-C, pp. 119–128.

Kelbaugh, D. (1978) "Kelbaugh House: Recent Performance," in *Proceedings of the Second National Passive Solar Conference, Passive Solar State of the Arts, Vol. 1* (Newark, DE: American Section, International Solar Energy Society), pp. 69–75.

Kelbaugh, D., and J. Tichy (1979) "A Proposed Simplified Thermal Load Analysis Technique for Trombe Wall Passive Solar Heating Systems," in *Proceedings of the Third National Passive Solar Conference, Vol. 3* (Newark, DE: American Section, International Solar Energy Society), pp. 403–409.

Keller, B., W. C. Johnson and A. Sedrick (1978) "Passive Solar Heated Warehouse," in *Proceedings of the Second National Passive Solar Conference, Passive Solar State of the Arts, Vol. 1* (Newark, DE: American Section, International Solar Energy Society), pp. 52–56.

Kieffer, B. D. (1979) "Lower Cost Passive Solar Homes," in *Proceedings of the Third National Passive Solar Conference, Vol. 3* (Newark, DE: American Section, International Solar Energy Society), pp. 367–372.

Kimball, H. H. (1954) "Variations in the Total Luminous Solar Radiation with Geographical Position in the United States," *Mon. Weather Rev.* 47:769–793.

Klein, W. H. (1978) "Calculation of Solar Radiation and the Solar Heat Load on Man," *J. Meteorol.* 5:119–129.

Kobayashi, A., and Y. Fujimoto (1954) "Study of Heat Dissipation by Natural Convection Between Parallel Vertical Plates," *Trans. Jap. Soc. Mech. Eng.* 20:233.

Klucher, T. M. "Evaluation of Models to Predict Insolation on Tilted Surfaces," DOE/NASA/1022-28, NASA TM-78842.

Kondratiev, K. Y. (1969) *Radiation in the Atmosphere,* Initial Geophysics Series, Vol. 12 (New York: Academic Press, Inc.), p. 912.

Lambeth, J. (1978) "Direct Gain Passive Design, Delap Residence," in *Proceedings of the Second National Passive Solar Conference, Passive Solar State of the Arts, Vol. 1* (Newark, DE: American Section, International Solar Energy Society), pp. 43–46.

List, R. J. (1968) *Smithsonian Meteorological Tables,* 6th rev. ed. (Washington, DC: Smithsonian Institution), p. 527.

Liu, B. Y. H., and R. C. Jordan (1960) "The Interrelationship and Characteristic Distribution of Direct, Diffuse and Total Solar Radiation," *Solar Energy* 4(3):1–19.

Liu, B. Y. H., and R. C. Jordan (1963) "The Long-Term Average Performance of Flat-Plate Solar Energy Collectors," *Solar Energy* 7:53.

Lof, G. O. G., J. A. Duffie and C. O. Smith (1966) "World Distribution of Solar Radiation," *Solar Energy* (10):27–37.

Loftness, V. (1979) "The Future of the HUD Passive Residential Design Competition," in *Proceedings of the Third National Passive Solar Conference, Vol. 3* (Newark, DE: American Section, International Solar Energy Society), pp. 22–25.

Maede, B. T., R. D. Anson and P. W. Grant (1979a) "Suncatcher Monitoring and Performance Evaluation Project," in *Proceedings of the Third National Passive Solar Conference, Vol. 3* (Newark, DE: American Section, International Solar Energy Society), pp. 606–612.

Maede, B. T., P. W. Grant and R. D. Anson (1979b) "Suncatcher Monitoring Project," DOE Report COO-4154-4.

Maloney, T. (1978) "Four Generations of Waterwall Design," in *Proceedings of the Second National Passive Solar Conference, Passive Solar State of the Arts, Vol. 2* (Newark, DE: American Section, International Solar Energy Society), pp. 489–492.

Maloney, T. (1979) "Comparative Performance Data for Side by Side Tests of Various Water Walls in a Low Sun Climate," in *Proceedings of the Third National Passive Solar Conference, Vol. 3* (Newark, DE: American Section, International Solar Energy Society), pp. 479–480.

Maloney, T. J., and V. Habib (1979) "Design, Fabrication and Testing of a Marketable Water Wall Component," DOE Report DSE-5171-2.

Mickelson, J. L., Jr. (1979) "The Ossobaw House: A Regionally Appropriate Design Solution," in *Proceedings of the Third National Passive Solar Conference, Vol. 3* (Newark, DE: American Section, International Solar Energy Society), pp. 325–329.

Mitalas, G. P., and D. G. Stephenson (1967a) "Cooling Load Calculations by Thermal Response Factor Method," *ASHRAE Trans.* 33(1).

Mitalas, G. P., and D. G. Stephenson (1976b) "Room Thermal Response Factors," *ASHRAE Trans.* 33(1).

Miyatake, O., and T. Fujii (1972) "Free Convective Heat Transfer Between Vertical Parallel Plates When One Plate Is Isothermally Heated and the Other Is Thermally Insulated," *Kagako Kogaku* 36:405.

Monson, W. A., S. A. Klein and W. A. Beckman (1981) "Prediction of Direct Gain Solar Heating System Performance," *Solar Energy* 27(2):143–147.

Moore, A. F., and Abbot, L. H. (1920) "The Brightness of the Sky," *Smithsonian Misc. Coll.* 71(4):1–36.

Morris, W. S. (1978) "Natural Convection Solar Collectors," in *Proceedings of the Second National Passive Solar Conference, Passive Solar State of the Arts, Vol. 2* (Newark, DE: American Section, International Solar Energy Society), pp. 596–601.

Morris, W. S. (1979) "Natural Convection Systems with Storage," in *Proceedings of the Third National Passive Solar Conference, Vol. 3* (Newark, DE: American Section, International Solar Energy Society), pp. 241–248.

Niles, P. W. (1975) "Thermal Evaluation of a House Using a Movable-Insulation Heating and Cooling System" in *Transactions of the 1975 International Solar Energy Congress* (Newark, DE: American Section, International Solar Energy Society), pp. 338–339.

Niles, P. W. B. (1978) "A Simple Direct Gain Passive House Performance Prediction Model," in *Proceedings of the Second National Passive Solar Conference, Passive Solar State of the Arts, Vol. 2* (Newark, DE: American Section, International Solar Energy Society), pp. 534–538.

Noll, S. A., and M. A. Thayer (1979) "Trombe Wall vs. Direct Gain: A Microeconomic Analysis for Albuquerque and Madison," in *Proceedings of the Third National Passive Solar Conference, Vol. 3* (Newark, DE: American Section, International Solar Energy Society), pp. 192–198.

Noll, S. A., J. F. Roach and S. Ben-David (1979) "Trombe Walls and Direct Gain: Patterns of Nationwide Applicability," in *Proceedings of the Third National Passive Solar Conference, Vol. 3* (Newark, DE: American Section, International Solar Energy Society), pp. 199–206.

Ohanessian, P., and W. S. Charters (1975) "Theoretical Performance of a Natural Solar Energy Collection System for House Heating," in *Transactions of the 1975 International Solar Energy Congress* (Newark, DE: American Section, International Solar Energy Society), pp. 301–302.

Ortega, J. K. E., C. E. Bingham and J. M. Connolly (1980) "Performance of Storage Walls with Highly Conductive Covering Plates and Connecting Fins," SERI Report SERI/TP-721-574.

Page, J. K. (1961a) "The Estimation of Monthly Mean Values of Daily Total Short-Wave Radiation on Vertical and Inclined Surfaces from Sunshine Records for Latitudes 40°N–40°S," in *Proceedings of the United Nations Conference on New Sources of Energy, Vol. 4* (Geneva, Switzerland: United Nations), p. 378.

Page, J. K. (1961b) "The Estimation of Monthly Mean Values of Daily Total Short-Wave Radiation on Vertical and Inclined Surfaces from Sunshine Records for Latitudes 60°N–40°S," Report BS32, Department of Building Science, University of Sheffield.

PASOLE (1978) "PASOLE: A General Simulation Program for Passive Solar Energy," Los Alamos Scientific Laboraty Report LA-7433-MS.

Parry, H. L., T. Haroldsen and L. Ziegenfuss (1979) "A Passively Heated Residence Designed for the Median Pacific Northwest Market," in *Proceedings of the Third National Passive Solar Conference, Vol. 3* (Newark, DE: American Section, International Solar Energy Society), pp. 210–216.

Peterson, J. T. (1980) Personal communication, as reported by Riches (1980).

Pfister, P. J. (1978) "The Lindeberg Residence: A DOE Funded Hybrid Solar House," in *Proceedings of the Second National Passive Solar Conference, Passive Solar State of the Arts, Vol. 1* (Newark, DE: American Section, International Solar Energy Society), pp. 122–127.

Pittinger, L., W. White and J. Yellott (1978) "The Energy Roof: A New Approach to Solar Heating and Cooling," in *Proceedings of the Second National Passive Solar Conference, Passive Solar State of the Arts, Vol. 1* (Newark, DE: American Section, International Solar Energy Society), pp. 218–222.

Pratt, R. G., and S. Karaki (1979) "Natural Convection Between Vertical Plates with External Frictional Losses—Application to Trombe Walls," in *Proceedings of the Third National Passive Solar Conference, Vol. 3* (Newark, DE: American Section, International Solar Energy Society), pp. 61–68.

Reid, R. L., et al. (1978) "Analysis and Design of a South Facing Hybrid Solar House," in *Proceedings of the 1978 Meeting of the International Solar Energy Society* (Newark, DE: American Section, International Solar Energy Society).

Riches, M. R. (1980) "An Introduction to Meteorological Measurements and Data Handling for Solar Energy Application," DOE Report DOE/ER-0084.

Robinson, N. (1966) *Solar Radiation* (New York: Elsevier Publishing Co.), p. 347.

Rogers, B. T. (1976) "Some Performance Estimates for the Wright House, Santa Fe, New Mexico," in *Proceedings of the Passive Solar Heating and Cooling Conference and Workshop,* ERDA Report LA-6637-C, pp. 189-199.

Sandia (1979) "Passive Solar Buildings," Sandia Laboratories Report SAND 79-0824.

Sasamori, T., J. London and D. V. Hoyt (1972) "Radiation Budget of the Southern Hemisphere," *Am. Meteorol. Soc. Monthly, Boston* 13:9.

Scully, D. (1978) "Knowing and Loving and Never Knowing: Two Houses," in *Proceedings of the Second National Passive Solar Conference, Passive Solar State of the Arts, Vol. 1* (Newark, DE: American Section, International Solar Energy Society), pp. 47-51.

Sebald, H. V., J. R. Clinton and F. Langenbacher (1979) "Control Considerations in the Trombe Wall," in *Proceedings of the Third National Passive Solar Conference, Vol. 3* (Newark, DE: American Section, International Solar Energy Society), pp. 48-53.

Seigel, R., and R. H. Norris (1957) "Test of Free Convection in a Partially Enclosed Space Between Two Heated Vertical Plates," *Trans. Am. Soc. Mech. Eng.* 79:663.

Skiles, A. (1979) "Performance of Attached Solar Greenhouses in the Ozarks," in *Proceedings of the Third National Passive Solar Conference, Vol. 3* (Newark, DE: American Section, International Solar Energy Society), pp. 678-682.

Skinner, S. M. (1964) *Control System Design* (New York: John Wiley & Sons, Inc.).

SOLMET (1977) "Solmet, Volume I—Users Manual," National Climatic Center.

Telkes, M. (1978) "Trombe Wall with Phase Change Storage Material," in *Proceedings of the Second National Passive Solar Conference, Passive Solar State of the Arts, Vol. 2* (Newark, DE: American Section, International Solar Energy Society), pp. 283-287.

Temps, R. C., and K. L. Coulson (1977) "Solar Radiation Incident upon Slopes of Different Orientations," *Solar Energy* 19:179.

Terry, K. (1976) "The Karen Terry House," in *Proceedings of the Passive Solar Heating and Cooling Conference and Workshop,* ERDA Report LA-6637-C, pp. 132-136.

Trombe, F., et al. (1975) "Some Performance Characteristics of the CNRS Solar Houses," in *Transactions of the 1975 International Solar Energy Congress* (Newark, DE: American Section, International Solar Energy Society), pp. 366-367.

Trombe, F., J. R. Robert, M. Cabanat and B. Sesolis (1976) "Some Performance Characteristics of the CNRS Solar House Collectors," in *Proceedings of the Heating and Cooling Conference and Workshop,* ERDA Report LA-6637-C, pp. 201-222.

Tukel, G., F. Catalioto and A. Marshall (1979) "Economic, Cultural, and Code Considerations in the Design and Retrofit Installation of Low-Cost Passive Solar Devices for Residential Space Heating," in *Proceedings of the Third National Passive Solar Conference, Vol. 3* (Newark, DE: American Section, International Solar Energy Society), pp. 362-366.

Wachtell, G. P. (1978a) "Self Pumping by Means of Power Cycles," in *Proceedings of the Second National Passive Solar Conference, Vol. 2* (Newark, DE: American Section, International Solar Energy Society), pp. 514-518.

Wachtell, G. P. (1978b) "Self Pumping Downward Heat Transport," in *Proceedings of the 1978 Annual Meeting of the American Section of the International Solar Energy Society, Vol. 2.1* (Newark, DE: American Section, International Solar Energy Society), pp. 615-620.

Walton, J. D., Jr. (1973) "Space Heating with Solar Energy at the CNRS Laboratory, Odeillo, France," in *Proceedings of the Solar Heating and Cooling for Buildings Workshop* (Washington, DC: National Science Foundation), pp. 127-139.

Watt, A. D. (1980) "The Sun and Its Radiation," in *An Introduction to Meteorological Measurement and Data Handling for Solar Energy Applications,* DOE Report DOE/ER-0084.

Whillier, A. (1953) "Solar Energy Collection and Its Utilization for House Heating," PhD Thesis, Massachusetts Institute of Technology, Cambridge, MA.

Whillier, A. (1965) "Solar Radiation Graphs," *Solar Energy* 9:165-166.

Wray, W. O., and J. D. Balcomb (1979) "Trombe Wall vs. Direct Gain: A Comparative Analysis of Passive Solar Heating Systems," in *Proceedings of the Third National Passive Solar Conference, Vol. 3* (Newark, DE: American Section, International Solar Energy Society), pp. 41-47.

Yellott, J. (1976) "Solar Roof Ponds, Early Tests of the Skytherm System," in *Proceedings of the Passive Solar Heating and Cooling Conference and Workshop,* ERDA Report LA-6637-C, pp. 54-62.

Zwarf, G. (1978) "A Hybrid Solar System in Los Alamos, New Mexico," in *Proceedings of the Second National Passive Solar Conference, Passive Solar State of the Arts, Vol. 1* (Newark, DE: American Section, International Solar Energy Society), pp. 128-132.

# APPENDIX A

# SOLAR HEATING FRACTION VS LOAD COLLECTOR RATIO

Solar heating fraction (SHF) vs load collector ratio (LCR) is given in Btu/ft$^2$-dd for water walls (WW), Trombe walls (TW) and direct gain (DG) passive solar heating systems, with and without R = 9 ft$^2$-hr-°F/Btu night insulation. The data are from DOE [1980].

SHF is defined here as the ratio of the reduction in auxiliary energy required (solar savings) to the auxiliary heat required for a conventional nonsolar building, assuming that the interior temperature is maintained at 65–75°F. This is the same as the solar savings fraction discussed in DOE [1980].

| | | SHF | | | | | | | | |
|---|---|---|---|---|---|---|---|---|---|---|
| | | **0.1** | **0.2** | **0.3** | **0.4** | **0.5** | **0.6** | **0.7** | **0.8** | **0.9** |
| Alabama | | | | | | | | | | |
| Birmingham | WW | 186 | 87 | 53 | 37 | 27 | 21 | 15 | 10 | 5 |
| 33.6°N | WWNI | 281 | 134 | 85 | 60 | 45 | 36 | 29 | 23 | 16 |
| 2844 dd | TW | 179 | 82 | 50 | 33 | 23 | 16 | 11 | 7 | 4 |
| | TWNI | 265 | 126 | 79 | 56 | 42 | 32 | 25 | 18 | 12 |
| | DG | 192 | 83 | 47 | 28 | 15 | | | | |
| | DGNI | 296 | 139 | 86 | 61 | 45 | 34 | 25 | 18 | 11 |
| Mobile | WW | 318 | 144 | 89 | 64 | 48 | 37 | 29 | 21 | 13 |
| 30.7°N | WWNI | 441 | 205 | 127 | 92 | 71 | 56 | 45 | 36 | 25 |
| 1684 dd | TW | 293 | 135 | 83 | 57 | 40 | 30 | 22 | 15 | 10 |
| | TWNI | 412 | 191 | 120 | 86 | 65 | 51 | 39 | 29 | 19 |
| | DG | 354 | 159 | 96 | 63 | 43 | 29 | 18 | 10 | |
| | DGNI | 469 | 216 | 135 | 96 | 72 | 55 | 42 | 30 | 20 |
| Montgomery | WW | 236 | 111 | 68 | 48 | 36 | 27 | 21 | 15 | 8 |
| 32.3°N | WWNI | 339 | 165 | 103 | 73 | 56 | 44 | 35 | 28 | 20 |

| | | SHF | | | | | | | | |
|---|---|---|---|---|---|---|---|---|---|---|
| | | **0.1** | **0.2** | **0.3** | **0.4** | **0.5** | **0.6** | **0.7** | **0.8** | **0.9** |
| 2269 dd | TW | 224 | 103 | 63 | 43 | 30 | 22 | 15 | 11 | 7 |
| | TWNI | 320 | 153 | 96 | 68 | 51 | 40 | 30 | 23 | 15 |
| | DG | 257 | 115 | 67 | 42 | 27 | 16 | 7 | | |
| | DGNI | 362 | 171 | 107 | 75 | 56 | 42 | 32 | 23 | 15 |
| Arizona | | | | | | | | | | |
| Phoenix | WW | 467 | 219 | 139 | 100 | 75 | 58 | 45 | 34 | 22 |
| 33.4°N | WWNI | 620 | 293 | 188 | 136 | 104 | 82 | 65 | 51 | 36 |
| 1552 dd | TW | 436 | 202 | 126 | 87 | 63 | 46 | 34 | 25 | 16 |
| | TWNI | 583 | 275 | 176 | 126 | 95 | 73 | 56 | 42 | 28 |
| | DG | 555 | 256 | 157 | 107 | 75 | 53 | 37 | 24 | 12 |
| | DGNI | 673 | 316 | 201 | 143 | 107 | 82 | 62 | 45 | 29 |
| Prescott | WW | 189 | 89 | 56 | 40 | 30 | 23 | 17 | 12 | 7 |
| 34.6°N | WWNI | 286 | 135 | 88 | 63 | 48 | 39 | 31 | 25 | 18 |
| 4456 dd | TW | 183 | 85 | 53 | 36 | 25 | 18 | 13 | 9 | 5 |
| | TWNI | 269 | 128 | 82 | 59 | 45 | 35 | 27 | 20 | 14 |
| | DG | 198 | 89 | 52 | 32 | 20 | 10 | | | |
| | DGNI | 300 | 142 | 90 | 64 | 49 | 37 | 28 | 20 | 13 |
| Tucson | WW | 425 | 199 | 127 | 92 | 70 | 55 | 43 | 32 | 21 |
| 32.1°N | WWNI | 571 | 268 | 172 | 125 | 97 | 77 | 62 | 49 | 36 |
| 1752 dd | TW | 394 | 185 | 116 | 81 | 59 | 43 | 32 | 23 | 16 |
| | TWNI | 533 | 252 | 161 | 116 | 89 | 69 | 54 | 40 | 27 |
| | DG | 498 | 231 | 143 | 98 | 69 | 49 | 34 | 22 | 12 |
| | DGNI | 613 | 289 | 185 | 132 | 100 | 77 | 59 | 43 | 29 |
| Winslow | WW | 165 | 78 | 49 | 34 | 25 | 19 | 14 | 9 | 4 |
| 35.0°N | WWNI | 255 | 123 | 79 | 57 | 43 | 34 | 27 | 21 | 15 |
| 4733 dd | TW | 162 | 75 | 46 | 31 | 22 | 15 | 10 | 7 | 4 |
| | TWNI | 242 | 116 | 74 | 53 | 40 | 31 | 24 | 18 | 12 |
| | DG | 168 | 74 | 42 | 24 | 12 | | | | |
| | DGNI | 268 | 127 | 81 | 57 | 43 | 32 | 24 | 17 | 11 |
| Yuma | WW | 728 | 342 | 219 | 155 | 116 | 89 | 70 | 52 | 35 |
| 32.7°N | WWNI | 932 | 442 | 283 | 204 | 154 | 119 | 94 | 74 | 53 |
| 1010 dd | TW | 670 | 313 | 194 | 135 | 97 | 72 | 53 | 38 | 25 |
| | TWNI | 877 | 413 | 264 | 187 | 140 | 108 | 82 | 61 | 40 |
| | DG | 887 | 412 | 254 | 174 | 124 | 89 | 64 | 44 | 26 |
| | DGNI | 1021 | 481 | 305 | 215 | 160 | 122 | 92 | 67 | 44 |
| Arkansas | | | | | | | | | | |
| Fort Smith | WW | 158 | 74 | 45 | 31 | 23 | 17 | 13 | 8 | |
| 35.3°N | WWNI | 246 | 119 | 75 | 53 | 40 | 32 | 26 | 20 | 14 |
| 3336 dd | TW | 153 | 70 | 43 | 29 | 20 | 14 | 9 | 6 | 3 |
| | TWNI | 233 | 111 | 70 | 50 | 37 | 29 | 22 | 17 | 11 |

| | | SHF | | | | | | | | |
|---|---|---|---|---|---|---|---|---|---|---|
| | | **0.1** | **0.2** | **0.3** | **0.4** | **0.5** | **0.6** | **0.7** | **0.8** | **0.9** |
| | DG | 156 | 67 | 36 | 20 | | | | | |
| | DGNI | 258 | 121 | 76 | 53 | 40 | 30 | 22 | 16 | 10 |
| Little Rock | WW | 157 | 72 | 44 | 31 | 22 | 17 | 12 | 8 | |
| 34.7°N | WWNI | 246 | 117 | 74 | 52 | 40 | 31 | 25 | 20 | 14 |
| 3354 dd | TW | 153 | 69 | 42 | 28 | 19 | 13 | 9 | 6 | 3 |
| | TWNI | 232 | 110 | 69 | 49 | 37 | 29 | 22 | 16 | 11 |
| | DG | 154 | 65 | 35 | 18 | | | | | |
| | DGNI | 257 | 120 | 75 | 53 | 39 | 29 | 22 | 15 | 10 |
| California | | | | | | | | | | |
| Bakersfield | WW | 323 | 143 | 89 | 63 | 46 | 35 | 26 | 18 | 10 |
| 35.4°N | WWNI | 449 | 203 | 127 | 91 | 69 | 54 | 42 | 32 | 22 |
| 2185 dd | TW | 297 | 135 | 81 | 55 | 39 | 28 | 20 | 14 | 8 |
| | TWNI | 418 | 191 | 119 | 85 | 63 | 48 | 36 | 27 | 17 |
| | DG | 359 | 158 | 93 | 60 | 40 | 26 | 15 | | |
| | DGNI | 475 | 216 | 135 | 94 | 69 | 52 | 39 | 27 | 17 |
| Daggett | WW | 360 | 165 | 103 | 73 | 55 | 42 | 32 | 24 | 15 |
| 34.9°N | WWNI | 491 | 228 | 144 | 103 | 79 | 62 | 49 | 39 | 27 |
| 2203 dd | TW | 334 | 153 | 94 | 65 | 46 | 34 | 25 | 17 | 11 |
| | TWNI | 461 | 214 | 135 | 96 | 72 | 56 | 43 | 32 | 21 |
| | DG | 411 | 185 | 112 | 74 | 51 | 35 | 23 | 13 | |
| | DGNI | 526 | 244 | 153 | 108 | 81 | 61 | 46 | 33 | 22 |
| Fresno | WW | 272 | 122 | 74 | 51 | 37 | 27 | 20 | 13 | 7 |
| 36.8°N | WWNI | 383 | 179 | 110 | 77 | 58 | 45 | 34 | 26 | 18 |
| 2650 dd | TW | 252 | 114 | 68 | 45 | 31 | 22 | 15 | 10 | 5 |
| | TWNI | 361 | 166 | 102 | 72 | 53 | 40 | 30 | 22 | 14 |
| | DG | 295 | 128 | 72 | 44 | 27 | 15 | | | |
| | DGNI | 408 | 186 | 114 | 79 | 57 | 42 | 31 | 22 | 13 |
| Long Beach | WW | 527 | 249 | 156 | 112 | 85 | 67 | 53 | 40 | 27 |
| 33.8°N | WWNI | 689 | 331 | 208 | 150 | 115 | 91 | 74 | 59 | 42 |
| 1606 dd | TW | 488 | 228 | 142 | 99 | 72 | 53 | 39 | 29 | 19 |
| | TWNI | 650 | 307 | 195 | 139 | 106 | 83 | 64 | 48 | 32 |
| | DG | 630 | 291 | 180 | 123 | 87 | 63 | 44 | 30 | 17 |
| | DGNI | 1753 | 354 | 224 | 159 | 120 | 92 | 70 | 52 | 34 |
| Los Angeles | WW | 563 | 259 | 161 | 115 | 87 | 68 | 54 | 41 | 27 |
| 33.9°N | WWNI | 737 | 342 | 215 | 153 | 117 | 93 | 75 | 60 | 43 |
| 1819 dd | TW | 513 | 238 | 147 | 101 | 73 | 54 | 40 | 29 | 20 |
| | TWNI | 687 | 320 | 200 | 143 | 108 | 84 | 65 | 49 | 33 |
| | DG | 665 | 304 | 187 | 127 | 90 | 65 | 46 | 31 | 18 |
| | DGNI | 793 | 369 | 231 | 163 | 123 | 94 | 72 | 53 | 35 |

| | | SHF | | | | | | | | |
|---|---|---|---|---|---|---|---|---|---|---|
| | | 0.1 | 0.2 | 0.3 | 0.4 | 0.5 | 0.6 | 0.7 | 0.8 | 0.9 |
| Mount Shasta | WW | 142 | 62 | 37 | 25 | 18 | 13 | 9 | 5 | |
| 41.3°N | WWNI | 230 | 106 | 66 | 46 | 35 | 27 | 21 | 16 | 11 |
| 5890 dd | TW | 137 | 61 | 36 | 23 | 15 | 10 | 7 | 4 | |
| | TWNI | 216 | 99 | 62 | 43 | 32 | 25 | 19 | 14 | 9 |
| | DG | 130 | 50 | 23 | | | | | | |
| | DGNI | 237 | 107 | 66 | 46 | 33 | 25 | 18 | 12 | 7 |
| Needles | WW | 508 | 239 | 152 | 108 | 81 | 62 | 47 | 35 | 23 |
| 34.8°N | WWNI | 668 | 317 | 202 | 147 | 111 | 86 | 68 | 53 | 37 |
| 1428 dd | TW | 474 | 220 | 136 | 94 | 67 | 49 | 36 | 26 | 17 |
| | TWNI | 630 | 297 | 189 | 134 | 100 | 77 | 59 | 44 | 29 |
| | DG | 608 | 280 | 171 | 116 | 81 | 57 | 40 | 26 | 13 |
| | DGNI | 729 | 342 | 217 | 153 | 114 | 86 | 65 | 47 | 30 |
| Oakland | WW | 348 | 170 | 107 | 75 | 56 | 42 | 32 | 23 | 14 |
| 37.7°N | WWNI | 472 | 234 | 150 | 106 | 80 | 62 | 49 | 38 | 27 |
| 2909 dd | TW | 327 | 155 | 96 | 66 | 47 | 34 | 24 | 17 | 11 |
| | TWNI | 446 | 219 | 139 | 98 | 73 | 56 | 43 | 31 | 20 |
| | DG | 405 | 189 | 115 | 76 | 51 | 35 | 22 | 12 | |
| | DGNI | 512 | 249 | 157 | 110 | 82 | 61 | 46 | 33 | 21 |
| Red Bluff | WW | 258 | 115 | 69 | 48 | 35 | 26 | 19 | 13 | 6 |
| 40.1°N | WWNI | 365 | 170 | 104 | 74 | 56 | 43 | 33 | 26 | 18 |
| 2688 dd | TW | 239 | 108 | 64 | 43 | 30 | 21 | 15 | 10 | 5 |
| | TWNI | 345 | 158 | 98 | 69 | 51 | 39 | 29 | 21 | 14 |
| | DG | 276 | 119 | 68 | 41 | 25 | 14 | | | |
| | DGNI | 389 | 177 | 109 | 76 | 55 | 41 | 30 | 21 | 13 |
| Sacramento | WW | 258 | 119 | 73 | 50 | 36 | 26 | 19 | 13 | 6 |
| 38.5°N | WWNI | 368 | 174 | 108 | 76 | 57 | 44 | 34 | 26 | 18 |
| 2843 dd | TW | 244 | 110 | 66 | 44 | 31 | 22 | 15 | 10 | 5 |
| | TWNI | 347 | 162 | 101 | 71 | 52 | 39 | 30 | 21 | 14 |
| | DG | 283 | 124 | 71 | 44 | 27 | 15 | | | |
| | DGNI | 393 | 182 | 112 | 78 | 57 | 42 | 31 | 22 | 13 |
| San Diego | WW | 612 | 284 | 179 | 129 | 98 | 77 | 61 | 46 | 31 |
| 32.7°N | WWNI | 796 | 373 | 235 | 170 | 131 | 104 | 84 | 67 | 48 |
| 1507 dd | TW | 562 | 261 | 163 | 113 | 82 | 61 | 46 | 33 | 23 |
| | TWNI | 744 | 348 | 220 | 158 | 120 | 94 | 73 | 54 | 37 |
| | DG | 734 | 338 | 210 | 144 | 103 | 75 | 53 | 37 | 22 |
| | DGNI | 864 | 403 | 255 | 181 | 137 | 105 | 80 | 59 | 40 |
| San Francisco | WW | 332 | 163 | 103 | 72 | 53 | 40 | 31 | 22 | 13 |
| 37.6°N | WWNI | 453 | 225 | 145 | 103 | 77 | 60 | 47 | 37 | 26 |
| 3042 dd | TW | 313 | 149 | 92 | 63 | 45 | 33 | 23 | 16 | 10 |
| | TWNI | 428 | 210 | 134 | 94 | 71 | 54 | 41 | 30 | 20 |

| | | SHF | | | | | | | | |
|---|---|---|---|---|---|---|---|---|---|---|
| | | **0.1** | **0.2** | **0.3** | **0.4** | **0.5** | **0.6** | **0.7** | **0.8** | **0.9** |
| | DG | 385 | 180 | 109 | 72 | 49 | 32 | 20 | 11 | |
| | DGNI | 491 | 239 | 151 | 106 | 79 | 59 | 44 | 32 | 20 |
| Santa Maria | WW | 327 | 164 | 107 | 77 | 58 | 46 | 35 | 26 | 17 |
| 34.9°N | WWNI | 448 | 224 | 148 | 108 | 83 | 66 | 53 | 42 | 30 |
| 3053 dd | TW | 311 | 152 | 97 | 67 | 49 | 36 | 27 | 19 | 12 |
| | TWNI | 423 | 211 | 138 | 100 | 76 | 59 | 46 | 34 | 23 |
| | DG | 383 | 185 | 116 | 79 | 55 | 38 | 26 | 16 | 7 |
| | DGNI | 485 | 241 | 156 | 112 | 85 | 65 | 50 | 36 | 24 |
| Colorado | | | | | | | | | | |
| Colorado | | | | | | | | | | |
| Springs | WW | 130 | 60 | 38 | 26 | 19 | 15 | 11 | 7 | |
| 38.8°N | WWNI | 211 | 102 | 65 | 47 | 36 | 29 | 23 | 18 | 13 |
| 6473 dd | TW | 128 | 59 | 36 | 24 | 17 | 11 | 8 | 5 | 2 |
| | TWNI | 201 | 96 | 61 | 44 | 33 | 26 | 20 | 15 | 10 |
| | DG | 120 | 51 | 26 | 10 | | | | | |
| | DGNI | 220 | 104 | 66 | 47 | 35 | 26 | 20 | 14 | 9 |
| Denver | WW | 136 | 63 | 39 | 27 | 20 | 15 | 11 | 7 | |
| 39.7°N | WWNI | 218 | 105 | 67 | 48 | 37 | 29 | 24 | 19 | 13 |
| 6016 dd | TW | 132 | 61 | 38 | 25 | 17 | 12 | 8 | 5 | 3 |
| | TWNI | 207 | 99 | 63 | 45 | 34 | 27 | 21 | 15 | 10 |
| | DG | 127 | 54 | 28 | 13 | | | | | |
| | DGNI | 227 | 108 | 68 | 48 | 36 | 27 | 20 | 14 | 9 |
| Eagle | WW | 95 | 43 | 26 | 17 | 12 | 8 | 5 | | |
| 39.6°N | WWNI | 172 | 81 | 52 | 37 | 28 | 22 | 17 | 13 | 9 |
| 8426 dd | TW | 96 | 43 | 25 | 16 | 10 | 7 | 4 | | |
| | TWNI | 163 | 77 | 49 | 34 | 26 | 20 | 15 | 11 | 7 |
| | DG | 72 | 22 | | | | | | | |
| | DGNI | 174 | 81 | 51 | 35 | 26 | 19 | 14 | 9 | 5 |
| Grand | | | | | | | | | | |
| Junction | WW | 135 | 61 | 37 | 25 | 18 | 13 | 9 | 5 | |
| 39.1°N | WWNI | 222 | 104 | 66 | 46 | 35 | 28 | 22 | 17 | 12 |
| 5605 dd | TW | 133 | 60 | 36 | 23 | 16 | 11 | 7 | 4 | 1 |
| | TWNI | 210 | 98 | 61 | 43 | 33 | 25 | 19 | 14 | 9 |
| | DG | 125 | 50 | 24 | | | | | | |
| | DGNI | 229 | 106 | 66 | 46 | 34 | 25 | 18 | 13 | 8 |
| Pueblo | WW | 145 | 67 | 41 | 29 | 21 | 16 | 12 | 8 | |
| 38.3°N | WWNI | 234 | 109 | 70 | 50 | 38 | 30 | 24 | 19 | 14 |
| 5394 dd | TW | 143 | 65 | 39 | 26 | 18 | 13 | 9 | 5 | 3 |
| | TWNI | 220 | 103 | 66 | 47 | 36 | 28 | 21 | 16 | 11 |
| | DG | 140 | 59 | 32 | 16 | | | | | |
| | DGNI | 242 | 113 | 71 | 50 | 38 | 28 | 21 | 15 | 9 |

| | | SHF | | | | | | | | |
|---|---|---|---|---|---|---|---|---|---|---|
| | | **0.1** | **0.2** | **0.3** | **0.4** | **0.5** | **0.6** | **0.7** | **0.8** | **0.9** |
| Connecticut | | | | | | | | | | |
| Hartford | WW | 62 | 26 | 14 | 9 | 5 | | | | |
| 41.9°N | WWNI | 134 | 62 | 39 | 28 | 21 | 16 | 13 | 10 | 7 |
| 6350 dd | TW | 66 | 28 | 16 | 9 | 5 | | | | |
| | TWNI | 127 | 59 | 37 | 26 | 19 | 15 | 11 | 8 | 5 |
| | DG | | | | | | | | | |
| | DGNI | 131 | 60 | 37 | 25 | 18 | 13 | 9 | 6 | 3 |
| Delaware | | | | | | | | | | |
| Wilmington | WW | 95 | 44 | 26 | 18 | 12 | 9 | 5 | | |
| 39.7°N | WWNI | 171 | 83 | 52 | 37 | 28 | 22 | 18 | 14 | 9 |
| 4940 dd | TW | 97 | 44 | 26 | 17 | 11 | 7 | 4 | | |
| | TWNI | 163 | 78 | 49 | 35 | 26 | 20 | 15 | 11 | 7 |
| | DG | 74 | 24 | | | | | | | |
| | DGNI | 174 | 82 | 51 | 36 | 26 | 19 | 14 | 10 | 5 |
| Washington, D.C. | | | | | | | | | | |
| | WW | 92 | 42 | 25 | 17 | 11 | 8 | 4 | | |
| 38.9°N | WWNI | 169 | 80 | 51 | 36 | 27 | 21 | 17 | 13 | 9 |
| 5010 dd | TW | 94 | 42 | 25 | 16 | 10 | 6 | 3 | | |
| | TWNI | 160 | 76 | 48 | 34 | 25 | 19 | 15 | 11 | 7 |
| | DG | 69 | 19 | | | | | | | |
| | DGNI | 171 | 80 | 50 | 35 | 25 | 19 | 13 | 9 | 5 |
| Florida | | | | | | | | | | |
| Apalachicola | WW | 405 | 182 | 114 | 81 | 61 | 48 | 37 | 27 | 18 |
| 29.7°N | WWNI | 547 | 249 | 156 | 113 | 87 | 68 | 55 | 44 | 31 |
| 1361 dd | TW | 371 | 170 | 104 | 72 | 51 | 38 | 28 | 20 | 13 |
| | TWNI | 511 | 233 | 147 | 105 | 79 | 62 | 48 | 36 | 24 |
| | DG | 464 | 208 | 126 | 84 | 59 | 41 | 28 | 17 | 8 |
| | DGNI | 585 | 267 | 168 | 119 | 89 | 68 | 52 | 38 | 25 |
| Daytona | | | | | | | | | | |
| Beach | WW | 603 | 281 | 180 | 130 | 100 | 79 | 62 | 48 | 32 |
| 29.2°N | WWNI | 784 | 367 | 235 | 172 | 133 | 106 | 86 | 69 | 49 |
| 902 dd | TW | 556 | 260 | 164 | 114 | 83 | 62 | 47 | 34 | 23 |
| | TWNI | 735 | 344 | 221 | 159 | 122 | 96 | 74 | 56 | 38 |
| | DG | 725 | 337 | 211 | 146 | 105 | 76 | 55 | 38 | 23 |
| | DGNI | 852 | 399 | 256 | 183 | 139 | 107 | 82 | 61 | 41 |
| Jacksonville | WW | 425 | 191 | 120 | 87 | 66 | 52 | 41 | 31 | 20 |
| 30.5°N | WWNI | 573 | 260 | 164 | 119 | 92 | 74 | 60 | 47 | 34 |
| 1327 dd | TW | 390 | 179 | 111 | 77 | 55 | 41 | 30 | 22 | 15 |
| | TWNI | 533 | 244 | 154 | 111 | 85 | 66 | 52 | 39 | 26 |
| | DG | 489 | 221 | 136 | 92 | 65 | 46 | 32 | 21 | 11 |
| | DGNI | 611 | 279 | 177 | 126 | 96 | 73 | 56 | 41 | 27 |

| | | SHF | | | | | | | | |
|---|---|---|---|---|---|---|---|---|---|---|
| | | **0.1** | **0.2** | **0.3** | **0.4** | **0.5** | **0.6** | **0.7** | **0.8** | **0.9** |
| Miami | WW | 2285 | 1138 | 731 | 516 | 389 | 307 | 242 | 186 | 130 |
| 25.8°N | WWNI | 2804 | 1401 | 906 | 641 | 483 | 382 | 307 | 242 | 174 |
| 206 dd | TW | 2101 | 1013 | 641 | 449 | 329 | 245 | 184 | 135 | 94 |
| | TWNI | 2638 | 1304 | 832 | 589 | 446 | 344 | 265 | 198 | 133 |
| | DG | 2912 | 1403 | 886 | 620 | 452 | 336 | 249 | 181 | 121 |
| | DGNI | 3119 | 1534 | 975 | 692 | 520 | 398 | 303 | 224 | 151 |
| Orlando | WW | 723 | 346 | 224 | 163 | 124 | 98 | 78 | 60 | 41 |
| 28.5°N | WWNI | 927 | 446 | 289 | 211 | 163 | 130 | 105 | 84 | 60 |
| 733 dd | TW | 663 | 319 | 202 | 142 | 104 | 78 | 58 | 43 | 30 |
| | TWNI | 867 | 418 | 270 | 195 | 149 | 117 | 91 | 68 | 46 |
| | DG | 879 | 421 | 265 | 185 | 134 | 99 | 72 | 51 | 32 |
| | DGNI | 1010 | 487 | 314 | 226 | 171 | 132 | 101 | 75 | 50 |
| Tallahassee | WW | 359 | 162 | 101 | 72 | 55 | 43 | 33 | 24 | 16 |
| 30.4°N | WWNI | 491 | 226 | 141 | 102 | 79 | 62 | 50 | 40 | 28 |
| 1563 dd | TW | 330 | 152 | 93 | 64 | 46 | 34 | 25 | 18 | 12 |
| | TWNI | 458 | 211 | 133 | 95 | 72 | 56 | 43 | 32 | 22 |
| | DG | 405 | 183 | 110 | 74 | 51 | 35 | 23 | 14 | 5 |
| | DGNI | 523 | 240 | 151 | 107 | 80 | 62 | 47 | 34 | 22 |
| Tampa | WW | 720 | 343 | 223 | 162 | 124 | 98 | 78 | 59 | 41 |
| 28.0°N | WWNI | 926 | 441 | 288 | 211 | 162 | 129 | 105 | 83 | 60 |
| 718 dd | TW | 663 | 317 | 201 | 141 | 104 | 78 | 58 | 43 | 30 |
| | TWNI | 866 | 415 | 269 | 195 | 149 | 117 | 90 | 68 | 46 |
| | DG | 878 | 418 | 264 | 184 | 134 | 98 | 72 | 50 | 32 |
| | DGNI | 1008 | 484 | 312 | 225 | 171 | 132 | 101 | 75 | 50 |
| West Palm Beach | WW | 1523 | 761 | 494 | 350 | 264 | 208 | 164 | 126 | 88 |
| 26.7°N | WWNI | 1886 | 943 | 619 | 441 | 331 | 261 | 211 | 167 | 120 |
| 299 dd | TW | 1407 | 682 | 433 | 304 | 223 | 167 | 125 | 91 | 63 |
| | TWNI | 1775 | 884 | 568 | 403 | 305 | 237 | 183 | 136 | 92 |
| | DG | 1930 | 935 | 592 | 415 | 302 | 224 | 165 | 119 | 79 |
| | DGNI | 2093 | 1038 | 663 | 471 | 355 | 272 | 207 | 153 | 103 |
| Georgia | | | | | | | | | | |
| Atlanta | WW | 172 | 79 | 48 | 33 | 25 | 19 | 14 | 9 | 4 |
| 33.6°N | WWNI | 264 | 126 | 79 | 56 | 42 | 33 | 27 | 21 | 15 |
| 3095 dd | TW | 166 | 75 | 46 | 31 | 21 | 15 | 10 | 7 | 4 |
| | TWNI | 249 | 118 | 74 | 52 | 39 | 30 | 23 | 17 | 11 |
| | DG | 173 | 74 | 41 | 23 | 10 | | | | |
| | DGNI | 276 | 129 | 80 | 56 | 42 | 32 | 23 | 17 | 10 |
| Augusta | WW | 213 | 101 | 62 | 43 | 32 | 25 | 19 | 13 | 7 |
| 33.4°N | WWNI | 312 | 152 | 95 | 67 | 51 | 41 | 33 | 26 | 18 |

| | | SHF | | | | | | | | |
|---|---|---|---|---|---|---|---|---|---|---|
| | | **0.1** | **0.2** | **0.3** | **0.4** | **0.5** | **0.6** | **0.7** | **0.8** | **0.9** |
| 2547 dd | TW | 204 | 94 | 58 | 39 | 27 | 20 | 14 | 9 | 6 |
| | TWNI | 295 | 141 | 89 | 63 | 48 | 37 | 28 | 21 | 14 |
| | DG | 228 | 101 | 59 | 37 | 22 | 12 | | | |
| | DGNI | 332 | 157 | 98 | 69 | 52 | 39 | 29 | 21 | 13 |
| Macon | WW | 244 | 114 | 70 | 49 | 37 | 28 | 21 | 15 | 9 |
| 32.7°N | WWNI | 349 | 169 | 105 | 74 | 57 | 45 | 36 | 28 | 20 |
| 2240 dd | TW | 230 | 106 | 65 | 44 | 31 | 22 | 16 | 11 | 7 |
| | TWNI | 330 | 156 | 98 | 69 | 52 | 41 | 31 | 23 | 16 |
| | DG | 266 | 119 | 70 | 44 | 28 | 17 | 9 | | |
| | DGNI | 373 | 175 | 109 | 77 | 57 | 43 | 33 | 24 | 15 |
| Savannah | WW | 278 | 131 | 81 | 57 | 43 | 33 | 26 | 19 | 11 |
| 32.1°N | WWNI | 389 | 189 | 118 | 84 | 65 | 51 | 41 | 32 | 23 |
| 1952 dd | TW | 260 | 122 | 75 | 51 | 37 | 26 | 19 | 13 | 9 |
| | TWNI | 367 | 175 | 110 | 79 | 59 | 46 | 36 | 27 | 18 |
| | DG | 309 | 141 | 84 | 55 | 37 | 24 | 14 | 6 | |
| | DGNI | 417 | 197 | 124 | 88 | 66 | 50 | 38 | 27 | 18 |
| Idaho | | | | | | | | | | |
| Boise | WW | 132 | 58 | 34 | 22 | 15 | 10 | 5 | | |
| 43.6°N | WWNI | 215 | 101 | 63 | 44 | 32 | 25 | 19 | 14 | 9 |
| 5833 dd | TW | 127 | 56 | 32 | 20 | 13 | 8 | 4 | | |
| | TWNI | 203 | 95 | 59 | 41 | 30 | 22 | 16 | 12 | 7 |
| | DG | 117 | 42 | | | | | | | |
| | DGNI | 221 | 102 | 62 | 42 | 30 | 22 | 15 | 10 | 5 |
| Lewiston | WW | 110 | 46 | 26 | 15 | 9 | 4 | | | |
| 46.4°N | WWNI | 192 | 88 | 54 | 37 | 27 | 20 | 15 | 11 | 7 |
| 5464 dd | TW | 108 | 46 | 25 | 15 | 9 | 4 | | | |
| | TWNI | 181 | 82 | 50 | 34 | 25 | 18 | 13 | 9 | 6 |
| | DG | 85 | | | | | | | | |
| | DGNI | 194 | 87 | 52 | 34 | 24 | 17 | 11 | 7 | 3 |
| Pocatello | WW | 105 | 47 | 28 | 18 | 12 | 8 | 3 | | |
| 42.9°N | WWNI | 182 | 88 | 55 | 39 | 29 | 22 | 17 | 13 | 9 |
| 7063 dd | TW | 104 | 47 | 27 | 17 | 11 | 6 | 3 | | |
| | TWNI | 173 | 82 | 51 | 36 | 26 | 20 | 15 | 11 | 7 |
| | DG | 84 | 27 | | | | | | | |
| | DGNI | 186 | 87 | 54 | 37 | 26 | 19 | 14 | 9 | 5 |
| Illinois | | | | | | | | | | |
| Chicago | WW | 73 | 31 | 17 | 11 | 6 | | | | |
| 41.8°N | WWNI | 149 | 69 | 43 | 30 | 22 | 17 | 14 | 10 | 7 |
| 6127 dd | TW | 78 | 33 | 18 | 11 | 6 | | | | |
| | TWNI | 141 | 65 | 40 | 28 | 21 | 16 | 12 | 9 | 5 |

| | | SHF | | | | | | | | |
|---|---|---|---|---|---|---|---|---|---|---|
| | | **0.1** | **0.2** | **0.3** | **0.4** | **0.5** | **0.6** | **0.7** | **0.8** | **0.9** |
| | DG | 34 | | | | | | | | |
| | DGNI | 148 | 67 | 41 | 28 | 20 | 14 | 10 | 7 | 3 |
| Moline | WW | 72 | 30 | 17 | 10 | 6 | | | | |
| 41.4°N | WWNI | 147 | 68 | 42 | 30 | 22 | 17 | 13 | 10 | 7 |
| 6395 dd | TW | 76 | 32 | 18 | 10 | 6 | | | | |
| | TWNI | 139 | 64 | 40 | 28 | 21 | 16 | 12 | 9 | 5 |
| | DG | 29 | | | | | | | | |
| | DGNI | 145 | 66 | 40 | 27 | 19 | 14 | 10 | 6 | 3 |
| Springfield | WW | 90 | 39 | 22 | 14 | 10 | 6 | | | |
| 39.8°N | WWNI | 168 | 78 | 49 | 34 | 25 | 20 | 16 | 12 | 8 |
| 5558 dd | TW | 92 | 39 | 23 | 14 | 9 | 5 | 2 | | |
| | TWNI | 159 | 74 | 46 | 32 | 24 | 18 | 14 | 10 | 6 |
| | DG | 61 | | | | | | | | |
| | DGNI | 169 | 77 | 47 | 32 | 23 | 17 | 12 | 8 | 4 |
| Indiana | | | | | | | | | | |
| Evansville | WW | 104 | 46 | 26 | 17 | 12 | 8 | 5 | | |
| 38.0°N | WWNI | 182 | 86 | 54 | 37 | 28 | 22 | 17 | 13 | 9 |
| 4629 dd | TW | 104 | 45 | 26 | 17 | 11 | 7 | 4 | | |
| | TWNI | 173 | 81 | 50 | 35 | 26 | 20 | 15 | 11 | 7 |
| | DG | 81 | 25 | | | | | | | |
| | DGNI | 186 | 85 | 52 | 36 | 26 | 19 | 14 | 9 | 5 |
| Fort Wayne | WW | 62 | 25 | 13 | 8 | | | | | |
| 41.0°N | WWNI | 136 | 62 | 39 | 27 | 20 | 16 | 12 | 9 | 6 |
| 6209 dd | TW | 67 | 28 | 15 | 8 | 4 | | | | |
| | TWNI | 128 | 59 | 37 | 25 | 19 | 14 | 11 | 8 | 5 |
| | DG | | | | | | | | | |
| | DGNI | 132 | 60 | 36 | 24 | 17 | 12 | 9 | 5 | 2 |
| Indianapolis | WW | 74 | 31 | 17 | 11 | 7 | | | | |
| 39.7°N | WWNI | 148 | 69 | 43 | 30 | 23 | 17 | 14 | 11 | 7 |
| 5577 dd | TW | 77 | 33 | 18 | 11 | 6 | 2 | | | |
| | TWNI | 141 | 65 | 41 | 28 | 21 | 16 | 12 | 9 | 6 |
| | DG | 35 | | | | | | | | |
| | DGNI | 147 | 67 | 41 | 28 | 20 | 14 | 10 | 7 | 3 |
| South Bend | WW | 60 | 24 | 12 | 6 | | | | | |
| 41.7°N | WWNI | 137 | 61 | 38 | 26 | 19 | 15 | 11 | 9 | 6 |
| 6462 dd | TW | 66 | 26 | 14 | 7 | | | | | |
| | TWNI | 129 | 58 | 36 | 25 | 18 | 13 | 10 | 7 | 5 |
| | DG | | | | | | | | | |
| | DGNI | 132 | 58 | 35 | 23 | 16 | 12 | 8 | 5 | |

| | | SHF | | | | | | | | |
|---|---|---|---|---|---|---|---|---|---|---|
| | | 0.1 | 0.2 | 0.3 | 0.4 | 0.5 | 0.6 | 0.7 | 0.8 | 0.9 |
| Iowa | | | | | | | | | | |
| Burlington | WW | 83 | 36 | 20 | 13 | 8 | 5 | | | |
| 40.8°N | WWNI | 159 | 74 | 46 | 32 | 24 | 19 | 15 | 11 | 8 |
| 6149 dd | TW | 85 | 36 | 21 | 13 | 7 | 4 | | | |
| | TWNI | 151 | 70 | 43 | 30 | 22 | 17 | 13 | 9 | 6 |
| | DG | 50 | | | | | | | | |
| | DGNI | 159 | 72 | 44 | 30 | 22 | 16 | 11 | 7 | 4 |
| Des Moines | WW | 78 | 33 | 18 | 11 | 7 | 3 | | | |
| 41.5°N | WWNI | 155 | 71 | 44 | 31 | 23 | 18 | 14 | 11 | 7 |
| 6710 dd | TW | 81 | 34 | 19 | 11 | 6 | 3 | | | |
| | TWNI | 146 | 67 | 41 | 29 | 21 | 16 | 12 | 9 | 6 |
| | DG | 41 | | | | | | | | |
| | DGNI | 153 | 69 | 42 | 29 | 20 | 15 | 11 | 7 | 3 |
| Mason City | WW | 68 | 27 | 14 | 8 | 4 | | | | |
| 43.1°N | WWNI | 143 | 65 | 40 | 28 | 21 | 16 | 12 | 9 | 6 |
| 7901 dd | TW | 72 | 29 | 16 | 9 | 4 | | | | |
| | TWNI | 136 | 62 | 38 | 26 | 19 | 15 | 11 | 8 | 5 |
| | DG | | | | | | | | | |
| | DGNI | 141 | 63 | 37 | 25 | 18 | 13 | 9 | 6 | 2 |
| Sioux City | WW | 77 | 32 | 17 | 11 | 7 | | | | |
| 42.4°N | WWNI | 153 | 70 | 44 | 30 | 22 | 17 | 14 | 10 | 7 |
| 6953 dd | TW | 80 | 33 | 18 | 11 | 6 | | | | |
| | TWNI | 144 | 66 | 41 | 28 | 21 | 16 | 12 | 9 | 6 |
| | DG | 37 | | | | | | | | |
| | DGNI | 151 | 68 | 41 | 28 | 20 | 14 | 10 | 7 | 3 |
| Kansas | | | | | | | | | | |
| Dodge City | WW | 140 | 64 | 39 | 27 | 19 | 15 | 10 | 6 | |
| 37.8°N | WWNI | 228 | 107 | 67 | 48 | 36 | 29 | 23 | 18 | 13 |
| 5046 dd | TW | 138 | 62 | 37 | 25 | 17 | 11 | 8 | 5 | 2 |
| | TWNI | 215 | 100 | 63 | 45 | 34 | 26 | 20 | 15 | 10 |
| | DG | 132 | 54 | 27 | 10 | | | | | |
| | DGNI | 236 | 109 | 68 | 47 | 35 | 26 | 20 | 14 | 8 |
| Goodland | WW | 120 | 55 | 33 | 23 | 17 | 12 | 8 | 5 | |
| 39.4°N | WWNI | 202 | 95 | 61 | 43 | 33 | 26 | 21 | 16 | 12 |
| 6119 dd | TW | 118 | 54 | 32 | 21 | 14 | 10 | 6 | 4 | 1 |
| | TWNI | 190 | 90 | 57 | 40 | 31 | 24 | 18 | 13 | 9 |
| | DG | 105 | 42 | 18 | | | | | | |
| | DGNI | 206 | 97 | 60 | 42 | 31 | 24 | 17 | 12 | 7 |
| Topeka | WW | 112 | 50 | 29 | 20 | 14 | 10 | 6 | | |
| 39.1°N | WWNI | 194 | 91 | 57 | 40 | 30 | 23 | 19 | 14 | 10 |

| | | SHF | | | | | | | | |
|---|---|---|---|---|---|---|---|---|---|---|
| | | **0.1** | **0.2** | **0.3** | **0.4** | **0.5** | **0.6** | **0.7** | **0.8** | **0.9** |
| 5243 dd | TW | 112 | 49 | 29 | 18 | 12 | 8 | 5 | 2 | |
| | TWNI | 183 | 85 | 53 | 37 | 28 | 21 | 16 | 12 | 8 |
| | DG | 93 | 33 | | | | | | | |
| | DGNI | 198 | 91 | 56 | 39 | 28 | 21 | 15 | 10 | 6 |
| Wichita | WW | 138 | 63 | 38 | 26 | 19 | 14 | 10 | 6 | |
| 37.6°N | WWNI | 224 | 106 | 66 | 47 | 35 | 28 | 22 | 17 | 12 |
| 4687 dd | TW | 135 | 61 | 36 | 24 | 16 | 11 | 7 | 4 | 2 |
| | TWNI | 212 | 99 | 62 | 44 | 33 | 25 | 19 | 14 | 9 |
| | DG | 128 | 52 | 25 | | | | | | |
| | DGNI | 232 | 107 | 66 | 46 | 34 | 26 | 19 | 13 | 8 |
| Kentucky | | | | | | | | | | |
| Lexington | WW | 96 | 42 | 24 | 16 | 11 | 7 | 4 | | |
| 38.0°N | WWNI | 174 | 82 | 51 | 36 | 27 | 21 | 17 | 13 | 9 |
| 4729 dd | TW | 98 | 42 | 25 | 15 | 10 | 6 | 3 | | |
| | TWNI | 165 | 77 | 48 | 34 | 25 | 19 | 15 | 11 | 7 |
| | DG | 71 | 17 | | | | | | | |
| | DGNI | 177 | 81 | 50 | 34 | 25 | 18 | 13 | 9 | 5 |
| Louisville | WW | 98 | 44 | 25 | 17 | 12 | 8 | 4 | | |
| 38.2°N | WWNI | 176 | 84 | 52 | 37 | 27 | 21 | 17 | 13 | 9 |
| 4645 dd | TW | 99 | 44 | 25 | 16 | 10 | 6 | 3 | | |
| | TWNI | 167 | 78 | 49 | 34 | 25 | 19 | 15 | 11 | 7 |
| | DG | 74 | 21 | | | | | | | |
| | DGNI | 179 | 83 | 51 | 35 | 25 | 19 | 14 | 9 | 5 |
| Louisiana | | | | | | | | | | |
| Baton Rouge | WW | 312 | 142 | 87 | 62 | 46 | 36 | 28 | 20 | 12 |
| 30.5°N | WWNI | 430 | 203 | 125 | 90 | 69 | 54 | 43 | 34 | 24 |
| 1670 dd | TW | 287 | 133 | 81 | 55 | 39 | 28 | 21 | 15 | 9 |
| | TWNI | 405 | 188 | 118 | 84 | 63 | 49 | 38 | 28 | 19 |
| | DG | 346 | 156 | 93 | 61 | 41 | 27 | 17 | 8 | |
| | DGNI | 460 | 213 | 133 | 94 | 70 | 53 | 40 | 29 | 19 |
| Lake Charles | WW | 330 | 144 | 89 | 63 | 48 | 37 | 28 | 21 | 13 |
| 30.1°N | WWNI | 457 | 205 | 127 | 92 | 70 | 55 | 44 | 35 | 25 |
| 1498 dd | TW | 301 | 136 | 83 | 56 | 40 | 29 | 21 | 15 | 10 |
| | TWNI | 425 | 192 | 120 | 85 | 64 | 50 | 39 | 29 | 19 |
| | DG | 364 | 160 | 95 | 62 | 42 | 28 | 18 | 9 | |
| | DGNI | 482 | 218 | 136 | 96 | 71 | 54 | 41 | 30 | 19 |
| New Orleans | WW | 374 | 169 | 104 | 74 | 56 | 44 | 34 | 25 | 16 |
| 30.0°N | WWNI | 506 | 235 | 146 | 105 | 80 | 64 | 51 | 40 | 29 |
| 1465 dd | TW | 342 | 158 | 97 | 66 | 47 | 35 | 25 | 18 | 12 |
| | TWNI | 474 | 219 | 137 | 98 | 75 | 57 | 44 | 33 | 22 |

| | | SHF | | | | | | | | |
|---|---|---|---|---|---|---|---|---|---|---|
| | | **0.1** | **0.2** | **0.3** | **0.4** | **0.5** | **0.6** | **0.7** | **0.8** | **0.9** |
| | DG | 423 | 191 | 115 | 76 | 52 | 36 | 25 | 14 | 6 |
| | DBNI | 542 | 249 | 156 | 110 | 83 | 63 | 48 | 35 | 23 |
| Shreveport | WW | 250 | 115 | 70 | 50 | 37 | 29 | 22 | 15 | 9 |
| 32.5°N | WWNI | 356 | 170 | 105 | 75 | 57 | 45 | 36 | 29 | 20 |
| 2167 dd | TW | 234 | 108 | 66 | 45 | 32 | 23 | 16 | 11 | 7 |
| | TWNI | 336 | 158 | 99 | 70 | 53 | 41 | 32 | 23 | 16 |
| | DG | 271 | 120 | 71 | 45 | 29 | 18 | 9 | | |
| | DGNI | 380 | 177 | 110 | 78 | 58 | 44 | 33 | 24 | 15 |
| Maine | | | | | | | | | | |
| Caribou | WW | 48 | 18 | 8 | | | | | | |
| 46.9°N | WWNI | 119 | 55 | 34 | 24 | 18 | 13 | 10 | 7 | 5 |
| 9632 dd | TW | 54 | 21 | 10 | 3 | | | | | |
| | TWNI | 113 | 52 | 32 | 22 | 16 | 12 | 9 | 6 | 4 |
| | DG | | | | | | | | | |
| | DGNI | 114 | 51 | 31 | 20 | 14 | 10 | 6 | 4 | |
| Portland | WW | 60 | 24 | 13 | 7 | | | | | |
| 43.6°N | WWNI | 133 | 61 | 38 | 27 | 20 | 15 | 12 | 9 | 6 |
| 7498 dd | TW | 65 | 27 | 14 | 8 | 3 | | | | |
| | TWNI | 126 | 58 | 36 | 25 | 19 | 14 | 11 | 8 | 5 |
| | DG | | | | | | | | | |
| | DGNI | 130 | 58 | 35 | 24 | 17 | 12 | 8 | 5 | 2 |
| Maryland | | | | | | | | | | |
| Baltimore | WW | 101 | 46 | 28 | 19 | 13 | 9 | 6 | | |
| 39.2°N | WWNI | 178 | 86 | 55 | 39 | 29 | 23 | 18 | 14 | 10 |
| 4729 dd | TW | 102 | 46 | 27 | 18 | 12 | 7 | 4 | 2 | |
| | TWNI | 169 | 81 | 51 | 36 | 27 | 21 | 16 | 12 | 8 |
| | DG | 81 | 29 | | | | | | | |
| | DGNI | 182 | 86 | 54 | 37 | 27 | 20 | 15 | 10 | 6 |
| Massachusetts | | | | | | | | | | |
| Boston | WW | 81 | 35 | 20 | 13 | 9 | 5 | | | |
| 42.4°N | WWNI | 159 | 73 | 46 | 32 | 24 | 19 | 15 | 11 | 8 |
| 5621 dd | TW | 85 | 36 | 21 | 13 | 8 | 4 | | | |
| | TWNI | 150 | 69 | 43 | 30 | 23 | 17 | 13 | 10 | 6 |
| | DG | 49 | | | | | | | | |
| | DGNI | 158 | 72 | 44 | 30 | 22 | 16 | 11 | 8 | 4 |
| Michigan | | | | | | | | | | |
| Alpena | WW | 53 | 19 | 8 | | | | | | |
| 45.1°N | WWNI | 126 | 57 | 35 | 24 | 17 | 13 | 10 | 7 | 5 |
| 8518 dd | TW | 58 | 22 | 10 | | | | | | |
| | TWNI | 119 | 54 | 33 | 22 | 16 | 12 | 9 | 6 | 4 |

| | | SHF | | | | | | | | |
|---|---|---|---|---|---|---|---|---|---|---|
| | | 0.1 | 0.2 | 0.3 | 0.4 | 0.5 | 0.6 | 0.7 | 0.8 | 0.9 |
| | DG | | | | | | | | | |
| | DGNI | 121 | 53 | 31 | 20 | 14 | 10 | 6 | 3 | |
| Detroit | WW | 62 | 26 | 14 | 8 | | | | | |
| 42.4°N | WWNI | 137 | 63 | 39 | 27 | 20 | 16 | 12 | 9 | 6 |
| 6228 dd | TW | 68 | 28 | 15 | 8 | 3 | | | | |
| | TWNI | 130 | 60 | 37 | 26 | 19 | 14 | 11 | 8 | 5 |
| | DG | | | | | | | | | |
| | DGNI | 134 | 60 | 36 | 25 | 17 | 12 | 9 | 5 | 2 |
| Flint | WW | 54 | 21 | 10 | | | | | | |
| 43.0°N | WWNI | 129 | 58 | 36 | 25 | 18 | 14 | 11 | 8 | 5 |
| 7041 dd | TW | 60 | 24 | 12 | 5 | | | | | |
| | TWNI | 122 | 55 | 34 | 23 | 17 | 13 | 9 | 7 | 4 |
| | DG | | | | | | | | | |
| | DGNI | 124 | 54 | 32 | 21 | 15 | 10 | 7 | 4 | |
| Grand Rapids | WW | 57 | 22 | 10 | | | | | | |
| 42.9°N | WWNI | 133 | 59 | 37 | 25 | 19 | 14 | 11 | 8 | 5 |
| 6801 dd | TW | 63 | 25 | 12 | 6 | | | | | |
| | TWNI | 125 | 56 | 34 | 24 | 17 | 13 | 10 | 7 | 4 |
| | DG | | | | | | | | | |
| | DGNI | 128 | 56 | 33 | 22 | 15 | 11 | 7 | 4 | |
| Sault Ste. Marie | WW | 45 | 15 | | | | | | | |
| 46.5°N | WWNI | 116 | 53 | 33 | 22 | 16 | 12 | 9 | 6 | 4 |
| 9193 dd | TW | 51 | 19 | 8 | | | | | | |
| | TWNI | 110 | 50 | 31 | 21 | 15 | 11 | 8 | 6 | 3 |
| | DG | | | | | | | | | |
| | DGNI | 110 | 49 | 29 | 19 | 12 | 8 | 5 | 2 | |
| Traverse City | WW | 51 | 18 | | | | | | | |
| 44.7°N | WWNI | 127 | 56 | 34 | 23 | 17 | 13 | 9 | 7 | 4 |
| 7698 dd | TW | 58 | 21 | 9 | | | | | | |
| | TWNI | 120 | 53 | 32 | 22 | 16 | 11 | 8 | 6 | 4 |
| | DG | | | | | | | | | |
| | DGNI | 121 | 52 | 30 | 20 | 13 | 9 | 6 | 3 | |
| Minnesota | | | | | | | | | | |
| Duluth | WW | 42 | 15 | | | | | | | |
| 46.8°N | WWNI | 113 | 52 | 32 | 22 | 16 | 12 | 9 | 7 | 4 |
| 9756 dd | TW | 49 | 18 | 8 | | | | | | |
| | TWNI | 107 | 49 | 30 | 21 | 15 | 11 | 8 | 6 | 3 |
| | DG | | | | | | | | | |
| | DGNI | 107 | 48 | 28 | 18 | 11 | 8 | 5 | 3 | |

| | | SHF | | | | | | | | |
|---|---|---|---|---|---|---|---|---|---|---|
| | | 0.1 | 0.2 | 0.3 | 0.4 | 0.5 | 0.6 | 0.7 | 0.8 | 0.9 |
| International | | | | | | | | | | |
| Falls | WW | 38 | 10 | | | | | | | |
| 48.6°N | WWNI | 109 | 49 | 30 | 21 | 15 | 11 | 8 | 6 | 4 |
| 10547 dd | TW | 45 | 16 | | | | | | | |
| | TWNI | 104 | 47 | 28 | 19 | 14 | 10 | 7 | 5 | 3 |
| | DG | | | | | | | | | |
| | DGNI | 103 | 45 | 26 | 16 | 11 | 7 | 4 | | |
| Minneapolis | WW | 54 | 21 | 10 | | | | | | |
| 44.9°N | WWNI | 126 | 58 | 36 | 25 | 18 | 14 | 11 | 8 | 5 |
| 8159 dd | TW | 59 | 24 | 12 | 5 | | | | | |
| | TWNI | 120 | 55 | 34 | 23 | 17 | 13 | 9 | 7 | 4 |
| | DG | | | | | | | | | |
| | DGNI | 122 | 54 | 32 | 22 | 15 | 10 | 7 | 4 | |
| Rochester | WW | 53 | 20 | 9 | | | | | | |
| 43.9°N | WWNI | 126 | 57 | 35 | 24 | 18 | 14 | 11 | 8 | 5 |
| 8227 dd | TW | 59 | 23 | 12 | 5 | | | | | |
| | TWNI | 120 | 54 | 33 | 23 | 17 | 13 | 9 | 7 | 4 |
| | DG | | | | | | | | | |
| | DGNI | 121 | 54 | 32 | 21 | 15 | 10 | 7 | 4 | |
| Mississippi | | | | | | | | | | |
| Jackson | WW | 230 | 108 | 66 | 46 | 34 | 26 | 20 | 14 | 8 |
| 32.3°N | WWNI | 331 | 161 | 100 | 71 | 54 | 43 | 34 | 27 | 19 |
| 2300 dd | TW | 218 | 101 | 62 | 42 | 29 | 21 | 15 | 10 | 6 |
| | TWNI | 313 | 149 | 94 | 66 | 50 | 39 | 30 | 22 | 15 |
| | DG | 248 | 111 | 65 | 41 | 26 | 15 | 5 | | |
| | DGNI | 354 | 167 | 104 | 73 | 55 | 41 | 31 | 22 | 14 |
| Meridian | WW | 216 | 103 | 63 | 44 | 33 | 25 | 19 | 13 | 7 |
| 32.3°N | WWNI | 315 | 154 | 97 | 69 | 53 | 41 | 33 | 26 | 19 |
| 2388 dd | TW | 206 | 96 | 59 | 40 | 28 | 20 | 14 | 10 | 6 |
| | TWNI | 298 | 144 | 90 | 64 | 48 | 38 | 29 | 21 | 14 |
| | DG | 233 | 104 | 61 | 38 | 24 | 13 | | | |
| | DGNI | 335 | 160 | 100 | 71 | 53 | 40 | 30 | 21 | 14 |
| Missouri | | | | | | | | | | |
| Columbia | WW | 102 | 45 | 26 | 17 | 12 | 8 | 5 | | |
| 38.8°N | WWNI | 182 | 85 | 53 | 37 | 28 | 22 | 17 | 13 | 9 |
| 5083 dd | TW | 103 | 45 | 26 | 16 | 10 | 6 | 3 | | |
| | TWNI | 173 | 80 | 50 | 35 | 26 | 20 | 15 | 11 | 7 |
| | DG | 79 | 23 | | | | | | | |
| | DGNI | 185 | 84 | 51 | 36 | 26 | 19 | 14 | 9 | 5 |
| Kansas City | WW | 102 | 45 | 26 | 17 | 12 | 8 | 5 | | |

| | | SHF | | | | | | | | |
|---|---|---|---|---|---|---|---|---|---|---|
| | | **0.1** | **0.2** | **0.3** | **0.4** | **0.5** | **0.6** | **0.7** | **0.8** | **0.9** |
| 39.3°N | WWNI | 182 | 85 | 53 | 37 | 28 | 22 | 17 | 14 | 9 |
| 5357 dd | TW | 103 | 45 | 26 | 17 | 11 | 7 | 4 | | |
| | TWNI | 172 | 80 | 50 | 35 | 26 | 20 | 15 | 11 | 7 |
| | DG | 79 | 25 | | | | | | | |
| | DGNI | 184 | 84 | 52 | 36 | 26 | 19 | 14 | 10 | 5 |
| Saint Louis | WW | 113 | 50 | 29 | 19 | 14 | 10 | 6 | | |
| 38.7°N | WWNI | 194 | 91 | 57 | 40 | 30 | 23 | 18 | 14 | 10 |
| 4750 dd | TW | 113 | 49 | 29 | 18 | 12 | 8 | 4 | 2 | |
| | TWNI | 184 | 86 | 53 | 37 | 28 | 21 | 16 | 12 | 8 |
| | DG | 94 | 32 | | | | | | | |
| | DGNI | 199 | 91 | 56 | 38 | 28 | 21 | 15 | 10 | 6 |
| Springfield | WW | 123 | 55 | 33 | 22 | 16 | 11 | 8 | 4 | |
| 37.2°N | WWNI | 207 | 97 | 61 | 43 | 32 | 25 | 20 | 16 | 11 |
| 4570 dd | TW | 122 | 54 | 32 | 21 | 14 | 9 | 6 | 3 | |
| | TWNI | 196 | 91 | 57 | 40 | 30 | 23 | 18 | 13 | 8 |
| | DG | 108 | 41 | 16 | | | | | | |
| | DGNI | 213 | 97 | 60 | 42 | 31 | 23 | 17 | 12 | 7 |
| Montana | | | | | | | | | | |
| Billings | WW | 91 | 41 | 23 | 15 | 9 | 6 | | | |
| 45.8°N | WWNI | 165 | 80 | 50 | 35 | 26 | 20 | 15 | 12 | 8 |
| 7265 dd | TW | 92 | 40 | 23 | 14 | 9 | 5 | | | |
| | TWNI | 158 | 75 | 47 | 32 | 24 | 18 | 14 | 10 | 6 |
| | DG | 64 | | | | | | | | |
| | DGNI | 168 | 78 | 48 | 33 | 12 | 17 | 12 | 8 | 4 |
| Cut Bank | WW | 77 | 33 | 18 | 10 | 5 | | | | |
| 48.6°N | WWNI | 153 | 71 | 44 | 31 | 23 | 17 | 13 | 9 | 6 |
| 9033 dd | TW | 80 | 34 | 18 | 11 | 5 | | | | |
| | TWNI | 144 | 67 | 42 | 29 | 21 | 15 | 11 | 8 | 5 |
| | DG | 40 | | | | | | | | |
| | DGNI | 151 | 69 | 42 | 28 | 20 | 14 | 9 | 6 | |
| Dillon | WW | 90 | 40 | 24 | 15 | 10 | 6 | | | |
| 45.2°N | WWNI | 168 | 78 | 50 | 35 | 26 | 20 | 16 | 12 | 8 |
| 8354 dd | TW | 92 | 40 | 23 | 15 | 9 | 5 | | | |
| | TWNI | 158 | 74 | 47 | 33 | 24 | 18 | 14 | 10 | 6 |
| | DG | 64 | | | | | | | | |
| | DGNI | 168 | 78 | 48 | 33 | 24 | 17 | 12 | 8 | 4 |
| Glasgow | WW | 60 | 23 | 10 | | | | | | |
| 48.2°N | WWNI | 130 | 61 | 38 | 26 | 19 | 14 | 10 | 8 | 5 |
| 8969 dd | TW | 64 | 25 | 13 | 5 | | | | | |
| | TWNI | 124 | 58 | 35 | 24 | 17 | 13 | 9 | 7 | 4 |

| | | SHF | | | | | | | | |
|---|---|---|---|---|---|---|---|---|---|---|
| | | **0.1** | **0.2** | **0.3** | **0.4** | **0.5** | **0.6** | **0.7** | **0.8** | **0.9** |
| | DG | | | | | | | | | |
| | DGNI | 128 | 58 | 34 | 22 | 15 | 10 | 7 | 4 | |
| Great Falls | WW | 86 | 38 | 21 | 13 | 7 | | | | |
| 47.5°N | WWNI | 161 | 77 | 48 | 33 | 25 | 19 | 14 | 10 | 7 |
| 7652 dd | TW | 88 | 38 | 21 | 13 | 7 | 3 | | | |
| | TWNI | 153 | 72 | 45 | 31 | 23 | 17 | 12 | 9 | 5 |
| | DG | 56 | | | | | | | | |
| | DGNI | 163 | 75 | 46 | 31 | 22 | 15 | 11 | 7 | 3 |
| Helena | WW | 77 | 34 | 19 | 11 | 6 | | | | |
| 46.6°N | WWNI | 151 | 71 | 45 | 31 | 23 | 17 | 13 | 10 | 6 |
| 8190 dd | TW | 80 | 34 | 19 | 11 | 6 | | | | |
| | TWNI | 144 | 67 | 42 | 29 | 21 | 16 | 12 | 8 | 5 |
| | DG | 41 | | | | | | | | |
| | DGNI | 151 | 69 | 42 | 29 | 20 | 14 | 10 | 6 | 2 |
| Lewistown | WW | 76 | 33 | 19 | 11 | 6 | | | | |
| 47.0°N | WWNI | 153 | 71 | 45 | 31 | 23 | 18 | 13 | 10 | 7 |
| 8586 dd | TW | 80 | 34 | 19 | 11 | 9 | | | | |
| | TWNI | 144 | 67 | 42 | 29 | 21 | 16 | 12 | 9 | 5 |
| | DG | 41 | | | | | | | | |
| | DGNI | 151 | 69 | 42 | 29 | 20 | 14 | 10 | 6 | 3 |
| Miles City | WW | 78 | 33 | 18 | 10 | 5 | | | | |
| 46.4°N | WWNI | 151 | 72 | 44 | 31 | 22 | 17 | 13 | 10 | 6 |
| 7889 dd | TW | 80 | 34 | 18 | 10 | 5 | | | | |
| | TWNI | 144 | 67 | 41 | 28 | 21 | 15 | 11 | 8 | 5 |
| | DG | 39 | | | | | | | | |
| | DGNI | 151 | 69 | 41 | 28 | 19 | 14 | 9 | 6 | 2 |
| Missoula | WW | 66 | 27 | 13 | | | | | | |
| 46.9°N | WWNI | 140 | 65 | 40 | 28 | 20 | 15 | 11 | 8 | 5 |
| 7931 dd | TW | 71 | 28 | 15 | 7 | | | | | |
| | TWNI | 133 | 61 | 38 | 26 | 18 | 13 | 10 | 7 | 4 |
| | DG | | | | | | | | | |
| | DGNI | 138 | 62 | 37 | 24 | 16 | 11 | 7 | 4 | |
| Nebraska | | | | | | | | | | |
| Grand Island | WW | 98 | 43 | 25 | 16 | 11 | 7 | 4 | | |
| 41.0°N | WWNI | 178 | 82 | 52 | 36 | 27 | 21 | 17 | 13 | 9 |
| 6425 dd | TW | 99 | 43 | 25 | 16 | 10 | 6 | 3 | | |
| | TWNI | 168 | 78 | 48 | 34 | 25 | 19 | 15 | 11 | 7 |
| | DG | 73 | 18 | | | | | | | |
| | DGNI | 179 | 82 | 50 | 34 | 25 | 18 | 13 | 9 | 5 |

| | | SHF | | | | | | | | |
|---|---|---|---|---|---|---|---|---|---|---|
| | | **0.1** | **0.2** | **0.3** | **0.4** | **0.5** | **0.6** | **0.7** | **0.8** | **0.9** |
| North Omaha | WW | 85 | 36 | 20 | 13 | 9 | 5 | | | |
| 41.4°N | WWNI | 163 | 75 | 47 | 33 | 24 | 19 | 15 | 12 | 8 |
| 6601 dd | TW | 87 | 37 | 21 | 13 | 8 | 4 | | | |
| | TWNI | 154 | 71 | 44 | 30 | 23 | 17 | 13 | 10 | 6 |
| | DG | 52 | | | | | | | | |
| | DGNI | 162 | 73 | 44 | 31 | 22 | 16 | 12 | 8 | 4 |
| North Platte | WW | 103 | 46 | 27 | 18 | 13 | 9 | 5 | | |
| 41.1°N | WWNI | 181 | 85 | 54 | 38 | 29 | 22 | 18 | 14 | 10 |
| 6743 dd | TW | 103 | 46 | 27 | 17 | 11 | 7 | 4 | 1 | |
| | TWNI | 172 | 80 | 50 | 35 | 27 | 20 | 16 | 11 | 7 |
| | DG | 81 | 27 | | | | | | | |
| | DGNI | 184 | 85 | 53 | 37 | 27 | 20 | 14 | 10 | 6 |
| Scottsbluff | WW | 103 | 47 | 28 | 19 | 13 | 9 | 6 | | |
| 41.9°N | WWNI | 180 | 86 | 55 | 39 | 29 | 23 | 18 | 14 | 10 |
| 6774 dd | TW | 103 | 46 | 28 | 18 | 12 | 7 | 4 | 2 | |
| | TWNI | 171 | 81 | 51 | 36 | 27 | 21 | 16 | 12 | 8 |
| | DG | 82 | 29 | | | | | | | |
| | DGNI | 183 | 86 | 54 | 37 | 27 | 20 | 15 | 10 | 6 |
| Nevada | | | | | | | | | | |
| Elko | WW | 113 | 52 | 31 | 21 | 15 | 10 | 7 | | |
| 40.8°N | WWNI | 195 | 92 | 58 | 42 | 31 | 24 | 19 | 15 | 10 |
| 7483 dd | TW | 114 | 51 | 30 | 20 | 13 | 8 | 5 | 2 | |
| | TWNI | 184 | 87 | 55 | 39 | 29 | 22 | 17 | 12 | 8 |
| | DG | 97 | 36 | | | | | | | |
| | DGNI | 199 | 93 | 58 | 40 | 29 | 22 | 16 | 11 | 6 |
| Ely | WW | 111 | 52 | 32 | 22 | 16 | 12 | 8 | 4 | |
| 39.3°N | WWNI | 191 | 91 | 59 | 42 | 32 | 26 | 20 | 16 | 11 |
| 7814 dd | TW | 111 | 51 | 31 | 20 | 14 | 9 | 6 | 3 | 1 |
| | TWNI | 180 | 86 | 55 | 39 | 30 | 23 | 18 | 13 | 9 |
| | DG | 96 | 38 | 16 | | | | | | |
| | DGNI | 195 | 92 | 58 | 41 | 31 | 23 | 17 | 12 | 7 |
| Las Vegas | WW | 311 | 144 | 90 | 64 | 48 | 37 | 28 | 20 | 12 |
| 36.1°N | WWNI | 430 | 204 | 129 | 92 | 70 | 56 | 44 | 35 | 24 |
| 2601 dd | TW | 291 | 134 | 83 | 56 | 40 | 29 | 21 | 15 | 9 |
| | TWNI | 405 | 191 | 120 | 86 | 64 | 50 | 38 | 28 | 19 |
| | DG | 350 | 158 | 95 | 62 | 42 | 28 | 17 | 9 | |
| | DGNI | 461 | 216 | 136 | 96 | 71 | 54 | 41 | 29 | 19 |
| Lovelock | WW | 160 | 73 | 45 | 31 | 22 | 16 | 12 | 7 | |
| 40.1°N | WWNI | 248 | 118 | 74 | 53 | 40 | 31 | 25 | 19 | 13 |

| | | SHF | | | | | | | | |
|---|---|---|---|---|---|---|---|---|---|---|
| | | 0.1 | 0.2 | 0.3 | 0.4 | 0.5 | 0.6 | 0.7 | 0.8 | 0.9 |
| 5990 dd | TW | 153 | 70 | 42 | 28 | 19 | 13 | 9 | 5 | 3 |
| | TWNI | 235 | 110 | 70 | 49 | 37 | 28 | 22 | 16 | 10 |
| | DG | 156 | 66 | 35 | 18 | | | | | |
| | DGNI | 259 | 121 | 75 | 53 | 39 | 29 | 21 | 15 | 9 |
| Reno | WW | 166 | 77 | 47 | 33 | 24 | 18 | 13 | 8 | |
| 39.5°N | WWNI | 258 | 122 | 77 | 55 | 42 | 33 | 26 | 20 | 14 |
| 6022 dd | TW | 161 | 74 | 45 | 30 | 21 | 14 | 10 | 6 | 3 |
| | TWNI | 243 | 115 | 73 | 51 | 39 | 30 | 23 | 17 | 11 |
| | DG | 166 | 71 | | 39 | 22 | | | | |
| | DGNI | 269 | 126 | 79 | 56 | 41 | 31 | 23 | 16 | 10 |
| Tonopah | WW | 163 | 75 | 47 | 33 | 24 | 18 | 13 | 9 | 4 |
| 38.1°N | WWNI | 251 | 120 | 76 | 55 | 42 | 33 | 26 | 21 | 15 |
| 5900 dd | TW | 156 | 72 | 44 | 30 | 21 | 14 | 10 | 6 | 3 |
| | TWNI | 238 | 113 | 72 | 51 | 39 | 30 | 23 | 17 | 11 |
| | DG | 161 | 70 | 39 | 22 | 9 | | | | |
| | DGNI | 263 | 124 | 78 | 55 | 41 | 31 | 23 | 16 | 10 |
| Winnemucca | WW | 131 | 60 | 37 | 25 | 18 | 13 | 9 | 5 | |
| 40.9°N | WWNI | 214 | 103 | 65 | 47 | 35 | 28 | 22 | 17 | 12 |
| 6629 dd | TW | 129 | 59 | 35 | 23 | 16 | 11 | 7 | 4 | 1 |
| | TWNI | 203 | 96 | 61 | 43 | 32 | 25 | 19 | 14 | 9 |
| | DG | 121 | 49 | 24 | | | | | | |
| | DGNI | 222 | 104 | 65 | 46 | 34 | 25 | 18 | 13 | 7 |
| New Hampshire | | | | | | | | | | |
| Concord | WW | 56 | 23 | 12 | 6 | | | | | |
| 43.2°N | WWNI | 129 | 59 | 37 | 26 | 19 | 15 | 12 | 9 | 6 |
| 7360 dd | TW | 62 | 25 | 13 | 7 | | | | | |
| | TWNI | 123 | 56 | 35 | 24 | 18 | 14 | 10 | 7 | 5 |
| | DG | | | | | | | | | |
| | DGNI | 125 | 56 | 34 | 23 | 16 | 12 | 8 | 5 | |
| New Jersey | | | | | | | | | | |
| Newark | WW | 91 | 42 | 25 | 16 | 11 | 8 | 4 | | |
| 40.7°N | WWNI | 167 | 80 | 51 | 36 | 27 | 21 | 17 | 13 | 9 |
| 5034 dd | TW | 93 | 42 | 25 | 16 | 10 | 6 | 3 | | |
| | TWNI | 158 | 76 | 48 | 34 | 25 | 19 | 15 | 11 | 7 |
| | DG | 67 | 18 | | | | | | | |
| | DGNI | 169 | 79 | 49 | 34 | 25 | 19 | 13 | 9 | 5 |
| New Mexico | | | | | | | | | | |
| Albuquerque | WW | 178 | 84 | 53 | 37 | 28 | 21 | 16 | 11 | 6 |
| 35.0°N | WWNI | 270 | 130 | 83 | 60 | 46 | 37 | 30 | 23 | 17 |
| 4292 dd | TW | 171 | 80 | 50 | 34 | 24 | 17 | 12 | 8 | 5 |

| | | SHF | | | | | | | | |
|---|---|---|---|---|---|---|---|---|---|---|
| | | **0.1** | **0.2** | **0.3** | **0.4** | **0.5** | **0.6** | **0.7** | **0.8** | **0.9** |
| | TWNI | 255 | 122 | 78 | 56 | 43 | 33 | 26 | 19 | 13 |
| | DG | 183 | 82 | 47 | 29 | 16 | | | | |
| | DGNI | 283 | 135 | 86 | 61 | 46 | 35 | 26 | 19 | 12 |
| Clayton | WW | 160 | 73 | 46 | 32 | 24 | 18 | 14 | 9 | 4 |
| 36.4°N | WWNI | 251 | 117 | 75 | 54 | 41 | 33 | 27 | 21 | 15 |
| 5121 dd | TW | 154 | 71 | 43 | 29 | 20 | 14 | 10 | 6 | 4 |
| | TWNI | 235 | 111 | 70 | 50 | 38 | 30 | 23 | 17 | 11 |
| | DG | 157 | 68 | 38 | 21 | 9 | | | | |
| | DGNI | 260 | 122 | 77 | 54 | 41 | 31 | 23 | 17 | 10 |
| Farmington | WW | 145 | 66 | 41 | 29 | 21 | 16 | 11 | 7 | |
| 36.7°N | WWNI | 234 | 108 | 70 | 50 | 38 | 30 | 24 | 19 | 13 |
| 5713 dd | TW | 142 | 64 | 39 | 26 | 18 | 13 | 8 | 5 | 3 |
| | TWNI | 220 | 103 | 65 | 47 | 35 | 27 | 21 | 16 | 10 |
| | DG | 138 | 58 | 31 | 15 | | | | | |
| | DGNI | 241 | 112 | 70 | 50 | 37 | 28 | 21 | 15 | 9 |
| Los Alamos | WW | 128 | 58 | 36 | 26 | 19 | 14 | 10 | 7 | |
| 35.9°N | WWNI | 210 | 100 | 64 | 46 | 35 | 28 | 23 | 18 | 13 |
| 6359 dd | TW | 125 | 58 | 35 | 24 | 16 | 11 | 8 | 5 | 2 |
| | TWNI | 199 | 94 | 60 | 43 | 33 | 26 | 20 | 15 | 10 |
| | DG | 116 | 49 | 25 | | | | | | |
| | DGNI | 217 | 102 | 64 | 46 | 34 | 26 | 19 | 14 | 9 |
| Roswell | WW | 200 | 95 | 59 | 42 | 32 | 24 | 18 | 13 | 7 |
| 33.4°N | WWNI | 299 | 142 | 92 | 66 | 50 | 40 | 32 | 25 | 18 |
| 3697 dd | TW | 194 | 89 | 55 | 38 | 27 | 19 | 14 | 9 | 6 |
| | TWNI | 283 | 134 | 86 | 61 | 47 | 36 | 28 | 21 | 14 |
| | DG | 214 | 95 | 56 | 35 | 22 | 12 | | | |
| | DGNI | 316 | 149 | 95 | 67 | 51 | 38 | 29 | 21 | 13 |
| Truth or Consequences | WW | 229 | 109 | 69 | 49 | 37 | 29 | 22 | 16 | 9 |
| 33.2°N | WWNI | 332 | 160 | 103 | 74 | 57 | 45 | 37 | 29 | 21 |
| 3392 dd | TW | 220 | 102 | 64 | 44 | 31 | 23 | 16 | 11 | 7 |
| | TWNI | 314 | 150 | 96 | 69 | 53 | 41 | 32 | 24 | 16 |
| | DG | 251 | 114 | 69 | 44 | 29 | 18 | 9 | | |
| | DGNI | 354 | 168 | 107 | 76 | 58 | 44 | 33 | 24 | 15 |
| Tucumcari | WW | 194 | 90 | 56 | 40 | 30 | 23 | 17 | 12 | 7 |
| 35.2°N | WWNI | 291 | 138 | 88 | 63 | 48 | 39 | 31 | 25 | 18 |
| 4047 dd | TW | 187 | 86 | 53 | 36 | 25 | 18 | 13 | 9 | 5 |
| | TWNI | 274 | 130 | 82 | 59 | 45 | 35 | 27 | 20 | 13 |
| | DG | 203 | 90 | 53 | 32 | 20 | 10 | | | |
| | DGNI | 306 | 144 | 91 | 65 | 49 | 37 | 28 | 20 | 13 |

| | | SHF | | | | | | | | |
|---|---|---|---|---|---|---|---|---|---|---|
| | | 0.1 | 0.2 | 0.3 | 0.4 | 0.5 | 0.6 | 0.7 | 0.8 | 0.9 |
| Zuni | WW | 144 | 66 | 41 | 29 | 22 | 16 | 12 | 8 | |
| 35.1°N | WWNI | 231 | 109 | 69 | 50 | 38 | 31 | 25 | 19 | 14 |
| 5815 dd | TW | 140 | 64 | 39 | 26 | 18 | 13 | 9 | 6 | 3 |
| | TWNI | 218 | 103 | 65 | 47 | 36 | 28 | 21 | 16 | 11 |
| | DG | 137 | 59 | 32 | 16 | | | | | |
| | DGNI | 238 | 112 | 71 | 50 | 38 | 28 | 21 | 15 | 9 |
| New York | | | | | | | | | | |
| Albany | WW | 56 | 23 | 12 | 6 | | | | | |
| 42.7°N | WWNI | 129 | 59 | 37 | 26 | 19 | 15 | 11 | 9 | 6 |
| 6888 dd | TW | 62 | 25 | 13 | 7 | | | | | |
| | TWNI | 123 | 56 | 35 | 24 | 18 | 14 | 10 | 7 | 5 |
| | DG | | | | | | | | | |
| | DGNI | 125 | 56 | 34 | 23 | 16 | 12 | 8 | 5 | |
| Binghamton | WW | 42 | 15 | | | | | | | |
| 42.2°N | WWNI | 115 | 52 | 32 | 22 | 16 | 12 | 10 | 7 | 5 |
| 7285 dd | TW | 50 | 19 | 8 | | | | | | |
| | TWNI | 109 | 49 | 30 | 21 | 15 | 11 | 8 | 6 | 4 |
| | DG | | | | | | | | | |
| | DGNI | 109 | 48 | 28 | 19 | 13 | 9 | 6 | 3 | |
| Buffalo | WW | 46 | 17 | 6 | | | | | | |
| 42.9°N | WWNI | 121 | 54 | 33 | 23 | 17 | 13 | 10 | 7 | 5 |
| 6927 dd | TW | 54 | 20 | 9 | | | | | | |
| | TWNI | 115 | 51 | 31 | 21 | 16 | 12 | 9 | 6 | 4 |
| | DG | | | | | | | | | |
| | DGNI | 115 | 50 | 29 | 20 | 13 | 9 | 6 | 3 | |
| Massena | WW | 42 | 14 | | | | | | | |
| 44.9°N | WWNI | 115 | 51 | 32 | 22 | 16 | 12 | 9 | 7 | 5 |
| 8237 dd | TW | 50 | 18 | 8 | | | | | | |
| | TWNI | 109 | 49 | 30 | 21 | 15 | 11 | 8 | 6 | 4 |
| | DG | | | | | | | | | |
| | DGNI | 109 | 47 | 28 | 18 | 13 | 9 | 6 | 3 | |
| New York | WW | 85 | 37 | 22 | 14 | 10 | 6 | | | |
| 40.8°N | WWNI | 159 | 76 | 48 | 34 | 25 | 20 | 16 | 12 | 8 |
| 4848 dd | TW | 87 | 38 | 22 | 14 | 8 | 5 | 2 | | |
| | TWNI | 151 | 72 | 45 | 32 | 24 | 18 | 14 | 10 | 6 |
| | DG | 56 | | | | | | | | |
| | DGNI | 161 | 74 | 46 | 32 | 23 | 17 | 12 | 8 | 4 |
| Rochester | WW | 50 | 18 | 8 | | | | | | |
| 43.1°N | WWNI | 124 | 55 | 34 | 24 | 17 | 13 | 10 | 8 | 5 |
| 6719 dd | TW | 56 | 22 | 10 | | | | | | |

| | | SHF | | | | | | | | |
|---|---|---|---|---|---|---|---|---|---|---|
| | | **0.1** | **0.2** | **0.3** | **0.4** | **0.5** | **0.6** | **0.7** | **0.8** | **0.9** |
| | TWNI | 117 | 53 | 32 | 22 | 16 | 12 | 9 | 6 | 4 |
| | DG | | | | | | | | | |
| | DGNI | 118 | 52 | 31 | 20 | 14 | 10 | 6 | 4 | |
| Syracuse | WW | 50 | 18 | 8 | | | | | | |
| 43.1°N | WWNI | 124 | 55 | 34 | 24 | 17 | 13 | 10 | 8 | 5 |
| 6678 dd | TW | 56 | 22 | 11 | 4 | | | | | |
| | TWNI | 117 | 53 | 32 | 22 | 16 | 12 | 9 | 6 | 4 |
| | DG | | | | | | | | | |
| | DGNI | 118 | 52 | 31 | 20 | 14 | 10 | 7 | 4 | |
| North Carolina | | | | | | | | | | |
| Asheville | WW | 138 | 64 | 39 | 27 | 20 | 15 | 11 | 7 | |
| 35.4°N | WWNI | 225 | 106 | 68 | 49 | 37 | 29 | 23 | 18 | 13 |
| 4237 dd | TW | 136 | 62 | 38 | 25 | 17 | 12 | 8 | 5 | 2 |
| | TWNI | 212 | 100 | 64 | 45 | 34 | 26 | 20 | 15 | 10 |
| | DG | 131 | 55 | 28 | 12 | | | | | |
| | DGNI | 232 | 109 | 68 | 48 | 36 | 27 | 20 | 14 | 9 |
| Cape Hatteras | WW | 214 | 97 | 60 | 42 | 31 | 23 | 18 | 12 | 7 |
| 35.3°N | WWNI | 312 | 148 | 93 | 66 | 50 | 39 | 31 | 25 | 18 |
| 2731 dd | TW | 200 | 92 | 56 | 38 | 26 | 19 | 13 | 9 | 5 |
| | TWNI | 294 | 138 | 87 | 61 | 46 | 36 | 27 | 20 | 13 |
| | DG | 223 | 98 | 56 | 34 | 21 | 10 | | | |
| | DGNI | 329 | 154 | 96 | 67 | 50 | 38 | 28 | 20 | 13 |
| Charlotte | WW | 177 | 82 | 50 | 35 | 25 | 19 | 14 | 9 | 4 |
| 35.2°N | WWNI | 270 | 129 | 81 | 57 | 43 | 34 | 27 | 21 | 15 |
| 3218 dd | TW | 170 | 78 | 47 | 31 | 22 | 15 | 10 | 7 | 4 |
| | TWNI | 255 | 121 | 76 | 53 | 40 | 31 | 24 | 18 | 12 |
| | DG | 180 | 77 | 43 | 24 | 12 | | | | |
| | DGNI | 283 | 133 | 82 | 58 | 43 | 32 | 24 | 17 | 11 |
| Greensboro | WW | 151 | 70 | 43 | 29 | 22 | 16 | 12 | 7 | |
| 36.1°N | WWNI | 239 | 113 | 72 | 51 | 39 | 31 | 24 | 19 | 14 |
| 3825 dd | TW | 147 | 67 | 41 | 27 | 19 | 13 | 9 | 5 | 3 |
| | TWNI | 226 | 107 | 67 | 48 | 36 | 28 | 21 | 16 | 10 |
| | DG | 147 | 62 | 33 | 16 | | | | | |
| | DGNI | 249 | 117 | 73 | 51 | 38 | 28 | 21 | 15 | 9 |
| Raleigh-Durham | WW | 155 | 73 | 45 | 31 | 23 | 17 | 12 | 8 | |
| 35.9°N | WWNI | 244 | 117 | 75 | 53 | 40 | 31 | 25 | 20 | 14 |
| 3514 dd | TW | 151 | 69 | 42 | 28 | 19 | 13 | 9 | 6 | 3 |
| | TWNI | 230 | 110 | 69 | 49 | 37 | 29 | 22 | 16 | 11 |

| | | SHF | | | | | | | | |
|---|---|---|---|---|---|---|---|---|---|---|
| | | 0.1 | 0.2 | 0.3 | 0.4 | 0.5 | 0.6 | 0.7 | 0.8 | 0.9 |
| | DG | 153 | 65 | 36 | 19 | | | | | |
| | DGNI | 254 | 120 | 75 | 53 | 39 | 29 | 22 | 15 | 9 |
| North Dakota | | | | | | | | | | |
| Bismarck | WW | 60 | 24 | 11 | 5 | | | | | |
| 46.8°N | WWNI | 132 | 61 | 38 | 26 | 19 | 14 | 11 | 8 | 5 |
| 9044 dd | TW | 64 | 26 | 13 | 7 | | | | | |
| | TWNI | 125 | 58 | 36 | 24 | 18 | 13 | 10 | 7 | 4 |
| | DG | | | | | | | | | |
| | DGNI | 129 | 58 | 34 | 23 | 16 | 11 | 7 | 4 | |
| Fargo | WW | 48 | 17 | | | | | | | |
| 46.9°N | WWNI | 119 | 55 | 34 | 23 | 17 | 12 | 9 | 7 | 5 |
| 9271 dd | TW | 54 | 20 | 9 | | | | | | |
| | TWNI | 114 | 52 | 31 | 21 | 15 | 11 | 8 | 6 | 4 |
| | DG | | | | | | | | | |
| | DGNI | 114 | 51 | 29 | 19 | 13 | 9 | 6 | 3 | |
| Minot | WW | 54 | 19 | 7 | | | | | | |
| 48.3°N | WWNI | 126 | 58 | 35 | 24 | 17 | 13 | 10 | 7 | 5 |
| 9407 dd | TW | 59 | 22 | 10 | | | | | | |
| | TWNI | 120 | 55 | 33 | 22 | 16 | 12 | 9 | 6 | 4 |
| | DG | | | | | | | | | |
| | DGNI | 122 | 54 | 31 | 20 | 14 | 9 | 6 | 3 | |
| Ohio | | | | | | | | | | |
| Akron-Canton | WW | 61 | 25 | 13 | 7 | | | | | |
| 40.9°N | WWNI | 137 | 62 | 39 | 27 | 20 | 15 | 12 | 9 | 6 |
| 6224 dd | TW | 67 | 27 | 14 | 8 | | | | | |
| | TWNI | 130 | 59 | 36 | 25 | 18 | 14 | 10 | 7 | 5 |
| | DG | | | | | | | | | |
| | DGNI | 133 | 59 | 35 | 24 | 17 | 12 | 8 | 5 | 2 |
| Cincinnati | WW | 81 | 36 | 20 | 13 | 8 | 5 | | | |
| 39.1°N | WWNI | 156 | 74 | 46 | 32 | 24 | 19 | 15 | 11 | 8 |
| 5070 dd | TW | 84 | 36 | 21 | 13 | 8 | 4 | | | |
| | TWNI | 148 | 70 | 43 | 30 | 22 | 17 | 13 | 9 | 6 |
| | DG | 49 | | | | | | | | |
| | DGNI | 157 | 72 | 44 | 30 | 22 | 16 | 11 | 8 | 4 |
| Cleveland | WW | 59 | 23 | 11 | 5 | | | | | |
| 41.4°N | WWNI | 135 | 60 | 37 | 26 | 19 | 14 | 11 | 8 | 6 |
| 6154 dd | TW | 65 | 26 | 13 | 7 | | | | | |
| | TWNI | 128 | 57 | 35 | 24 | 18 | 13 | 10 | 7 | 4 |
| | DG | | | | | | | | | |
| | DGNI | 130 | 57 | 34 | 23 | 16 | 11 | 8 | 5 | |

| | | SHF | | | | | | | | |
|---|---|---|---|---|---|---|---|---|---|---|
| | | 0.1 | 0.2 | 0.3 | 0.4 | 0.5 | 0.6 | 0.7 | 0.8 | 0.9 |
| Columbus | WW | 67 | 28 | 15 | 9 | 5 | | | | |
| 40.0°N | WWNI | 141 | 65 | 41 | 29 | 21 | 16 | 13 | 10 | 7 |
| 5702 dd | TW | 71 | 30 | 16 | 9 | 5 | | | | |
| | TWNI | 133 | 62 | 38 | 27 | 20 | 15 | 11 | 8 | 5 |
| | DG | | | | | | | | | |
| | DGNI | 138 | 63 | 38 | 26 | 19 | 13 | 9 | 6 | 3 |
| Dayton | WW | 72 | 30 | 17 | 10 | 6 | | | | |
| 39.9°N | WWNI | 146 | 68 | 43 | 30 | 22 | 17 | 13 | 10 | 7 |
| 5641 dd | TW | 76 | 32 | 18 | 10 | 6 | | | | |
| | TWNI | 139 | 64 | 40 | 28 | 21 | 16 | 12 | 9 | 6 |
| | DG | 30 | | | | | | | | |
| | DGNI | 145 | 66 | 40 | 27 | 20 | 14 | 10 | 7 | 3 |
| Toledo | WW | 62 | 25 | 13 | 7 | | | | | |
| 41.6°N | WWNI | 138 | 62 | 39 | 27 | 20 | 15 | 12 | 9 | 6 |
| 6381 dd | TW | 68 | 27 | 15 | 8 | 3 | | | | |
| | TWNI | 130 | 59 | 36 | 25 | 19 | 14 | 10 | 8 | 5 |
| | DG | | | | | | | | | |
| | DGNI | 134 | 60 | 36 | 24 | 17 | 12 | 8 | 5 | 2 |
| Youngstown | WW | 52 | 20 | 9 | | | | | | |
| 41.3°N | WWNI | 126 | 57 | 35 | 24 | 18 | 14 | 10 | 8 | 5 |
| 6224 dd | TW | 58 | 23 | 11 | 5 | | | | | |
| | TWNI | 120 | 54 | 33 | 23 | 17 | 12 | 9 | 7 | 4 |
| | DG | | | | | | | | | |
| | DGNI | 121 | 53 | 32 | 21 | 15 | 10 | 7 | 4 | |
| Oklahoma | | | | | | | | | | |
| Oklahoma City | WW | 161 | 74 | 45 | 31 | 23 | 17 | 13 | 8 | |
| 35.4°N | WWNI | 251 | 119 | 75 | 53 | 40 | 32 | 26 | 20 | 14 |
| 3695 dd | TW | 156 | 71 | 43 | 28 | 20 | 14 | 9 | 6 | 3 |
| | TWNI | 237 | 111 | 70 | 50 | 37 | 29 | 22 | 16 | 11 |
| | DG | 158 | 67 | 36 | 19 | | | | | |
| | DGNI | 262 | 122 | 76 | 53 | 40 | 30 | 22 | 16 | 10 |
| Tulsa | WW | 147 | 67 | 41 | 28 | 21 | 15 | 11 | 7 | |
| 36.2°N | WWNI | 235 | 111 | 70 | 49 | 38 | 30 | 24 | 19 | 13 |
| 3680 dd | TW | 144 | 65 | 39 | 26 | 18 | 12 | 8 | 5 | 3 |
| | TWNI | 222 | 104 | 65 | 46 | 35 | 27 | 21 | 15 | 10 |
| | DG | 141 | 58 | 30 | 14 | | | | | |
| | DGNI | 245 | 113 | 70 | 49 | 37 | 28 | 20 | 14 | 9 |
| Oregon | | | | | | | | | | |
| Astoria | WW | 122 | 59 | 36 | 24 | 17 | 11 | 7 | | |
| 46.1°N | WWNI | 201 | 100 | 64 | 46 | 34 | 26 | 20 | 15 | 10 |

| | | SHF | | | | | | | | |
|---|---|---|---|---|---|---|---|---|---|---|
| | | **0.1** | **0.2** | **0.3** | **0.4** | **0.5** | **0.6** | **0.7** | **0.8** | **0.9** |
| 5295 dd | TW | 121 | 56 | 34 | 22 | 14 | 9 | 6 | 2 | |
| | TWNI | 191 | 94 | 60 | 42 | 31 | 23 | 17 | 13 | 8 |
| | DG | 112 | 46 | 19 | | | | | | |
| | DGNI | 208 | 101 | 64 | 44 | 32 | 23 | 17 | 11 | 6 |
| Burns | WW | 100 | 44 | 26 | 17 | 11 | 7 | | | |
| 43.6°N | WWNI | 179 | 84 | 52 | 37 | 28 | 21 | 16 | 12 | 8 |
| 7212 dd | TW | 101 | 44 | 25 | 16 | 10 | 6 | 2 | | |
| | TWNI | 170 | 79 | 49 | 34 | 25 | 19 | 14 | 10 | 6 |
| | DG | 76 | 19 | | | | | | | |
| | DGNI | 182 | 83 | 51 | 35 | 25 | 18 | 13 | 8 | 4 |
| Medford | WW | 134 | 57 | 34 | 22 | 15 | 9 | 5 | | |
| 42.4°N | WWNI | 222 | 100 | 62 | 44 | 32 | 25 | 19 | 14 | 9 |
| 4930 dd | TW | 130 | 56 | 32 | 20 | 13 | 8 | 4 | | |
| | TWNI | 209 | 94 | 58 | 40 | 29 | 22 | 16 | 12 | 7 |
| | DG | 118 | 42 | | | | | | | |
| | DGNI | 227 | 102 | 62 | 42 | 30 | 21 | 15 | 10 | 5 |
| North Bend | WW | 172 | 86 | 55 | 39 | 29 | 21 | 15 | 10 | 5 |
| 43.4°N | WWNI | 260 | 130 | 86 | 63 | 48 | 37 | 29 | 23 | 16 |
| 6224 dd | TW | 168 | 81 | 51 | 34 | 24 | 17 | 12 | 8 | 4 |
| | TWNI | 247 | 123 | 80 | 58 | 44 | 33 | 25 | 19 | 12 |
| | DG | 181 | 84 | 49 | 30 | 17 | | | | |
| | DGNI | 275 | 137 | 88 | 63 | 47 | 35 | 26 | 18 | 11 |
| Pendleton | WW | 117 | 49 | 28 | 17 | 10 | 5 | | | |
| 45.7°N | WWNI | 204 | 90 | 56 | 39 | 28 | 21 | 15 | 11 | 7 |
| 5240 dd | TW | 115 | 48 | 26 | 16 | 9 | 5 | | | |
| | TWNI | 190 | 85 | 52 | 35 | 25 | 19 | 14 | 10 | 6 |
| | DG | 94 | 22 | | | | | | | |
| | DGNI | 205 | 91 | 54 | 36 | 25 | 17 | 12 | 8 | 3 |
| Portland | WW | 135 | 56 | 32 | 20 | 13 | 8 | | | |
| 45.6°N | WWNI | 223 | 100 | 61 | 42 | 31 | 23 | 17 | 13 | 8 |
| 4792 dd | TW | 130 | 55 | 31 | 19 | 12 | 7 | 3 | | |
| | TWNI | 209 | 94 | 57 | 39 | 28 | 21 | 15 | 11 | 7 |
| | DG | 117 | 38 | | | | | | | |
| | DGNI | 228 | 100 | 60 | 40 | 28 | 20 | 14 | 9 | 4 |
| Redmond | WW | 125 | 56 | 33 | 22 | 15 | 10 | 6 | | |
| 44.3°N | WWNI | 209 | 98 | 61 | 43 | 32 | 25 | 19 | 15 | 10 |
| 6643 dd | TW | 122 | 54 | 32 | 20 | 13 | 9 | 5 | 2 | |
| | TWNI | 196 | 92 | 57 | 40 | 30 | 22 | 17 | 12 | 8 |
| | DG | 110 | 41 | 12 | | | | | | |
| | DGNI | 213 | 98 | 61 | 42 | 30 | 22 | 16 | 11 | 6 |

| | | SHF | | | | | | | | |
|---|---|---|---|---|---|---|---|---|---|---|
| | | **0.1** | **0.2** | **0.3** | **0.4** | **0.5** | **0.6** | **0.7** | **0.8** | **0.9** |
| Salem | WW | 137 | 57 | 34 | 22 | 15 | 9 | 5 | | |
| 44.9°N | WWNI | 226 | 101 | 62 | 43 | 32 | 24 | 18 | 14 | 9 |
| 4852 dd | TW | 133 | 56 | 32 | 20 | 13 | 8 | 4 | | |
| | TWNI | 212 | 95 | 58 | 40 | 29 | 22 | 16 | 11 | 7 |
| | DG | 121 | 41 | | | | | | | |
| | DGNI | 231 | 102 | 62 | 42 | 30 | 21 | 15 | 10 | 5 |
| Pennsylvania | | | | | | | | | | |
| Allentown | WW | 76 | 33 | 19 | 12 | 8 | 5 | | | |
| 40.6°N | WWNI | 152 | 71 | 45 | 32 | 24 | 18 | 15 | 11 | 8 |
| 5827 dd | TW | 80 | 35 | 20 | 12 | 7 | 4 | | | |
| | TWNI | 143 | 67 | 42 | 30 | 22 | 17 | 13 | 9 | 6 |
| | DG | 43 | | | | | | | | |
| | DGNI | 150 | 69 | 43 | 29 | 21 | 16 | 11 | 7 | 4 |
| Erie | WW | 53 | 19 | 8 | | | | | | |
| 42.1°N | WWNI | 129 | 57 | 35 | 24 | 17 | 13 | 10 | 7 | 5 |
| 6851 dd | TW | 59 | 22 | 11 | 4 | | | | | |
| | TWNI | 122 | 54 | 33 | 22 | 16 | 12 | 9 | 6 | 4 |
| | DG | | | | | | | | | |
| | DGNI | 124 | 53 | 31 | 21 | 14 | 10 | 6 | 4 | |
| Harrisburg | WW | 83 | 37 | 22 | 14 | 10 | 6 | | | |
| 40.2°N | WWNI | 158 | 75 | 47 | 34 | 25 | 20 | 16 | 12 | 8 |
| 5224 dd | TW | 86 | 38 | 22 | 14 | 8 | 5 | 2 | | |
| | TWNI | 150 | 71 | 44 | 31 | 23 | 18 | 14 | 10 | 6 |
| | DG | 55 | | | | | | | | |
| | DGNI | 158 | 74 | 46 | 32 | 23 | 17 | 12 | 8 | 4 |
| Philadelphia | WW | 95 | 43 | 26 | 17 | 12 | 8 | 5 | | |
| 39.9°N | WWNI | 171 | 82 | 52 | 37 | 28 | 22 | 17 | 13 | 9 |
| 4865 dd | TW | 96 | 43 | 25 | 16 | 10 | 6 | 4 | | |
| | TWNI | 162 | 77 | 49 | 34 | 26 | 20 | 15 | 11 | 7 |
| | DG | 72 | 22 | | | | | | | |
| | DGNI | 174 | 81 | 51 | 35 | 26 | 19 | 14 | 9 | 5 |
| Pittsburgh | WW | 62 | 25 | 13 | 7 | | | | | |
| 40.5°N | WWNI | 137 | 62 | 39 | 27 | 20 | 15 | 12 | 9 | 6 |
| 6643 dd | TW | 68 | 28 | 15 | 8 | 3 | | | | |
| | TWNI | 130 | 59 | 37 | 25 | 19 | 14 | 11 | 8 | 5 |
| | DG | | | | | | | | | |
| | DGNI | 134 | 60 | 36 | 24 | 17 | 12 | 8 | 5 | 2 |
| Scranton | WW | 63 | 26 | 14 | 8 | 4 | | | | |
| 41.3°N | WWNI | 137 | 63 | 40 | 28 | 20 | 16 | 12 | 9 | 6 |
| 6277 dd | TW | 68 | 28 | 15 | 9 | 4 | | | | |

| | | SHF | | | | | | | | |
|---|---|---|---|---|---|---|---|---|---|---|
| | | **0.1** | **0.2** | **0.3** | **0.4** | **0.5** | **0.6** | **0.7** | **0.8** | **0.9** |
| | TWNI | 130 | 60 | 37 | 26 | 19 | 14 | 11 | 8 | 5 |
| | DG | | | | | | | | | |
| | DGNI | 134 | 61 | 37 | 25 | 18 | 13 | 9 | 6 | 2 |
| Rhode Island | | | | | | | | | | |
| Providence | WW | 77 | 34 | 20 | 13 | 8 | 5 | | | |
| 41.7°N | WWNI | 153 | 71 | 45 | 32 | 24 | 19 | 15 | 11 | 8 |
| 5972 dd | TW | 81 | 35 | 20 | 12 | 7 | 4 | | | |
| | TWNI | 145 | 67 | 42 | 30 | 22 | 17 | 13 | 9 | 6 |
| | DG | 44 | | | | | | | | |
| | DGNI | 152 | 69 | 43 | 30 | 22 | 16 | 11 | 8 | 4 |
| South Carolina | | | | | | | | | | |
| Charleston | WW | 252 | 118 | 72 | 51 | 38 | 29 | 22 | 16 | 9 |
| 32.9°N | WWNI | 358 | 173 | 108 | 76 | 58 | 46 | 37 | 29 | 21 |
| 2146 dd | TW | 238 | 110 | 67 | 46 | 32 | 23 | 17 | 11 | 7 |
| | TWNI | 339 | 161 | 101 | 71 | 54 | 42 | 32 | 24 | 16 |
| | DG | 276 | 124 | 73 | 47 | 30 | 19 | 10 | | |
| | DGNI | 384 | 180 | 113 | 79 | 59 | 45 | 34 | 24 | 16 |
| Columbia | WW | 215 | 102 | 62 | 43 | 32 | 25 | 19 | 13 | 7 |
| 33.9°N | WWNI | 315 | 153 | 96 | 68 | 52 | 41 | 33 | 26 | 18 |
| 2598 dd | TW | 206 | 95 | 58 | 39 | 28 | 20 | 14 | 9 | 6 |
| | TWNI | 298 | 142 | 89 | 63 | 48 | 37 | 28 | 21 | 14 |
| | DG | 231 | 102 | 60 | 37 | 23 | 12 | | | |
| | DGNI | 335 | 158 | 99 | 69 | 52 | 39 | 29 | 21 | 13 |
| Greenville | WW | 178 | 83 | 51 | 35 | 26 | 20 | 14 | 10 | 4 |
| 34.9°N | WWNI | 272 | 129 | 82 | 58 | 44 | 35 | 28 | 22 | 15 |
| 3163 dd | TW | 172 | 78 | 48 | 32 | 22 | 16 | 11 | 7 | 4 |
| | TWNI | 257 | 121 | 76 | 54 | 41 | 31 | 24 | 18 | 12 |
| | DG | 182 | 78 | 44 | 25 | 13 | | | | |
| | DGNI | 285 | 134 | 83 | 58 | 43 | 33 | 24 | 17 | 11 |
| South Dakota | | | | | | | | | | |
| Huron | WW | 63 | 25 | 12 | 6 | | | | | |
| 44.4°N | WWNI | 136 | 62 | 39 | 27 | 19 | 15 | 11 | 9 | 6 |
| 8054 dd | TW | 67 | 27 | 14 | 7 | | | | | |
| | TWNI | 129 | 59 | 36 | 25 | 18 | 14 | 10 | 7 | 5 |
| | DG | | | | | | | | | |
| | DGNI | 133 | 59 | 35 | 24 | 16 | 12 | 8 | 5 | |
| Pierre | WW | 77 | 32 | 17 | 10 | 6 | | | | |
| 44.4°N | WWNI | 153 | 70 | 44 | 30 | 22 | 17 | 13 | 10 | 7 |
| 7677 dd | TW | 80 | 33 | 18 | 10 | 6 | | | | |
| | TWNI | 144 | 67 | 41 | 28 | 21 | 16 | 12 | 8 | 5 |

| | | SHF | | | | | | | | |
|---|---|---|---|---|---|---|---|---|---|---|
| | | 0.1 | 0.2 | 0.3 | 0.4 | 0.5 | 0.6 | 0.7 | 0.8 | 0.9 |
| | DG | 36 | | | | | | | | |
| | DGNI | 151 | 68 | 41 | 28 | 20 | 14 | 10 | 6 | 3 |
| Rapid City | WW | 91 | 40 | 23 | 15 | 10 | 6 | | | |
| 44.0°N | WWNI | 166 | 79 | 50 | 35 | 26 | 20 | 16 | 12 | 8 |
| 7324 dd | TW | 92 | 40 | 23 | 14 | 9 | 5 | 2 | | |
| | TWNI | 158 | 75 | 47 | 33 | 24 | 18 | 14 | 10 | 6 |
| | DG | 64 | | | | | | | | |
| | DGNI | 168 | 78 | 48 | 33 | 24 | 17 | 12 | 8 | 4 |
| Sioux Falls | WW | 68 | 28 | 15 | 8 | 4 | | | | |
| 43.6°N | WWNI | 143 | 66 | 41 | 28 | 21 | 16 | 12 | 9 | 6 |
| 7838 dd | TW | 72 | 30 | 16 | 9 | 4 | | | | |
| | TWNI | 135 | 62 | 38 | 26 | 19 | 15 | 11 | 8 | 5 |
| | DG | | | | | | | | | |
| | DGNI | 140 | 63 | 38 | 25 | 18 | 13 | 9 | 6 | 2 |
| Tennessee | | | | | | | | | | |
| Chattanooga | WW | 136 | 63 | 38 | 26 | 19 | 14 | 10 | 6 | |
| 35.0°N | WWNI | 220 | 106 | 67 | 47 | 35 | 28 | 22 | 17 | 12 |
| 3505 dd | TW | 133 | 61 | 36 | 24 | 16 | 11 | 7 | 4 | 2 |
| | TWNI | 208 | 99 | 62 | 44 | 33 | 25 | 19 | 14 | 9 |
| | DG | 127 | 52 | 25 | | | | | | |
| | DGNI | 228 | 108 | 67 | 47 | 34 | 26 | 19 | 13 | 8 |
| Knoxville | WW | 143 | 66 | 39 | 27 | 20 | 14 | 10 | 6 | |
| 35.8°N | WWNI | 230 | 110 | 69 | 48 | 37 | 29 | 23 | 18 | 13 |
| 3478 dd | TW | 140 | 63 | 38 | 25 | 17 | 11 | 8 | 5 | 2 |
| | TWNI | 217 | 103 | 64 | 45 | 34 | 26 | 20 | 15 | 10 |
| | DG | 136 | 56 | 28 | 10 | | | | | |
| | DGNI | 238 | 111 | 69 | 48 | 35 | 26 | 19 | 14 | 8 |
| Memphis | WW | 161 | 74 | 44 | 31 | 22 | 17 | 12 | 8 | |
| 35.0°N | WWNI | 251 | 119 | 75 | 52 | 40 | 31 | 25 | 20 | 14 |
| 3227 dd | TW | 156 | 70 | 42 | 28 | 19 | 13 | 9 | 6 | 3 |
| | TWNI | 237 | 112 | 70 | 49 | 37 | 28 | 22 | 16 | 11 |
| | DG | 159 | 66 | 35 | 18 | | | | | |
| | DGNI | 263 | 122 | 75 | 53 | 39 | 29 | 22 | 15 | 9 |
| Nashville | WW | 124 | 56 | 32 | 22 | 16 | 11 | 8 | 4 | |
| 36.1°N | WWNI | 207 | 98 | 61 | 42 | 32 | 25 | 20 | 16 | 11 |
| 3696 dd | TW | 122 | 54 | 32 | 21 | 14 | 9 | 6 | 3 | |
| | TWNI | 195 | 92 | 57 | 40 | 30 | 23 | 17 | 13 | 8 |
| | DG | 108 | 41 | 15 | | | | | | |
| | DGNI | 212 | 98 | 60 | 42 | 31 | 23 | 17 | 11 | 7 |

| | | SHF | | | | | | | | |
|---|---|---|---|---|---|---|---|---|---|---|
| | | 0.1 | 0.2 | 0.3 | 0.4 | 0.5 | 0.6 | 0.7 | 0.8 | 0.9 |
| Texas | | | | | | | | | | |
| Abileen | WW | 236 | 111 | 69 | 49 | 37 | 28 | 22 | 15 | 9 |
| 32.4°N | WWNI | 339 | 164 | 104 | 74 | 57 | 45 | 36 | 29 | 20 |
| 2610 dd | TW | 224 | 104 | 64 | 44 | 31 | 22 | 16 | 11 | 7 |
| | TWNI | 321 | 153 | 97 | 69 | 52 | 41 | 31 | 23 | 16 |
| | DG | 257 | 116 | 69 | 44 | 29 | 18 | 9 | | |
| | DGNI | 362 | 171 | 108 | 77 | 57 | 44 | 33 | 24 | 15 |
| Amarillo | WW | 178 | 83 | 52 | 36 | 27 | 21 | 16 | 11 | 5 |
| 35.2°N | WWNI | 271 | 130 | 83 | 59 | 45 | 36 | 29 | 23 | 16 |
| 4183 dd | TW | 173 | 79 | 49 | 33 | 23 | 16 | 11 | 8 | 5 |
| | TWNI | 256 | 122 | 77 | 55 | 42 | 33 | 25 | 19 | 12 |
| | DG | 183 | 80 | 46 | 27 | 15 | | | | |
| | DGNI | 285 | 134 | 85 | 60 | 45 | 34 | 25 | 18 | 12 |
| Austin | WW | 311 | 143 | 89 | 63 | 48 | 37 | 28 | 21 | 13 |
| 30.3°N | WWNI | 432 | 203 | 127 | 91 | 70 | 55 | 45 | 35 | 25 |
| 1737 dd | TW | 288 | 134 | 82 | 56 | 40 | 29 | 21 | 15 | 10 |
| | TWNI | 404 | 189 | 119 | 85 | 64 | 50 | 39 | 29 | 19 |
| | DG | 348 | 157 | 95 | 62 | 42 | 28 | 18 | 9 | |
| | DGNI | 460 | 214 | 135 | 95 | 71 | 54 | 41 | 30 | 19 |
| Brownsville | WW | 656 | 308 | 192 | 137 | 105 | 82 | 65 | 49 | 33 |
| 25.9°N | WWNI | 846 | 402 | 252 | 180 | 138 | 111 | 89 | 70 | 50 |
| 650 dd | TW | 609 | 280 | 175 | 121 | 88 | 65 | 48 | 35 | 24 |
| | TWNI | 797 | 373 | 235 | 168 | 128 | 99 | 77 | 57 | 38 |
| | DG | 799 | 365 | 226 | 155 | 111 | 80 | 58 | 40 | 24 |
| | DGNI | 929 | 432 | 272 | 194 | 146 | 112 | 85 | 63 | 42 |
| Corpus Christi | WW | 469 | 225 | 146 | 105 | 80 | 62 | 49 | 37 | 24 |
| 27.8°N | WWNI | 621 | 299 | 195 | 141 | 109 | 86 | 69 | 55 | 39 |
| 930 dd | TW | 442 | 208 | 131 | 92 | 67 | 50 | 37 | 26 | 18 |
| | TWNI | 586 | 282 | 182 | 131 | 100 | 78 | 60 | 45 | 30 |
| | DG | 564 | 264 | 165 | 113 | 81 | 58 | 41 | 27 | 15 |
| | DGNI | 677 | 325 | 208 | 149 | 113 | 87 | 66 | 48 | 32 |
| Dallas | WW | 237 | 109 | 68 | 48 | 36 | 28 | 21 | 15 | 9 |
| 32.8°N | WWNI | 343 | 162 | 102 | 73 | 56 | 45 | 36 | 28 | 20 |
| 2290 dd | TW | 223 | 103 | 64 | 43 | 31 | 22 | 16 | 11 | 7 |
| | TWNI | 321 | 151 | 95 | 68 | 52 | 40 | 31 | 23 | 15 |
| | DG | 255 | 114 | 68 | 43 | 28 | 17 | 8 | | |
| | DGNI | 362 | 169 | 106 | 75 | 57 | 43 | 32 | 23 | 15 |
| Del Rio | WW | 375 | 167 | 105 | 75 | 57 | 44 | 34 | 25 | 16 |
| 29.4°N | WWNI | 512 | 232 | 246 | 106 | 81 | 64 | 51 | 40 | 29 |

| | | SHF | | | | | | | | |
|---|---|---|---|---|---|---|---|---|---|---|
| | | **0.1** | **0.2** | **0.3** | **0.4** | **0.5** | **0.6** | **0.7** | **0.8** | **0.9** |
| 1523 dd | TW | 343 | 158 | 97 | 66 | 48 | 35 | 26 | 18 | 12 |
| | TWNI | 476 | 218 | 138 | 98 | 74 | 58 | 44 | 33 | 22 |
| | DG | 424 | 191 | 115 | 77 | 53 | 36 | 24 | 14 | 5 |
| | DGNI | 543 | 248 | 157 | 111 | 83 | 63 | 48 | 35 | 23 |
| El Paso | WW | 274 | 131 | 82 | 58 | 44 | 34 | 26 | 19 | 12 |
| 31.8°N | WWNI | 384 | 189 | 119 | 85 | 65 | 52 | 42 | 33 | 24 |
| 2678 dd | TW | 258 | 122 | 76 | 52 | 37 | 27 | 19 | 14 | 9 |
| | TWNI | 363 | 175 | 111 | 79 | 60 | 47 | 36 | 27 | 18 |
| | DG | 307 | 141 | 85 | 56 | 37 | 25 | 15 | 7 | |
| | DGNI | 413 | 197 | 125 | 89 | 66 | 51 | 38 | 28 | 18 |
| Fort Worth | WW | 225 | 104 | 65 | 46 | 34 | 26 | 20 | 14 | 8 |
| 32.8°N | WWNI | 328 | 155 | 98 | 71 | 54 | 43 | 34 | 27 | 19 |
| 2382 dd | TW | 212 | 99 | 61 | 41 | 29 | 21 | 15 | 10 | 6 |
| | TWNI | 307 | 146 | 92 | 66 | 50 | 39 | 30 | 22 | 15 |
| | DG | 240 | 108 | 64 | 40 | 25 | 15 | 6 | | |
| | DGNI | 345 | 162 | 102 | 73 | 54 | 41 | 31 | 22 | 14 |
| Houston | WW | 336 | 148 | 93 | 66 | 50 | 39 | 30 | 22 | 14 |
| 30.0°N | WWNI | 466 | 209 | 131 | 95 | 73 | 58 | 46 | 36 | 26 |
| 1434 dd | TW | 309 | 140 | 86 | 59 | 42 | 31 | 22 | 16 | 10 |
| | TWNI | 433 | 196 | 124 | 88 | 67 | 52 | 40 | 30 | 20 |
| | DG | 375 | 166 | 99 | 66 | 45 | 30 | 19 | 11 | |
| | DGNI | 492 | 223 | 140 | 99 | 74 | 57 | 43 | 31 | 20 |
| Laredo | WW | 528 | 252 | 163 | 115 | 87 | 67 | 52 | 39 | 26 |
| 27.5°N | WWNI | 693 | 331 | 216 | 156 | 117 | 92 | 74 | 58 | 41 |
| 876 dd | TW | 495 | 231 | 145 | 101 | 73 | 54 | 40 | 28 | 19 |
| | TWNI | 652 | 312 | 200 | 143 | 108 | 83 | 64 | 48 | 32 |
| | DG | 639 | 297 | 184 | 126 | 89 | 64 | 45 | 30 | 17 |
| | DGNI | 756 | 360 | 230 | 163 | 122 | 93 | 70 | 51 | 34 |
| Lubbock | WW | 206 | 97 | 61 | 43 | 32 | 25 | 19 | 13 | 8 |
| 33.6°N | WWNI | 306 | 146 | 94 | 67 | 51 | 41 | 33 | 26 | 19 |
| 3545 dd | TW | 198 | 92 | 57 | 39 | 28 | 20 | 14 | 10 | 6 |
| | TWNI | 288 | 137 | 87 | 63 | 48 | 37 | 29 | 21 | 14 |
| | DG | 220 | 99 | 58 | 37 | 23 | 13 | | | |
| | DGNI | 323 | 153 | 97 | 69 | 52 | 39 | 30 | 21 | 14 |
| Lufkin | WW | 273 | 125 | 78 | 55 | 42 | 32 | 25 | 18 | 11 |
| 31.2°N | WWNI | 385 | 182 | 113 | 81 | 63 | 50 | 40 | 32 | 22 |
| 1940 dd | TW | 254 | 118 | 73 | 49 | 35 | 25 | 18 | 13 | 8 |
| | TWNI | 361 | 170 | 107 | 76 | 58 | 45 | 35 | 26 | 17 |
| | DG | 299 | 135 | 80 | 52 | 34 | 22 | 13 | | |
| | DGNI | 409 | 191 | 120 | 85 | 63 | 48 | 36 | 26 | 17 |

| | | SHF | | | | | | | | |
|---|---|---|---|---|---|---|---|---|---|---|
| | | 0.1 | 0.2 | 0.3 | 0.4 | 0.5 | 0.6 | 0.7 | 0.8 | 0.9 |
| Midland- | | | | | | | | | | |
| Odessa | WW | 265 | 127 | 79 | 56 | 43 | 33 | 26 | 19 | 11 |
| 31.9°N | WWNI | 373 | 182 | 115 | 83 | 64 | 51 | 41 | 32 | 23 |
| 2621 dd | TW | 249 | 118 | 74 | 50 | 36 | 26 | 19 | 13 | 9 |
| | TWNI | 352 | 170 | 108 | 77 | 59 | 46 | 35 | 27 | 18 |
| | DG | 294 | 136 | 82 | 54 | 36 | 24 | 14 | 6 | |
| | DGNI | 400 | 191 | 121 | 86 | 65 | 50 | 37 | 27 | 18 |
| Port Arthur | WW | 339 | 153 | 95 | 67 | 51 | 40 | 31 | 22 | 14 |
| 29.9°N | WWNI | 466 | 215 | 134 | 96 | 74 | 59 | 47 | 37 | 27 |
| 1518 dd | TW | 311 | 143 | 88 | 60 | 43 | 31 | 23 | 16 | 11 |
| | TWNI | 435 | 201 | 126 | 90 | 68 | 53 | 41 | 30 | 20 |
| | DG | 380 | 170 | 102 | 68 | 46 | 31 | 20 | 11 | |
| | DGNI | 496 | 228 | 143 | 101 | 76 | 58 | 44 | 32 | 21 |
| San Angelo | WW | 269 | 129 | 80 | 57 | 43 | 33 | 26 | 19 | 11 |
| 31.4°N | WWNI | 377 | 185 | 117 | 84 | 65 | 51 | 41 | 33 | 23 |
| 2240 dd | TW | 253 | 120 | 75 | 51 | 36 | 26 | 19 | 13 | 9 |
| | TWNI | 357 | 172 | 109 | 78 | 59 | 46 | 36 | 27 | 18 |
| | DG | 300 | 138 | 84 | 55 | 37 | 24 | 15 | 6 | |
| | DGNI | 405 | 194 | 123 | 87 | 66 | 50 | 38 | 27 | 18 |
| San Antonio | WW | 345 | 156 | 97 | 70 | 52 | 41 | 31 | 23 | 14 |
| 29.5°N | WWNI | 474 | 219 | 137 | 99 | 76 | 60 | 48 | 38 | 27 |
| 1570 dd | TW | 318 | 146 | 90 | 62 | 44 | 32 | 24 | 17 | 11 |
| | TWNI | 443 | 204 | 129 | 92 | 70 | 54 | 42 | 31 | 21 |
| | DG | 389 | 175 | 105 | 70 | 48 | 33 | 21 | 12 | |
| | DGNI | 505 | 232 | 146 | 103 | 78 | 59 | 45 | 33 | 21 |
| Sherman | WW | 191 | 88 | 54 | 38 | 28 | 21 | 16 | 11 | 6 |
| 33.7°N | WWNI | 286 | 136 | 85 | 61 | 47 | 37 | 30 | 23 | 17 |
| 2864 dd | TW | 182 | 83 | 51 | 34 | 24 | 17 | 12 | 8 | 5 |
| | TWNI | 271 | 127 | 80 | 57 | 43 | 33 | 26 | 19 | 13 |
| | DG | 197 | 86 | 49 | 29 | 17 | | | | |
| | DGNI | 302 | 141 | 88 | 62 | 46 | 35 | 26 | 19 | 12 |
| Waco | WW | 263 | 121 | 75 | 53 | 40 | 31 | 24 | 17 | 10 |
| 31.6°N | WWNI | 373 | 176 | 110 | 79 | 61 | 48 | 39 | 30 | 22 |
| 2058 dd | TW | 245 | 114 | 70 | 47 | 34 | 24 | 18 | 12 | 8 |
| | TWNI | 350 | 164 | 103 | 74 | 56 | 43 | 33 | 25 | 17 |
| | DG | 287 | 129 | 77 | 49 | 32 | 21 | 12 | | |
| | DGNI | 396 | 185 | 116 | 82 | 61 | 47 | 35 | 25 | 16 |
| Wichita Falls | WW | 207 | 96 | 59 | 41 | 31 | 24 | 18 | 13 | 7 |
| 34.0°N | WWNI | 304 | 145 | 91 | 65 | 50 | 40 | 32 | 25 | 18 |
| 2904 dd | TW | 197 | 90 | 55 | 37 | 26 | 19 | 13 | 9 | 5 |

| | | SHF | | | | | | | | |
|---|---|---|---|---|---|---|---|---|---|---|
| | | 0.1 | 0.2 | 0.3 | 0.4 | 0.5 | 0.6 | 0.7 | 0.8 | 0.9 |
| | TWNI | 288 | 136 | 85 | 61 | 46 | 36 | 28 | 21 | 14 |
| | DG | 217 | 96 | 56 | 34 | 21 | 11 | | | |
| | DGNI | 322 | 151 | 94 | 67 | 50 | 38 | 28 | 20 | 13 |
| Utah | | | | | | | | | | |
| Bryce Canyon | WW | 98 | 47 | 29 | 20 | 15 | 11 | 7 | 3 | |
| 37.7°N | WWNI | 171 | 85 | 55 | 40 | 30 | 24 | 19 | 15 | 11 |
| 9133 dd | TW | 99 | 46 | 28 | 19 | 12 | 8 | 5 | 3 | |
| | TWNI | 163 | 80 | 52 | 37 | 28 | 22 | 17 | 12 | 8 |
| | DG | 80 | 32 | | | | | | | |
| | DGNI | 175 | 85 | 54 | 39 | 29 | 22 | 16 | 11 | 7 |
| Cedar City | WW | 139 | 64 | 39 | 27 | 20 | 15 | 11 | 7 | |
| 37.7°N | WWNI | 223 | 106 | 68 | 49 | 37 | 29 | 23 | 18 | 13 |
| 6137 dd | TW | 135 | 62 | 38 | 25 | 17 | 12 | 8 | 5 | 2 |
| | TWNI | 211 | 100 | 64 | 45 | 34 | 27 | 20 | 15 | 10 |
| | DG | 130 | 55 | 29 | 12 | | | | | |
| | DGNI | 231 | 109 | 68 | 48 | 36 | 27 | 20 | 14 | 9 |
| Salt Lake City | WW | 131 | 59 | 35 | 23 | 16 | 11 | 7 | 3 | |
| 40.8°N | WWNI | 215 | 101 | 64 | 45 | 33 | 26 | 20 | 15 | 11 |
| 5983 dd | TW | 127 | 57 | 34 | 22 | 14 | 9 | 6 | 3 | |
| | TWNI | 203 | 95 | 59 | 42 | 31 | 23 | 18 | 13 | 8 |
| | DG | 118 | 45 | 18 | | | | | | |
| | DGNI | 221 | 102 | 63 | 44 | 32 | 23 | 17 | 11 | 6 |
| Vermont | | | | | | | | | | |
| Burlington | WW | 42 | 14 | | | | | | | |
| 44.5°N | WWNI | 115 | 51 | 32 | 22 | 16 | 12 | 9 | 7 | 5 |
| 7876 dd | TW | 50 | 18 | 8 | | | | | | |
| | TWNI | 109 | 49 | 30 | 21 | 15 | 11 | 8 | 6 | 4 |
| | DG | | | | | | | | | |
| | DGNI | 109 | 47 | 28 | 19 | 13 | 9 | 6 | 3 | |
| Virginia | | | | | | | | | | |
| Norfolk | WW | 162 | 75 | 46 | 32 | 23 | 17 | 13 | 8 | |
| 36.9°N | WWNI | 251 | 120 | 76 | 54 | 41 | 32 | 26 | 20 | 14 |
| 3488 dd | TW | 156 | 72 | 43 | 29 | 20 | 14 | 9 | 6 | 3 |
| | TWNI | 237 | 113 | 71 | 50 | 38 | 29 | 22 | 17 | 11 |
| | DG | 160 | 68 | 37 | 20 | | | | | |
| | DGNI | 263 | 123 | 77 | 54 | 40 | 30 | 22 | 16 | 10 |
| Richmond | WW | 132 | 61 | 37 | 25 | 18 | 13 | 9 | 5 | |
| 37.5°N | WWNI | 216 | 103 | 65 | 46 | 35 | 27 | 22 | 17 | 12 |
| 3939 dd | TW | 130 | 59 | 35 | 23 | 16 | 11 | 7 | 4 | 2 |

| | | SHF | | | | | | | | |
|---|---|---|---|---|---|---|---|---|---|---|
| | | **0.1** | **0.2** | **0.3** | **0.4** | **0.5** | **0.6** | **0.7** | **0.8** | **0.9** |
| | TWNI | 205 | 97 | 61 | 43 | 32 | 25 | 19 | 14 | 9 |
| | DG | 122 | 49 | 24 | | | | | | |
| | DGNI | 223 | 105 | 65 | 45 | 34 | 25 | 18 | 13 | 8 |
| Roanoke | WW | 124 | 58 | 35 | 24 | 18 | 13 | 9 | 5 | |
| 37.3°N | WWNI | 206 | 99 | 63 | 45 | 34 | 27 | 21 | 17 | 12 |
| 4307 dd | TW | 123 | 56 | 34 | 22 | 15 | 10 | 7 | 4 | 1 |
| | TWNI | 195 | 93 | 59 | 42 | 32 | 24 | 19 | 14 | 9 |
| | DG | 113 | 46 | 21 | | | | | | |
| | DGNI | 212 | 100 | 63 | 44 | 33 | 24 | 18 | 13 | 7 |
| Washington, DC; *See* DC | | | | | | | | | | |
| Washington | | | | | | | | | | |
| Olympia | WW | 112 | 48 | 28 | 17 | 10 | 5 | | | |
| 47.0°N | WWNI | 191 | 90 | 55 | 38 | 28 | 21 | 16 | 11 | 7 |
| 5530 dd | TW | 109 | 48 | 27 | 16 | 10 | 5 | | | |
| | TWNI | 181 | 84 | 52 | 36 | 26 | 19 | 14 | 10 | 6 |
| | DG | 90 | 23 | | | | | | | |
| | DGNI | 195 | 89 | 54 | 36 | 25 | 18 | 12 | 8 | 3 |
| Seattle-Tacoma | WW | 128 | 54 | 30 | 19 | 11 | 6 | | | |
| 47.4°N | WWNI | 213 | 98 | 59 | 41 | 30 | 22 | 16 | 11 | 7 |
| 5185 dd | TW | 123 | 53 | 29 | 18 | 11 | 6 | | | |
| | TWNI | 199 | 91 | 55 | 38 | 27 | 20 | 14 | 10 | 6 |
| | DG | 108 | 33 | | | | | | | |
| | DGNI | 217 | 97 | 58 | 38 | 27 | 19 | 13 | 8 | 3 |
| Spokane | WW | 91 | 37 | 20 | 10 | | | | | |
| 47.6°N | WWNI | 169 | 78 | 47 | 32 | 23 | 17 | 12 | 9 | 6 |
| 6835 dd | TW | 92 | 38 | 20 | 11 | 5 | | | | |
| | TWNI | 161 | 73 | 44 | 30 | 21 | 15 | 11 | 8 | 4 |
| | DG | 56 | | | | | | | | |
| | DGNI | 171 | 75 | 45 | 29 | 20 | 13 | 9 | 5 | |
| Yakima | WW | 117 | 48 | 26 | 15 | 8 | | | | |
| 46.6°N | WWNI | 201 | 90 | 55 | 38 | 27 | 20 | 14 | 10 | 7 |
| 6009 dd | TW | 114 | 47 | 25 | 15 | 8 | 4 | | | |
| | TWNI | 190 | 85 | 51 | 35 | 25 | 18 | 13 | 9 | 5 |
| | DG | 92 | | | | | | | | |
| | DGNI | 205 | 89 | 53 | 35 | 24 | 16 | 11 | 7 | 3 |
| West Virginia | | | | | | | | | | |
| Charleston | WW | 93 | 41 | 23 | 15 | 10 | 7 | 3 | | |
| 38.4°N | WWNI | 170 | 80 | 50 | 35 | 26 | 20 | 16 | 12 | 9 |

| | | SHF | | | | | | | | |
|---|---|---|---|---|---|---|---|---|---|---|
| | | **0.1** | **0.2** | **0.3** | **0.4** | **0.5** | **0.6** | **0.7** | **0.8** | **0.9** |
| 4590 dd | TW | 94 | 41 | 24 | 15 | 9 | 5 | 2 | | |
| | TWNI | 161 | 75 | 47 | 33 | 24 | 19 | 14 | 10 | 7 |
| | DG | 66 | | | | | | | | |
| | DGNI | 172 | 79 | 48 | 33 | 24 | 18 | 13 | 8 | 5 |
| Huntington | WW | 99 | 44 | 26 | 17 | 12 | 8 | 4 | | |
| 38.4°N | WWNI | 178 | 84 | 53 | 37 | 28 | 21 | 17 | 13 | 9 |
| 4624 dd | TW | 101 | 44 | 26 | 16 | 10 | 6 | 3 | | |
| | TWNI | 169 | 79 | 49 | 34 | 26 | 20 | 15 | 11 | 7 |
| | DG | 76 | 22 | | | | | | | |
| | DGNI | 181 | 83 | 51 | 35 | 26 | 19 | 14 | 9 | 5 |
| Wisconsin | | | | | | | | | | |
| Eau Claire | WW | 50 | 19 | 8 | | | | | | |
| 44.9°N | WWNI | 121 | 56 | 34 | 24 | 17 | 13 | 10 | 8 | 5 |
| 8388 dd | TW | 56 | 22 | 11 | 4 | | | | | |
| | TWNI | 115 | 53 | 32 | 22 | 16 | 12 | 9 | 6 | 4 |
| | DG | | | | | | | | | |
| | DGNI | 117 | 52 | 31 | 20 | 14 | 10 | 7 | 4 | |
| Green Bay | WW | 57 | 22 | 11 | 5 | | | | | |
| 44.5°N | WWNI | 132 | 59 | 37 | 26 | 19 | 14 | 11 | 8 | 5 |
| 8098 dd | TW | 63 | 25 | 13 | 6 | | | | | |
| | TWNI | 125 | 56 | 35 | 24 | 17 | 13 | 10 | 7 | 4 |
| | DG | | | | | | | | | |
| | DGNI | 127 | 56 | 34 | 22 | 16 | 11 | 7 | 4 | |
| La Crosse | WW | 59 | 23 | 12 | 6 | | | | | |
| 43.9°N | WWNI | 133 | 61 | 37 | 26 | 19 | 15 | 11 | 9 | 6 |
| 7417 dd | TW | 64 | 26 | 13 | 7 | | | | | |
| | TWNI | 126 | 57 | 35 | 24 | 18 | 13 | 10 | 7 | 5 |
| | DG | | | | | | | | | |
| | DGNI | 129 | 57 | 34 | 23 | 16 | 11 | 8 | 5 | |
| Madison | WW | 62 | 25 | 13 | 7 | | | | | |
| 43.1°N | WWNI | 137 | 62 | 39 | 27 | 20 | 15 | 12 | 9 | 6 |
| 7730 dd | TW | 67 | 27 | 15 | 8 | 3 | | | | |
| | TWNI | 130 | 59 | 36 | 25 | 19 | 14 | 11 | 8 | 5 |
| | DG | | | | | | | | | |
| | DGNI | 133 | 59 | 36 | 24 | 17 | 12 | 8 | 5 | 2 |
| Milwaukee | WW | 64 | 26 | 14 | 8 | | | | | |
| 42.9°N | WWNI | 140 | 63 | 39 | 27 | 20 | 16 | 12 | 9 | 6 |
| 7444 dd | TW | 69 | 28 | 15 | 8 | 4 | | | | |
| | TWNI | 132 | 60 | 37 | 26 | 19 | 14 | 11 | 8 | 5 |
| | DG | | | | | | | | | |
| | DGNI | 136 | 60 | 36 | 25 | 17 | 12 | 9 | 5 | 2 |

| | | SHF | | | | | | | | |
|---|---|---|---|---|---|---|---|---|---|---|
| | | **0.1** | **0.2** | **0.3** | **0.4** | **0.5** | **0.6** | **0.7** | **0.8** | **0.9** |
| Wyoming | | | | | | | | | | |
| Casper | WW | 107 | 49 | 30 | 20 | 14 | 10 | 7 | | |
| 42.9°N | WWNI | 184 | 90 | 57 | 41 | 31 | 24 | 19 | 15 | 10 |
| 7555 dd | TW | 107 | 49 | 29 | 19 | 12 | 8 | 5 | 2 | |
| | TWNI | 175 | 84 | 53 | 38 | 28 | 22 | 17 | 12 | 8 |
| | DG | 90 | 34 | | | | | | | |
| | DGNI | 190 | 90 | 56 | 39 | 29 | 21 | 16 | 11 | 6 |
| Cheyenne | WW | 111 | 52 | 32 | 22 | 16 | 12 | 8 | 5 | |
| 41.1°N | WWNI | 190 | 91 | 58 | 42 | 32 | 25 | 21 | 16 | 11 |
| 7255 dd | TW | 112 | 51 | 31 | 20 | 14 | 9 | 6 | 3 | 1 |
| | TWNI | 181 | 86 | 55 | 39 | 30 | 23 | 18 | 13 | 9 |
| | DG | 96 | 38 | 16 | | | | | | |
| | DGNI | 195 | 92 | 58 | 41 | 31 | 23 | 17 | 12 | 7 |
| Rock Springs | WW | 98 | 45 | 28 | 19 | 13 | 9 | 6 | | |
| 41.6°N | WWNI | 176 | 84 | 54 | 38 | 29 | 23 | 18 | 14 | 10 |
| 8410 dd | TW | 100 | 45 | 27 | 17 | 11 | 7 | 4 | 2 | |
| | TWNI | 167 | 79 | 50 | 36 | 27 | 21 | 16 | 12 | 8 |
| | DG | 78 | 28 | | | | | | | |
| | DGNI | 179 | 84 | 53 | 37 | 27 | 20 | 15 | 10 | 6 |
| Sheridan | WW | 86 | 38 | 22 | 14 | 9 | 5 | | | |
| 44.8°N | WWNI | 161 | 77 | 48 | 34 | 25 | 19 | 15 | 12 | 8 |
| 7708 dd | TW | 88 | 38 | 22 | 14 | 8 | 4 | | | |
| | TWNI | 153 | 72 | 45 | 32 | 23 | 18 | 13 | 10 | 6 |
| | DG | 57 | | | | | | | | |
| | DGNI | 163 | 75 | 46 | 32 | 23 | 17 | 12 | 8 | 4 |
| Alberta | | | | | | | | | | |
| Edmonton | WW | 66 | 26 | 10 | | | | | | |
| 53.6°N | WWNI | 139 | 65 | 39 | 27 | 19 | 10 | 7 | 4 | |
| 10268 dd | TW | 69 | 27 | 13 | | | | | | |
| | TWNI | 132 | 61 | 37 | 25 | 17 | 12 | 9 | 3 | |
| | DG | | | | | | | | | |
| | DGNI | 136 | 61 | 35 | 23 | 15 | 10 | 6 | 3 | |
| Suffield | WW | 92 | 40 | 23 | 14 | 8 | 4 | | | |
| 50.3°N | WWNI | 170 | 79 | 50 | 35 | 26 | 19 | 15 | 11 | 7 |
| 8644 dd | TW | 93 | 40 | 23 | 14 | 8 | 4 | | | |
| | TWNI | 160 | 75 | 46 | 32 | 23 | 17 | 13 | 9 | 6 |
| | DG | 64 | | | | | | | | |
| | DGNI | 170 | 78 | 48 | 32 | 23 | 16 | 11 | 7 | 3 |
| British Columbia | | | | | | | | | | |
| Nanaimo | WW | 140 | 61 | 35 | 21 | 13 | 7 | | | |

| | | SHF | | | | | | | | |
|---|---|---|---|---|---|---|---|---|---|---|
| | | 0.1 | 0.2 | 0.3 | 0.4 | 0.5 | 0.6 | 0.7 | 0.8 | 0.9 |
| 49.2°N | WWNI | 229 | 105 | 65 | 44 | 32 | 23 | 17 | 12 | 8 |
| 5515 dd | TW | 135 | 58 | 32 | 20 | 12 | 7 | | | |
| | TWNI | 214 | 98 | 60 | 40 | 29 | 21 | 15 | 10 | 6 |
| | DG | 126 | 43 | | | | | | | |
| | DGNI | 233 | 106 | 63 | 42 | 29 | 20 | 14 | 9 | 4 |
| Vancouver | WW | 111 | 47 | 26 | 15 | 9 | 4 | | | |
| 49.3°N | WWNI | 193 | 89 | 54 | 37 | 27 | 20 | 15 | 11 | 7 |
| 5515 dd | TW | 109 | 46 | 25 | 15 | 8 | 4 | | | |
| | TWNI | 181 | 83 | 50 | 34 | 24 | 18 | 13 | 9 | 6 |
| | DG | 86 | | | | | | | | |
| | DGNI | 195 | 88 | 52 | 34 | 24 | 17 | 11 | 7 | 3 |
| Manitoba | | | | | | | | | | |
| Winnipeg | WW | 53 | 21 | 9 | | | | | | |
| 49.9°N | WWNI | 125 | 58 | 36 | 25 | 18 | 13 | 10 | 7 | 5 |
| 10679 dd | TW | 59 | 23 | 11 | 4 | | | | | |
| | TWNI | 119 | 55 | 34 | 23 | 17 | 12 | 9 | 6 | 4 |
| | DG | | | | | | | | | |
| | DGNI | 121 | 54 | 32 | 21 | 15 | 10 | 6 | 3 | |
| Nova Scotia | | | | | | | | | | |
| Dartmouth | WW | 73 | 31 | 18 | 11 | 7 | 4 | | | |
| 44.6°N | WWNI | 148 | 68 | 43 | 30 | 23 | 18 | 14 | 11 | 7 |
| 7361 dd | TW | 76 | 33 | 18 | 11 | 6 | 3 | | | |
| | TWNI | 140 | 64 | 40 | 28 | 21 | 16 | 12 | 9 | 6 |
| | DG | 34 | | | | | | | | |
| | DGNI | 146 | 66 | 41 | 28 | 20 | 15 | 11 | 7 | 3 |
| Ontario | | | | | | | | | | |
| Moosonee | WW | 34 | 11 | | | | | | | |
| 51.3°N | WWNI | 102 | 48 | 30 | 21 | 15 | 11 | 8 | 6 | 4 |
| 11572 dd | TW | 42 | 15 | | | | | | | |
| | TWNI | 98 | 45 | 28 | 19 | 14 | 10 | 7 | 5 | 3 |
| | DG | | | | | | | | | |
| | DGNI | 96 | 43 | 26 | 17 | 11 | 7 | 4 | | |
| Ottawa | WW | 65 | 26 | 14 | 8 | | | | | |
| 45.5°N | WWNI | 140 | 63 | 39 | 27 | 20 | 16 | 12 | 9 | 6 |
| 8735 dd | TW | 69 | 28 | 15 | 8 | 3 | | | | |
| | TWNI | 133 | 60 | 37 | 26 | 19 | 14 | 11 | 8 | 5 |
| | DG | | | | | | | | | |
| | DGNI | 137 | 60 | 36 | 25 | 17 | 12 | 9 | 5 | 2 |
| Toronto | WW | 73 | 31 | 17 | 11 | 7 | | | | |
| 43.7°N | WWNI | 148 | 68 | 43 | 30 | 22 | 17 | 14 | 10 | 7 |

| | | SHF | | | | | | | | |
|---|---|---|---|---|---|---|---|---|---|---|
| | | **0.1** | **0.2** | **0.3** | **0.4** | **0.5** | **0.6** | **0.7** | **0.8** | **0.9** |
| 6827 dd | TW | 76 | 32 | 18 | 11 | 6 | 2 | | | |
| | TWNI | 140 | 65 | 40 | 28 | 21 | 16 | 12 | 9 | 6 |
| | DG | 32 | | | | | | | | |
| | DGNI | 146 | 66 | 40 | 28 | 20 | 14 | 10 | 7 | 3 |
| Quebec | | | | | | | | | | |
| Normandin | WW | 49 | 19 | 9 | | | | | | |
| 48.8°N | WWNI | 118 | 56 | 35 | 24 | 18 | 13 | 10 | 7 | 5 |
| 10528 dd | TW | 54 | 22 | 11 | 4 | | | | | |
| | TWNI | 112 | 52 | 33 | 23 | 16 | 12 | 9 | 6 | 4 |
| | DG | | | | | | | | | |
| | DGNI | 113 | 52 | 31 | 21 | 14 | 10 | 6 | 4 | |

# APPENDIX B

# ABSORPTION AND TRANSMISSION OF SOLAR RADIATION

When solar radiation impinges on a surface, it is absorbed, transmitted and/or reflected. Reflection may be specular (angle of incidence equals angle of reflection), diffuse, or partly specular and partly diffuse. The absorptance $\alpha$ (not to be confused with the surface azimuth angle $\alpha$) of a surface is the ratio of the energy absorbed to the energy incident on it. The transmittance $\tau$ of an object (such as a pane of glass) is the ratio of the energy transmitted through to the incident energy, and the reflectance $\rho$ is the ratio of the energy reflected off the surface to the energy incident. Since all the energy incident on a surface is either absorbed, reflected or transmitted:

$$\alpha + \tau + \rho = 1 \tag{B.1}$$

$\alpha$, $\tau$ and $\rho$ are usually all functions of wavelength, so their values depend on the spectrum of the incident radiation. For an opaque object ($\tau = 0$), the above equation reduces to:

$$\alpha + \rho = 1 \tag{B.2}$$

Many solar systems involve transmission of solar radiation through one or more sheets of transparent glazing and subsequent absorption on a surface. In this case, the effective transmittance-absorptance product is found from:

$$(\tau\alpha)_e = \frac{\tau\alpha}{1 - (1 - \alpha)\rho_d} \tag{B.3}$$

where $\alpha$ = absorptance of the absorbing surface
$\rho_d$ = diffuse reflectance of the covers, estimated by calculating $\rho$ for an incidence angle of 60°
$\tau$ = transmittance of the transparent panes

$$\tau = \frac{1}{2}\left[\frac{1-\rho_p}{1+(2N-1)\rho_p} + \frac{1-\rho_s}{1+(2N-1)\rho_s}\right]\exp\left(\frac{-KX}{\cos\psi'}\right) \qquad (B.4)$$

where K = extinction coefficient of the transparent panes
X = total thickness of the N transparent panes
$\psi'$ = angle of refraction

The angle of refraction $\psi'$ is given by Snell's law:

$$\sin\psi' = \frac{\sin\psi}{n} \qquad (B.5)$$

where $\psi$ = the angle of incidence
n = the index of refraction of the transparent panes

The reflectance from a transparent surface is different for the parallel ($\rho_p$) and perpendicular ($\rho_s$) components of the radiation striking the surface:

$$\rho_p = \frac{\tan^2(\psi - \psi')}{\tan^2(\psi + \psi')} \qquad (B.6)$$

$$\rho_s = \frac{\sin^2(\psi - \psi')}{\sin^2(\psi + \psi')} \qquad (B.7)$$

For unpolarized light, the two components of the incident light are equal, so:

$$\rho = \frac{1}{2}\frac{\tan^2(\psi - \psi')}{\tan^2(\psi + \psi')} + \frac{1}{2}\frac{\sin^2(\psi - \psi')}{\sin^2(\psi + \psi')} \qquad (B.8)$$

For normal incidence radiation, the two components are reflected equally, and

$$\rho = \frac{(n-1)^2}{(n+1)^2} \qquad (B.9)$$

## EXAMPLE

What fraction of the incident solar radiation is transmitted through three glass plates of 1.526 index of refraction, extinction coefficient of

0.2/cm and thickness of 2 mm (each) for incidence angles of 10°, 30°, 50° and 70°?

## Solution

Use Equation B.4 after first calculating $\psi'$, $\rho_p$ and $\rho_s$ from Equations B.5–B.7. Kx is 0.12. The results are

| $\psi'$ | $\psi'$ | $\rho_s$ | $\rho_p$ | $\exp \frac{-KX}{\cos \psi'}$ | $\tau$ |
|---|---|---|---|---|---|
| 10° | 6.53° | 0.0451 | 0.0416 | 0.886 | 0.697 |
| 30° | 19.1° | 0.0622 | 0.0276 | 0.881 | 0.691 |
| 50° | 30.1° | 0.1190 | 0.0040 | 0.871 | 0.666 |
| 70° | 38.0° | 0.3103 | 0.0412 | 0.858 | 0.457 |

# APPENDIX C

# UTILIZABILITY

Klein [1978] refined the Φ-curve method of Whillier [1953] and Liu [1963]. The utilizability, $\phi$ [Klein 1978], is the fraction of the long-term solar radiation ($\overline{H}_T$) which is above the threshold level ($H_{TC}$) for solar collector operation for a given hour of the day summed over N days.

$$\Phi = \frac{1}{N} \sum_{i=1}^{N} \frac{(H_T - H_{TC})^+}{\overline{H}_T} \qquad (C.1)$$

where $H_T$ = the hourly solar radiation on the collector aperture
$H_{TC}$ = the hourly solar radiation on the collector aperture that is above the threshold
$\overline{H}_T$ = the average hourly radiation on the collector aperture

The "+" superscript indicates that only positive values of $(H_T - H_{TC})$ are included in the sum. The threshold value of $H_{TC}$ is found from

$$H_{TC} = \frac{F_R U_L (T_i - T_a)}{F_R(\tau\alpha)_e} = \frac{U_L(T_i - T_a)}{(\tau\alpha)_e} \qquad (C.2)$$

where $U_L$ is the loss coefficient.
$(\tau\alpha)_e$ is the effective transmittance-absorptance product (Eq. B.3) so

$$Q_u/A_c = F_R(\tau\alpha)_e(H_T - H_{TC}) \qquad (C.3)$$

The Φ-curve method uses Equation C.3 to determine the useful energy collected for a given hour of the day averaged over N days. The long-term average useful energy collected during a given hour of the day over a month can be expressed in terms of the utilizability Φ,

$$\overline{Q_i} = A_C F_R (\tau\alpha)_e \overline{H_T} \Phi \tag{C.4}$$

where $A_c$ = the solar collector aperture area
$F_R$ = the heat removal factor
$\overline{H_T}$ = the average solar radiation on the collector aperture and the total useful energy collected is

$$Q_u = N \sum_{i=1}^{n} \overline{Q_i} \tag{C.5}$$

where n is the number of hours between sunrise and sunset.

Whillier developed graphs of $\Phi$ as a function of $H_{TC}/\overline{H_T}$ for each month and showed that it is necessary only to determine $\Phi$ for each hourly interval on either side of solar noon rather than for each hour of the day. Liu and Jordan [1960] later showed that the plots of $\Phi$ vs $H_{TC}/\overline{H_T}$ are unique functions of $\overline{K_T}$, the ratio of monthly average daily global radiation on a horizontal surface to the monthly average daily extraterrestrial radiation on a horizontal surface. The result was a set of generalized $\Phi$-curves applicable to any south-facing solar collector in the northern hemisphere.

An assumption of the $\Phi$-curve method is that $H_{TC}$ (Equation C.2) is the same for any one hour of the day during the N-day time period (usually a month). Thus, the method is less accurate if collector operating temperatures vary by large amounts from day to day. For hot water and space heating systems, reasonable assumptions can be made as to the average operating temperature during a given hour of the day.

Combining Equations C.4 and C.5, the useful energy gain over a period of N days can be written

$$Q_u = A_c F_R (\overline{\tau\alpha})_e \sum^{N} \sum^{n} (H_T - H_{TC})^+ \tag{C.6}$$

where $(\overline{\tau\alpha})_e$ is the monthly weighted-average value of $(\tau\alpha)_e$. $H_{TC}$ is evaluated using the average daytime ambient temperature. The monthly average daily utilizability is given by

$$\Phi = \frac{\sum^{N} \sum^{n} (H_T - H_{TC})^+}{\sum^{N} \sum^{n} H_T} \tag{C.7}$$

However, the denominator is merely the total solar radiation falling on the collector during the N-day period, which is $\overline{H_T}N$, where $\overline{H_T}$ is the monthly average daily total solar radiation on the collector aperture tabulated in the tables in Chapter 7. Thus, combining C.7 with C.6 leads to

$$Q_u = A_c F_R (\overline{\tau\alpha})_e \bar{\Phi} \overline{H_T} N \tag{C.8}$$

The utilizability $\bar{\Phi}$ for a month is a function of $H_{TC}$, the collector location and orientation, the month of the year, and the monthly average cloudiness index $\overline{K_T}$. The effects of collector orientation, location and month of the year may be accounted for by a single variable $\bar{F}/F_n$, where $\bar{F}$ is the ratio of average daily radiation on the tilted surface to the horizontal daily average radiation, and $F_n$ is the ratio of radiation intensity at noon on the tilted surface to that on a horizontal surface for an average day of the month. $X_c$ is the ratio of $H_{TC}$ to the horizontal radiation intensity at noon for an average day during the month for which the total radiation for the day is the same as the average for the month.

$$X_c = \frac{H_{TC}}{R_{Tn} F_n \bar{H}} = \frac{H_{TC}}{R_{Tn} F_n \overline{K_T} H_o} \tag{C.9}$$

where $R_{Tn}$, the ratio of the solar radiation intensity at noon to the daily total radiation, is given by

$$R_{Tn} = R_{dn}[1.07 + 0.025 \sin(\omega_s - 60)] \tag{C.10}$$

where $R_{dn}$, the ratio of the diffuse radiation at noon to the daily diffuse radiation, is found from

$$R_{dn} = \left(\frac{\pi}{24}\right)\left(\frac{1 - \cos \omega_s}{\sin \omega_s - (\pi/180)\omega_s \cos \omega_s}\right) \tag{C.11}$$

and $\omega_s$ is the sunset hour angle found from

$$\omega_s = \arccos(-\tan \phi \tan \delta) \tag{C.12}$$

$F_n$ may be calculated from

$$F_n = \left(1 - \frac{R_{dn}}{R_{Tn}}\left(\frac{D}{H}\right)\right)F_{bn} + \frac{R_{dn}}{R_{Tn}}\left(\frac{D}{H}\right)\left(\frac{1 + \cos \beta}{2}\right) + a\left(\frac{1 - \cos \beta}{2}\right) \tag{C.13}$$

where for surfaces facing toward the equator the ratio of beam radiation on a tilted surface to that on a horizontal surface at noon $F_{bn}$ is

$$F_{bn} = \frac{\cos(\phi - \beta) \cos \delta + \sin(\phi - \beta) \sin \delta}{\cos \phi \cos \delta + \sin \phi \sin \delta} \tag{C.14}$$

and D/H is given in Chapter 7. Klein [1981] found the following correlation for the monthly average value of $\phi$

$$\bar{\Phi} = \exp[[A + B(F_n/\bar{F})](X_c + CX_c^2)] \tag{C.15}$$

when

$$A = 2.943 - 9.271\overline{K_T} + 4.031\overline{K_T}^2 \tag{C.16}$$

$$B = -4.34 + 8.853\overline{K_T} - 3.602\overline{K_T}^2 \tag{C.17}$$

$$C = -0.170 - 0.306\overline{K_T} + 2.936\overline{K_T}^2 \tag{C.18}$$

$$\bar{F} = (1 - \bar{D}/\bar{H})\overline{F_b} + (\bar{D}/\bar{H})(1 + \cos\beta)/2 + a(1 - \cos\beta)/2 \tag{C.19}$$

$$\bar{D}/\bar{H} = 1.39 - 4.03\overline{K_T} + 5.53\overline{K_T}^2 - 3.11\overline{K_T}^3 \tag{C.20}$$

$$\overline{F_b} = \frac{\cos(\phi - \beta)\cos\delta\sin\omega_s' + (\pi/180)\omega_s'\sin(\phi - \beta)\sin\delta}{\cos\phi\cos\delta\sin\omega_s + (\pi/180)\omega_s\sin\phi\sin\delta} \tag{C.21}$$

$$\omega_s' = \text{lesser of } \omega_s \text{ and } \arccos(-\tan(\phi - \beta)\tan\delta)$$

$$a = \text{albedo} = \text{reflectance of the earth}$$

Figures C.1–C.5 are plots of $\bar{\Phi}$ vs $X_c$ for various values of $\bar{F}/Fn$. $\bar{\Phi}$ is the monthly average daily utilizability.

The following example by Klein illustrates the utility of this method.

## Example: Using Utilizability Method

A solar energy system in Miami (latitude = 25.7°) with 50 m$^2$ of conventional double-glazed flat-plate solar collectors facing south at a 20° slope operates with an inlet temperature of 80°C. The pertinent collector parameters are $F_R(\tau\alpha)_e = 0.5985$ and $F_R U_L = 4.6$ W/m$^2$-°C, both of which are considered to be constant. During July the average ambient temperature is 27°C, the average daily solar radiation on a horizontal surface is 22.5 MJ/m$^2$, the average value of the cloudiness index $\overline{K_T}$ is 0.57, and the average reflectance of the ground (surface albedo) is 0.2. Using the utilizability method, calculate the energy supplied by the solar collector in July.

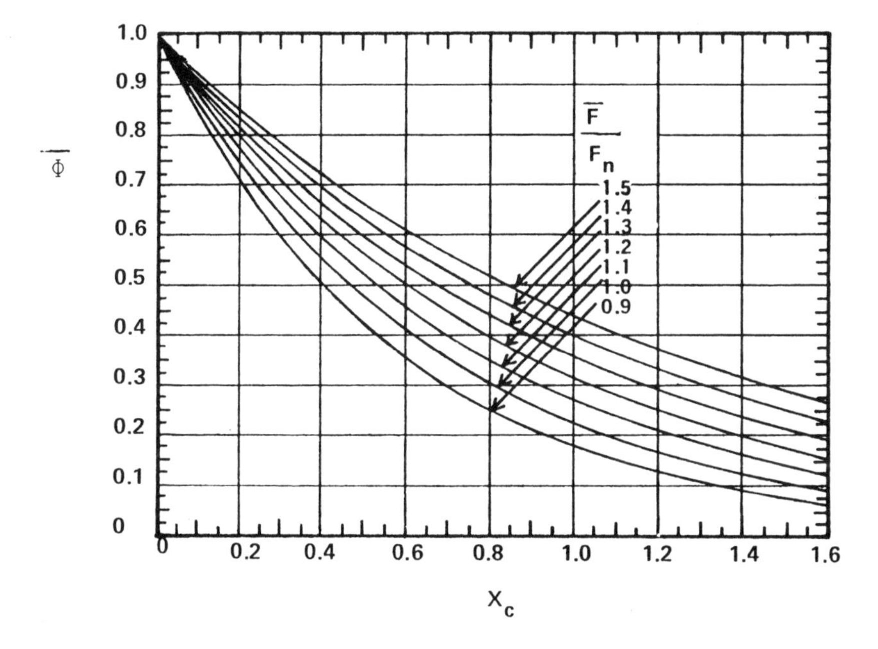


**Figure C.1.** $\bar{\Phi}$ vs $X_c$ for $\overline{K_T} = 0.3$.

## *Solution*

The problem is to determine the useful energy supplied by the collector $Q_u$ given by:

$$Q_u = A_c F_R(\overline{\tau\alpha})_e \bar{\Phi} \overline{H_T} N \qquad \text{(C.8)}$$

where

$$A_c = 50 \text{ m}^2 \qquad \text{(given)}$$

$$F_R(\overline{\tau\alpha})_e = 0.5985 \qquad \text{(given)}$$

$$N = 31 \qquad \text{(given)}$$

$$\overline{H_T} = \bar{F}\bar{H} \qquad \text{(12)}$$

$\bar{\Phi}$ is determined from Figures C.1–C.5 or Equations C.15–C.21. In order to determine $\overline{H_T}$, the value of $\bar{F}$ must be calculated

$$\bar{F} = (1 - \bar{D}/\bar{H})\overline{F_b} + (\bar{D}/\bar{H})(1 + \cos\beta)/2 + a(1 - \cos\beta)/2 \qquad \text{(C.19)}$$

where

$$\bar{D}/\bar{H} = 1.39 - 4.03\overline{K_T} + 5.53\overline{K_T}^2 - 3.11\overline{K_T}^3 \qquad \text{(C.20)}$$

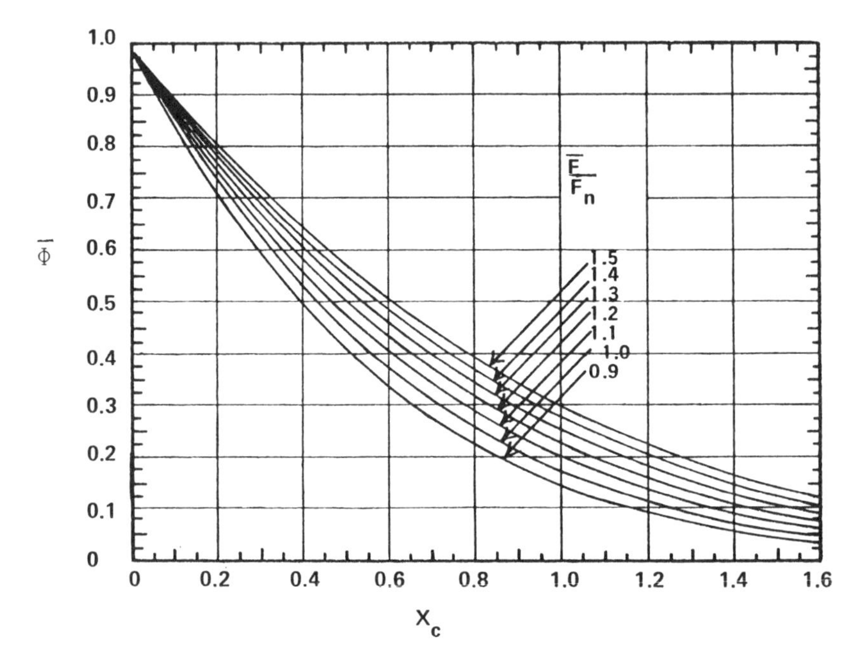


**Figure C.2.** $\bar{\Phi}$ vs $X_c$ for $\overline{K_T} = 0.4$.

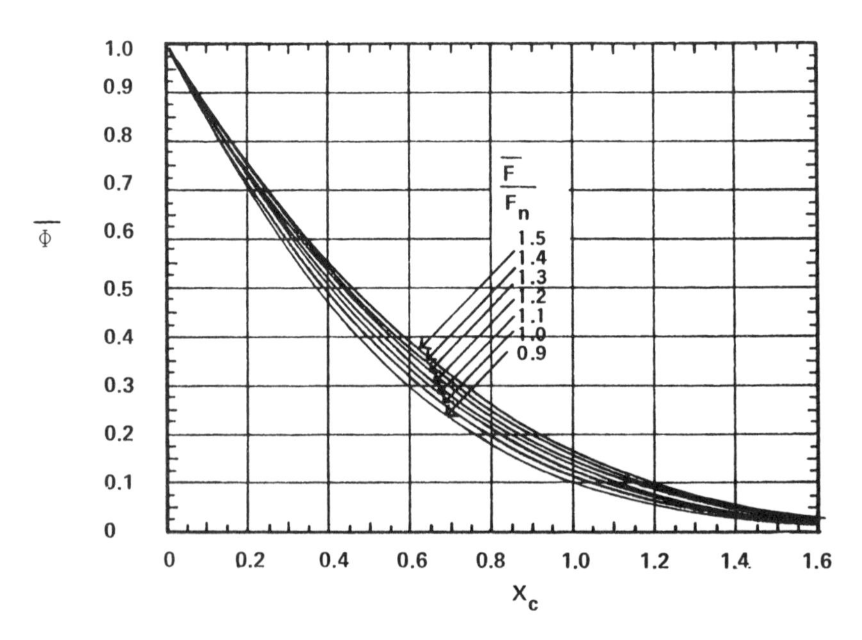


**Figure C.3.** $\bar{\Phi}$ vs $X_c$ for $\overline{K_T} = 0.5$.

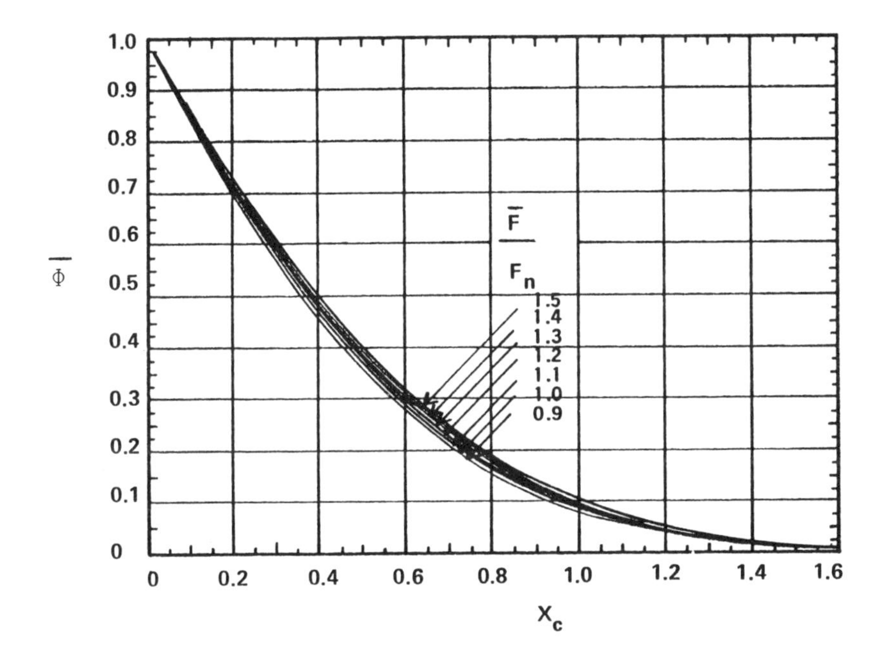


**Figure C.4.** $\bar{\Phi}$ vs $X_c$ for $\overline{K_T} = 0.6$.

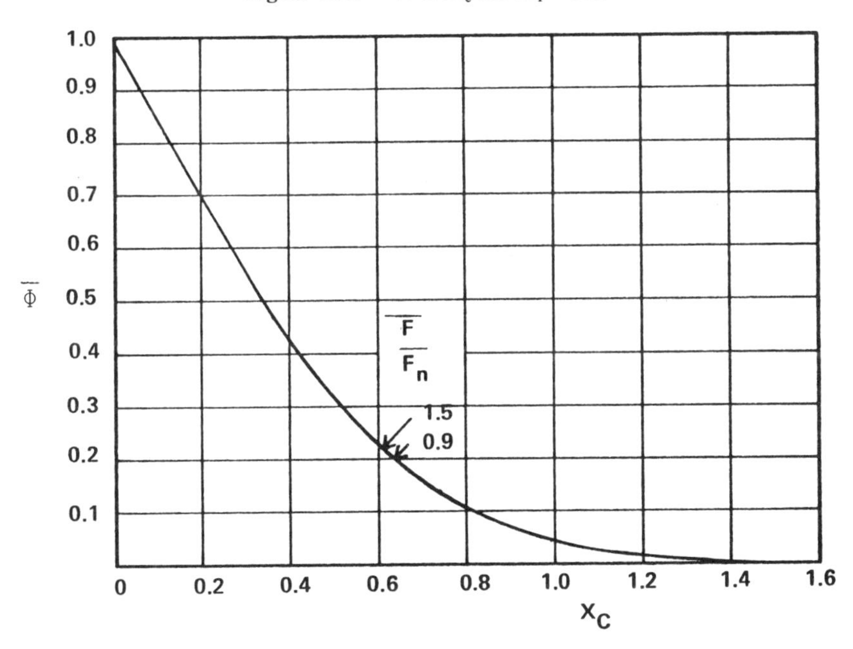


**Figure C.5.** $\bar{\Phi}$ vs $X_c$ for $\overline{K_T} = 0.7$.

$\overline{K_T} = 0.57$ (given)

$$\overline{F_b} = \frac{\cos(\phi - \beta)\cos\delta\sin\omega_s' + (\pi/180)\omega_s'\sin(\phi - \beta)\sin\delta}{\cos\phi\cos\delta\sin\omega_s + (\pi/180)\omega_s\sin\phi\sin\delta} \quad \text{(C.21)}$$

$\omega_s'$ = lessor of $\omega_s$ and $\cos^{-1}[-\tan(\phi - \beta)\tan\delta]$

a = albedo = reflectance of the earth = 0.2 (given)

$\phi$ = latitude = 25.7° (given)

$\beta$ = slope = 20° (given)

$$\delta = 0.36 - 22.96\cos(0.9856n) - 0.37\cos(2 \times 0.9856n) - 0.15\cos(3 \times 0.9856n) + 4\sin 0.9856n \quad (141)$$

n = 197 (from Table 1.1) (Table XIV)

So, from Equation 141,

$$\delta = 0.36 + 22.26 - 0.33 + 0.11 - 0.98 = 21.4°$$

$$\omega_s = \cos^{-1}(-\tan\phi\tan\delta) = \cos^{-1}[-\tan(25.7)\tan(21.4)] = \cos^{-1}(-0.1886) = 100.9° \quad (147)$$

$$\omega_s' = \cos^{-1}[-\tan(25.7 - 20)\tan(21.4)] = \cos^{-1}(-0.039) = 92.2°$$

$$\overline{F_b} = \frac{\cos(5.7)\cos(21.4)\sin(92.2) + (\pi/180)(92.2)\sin(5.7)\sin(21.4)}{\cos(25.7)\cos(21.4)\sin(100.9) + (\pi/180)(100.9)\sin(25.7)\sin(21.4)} = \frac{0.926 + 0.058}{0.824 + 0.279} = 0.89 \quad \text{(C.21)}$$

Now, $\bar{D}/\bar{H}$ and the $\bar{F}$ are calculated, from which $\overline{H_T}$ is determined.

$$\bar{D}/\bar{H} = 1.39 - 4.03(0.57) + 5.53(0.57)^2 - 3.11(0.57)^3 = 0.314$$

$$\bar{F} = (1 - 0.314)(0.89) + 0.314[1 + \cos(20)]/2 + 0.2[1 - \cos(20)]/2 = 0.611 + 0.305 + 0.006 = 0.922 \quad \text{(C.19)}$$

$$\bar{H} = 22.5 \text{ MJ/m}^2 \qquad \text{(given)}$$

$$\overline{H_T} = \bar{F}\bar{H} = 0.922(22.5) = 20.75 \text{ MJ/m}^2 \qquad (12)$$

To calculate $\phi$, $X_c$ must be calculated from:

$$X_c = H_{TC}/(R_{Tn} F_n \bar{H}) \qquad (C.9)$$

$R_{dn}$ is needed to get $R_{Tn}$.

$$R_{dn} = (\pi/24)\left[\frac{1 - \cos\omega_s}{\sin\omega_s - (\pi/180)\omega_s \cos\omega_s}\right]$$

$$= \frac{(\pi/24)[1 - \cos(100.9)]}{\sin(100.9) - (\pi/180)(100.9)\cos(100.9)} = \frac{(\pi/24)(1.189)}{0.982 + 0.333} \qquad (C.11)$$

$$= 0.118$$

$$R_{Tn} = R_{dn}[1.07 + 0.025\sin(\omega_s - 60)]$$

$$= 0.118[1.07 + 0.025\sin(100.9 - 60)] = 0.128 \qquad (C.10)$$

Now $F_n$ may be calculated

$$F_n = \left[1 - \frac{R_{dn}}{R_{Tn}}\left(\frac{D}{H}\right)\right]F_{bn} + \frac{R_{dn}}{R_{Tn}}\left(\frac{D}{H}\right)\left(\frac{1 + \cos\beta}{2}\right) + a\left(\frac{1 - \cos\beta}{2}\right) \qquad (C.13)$$

where $K_T = 0.57$ (given), and:

$$F_{bn} = \frac{\cos(\phi - \beta)\cos\delta + \sin(\phi - \beta)\sin\delta}{\cos\phi\cos\delta - \sin\phi\sin\delta} \qquad (C.14)$$

$$= \frac{\cos(5.7)\cos(21.4) + \sin(5.7)\sin(21.4)}{\cos(25.7)\cos(21.4) + \sin(25.7)\sin(21.4)} = \frac{0.9265 + 0.0362}{0.8390 + 0.1582} = 0.965$$

$$D/H = 1.0045 + 0.04349K_T - 3.5227K_T^2 + 2.6313K_T^3$$

$$D/H = 1.0045 + 0.0248 - 1.1445 + 0.4873 = 0.3721$$

$$F_n = \left[1 - \frac{0.118}{0.128}(0.314)\right](0.965) + \frac{0.118}{0.128}(0.314)$$

$$\times [1 + \cos(20)]/2 + 0.2[1 - \cos(20)]2 \quad (C.13)$$

$$= 0.6857 + 0.2807 + 0.0060 = 0.972$$

$$H_{TC} = \frac{F_R U_L (T_i - T_a)}{F_R(\overline{\tau\alpha})_e} = \frac{(4.6 \text{ W/m}^2\text{-°C})(80 - 27°\text{C})}{(0.5985)} = 407.35 \text{ W/m}^2 \quad (C.2)$$

so

$$X_c = \frac{H_{TC}}{R_{Tn} F_n \bar{H}} = \frac{407.35 \text{ J/m}^2\text{-sec } (3600 \text{ sec/hr})}{0.128(0.972)(22.5 \times 10^6 \text{ J/m}^2)} = 0.524 \quad (C.9)$$

$R_{Tn}$ converts the daily radiation, $\bar{H}$, into a hourly value, so for dimensional consistency, $H_{TC}$ in J/m$^2$-sec must be multiplied by 3600 sec/hr to convert $H_{TC}$ to J/m$^2$-hr.

$$\bar{\Phi} = \exp\{[A + B(F_n/\bar{F})](X_c + CX_c^2)\} \quad (C.15)$$

where $\overline{K_T} = 0.57$

$$A = 2.943 - 9.271\overline{K_T} + 4.031\overline{K_T}^2 = -1.032 \quad (C.16)$$

$$B = -4.34 + 8.853\overline{K_T} - 3.602\overline{K_T}^2 = -0.464 \quad (C.17)$$

$$C = -0.170 - 0.306\overline{K_T} + 2.936\overline{K_T}^2 = 0.6095 \quad (C.18)$$

so

$$\bar{\Phi} = \exp\left\{\left[-1.032 - 0.464\left(\frac{0.972}{0.922}\right)\right] \times [0.524 + 0.6095(0.524)^2]\right\}$$

$$= \exp[(-1.521)(0.691)] = 0.349$$

The useful energy supplied by the collector in July may now be calculated.

$$Q_u = A_c F_R(\overline{\tau\alpha})_e \bar{\Phi} \overline{H_T} N$$
$$= (50 \text{ m}^2)(0.5985)(0.349)(20.75 \text{ MJ/m}^2)(31) = 6718 \text{ MJ} \quad (C.8)$$

# APPENDIX D

# EQUIPMENT MANUFACTURERS

The following is a list of some passive solar equipment manufacturers. It does not include all manufacturers, nor does it necessarily include all of the product lines of those that are listed. Listing of a manufacturer does not constitute an endorsement of its products. For more recent information on solar equipment manufacturers, contact the Solar Energy Industries Association, 1001 Connecticut Avenue, N.W., Suite 800, Washington, DC, 20036, (202) 293-2981.

**Appropriate Technology Corp.**
Old Ferry Road
Brattleboro, VT 05301
(802) 257-4501
Insulating shades or curtains

**Bio-Energy Systems Inc.**
221 Canal Street
Ellenville, NY 12428
(914) 647-6700
Greenhouses

**J. R. Friedrich Builder**
CR352, P.O. Box 160-A
Lawton, MI 49065
(616) 624-6866
Insulating shades or curtains;
shutters; greenhouses

**Habitat**
123 Elm Street
S. Deerfield, MA 01373
(413) 665-4006
Greenhouses

**Homesworth Corp.**
18 Main Street
Yarmouth, ME 04096
(207) 846-9934
Insulating shades or curtains;
shutters

**Hordis Brothers Inc.**
825 Hylton Road
Pennsauken, NJ 08110
(609) 662-0400
Greenhouses

**Idea Development Co.**
P.O. Box 44
Antrim, NH 03440
(603) 525-2038
Greenhouses

**Kenergy Corp.**
**Kennedy Sky-Lites Div.**
3647 All-American Blvd.
Orlando, FL 32810
(305) 293-3880

Insulating shades or curtains;
shutters

**One Design, Inc.**
Mountain Falls Route
Winchester, VA 22601
(703) 887-2172
Waterwalls; greenhouses

**Otto Fabric Inc.**
P.O. Box 18361
Wichita, KS 67218
(316) 686-2010
Insulating shades or curtains

**P. & S. Hardware**
905 W. 5th Street
Reno, NV 89503
(702) 329-1392
Greenhouses

**Pace Corp.**
555 Two Mile Road
Appleton, WI 54911
(414) 731-5281
Greenhouses

**Plastic-View, Inc.**
15468 Cabrito Road
Van Nuys, CA 91408
(213) 786-2801
Insulating shades or curtains

**Roche Industrial Fabrics, Ltd.**
8118 3rd Ave.
Brooklyn, NY 11209
(212) 238-0500
Insulating shades or curtains

**Rocky Mountain Solar Glass**
7165 Arapahoe
Boulder, CO 80303
(303) 442-4277
Waterwalls

**Solar Design Associates, Inc.**
205 W. John Street
Champaign, IL 61820
(217) 359-5748
Shutters

**Solar Energy Sales, Inc.**
2499 N. Main Street
Walnut Creek, CA 94596
(415) 939-8838
Greenhouses

**Solar Resources, Inc.**
South Santa Fe Highway
Taos, NM 87571
(505) 758-9344
Insulating shades or curtains

**Solar Screen Company**
53-11 105th Street
Corona, NY 11368
(212) 592-8222
Insulating shades or curtains

**Somfy Systems**
1445 Raritan Road
Clark, New Jersey 07006
(201) 382-4650
Insulating shades or curtains;
shutters; greenhouses

**Sungrabber Energy, Inc.**
5010 Cook Street
Denver, CO 80216
(303) 825-0203
Insulating shades or curtains;
shutters

**Sunray Works Co.**
P.O. Box 341
Mendham, NJ 07945
(201) 543-4462
Insulating shades or curtains;
shutters

**Sun Source Inc.**
P.O. Box 701
Metuchen, NJ 08840
(201) 752-0666
Insulating shades or curtains

**Sunwest Solar Systems, Inc.**
4024 E. Broadway Road, Ste. 1001
Phoenix, AZ 85040
(602) 243-6171
Greenhouses

**Thermal Technology Corporation of Aspen, Inc.**
600 Alter Street
Broomfield, CO 80302
(303) 466-1848
Insulating shades or curtains

**Window Blanket Co., Inc.**
107 Kingston Street
Lenoir City, TN 37771
(615) 986-3125
Insulating shades or curtains

**Zomeworks Corp.**
1221 Edith Blvd. N.E.
P.O. Box 25805
Albuquerque, NM 87125
(505) 242-5354
Insulating shades or curtains
shutters

# APPENDIX E

# CONVERSION FACTORS

| To Convert from | To | Multiply by |
|---|---|---|
| acre-ft | $ft^3$ | 43,560 |
| acre-ft | $m^3$ | 1,233.482 |
| acre-ft | $yd^3$ | 1,613.333 |
| acre-in. | $ft^3$ | 3,630 |
| acre-in. | $m^3$ | 102.7903 |
| acre-in. | gal (U.S., liquid) | 27,154.28 |
| acres | $ft^2$ | 43,560 |
| acres | $in.^2$ | 6,272,640 |
| acres | $km^2$ | 0.004046856 |
| acres | $m^2$ | 4,046.856 |
| acres | $mi^2$ | 0.0015625 |
| acres | $yd^2$ | 4,840 |
| angstroms | cm | $1 \times 10^{-8}$ |
| angstroms | in. | $3.937 \times 10^{-9}$ |
| angstroms | $\mu$ | 0.0001 |
| astronomical units | m | $1.496 \times 10^{11}$ |
| atmospheres | bars | 1.01325 |
| atmospheres | cm Hg (0°C) | 76 |
| atmospheres | cm of $H_2O$ (4°C) | 1,033.26 |
| atmospheres | $dyn/cm^2$ | $1.01325 \times 10^6$ |
| atmospheres | ft $H_2O$ (4°C) | 33.8995 |
| atmospheres | $g/cm^2$ | 1,033.23 |
| atmospheres | in. Hg (0°C) | 29.9213 |
| atmospheres | in. $H_2O$ (4°C) | 406.8 |
| atmospheres | $kg/cm^2$ | 1.03323 |
| atmospheres | mm Hg (0°C) | 760 |
| atmospheres | $N/m^2$ | 101,325 |
| atmospheres | $lb/in.^2$ | 14.6960 |
| atmospheres | $lb/ft^2$ | 2,116.22 |
| atmospheres | tons (short)/$ft^2$ | 1.05811 |

| To Convert from | To | Multiply by |
|---|---|---|
| atmospheres | torrs | 760 |
| atomic mass units | kg | $1.660 \times 10^{-27}$ |
| atomic mass units | lb | $3.660 \times 10^{-27}$ |
| atomic mass units | Btu ($E = mc^2$) | $1.415 \times 10^{-13}$ |
| atomic mass units | J ($E = mc^2$) | $1.492 \times 10^{-10}$ |
| atomic mass units | ft-lb ($E = mc^2$) | $1.100 \times 10^{-10}$ |
| atomic mass units | cal ($E = mc^2$) | $3.564 \times 10^{-11}$ |
| atomic mass units | kWh ($E = mc^2$) | $4.145 \times 10^{-17}$ |
| atomic mass units | MeV ($E = mc^2$) | 931.0 |
| barrels (petroleum, U.S.) | $ft^3$ | 5.614583 |
| barrels (petroleum, U.S.) | $m^3$ | 0.1589873 |
| barrels (petroleum, U.S.) | gal (U.S.) | 42 |
| barrels (petroleum, U.S.) | gal (Imperial) | 35 |
| barrels (petroleum, U.S.) | liters | 158.9828 |
| barrels (petroleum, U.S.) | Btu (typ. energy equiv.) | $5.8 \times 10^6$ |
| bars | atmo | 0.986923 |
| bars | cm Hg (0°C) | 75.0062 |
| bars | $dyn/cm^2$ | $1 \times 10^6$ |
| bars | ft $H_2O$ (60°F) | 33.4883 |
| bars | $g/cm^2$ | 1,019.716 |
| bars | in. Hg (0°C) | 29.5300 |
| bars | $kg/cm^2$ | 1.019716 |
| bars | mbars | 1,000 |
| bars | $N/m^2$ | 100,000 |
| bars | lb/in.$^2$ | 14.5038 |
| board feet | $cm^3$ | 2,359.737 |
| board feet | $ft^3$ | 0.083333 |
| board feet | in.$^3$ | 144 |
| board feet | $m^3$ | 0.002359737 |
| Btu | cal | 252.1607 |
| Btu | eV | $6.585 \times 10^{21}$ |
| Btu | ergs | $1.05504 \times 10^{10}$ |
| Btu | ft-lb | 778.1579 |
| Btu | G-cm | $1.07584 \times 10^7$ |
| Btu | hp-hr | 0.000393009 |
| Btu | J | 1,055.056 |
| Btu (mass equiv.) | amu ($m = E/c^2$) | $7.074 \times 10^{12}$ |
| Btu (mass equiv.) | kg ($m = E/c^2$) | $1.174 \times 10^{-14}$ |
| Btu | kg-m | 107.584 |
| Btu | kw-h | 0.000293067 |
| Btu | MeV | $6.585 \times 10^{15}$ |
| Btu | w-sec | 1,055.04 |
| Btu/ft-hr-°F | cal/cm-hr-°C | 14.88 |
| Btu/ft-hr-°F | W/cm-°C | 0.01731 |
| Btu/ft$^2$-hr-°F | cal/cm$^2$-hr-°C | 0.4882 |
| Btu/ft$^2$-hr-°F | cal/m$^2$-sec-°C | 1.3573 |
| Btu/ft$^2$-hr-°F | W/m$^2$-°C | 5.6820 |
| Btu/hr | erg/sec | $2.930668 \times 10^6$ |
| Btu/hr | ft-lb/hr | 778.158 |

| To Convert from | To | Multiply by |
|---|---|---|
| Btu/hr | hp | 0.000393009 |
| Btu/hr | kW | 0.000293067 |
| Btu/hr | tons of refrig | $8.33333 \times 10^{-5}$ |
| Btu/hr | W | 0.293067 |
| Btu/hr | cal/hr | 252.161 |
| Btu/lb | cal/g | 0.555555 |
| Btu/lb | ft-lb/lb | 778.158 |
| Btu/lb | hp-hr/lb | 0.000393009 |
| Btu/lb | J/g | 2.32596 |
| Btu/lb-°F | J/kg-°C | 4,189.6 |
| Btu/ft$^2$ | cal/cm$^2$ | 0.271442 |
| Btu/ft$^2$ | W-hr/ft$^2$ | 0.293087 |
| Btu/ft$^2$ | Langley | 0.271447 |
| Btu/ft$^2$-hr | W/cm$^2$ | 0.0003154 |
| Btu/ft$^2$-hr | W/m$^2$ | 3.1544 |
| Btu/ft$^2$-hr | cal/cm$^2$-sec | 0.00007535 |
| Btu/ft$^2$-hr | cal/cm$^2$-min | 0.0045208 |
| Btu/ft$^2$-hr | Langley/min | 0.0045208 |
| Btu/ft$^2$-hr | cal/cm$^2$-hr | 0.271246 |
| bushel (US) | m$^3$ | 0.03523907 |
| calories | Btu | 0.00396573 |
| Calories (mass equiv.) | atomic mass units ($m = E/c^2$) | $2.807 \times 10^{10}$ |
| calories | ergs | $4.184 \times 10^{7}$ |
| calories | ft-lb | 3.08596 |
| calories | hp-hr | $1.55857 \times 10^{-6}$ |
| calories | J | 4.18400 |
| calories (mass equiv.) | kg ($m = E/c^2$) | $4.659 \times 10^{-17}$ |
| calories | kg-m | 0.426649 |
| calories | KwH | $1.162222 \times 10^{-6}$ |
| calories | MeV | $2.613 \times 10^{13}$ |
| calories | w-hr | 0.001162222 |
| calories/cm$^2$-hr-°C | W/cm$^2$-°C | 0.001163 |
| calories/cm$^2$-hr-°C | Btu/ft$^2$-hr-°F | 2.048 |
| calories/cm$^2$-hr | W/cm$^2$ | 0.001163 |
| calories/cm$^2$-hr | Btu/ft$^2$-hr | 3.687 |
| calories/cm$^2$ | Btu/ft$^2$ | 3.68428 |
| calories/hr-cm-°C | W/cm-°C | 0.001163 |
| calories/hr-cm-°C | Btu/hr-ft-°F | 0.0672 |
| calorie/g | Btu/lb | 1.8 |
| calorie/cm-sec-°C | W/cm-°C | 4.187 |
| calorie/cm-sec-°C | Btu/ft-hr-°F | 241.9 |
| calorie/cm$^2$ | Langleys | 1 |
| calorie/cm$^2$-sec | W/cm$^2$ | 4.187 |
| calorie/cm$^2$-sec | Btu/ft$^2$-hr | 13,272 |
| calorie/min | W | 0.06973 |
| candle power | lumens | 12.566 |
| centimeters | angstroms | $1 \times 10^{8}$ |
| centimeters | ft | 0.0328084 |
| centimeters | in. | 0.39370 |

| To Convert from | To | Multiply by |
|---|---|---|
| centimeters | m | 0.01 |
| centimeters | $\mu$ | 10,000 |
| centimeters | mi | $6.213712 \times 10^{-6}$ |
| centimeters | mm | 10 |
| centimeters | yd | 0.01093613 |
| centimeter Hg (0°C) | atmo | 0.01315789 |
| centimeter Hg (0°C) | bars | 0.0133322 |
| centimeter Hg (0°C) | dyn/cm$^2$ | 13332.2 |
| centimeter Hg (0°C) | ft $H_2O$ (4°C) | 0.446050 |
| centimeter Hg (0°C) | ft $H_2O$ (60°F) | 0.446474 |
| centimeter Hg (0°C) | in. Hg (0°C) | 0.3937008 |
| centimeter Hg (0°C) | kg/m$^2$ | 135.951 |
| centimeter Hg (0°C) | N/m$^2$ | 1,333.22 |
| centimeter Hg (0°C) | lb/ft$^2$ | 27.8450 |
| centimeter Hg (0°C) | lb/in.$^2$ | 0.193368 |
| centimeter Hg (0°C) | torr | 10 |
| centimeter $H_2O$ (4°C) | atm | 0.000967814 |
| centimeter $H_2O$ (4°C) | dyn/cm$^2$ | 980.638 |
| centimeter $H_2O$ (4°C) | lb/in.$^2$ | 0.0142229 |
| centimeter/sec | ft/min | 1.968504 |
| centimeter/sec | ft/sec | 0.0328084 |
| centimeter/sec | km/hr | 0.036 |
| centimeter/sec | mi/hr | 0.02236936 |
| centimeter/sec$^2$ | ft/sec$^2$ | 0.03281 |
| centimeter/sec | mi/hr | 0.02237 |
| centipoise | lb-sec/ft$^2$ | $2.083 \times 10^{-5}$ |
| centipoise | poise | 0.01 |
| centipoise | N-sec/m$^2$ | 0.001 |
| centistoke | ft$^2$/sec | $1.076 \times 10^{-5}$ |
| centistoke | m$^2$/sec | $1 \times 10^{-6}$ |
| cords | cord-feet | 8 |
| cords | ft$^3$ | 128 |
| cords | m$^3$ | 3.6245563 |
| Cord-ft | cords | 0.125 |
| Cord-ft | ft$^3$ | 16 |
| cubic centimeters | board feet | 0.0004237760 |
| cubic centimeters | bushels (U.S.) | $2.837759 \times 10^{-5}$ |
| cubic centimeters | ft$^3$ | $3.5314667 \times 10^{-5}$ |
| cubic centimeters | in.$^3$ | 0.06102374 |
| cubic centimeters | m$^3$ | $1 \times 10^{-6}$ |
| cubic centimeters | yd$^3$ | $1.3079506 \times 10^{-8}$ |
| cubic centimeters | gal (Imperial) | 0.00021997 |
| cubic centimeters | gal (U.S., liquid) | 0.000264172 |
| cubic centimeters | liters | 0.001 |
| cubic centimeters | oz (U.S.) | 0.033814 |
| cubic centimeters | pt (U.S.) | 0.002113376 |
| cubic centimeters | qt (U.S.) | 0.001056688 |
| cubic centimeter/g | ft$^3$/lb | 0.01601846 |

| To Convert from | To | Multiply by |
|---|---|---|
| cubic centimeter/sec | $ft^3$/min | 0.00211888 |
| cubic centimeter/sec | gal (U.S., liquid)/min | 0.01585032 |
| cubic feet | ac-feet | $2.295684 \times 10^{-5}$ |
| cubic feet | board-ft | 12 |
| cubic feet | cords (wood) | 0.0078125 |
| cubic feet | cord-feet | 0.0625 |
| cubic feet | $cm^3$ | 28,316.85 |
| cubic feet | $m^3$ | 0.02831685 |
| cubic feet | $yd^3$ | 0.037037 |
| cubic feet | gal (U.S., liquid) | 7.480520 |
| cubic feet | liters | 28.31685 |
| cubic feet | oz (U.S.) | 957.5065 |
| cubic feet | qt (U.S.) | 29.92208 |
| cubic feet of water (4°C) | lb water | 62.4262 |
| cubic feet of water (60°F) | lb water | 62.366 |
| cubic feet/lb | $cm^3$/g | 62.42796 |
| cubic feet/sec | ac-in./hr | 0.9917355 |
| cubic feet/sec | $cm^3$/sec | 28,316.85 |
| cubic feet/sec | gal (U.S., liquid)/min | 448.8312 |
| cubic feet/sec | liter/sec | 28.3160 |
| cubic inches | $cm^3$ | 16.38706 |
| cubic inches | $ft^3$ | 0.0005787037 |
| cubic inches | $m^3$ | $1.638706 \times 10^{-5}$ |
| cubic inches | $yd^3$ | $2.143347 \times 10^{-5}$ |
| cubic inches | gal (U.S., liquid) | 0.004329004 |
| cubic inches | liters | 0.01638706 |
| cubic inches | ml | 16.38706 |
| cubic inches | oz (U.S.) | 0.5541125 |
| cubic inches | qt (U.S.) | 0.01731602 |
| cubic meters | ac-ft | 0.0008107132 |
| cubic meters | bbl (U.S.) | 8.386415 |
| cubic meters | $cm^3$ | 1,000,000 |
| cubic meters | $ft^3$ | 35.31467 |
| cubic meters | in.$^3$ | 61,023.74 |
| cubic meters | $yd^3$ | 1.307951 |
| cubic meters | gal (U.S., liquid) | 264.1721 |
| cubic meters | liters | 1000 |
| cubic meters | qt (US) | 1,056.688 |
| cubic meters/min | gal (U.S., liquid)/min | 264.1721 |
| cubic millimeters | in.$^3$ | $6.102374 \times 10^{-5}$ |
| cubic yards | $cm^3$ | 764,554.9 |
| cubic yards | $ft^3$ | 27 |
| cubic yards | in.$^3$ | 46,656 |
| cubic yards | $m^3$ | 0.7645549 |
| cubic yards | gal (U.S., liquid) | 201.9740 |
| cubic yards | liters | 764.5549 |
| cubic yards | qt (U.S.) | 807.8961 |
| cubic yard/min | $ft^3$/sec | 0.45 |

| To Convert from | To | Multiply by |
|---|---|---|
| cubic yard/min | gal (U.S., liquid)/sec | 3.366234 |
| cubic yard/min | liter/sec | 12.74222 |
| days (mean solar) | days (sidereal) | 1.002738 |
| days (mean solar) | years (calendar) | 0.002739726 |
| days (sidereal) | days (mean solar) | 0.9972696 |
| degrees | minutes | 60 |
| degrees | quadrants | 0.0111111 |
| degrees | radians | 0.01745329 |
| degrees | revolutions | 0.00277778 |
| degrees | seconds | 3,600 |
| dynes | N | $1 \times 10^{-5}$ |
| dynes | lb | $2.248 \times 10^{-6}$ |
| dynes | poundal | $7.233 \times 10^{-5}$ |
| dynes | kg (force) | $1.020 \times 10^{-6}$ |
| electron-volts | J | $1.6021 \times 10^{-19}$ |
| ergs | Btu | $9.47831 \times 10^{-8}$ |
| ergs | Cal | $2.39006 \times 10^{-10}$ |
| ergs | ft-lb | $7.376 \times 10^{-8}$ |
| ergs | hp-hr | $3.725 \times 10^{-14}$ |
| ergs | J | $1 \times 10^{-7}$ |
| ergs | kWh | $2.778 \times 10^{-14}$ |
| ergs | MeV | $6.242 \times 10^{5}$ |
| ergs (mass equiv.) | kg ($m = E/c^2$) | $1.113 \times 10^{-24}$ |
| ergs (mass equiv.) | amu ($m = E/c^2$) | 670.5 |
| feet | cm | 30.48 |
| feet | in. | 12 |
| feet | m | 0.3048 |
| feet | $\mu$ | 304800 |
| feet | mi | 0.000189393 |
| feet | yd | 0.333333 |
| feet of air (1 atm, 60°F) | atm | $3.6083 \times 10^{-5}$ |
| feet of air (1 atm, 60°F) | ft Hg (0°C) | 0.00089970 |
| feet of air (1 atm, 60°F) | ft $H_2O$ (60°F) | 0.0012244 |
| feet of air (1 atm, 60°F) | in. Hg (0°F) | 0.0010796 |
| feet of air (1 atm, 60°F) | lb/in.$^2$ | 0.00053027 |
| feet of $H_2O$ (4°C) | atm | 0.0294990 |
| feet of $H_2O$ (4°C) | cm Hg (0°C) | 2.24192 |
| feet of $H_2O$ (4°C) | dyn/cm$^2$ | 29,889.8 |
| feet of $H_2O$ (4°C) | g/cm$^2$ | 30.4791 |
| feet of $H_2O$ (4°C) | in. Hg (0°C) | 0.882646 |
| feet of $H_2O$ (4°C) | kg/m$^2$ | 304.791 |
| feet of $H_2O$ (4°C) | lb/in.$^2$ | 0.433515 |
| feet of $H_2O$ (4°C) | N/m$^2$ | 2,988.98 |
| feet/hr | cm/sec | 0.0084666 |
| feet/hr | km/hr | 0.0003048 |
| feet/hr | mi/hr | 0.000189393 |
| feet/min | cm/sec | 0.508 |
| feet/min | km/hr | 0.018288 |

| To Convert from | To | Multiply by |
|---|---|---|
| feet/min | m/sec | 0.00508 |
| feet/min | mi/hr | 0.01136363 |
| feet/sec | cm/sec | 30.48 |
| feet/sec | km/hr | 1.09728 |
| feet/sec | m/sec | 0.3048 |
| feet/sec | mi/hr | 0.6818182 |
| foot-candles | lumen/$ft^2$ | 1 |
| foot-candles | lumen/$m^2$ | 10.76391 |
| foot-lb (mass equiv.) | atomic mass units ($m = E/c^2$) | $9.092 \times 10^9$ |
| foot-lb | Btu | 0.00128509 |
| foot-lb | cal | 0.324048 |
| foot-lb | ergs | $1.35582 \times 10^7$ |
| foot-lb | eV | $8.464 \times 10^{18}$ |
| foot-lb | hp-hr | $5.05050 \times 10^{-7}$ |
| foot-lb | J | 1.35582 |
| foot-lb (mass equiv.) | kg ($m = E/c^2$) | $1.509 \times 10^{-17}$ |
| foot-lb | kg-m | 0.138255 |
| foot-lb | kW | $3.76616 \times 10^{-7}$ |
| foot-lb | MeV | $8.464 \times 10^{12}$ |
| foot-lb | W-hr | 0.000376616 |
| furlongs | ft | 660 |
| furlongs | m | 201.168 |
| furlongs | mi | 0.125 |
| gallons (U.S., dry) | gal (U.S., liquid) | 1.1636472 |
| gallons (U.S., liquid) | ac-ft | $3.068883 \times 10^{-6}$ |
| gallons (U.S., liquid) | $cm^3$ | 3785.412 |
| gallons (U.S., liquid) | $ft^3$ | 0.1336806 |
| gallons (U.S., liquid) | $in^3$ | 231 |
| gallons (U.S., liquid) | $m^3$ | 0.003785412 |
| gallons (U.S., liquid) | $yd^3$ | 0.004951132 |
| gallons (U.S., liquid) | kg of water | 3.7852 |
| gallons (U.S., liquid) | liters | 3.785412 |
| gallons (U.S., liquid) | lb of water | 8.34517 |
| gallons (U.S., liquid) | oz (U.S.) | 128 |
| gallons (U.S., liquid) | qt | 4 |
| gallons of water (4°C) | lb of water | 8.33585 |
| gallons of water (60°F) | lb of water | 8.32823 |
| grads | degrees | 0.9 |
| grads | minutes | 54 |
| grads | radians | 0.01570796 |
| grams | kg | 0.001 |
| grams | oz | 0.03527396 |
| grams | lb | 0.002204623 |
| grams (force) | N | 0.009807 |
| grams/$cm^3$ | lb/$ft^3$ | 62.42796 |
| grams/$cm^3$ | lb/gal (U.S., liquid) | 8.345404 |
| grams/$cm^2$ | atmo | 0.000967841 |
| grams/$cm^2$ | bars | 0.000980665 |

| To Convert from | To | Multiply by |
|---|---|---|
| grams/cm$^2$ | cm Hg | 0.0735559 |
| grams/cm$^2$ | in. Hg (0°C) | 0.0289590 |
| grams/cm$^2$ | lb/in. | 0.01422334 |
| grams/cm$^2$ | lb/in. | 0.000341717 |
| gravitational acceleration (*g*) | feet/sec$^2$ | 32.1740 |
| gravitational acceleration (*g*) | meters/sec$^2$ | 9.80665 |
| gravitational constant | cm/sec$^2$ | 980.621 |
| gravitational constant | ft/sec$^2$ | 32.1725 |
| hectares | ac | 2.471054 |
| horsepower | hp (metric) | 1.01387 |
| horsepower | Btu/hr | 2544.47 |
| horsepower | erg/sec | $7.45700 \times 10^9$ |
| horsepower | foot-lb/sec | 550 |
| horsepower | kW | 0.7456999 |
| horsepower | W | 745.69987 |
| horsepower-hr | Btu | 2,544.47 |
| horsepower-hr (mass equiv.) | amu ($m = E/c^2$) | $1.800 \times 10^{16}$ |
| horsepower-hr | cal | 641,616 |
| horsepower-hr | foot-lb | 1,980,000 |
| horsepower-hr | J | 2,684,520 |
| horsepower-hr | kWh | 0.745700 |
| horsepower-hr (mass equiv.) | kg ($m = E/c^2$) | $2.988 \times 10^{-11}$ |
| horsepower-hr | MeV | $1.676 \times 10^{19}$ |
| hours | days | 0.0416666 |
| hours | minutes | 60 |
| hours | seconds | 3,600 |
| inches | an | $2.54 \times 10^8$ |
| inches | cm | 2.54 |
| inches | ft | 0.083333 |
| inches | m | 0.0254 |
| inches | yd | 0.027777 |
| inches of Hg (0°C) | atmo | 0.0334211 |
| inches of Hg (0°C) | bars | 0.0338639 |
| inches of Hg (0°C) | ft air (60°F) | 926.24 |
| inches of Hg (0°C) | ft $H_2O$ (4°C) | 1.132957 |
| inches of Hg (0°C) | mm Hg (0°C) | 25.4 |
| inches of Hg (0°C) | N/sq meter | 3,386.389 |
| inches of Hg (0°C) | lb/ft$^2$ | 70.7262 |
| inches of $H_2O$ (4°C) | atmo | 0.0024582 |
| inches of $H_2O$ (4°C) | dyn/cm$^2$ | 2,490.82 |
| inches of $H_2O$ (4°C) | in. Hg (0°C) | 0.0735539 |
| inches of $H_2O$ (4°C) | N/m$^2$ | 249.082 |
| inches of $H_2O$ (4°C) | lb/in.$^2$ | 0.03612628 |
| joules | Btu | 0.000947831 |
| joules | cal | 0.239006 |
| joules | ergs | $1 \times 10^7$ |
| joules | foot-lb | 0.737562 |
| joules | g-cm | 10,197.16 |

| To Convert from | To | Multiply by |
|---|---|---|
| joules | hp-hr | $3.72506 \times 10^{-7}$ |
| joules | kW-h | $2.7777 \times 10^{-7}$ |
| joules | MeV | $6.242 \times 10^{12}$ |
| joules | W-hr | 0.0002777777 |
| joules | W-sec | 1 |
| joules (mass equiv.) | kg ($m = E/c^2$) | $1.113 \times 10^{-17}$ |
| joules (mass equiv.) | amu ($m = E/c^2$) | $6.705 \times 10^{9}$ |
| joules/°C | Btu/°F | 0.000526572 |
| joules/sec | Btu/min | 0.0568699 |
| joules/sec | hp | 0.00134102 |
| joules/sec | W | 1 |
| kilocalories | J | 4186.8 |
| kilocalories/g | Btu/lb | 1,378.54 |
| kilograms | oz | 35.27396 |
| kilograms | amu | $6.025 \times 10^{26}$ |
| kilograms | lb | 2.204623 |
| kilograms | tons (long) | 0.0009842065 |
| kilograms | tons (metric) | 0.001 |
| kilograms | tons (short) | 0.0011023113 |
| kilograms (energy equiv.) | Btu ($E = mc^2$) | $8.521 \times 10^{13}$ |
| kilograms (energy equiv.) | ft-lb ($E = mc^2$) | $6.629 \times 10^{16}$ |
| kilograms (energy equiv.) | hp-hr ($E = mc^2$) | $3.348 \times 10^{10}$ |
| kilograms (energy equiv.) | J ($E = mc^2$) | $8.987 \times 10^{16}$ |
| kilograms (energy equiv.) | cal ($E = mc^2$) | $2.147 \times 10^{16}$ |
| kilograms (energy equiv.) | kWh ($E = mc^2$) | $2.497 \times 10^{10}$ |
| kilograms (force) | N | 9.80665 |
| kilograms/$m^3$ | lb/$ft^3$ | 0.06242796 |
| kilograms/$m^2$ | atmo | $9.67841 \times 10^{-5}$ |
| kilograms/$m^2$ | ft $H_2O$ (4°C) | 0.00328093 |
| kilograms/$m^2$ | lb/$ft^2$ | 0.2048161 |
| kilograms/$m^2$ | lb/in.$^2$ | 0.001422334 |
| kilojoules/$m^2$ | Btu/$ft^2$ | 0.0880563 |
| kilojoules/$m^2$ | cal/$cm^2$ | 0.023901 |
| kilojoules/$m^2$ | kcal/$m^2$ | 0.23901 |
| kilometers | cm | 100,000 |
| kilometers | ft | 3,280.840 |
| kilometers | mi | 0.6213712 |
| kilometers | yd | 1,093.613 |
| kilometer/hr | cm/sec | 27.7777 |
| kilometer/hr | ft/min | 54.68066 |
| kilometer/hr | m/sec | 0.277777 |
| kilometer/hr | mi/hr | 0.6213712 |
| kilowatts | Btu/hr | 3,412.19 |
| kilowatts | ft-lb/hr | $2.65522 \times 10^{6}$ |
| kilowatts | ft-lb/sec | 737.5611 |
| kilowatts | hp | 1.34102 |
| kilowatts | J/hr | $3.6 \times 10^{6}$ |
| kilowatt-hr | Btu | 3,412.19 |

| To Convert from | To | Multiply by |
|---|---|---|
| kilowatt-hr | ft-lb | $2.65522 \times 10^{6}$ |
| kilowatt-hr | hp-hr | 1.34102 |
| kilowatt-hr | J | $3.6 \times 10^{6}$ |
| kilowatt-hr | MeV | $2.270 \times 10^{19}$ |
| kilowatt-hr (mass equiv.) | amu ($m = E/c^2$) | $2.414 \times 10^{16}$ |
| kilowatt-hr (mass equiv.) | kg ($m = E/c^2$) | $4.007 \times 10^{-11}$ |
| lamberts | candle/cm$^2$ | 0.3183099 |
| lamberts | candle/in.$^2$ | 2.053608 |
| lamberts | lumens/cm$^2$ | 1 |
| langleys | J/m$^2$ | 41,840 |
| langleys | Btu/ft | 3.6866 |
| langleys | cal/cm$^2$ | 1 |
| langleys/min | W/cm$^2$ | 0.00698 |
| light years | astronomical units | 63,279.5 |
| light years | km | $9.46055 \times 10^{12}$ |
| light years | mi | $5.87851 \times 10^{12}$ |
| liters | cm$^3$ | 1000 |
| liters | ft$^3$ | 0.0353157 |
| liters | in.$^3$ | 61.02545 |
| liters | m$^3$ | 0.001 |
| liters | yd$^3$ | 0.001307987 |
| liters | gal (U.S., liquid) | 0.2641794 |
| liters | oz (US) | 33.81497 |
| liters | qt (US) | 1.056718 |
| lumens | candle power | 0.07957747 |
| lumens | ft-candles | 1 |
| lumens (5550 Å) | W | 0.0014706 |
| lux | ft-candles | 0.09290304 |
| lux | lumen/m$^2$ | 1 |
| megatons (nuclear) | J | $4.2 \times 10^{15}$ |
| meters | cm | 100 |
| meters | ft | 3.280840 |
| meters | in. | 39.37008 |
| meters | km | 0.001 |
| meters | mi | 0.0006213712 |
| meters | yd | 1.093613 |
| meters of Hg (0°C) | atmo | 1.315789 |
| meters of Hg (0°C) | ft $H_2O$ (60°F) | 44.6474 |
| meters of Hg (0°C) | in. Hg (0°C) | 39.37008 |
| meters of Hg (0°C) | lb/in.$^2$ | 19.3368 |
| meter/sec | km/hr | 3.6 |
| meter/sec | mi/hr | 2.236936 |
| microns | Å | 10,000 |
| microns | cm | 0.0001 |
| microns | in. | $3.937008 \times 10^{-5}$ |
| microns | m | $1 \times 10^{-6}$ |
| miles | cm | 160,934.4 |
| miles | ft | 5,280 |

| To Convert from | To | Multiply by |
|---|---|---|
| miles | in. | 63,360 |
| miles | km | 1.609344 |
| miles | m | 1,609.344 |
| miles | yd | 1,760 |
| mile/hr | cm/sec | 44.704 |
| mile/hr | ft/sec | 1.466666 |
| mile/hr | km/hr | 1.609344 |
| millibars | atmo | 0.000986923 |
| millibars | bars | 0.001 |
| millibars | in. Hg (0°C) | 0.0295300 |
| millibars | lb/in. | 0.0145038 |
| milliliters | $cm^3$ | 1 |
| milliliters | $in.^3$ | 0.06102545 |
| milliliters | oz (U.S.) | 0.03381497 |
| millimeters | Å | $1 \times 10^7$ |
| millimeters | ft | 0.0032808400 |
| millimeters | in. | 0.03937008 |
| millimeters | m | 0.001 |
| millimeters | $\mu$ | 1,000 |
| millimeters | mils | 39.37008 |
| millimeters of Hg (0°C) | atmo | 0.001315789 |
| millimeters of Hg (0°C) | bars | 0.00133322 |
| millimeters of Hg (0°C) | lb/sq inch | 0.0193368 |
| millimeters of Hg (0°C) | torrs | 1 |
| million electron volts | Btu | $1.519 \times 10^{-16}$ |
| million electron volts | ft-lb | $1.182 \times 10^{-13}$ |
| million electron volts | hp-hr | $5.967 \times 10^{-20}$ |
| million electron volts | J | $1.602 \times 10^{-13}$ |
| million electron volts | cal | $3.827 \times 10^{-14}$ |
| million electron volts | kWh | $4.450 \times 10^{-20}$ |
| MeV (mass equiv.) | amu ($m = E/c^2$) | 0.001074 |
| MeV (mass equiv.) | kg ($m = E/c^2$) | $1.783 \times 10^{-30}$ |
| minutes (angular) | degrees | 0.0166666 |
| minutes (angular) | radians | 0.0002908882 |
| minutes (angular) | revolutions | 0.0000462963 |
| minutes (angular) | seconds (angular) | 60 |
| minutes | days | 0.0006944444 |
| minutes | hours | 0.0166666 |
| months | days | 30.41667 |
| months | hours | 730 |
| newtons | dyn | 100,000 |
| newtons | lb | 0.2248089 |
| newton-m | dyn-cm | $1 \times 10^7$ |
| newton-m | lb-feet | 0.7375621 |
| newton-sec/$m^2$ | cP | 1,000 |
| ounces (U.S.) | $cm^3$ | 29.57373 |
| ounces (U.S.) | $in.^3$ | 1.804687 |
| ounces (U.S.) | gal | 0.0078125 |

| To Convert from | To | Multiply by |
|---|---|---|
| ounces (U.S.) | liters | 0.02957270 |
| ounces (U.S.) | qt (U.S.) | 0.03125 |
| parsec | m | $3.0857 \times 10^{16}$ |
| pascal | $N/m^2$ | 1 |
| poise | cP | 100 |
| poise | $N\text{-sec}/m^2$ | 0.1 |
| pounds | kg | 0.45359237 |
| pounds (force) | N | 4.4482216 |
| pounds | oz | 16 |
| pounds | tons (long) | 0.0004464286 |
| pounds | tons (metric) | 0.0004535924 |
| pounds | tons (short) | 0.0005 |
| pounds of water (4°C) | $ft^3$ | 0.01601891 |
| pounds of water (4°C) | gal (U.S., liquid) | 0.1198298 |
| pounds of water (4°C) | liters | 0.4535924 |
| poundals | N | 0.13825495 |
| pounds/$ft^3$ | g/$cm^3$ | 0.01601846 |
| pounds/$ft^3$ | kg/$meter^3$ | 16.01846 |
| pounds/gal | lb/$ft^3$ | 7.480519 |
| pounds-sec/$ft^2$ | cP | 48,008 |
| pounds/in.$^2$ | atmo | 0.0680460 |
| pounds/in.$^2$ | bars | 0.0689476 |
| pounds/in.$^2$ | cm Hg (0°C) | 5.17149 |
| pounds/in.$^2$ | cm $H_2O$ (4°C) | 70.3089 |
| pounds/in.$^2$ | in. Hg (0°C) | 2.03602 |
| pounds/in.$^2$ | in. $H_2O$ (4°C) | 27.6807 |
| pounds/in.$^2$ | kg/$cm^2$ | 0.07030696 |
| pounds/in.$^2$ | mm Hg (0°C) | 51.7149 |
| pounds/in.$^2$ | $N/m^2$ | 6,895 |
| quarts (U.S.) | $cm^3$ | 946.3529 |
| quarts (U.S.) | $ft^3$ | 0.03342014 |
| quarts (U.S.) | in.$^3$ | 57.75 |
| quarts (U.S.) | $m^3$ | 0.000946359 |
| quarts (U.S.) | gal (U.S.) | 0.25 |
| quarts (U.S.) | liters | 0.9463264 |
| quarts (U.S.) | oz (US) | 32 |
| rads | J/kg | 0.01 |
| radians | degrees | 57.295788 |
| radians | minutes | 3,437.747 |
| radians | seconds | 206,264.8 |
| radians | revolutions | 0.1591549 |
| revolutions | radians | 6.2831853 |
| revolutions | degrees | 360 |
| slug/$ft^3$ | kg/$m^3$ | 515.379 |
| slug | kg | 14.5939029 |
| stokes | $m^2$/sec | $1 \times 10^{-4}$ |
| square centimeters | $ft^2$ | 0.001076391 |
| square centimeters | in.$^2$ | 0.1550003 |

| To Convert from | To | Multiply by |
|---|---|---|
| square centimeters | $m^2$ | 0.0001 |
| square feet | ac | $2.295684 \times 10^{-5}$ |
| square feet | $cm^2$ | 929.0304 |
| square feet | in.$^2$ | 144 |
| square feet | $m^2$ | 0.09290304 |
| square feet | $mi^2$ | $3.587006 \times 10^{-8}$ |
| square feet/sec | cS | 92,937 |
| square feet/sec | $m^2$/sec | 0.09290304 |
| square inches | $cm^2$ | 6.4516 |
| square inches | $ft^2$ | 0.0069444 |
| square inches | $m^2$ | 0.00064516 |
| square inches | $mi^2$ | $2.490977 \times 10^{-10}$ |
| square kilometers | ac | 247.1054 |
| square kilometers | $ft^2$ | $1.076391 \times 10^7$ |
| square kilometers | in.$^2$ | $1.550003 \times 10^9$ |
| square kilometers | $m^2$ | $1 \times 10^6$ |
| square kilometers | $mi^2$ | 0.3861022 |
| square meters | ac | 0.0002471054 |
| square meters | $cm^2$ | 10,000 |
| square meters | $ft^2$ | 10.76391 |
| square meters | in.$^2$ | 1,550.003 |
| square meters | $mi^2$ | $3.861022 \times 10^{-7}$ |
| square meters | $yd^2$ | 1.19599 |
| square meters/sec | cS | 1,000,000 |
| square meters/sec | St | 10,000 |
| square meters/sec | $ft^2$/sec | 10.763915 |
| square miles | ac | 640 |
| square miles | $ft^2$ | $2.787829 \times 10^7$ |
| square miles | $km^2$ | 2.589988 |
| square miles | $m^2$ | 2,589,988 |
| square yards | $m^2$ | 0.83613 |
| therms | Btu | 100,000 |
| therms | MBtu | 0.1 |
| therms | kWh | 29.28 |
| tons (long) | kg | 1,016.047 |
| tons (long) | lb | 2,240 |
| tons (metric) | kg | 1000 |
| tons (metric) | lb | 2,204.623 |
| tons (short) | kg | 907.1848 |
| tons (short) | lb | 2,000 |
| tons of refrig | Btu/hr | 12,000 |
| tons of refrig | hp | 4.71611 |
| tons of refrig | kg of ice melted/hr | 37.971 |
| tons of refrig | lb of ice melted/hr | 83.711 |
| watts | Btu/hr | 3.41220 |
| watts | cal/hr | 860.421 |
| watts | ft-lb/min | 44.2537 |
| watts | hp | 0.00134102 |

| To Convert from | To | Multiply by |
|---|---|---|
| watts | J/sec | 1 |
| watts/cm$^2$ | Btu/ft$^2$-hr | 3,170.03 |
| watts/cm$^2$ | cal/cm$^2$-hr | 860.421 |
| watts/cm-°C | cal/hr-cm-°C | 860 |
| watts/cm-°C | Btu/hr-ft-°F | 57.79 |
| watts/cm$^2$-°C | cal/cm$^2$-hr-°C | 860 |
| watts/cm$^2$-°C | Btu/ft$^2$-hr-°F | 1761 |
| watt-hr | Btu | 3.41443 |
| watt-hr | cal | 860.421 |
| watt-hr | ft-lb | 2,655.22 |
| watt-hr | hp-hr | 0.00134102 |
| watt-hr | J | 3,600 |
| watt-hr | kWh | 0.001 |
| weeks | days | 7 |
| weeks | hr | 168 |
| weeks | min | 10,080 |
| weeks | mo | 0.2301370 |
| yards | cm | 91.44 |
| yards | ft | 3 |
| yards | in. | 36 |
| yards | m | 0.9144 |
| years | days | 365 |
| years | hr | 8,760 |
| years | min | 525,600 |
| years | sec | $3.1536 \times 10^7$ |
| years (leap) | days | 366 |

# TEMPERATURE CONVERSIONS

| | |
|---|---|
| Celsius to Kelvin | °K = °C + 273.15 |
| Celsius to Fahrenheit | °F = (9/5)°C + 32 |
| Celsius to Rankine | °R = (9/5)°C + 491.67 |
| Fahrenheit to Celsius | °C = (5/9) (°F − 32) |
| Fahrenheit to Kelvin | °K = (5/9) (°F + 459.67) |
| Fahrenheit to Rankine | °R = °F + 459.67 |
| Kelvin to Fahrenheit | °F = (9/5)°K − 459.67 |
| Kelvin to Celsius | °C = °K − 273.15 |
| Kelvin to Rankine | °R = (9/5)°K |
| Rankine to Celsius | °C = (5/9)°R − 273.15 |
| Rankine to Fahrenheit | °F = °R − 459.67 |
| Rankine to Kelvin | °K = (5/9)°R |

# INDEX

## SOLAR-ELECTRICS: RESEARCH AND DEVELOPMENT

By **Robert L. Bailey,** U. of Florida

Written by one of the leading experts in the field of solar-electric technology. The author examines research and developments in solar-electricity generation, and also looks into the areas where future research is needed. Realistically reveals what can be done to transform the now miniscule solar-electric industry into a future power giant.

1980 372 pages (8½ x 11") 75 fig. 12 tab. 879 ref.
**ISBN 0-250-40346-3**

## SOLAR HEATING AND COOLING OF BUILDINGS

By **Richard S. Greeley, Robert P. Ouellette,** MITRE Corp., and **Paul N. Cheremisinoff,** New Jersey Institute of Technology

Solar energy is generally considered clean and nonpolluting. On the other hand, it is also intermittent and diffuse. This book dispels some of the uncertainties concerning solar energy, clarifies others, and shows how to take advantage of solar energy incentives. Begins with the basics—the sun—and proceeds through equipment, economics, and examples of solar systems. For the practicing or would-be solar energy engineer...an exhaustive treatment of this important subject.

1981 502 pages 89 fig. 77 tab. 122 ref. **ISBN 0-250-40353-6**

## FUELS FROM BIOMASS AND WASTES

**Donald L. Klass,** Institute of Gas Technology, and **George H. Emert,** U. of Arkansas, Editors

A timely discussion of the use of biomass (land- and water-based vegetation), as well as raw materials to make useful energy forms. Concise and well-organized, the absolute currency of the references makes this major work of top interest to energy suppliers, scientists and chemical engineers.

1981 592 pages 150 fig. 158 tab. 635 ref. **ISBN 0-250-40418-4**

# THE ENERGY CRISIS, CONSERVATION AND SOLAR

By **Harvey Rose** and **Amy Pinkerton,** Solar Energy Research Institute, Golden, Colorado

This book addresses the efficient use of energy without curtailing services or amenities. Explains how to save energy, as well as how to use solar energy efficiently. The authors show how conservation could reduce energy consumption by reducing waste. Gives numerous real-life examples which prove that some solar technologies are economically ready, and others nearly ready. An in-depth analysis of the many controversies surrounding solar technologies.

1981 210 pages 35 fig. 11 tab. 546 ref. **Hardcover ISBN 0-250-40460-5**
**Softcover ISBN 0-250-40482-6**

# GASOHOL FOR ENERGY PRODUCTION

By **Nicholas P. Cheremisinoff,** Exxon Research and Engineering

Complete coverage of mass production of organic wastes for energy. Examines the impact of gasohol production on U.S. energy demand along with other fuels that can be produced from biomass. A solid overview of the entire gasohol picture.

1979,80 140 pages 33 fig. 38 tab. 81 ref. **ISBN 0-250-40325-0**

# SOLAR ARCHITECTURE

By **Gregory E. Franta** and **Kenneth R. Olson,** Roaring Fork Research Center, Aspen, Colorado

A necessary addition to the bookshelf of anyone considering solar heating for a new home. Contains many examples and case histories of passive solar designs and includes procedures for determining heat loss and heat transfer coefficients. Also features greenhouse design. Discusses the techniques, methods and materials used in energy-conscious design and construction concepts. Gives you the best ideas – in language that anyone interested or involved in solar can readily utilize.

1978,79 331 pages 140 fig. 6 tab. 64 ref. **ISBN 0-250-40233-5**